THE ART OF DIPLOMACY

Tobias Bunde & Benedikt Franke (Eds.)

THE ART OF DIPLOMACY

75+ Views Behind the Scenes of World Politics

Econ

Content

11 Speak Softly and Carry a Big Book
Tobias Bunde and Benedikt Franke

Elements of Diplomacy

17 A Walk to the Garden
Javier Solana

21 The Test of Trust
Patricia Espinosa

23 The Human Touch
Atifete Jahjaga

25 Personal Connections
Børge Brende

27 The Utility of Ambassadors
Robert Cooper

33 International Law and Diplomacy
Fatou Bensouda

37 Military Power and Diplomacy
James G. Stavridis

39 The Language of Power
Josep Borrell

45 The Power of Language
Jasmine M. El-Gamal

47 Tea Diplomacy
Siemtje Möller

49 Jazz and Diplomacy
Sebastian Groth

53 The Right Venue
Benedikt Franke

59 The Mental Maps of Diplomats
Joseph S. Nye

63 Risk Management in Politics and Diplomacy
Nikolaus von Bomhard

67 Back-Channel Diplomacy
Karl Kaiser

69 Parliamentary Diplomacy
Elmar Brok

75 Track Two Diplomacy
Sam Nunn

77 The Younger Generation
Desmond Browne

79 People's Diplomacy
Izumi Nakamitsu

Challenges for Diplomacy

83 Choosing the Right Historical Analogies
Ivan Krastev

85 Learning from Our Experience
John Scarlett

87 Reviving the Helsinki Spirit
Sauli Niinistö

89 Securing Fragile Peace
Charles A. Kupchan

93 Pursuing Diplomacy in a G-Zero World
Ian Bremmer

97 Preparing for a World without Order
Klaus Naumann

103 Dealing with Difficult Partners in Central Europe
Wolfgang Schüssel

107 Putting Ourselves in Others' Shoes
Sigmar Gabriel

113 Keeping Communication Channels Open
Nora Müller

117 Promoting Mutual Understanding between China and the West
Fu Ying

125 Managing U.S.-China Strategic Competition
Kevin Rudd

129 Standing Up to China
Kenneth Roth

133 Protecting Liberal-Democratic Values
Nathalie Tocci

135 Sustaining Liberal Democracy
Ana Palacio

137 Not Giving Up on Democracy and Equality in the Middle East
Tawakkol Karman

143 Building a Global Alliance of Democracies
Anders Fogh Rasmussen

147 Rethinking the Transatlantic Community
Anne-Marie Slaughter

149 Recalibrating Western Ambition
Thomas Kleine-Brockhoff

151 Overcoming Westlessness
Tobias Bunde

161 Developing a Weltpolitikfähigkeits-verlustvermeidungsstrategie
Timothy Garton Ash

163 Demonstrating Courage and Determination
Markus Söder

165 Forging a Common European Strategic Culture
Franziska Brantner

167 Making the Case for Defense
Frederick "Ben" Hodges

169 Securing Public Support
Norbert Röttgen

171 Reforming Germany's National Security Architecture
Boris Ruge

173 Navigating Propaganda and Social Media
Steven Erlanger

175 Mitigating Hybrid Threats
Teija Tiilikainen

181 Understanding the Digitization of War
Toomas Hendrik Ilves

189 Mastering the Art of Deniability
Thomas Rid

195 Treating Cyber Problems as Geopolitical Problems
Dmitri Alperovitch

199 Maintaining the Negotiating Edge in the Age of Tech-Geopolitics
Sorin Ducaru

205 Deploying an Effective Technology Diplomacy
Manuel Muñiz Villa

211 Paving the Way for a Free and Democratic Digital Future
Kersti Kaljulaid

217 Balancing the Geopolitical Power of Tech Companies
Marietje Schaake

219 Reversing the Tide of Impunity
David Miliband

221 Understanding Security Comprehensively
Achim Steiner

223 Charting a Path to Lasting Food Security and Peace
David Beasley

225 Investing in Pandemic Preparedness
Tedros Adhanom Ghebreyesus

227 Making Sense of the Quantum World
Armen Sarkissian

235 Adapting Diplomatic Tools and Structures
Cathryn Clüver Ashbrook

Episodes of Diplomacy

241 Negotiating German Unity: The Art of Pragmatic Diplomacy
Robert B. Zoellick

247 Benefiting from Cross-Departmental Teamwork
Theo Waigel

249 Taking Sides as Mediators
Carl Bildt

253 Pursuing Peace Against All Odds
Nasser bin Nasser

255 Conducting the Concert of Nations
Peter Ricketts

259 Dreaming of Dayton 30 Years On
Igor Ivanov

261 Ending a War
Strobe Talbott

265 Reflecting on Journalistic Responsibility
Constanze Stelzenmüller

267 Trying to Rein in the Executive
Jane Harman

269 Setting the Agenda of the United Nations General Assembly
Srgjan Kerim

273 Surviving Difficult Diplomatic Visits
Louise Mushikiwabo

277 Raising Interest for the Arctic
Ólafur Ragnar Grímsson

279 Negotiating the Status of Kosovo
Frank G. Wisner

283 Pursuing a European Future for Georgia
Eka Tkeshelashvili

285 Tearing Down Walls
Radosław Sikorski

287 Negotiating the New START Treaty
Rose Gottemoeller

293 Building NATO Consensus on Libya
Ivo H. Daalder

297 Reaching a Nuclear Deal with Iran
Helga Maria Schmid

301 Paving the Way for a Robust Diplomatic Process
Thomas Greminger

305 Making Use of Track Two Diplomacy
Alexander Dynkin

309 Conducting Small Power Diplomacy in an Age of Great Power Rivalry
Ine Eriksen Søreide

313 Fighting Terrorism
Peter Neumann

317 Accepting Failure in Cyprus
Espen Barth Eide

325 Saying No to Turkey
Alexander Graf Lambsdorff

327 Paving the Way for the Agreement between Greece and North Macedonia
Johannes Hahn

329 Moving from Enmity to Accountability
Ottilia Anna Maunganidze

335 Futureproofing NATO
Benedetta Berti

339 Building Institutions in the Realm of Economic and Monetary Policy
Christine Lagarde

347 Bringing a Breath of Fresh Air to the United Nations Security Council
Christoph Heusgen

Lessons for Diplomacy

353 The EU and Three Lessons in Foreign Policy
Catherine Ashton

361 Has Diplomacy Had Its Day?
Jens Stoltenberg

363 Why Do We Succeed or Fail in Negotiation and Mediation?
Jan Eliasson

367 The Diplomatic Toolbox
Wolfgang Ischinger

Addendum

372 Acknowledgments
373 Image Sources
374 Photo Captions
378 Endnotes
392 Imprint

The Right Venue

Benedikt Franke

Successful diplomacy has a lot to do with creating and controlling powerful emotions—as has been underscored by many authors in this book. Aside from timing (anniversaries usually do the trick) or attendance (a conflict survivor or a member of the next generation can help to remind everyone present of what is at stake), a particular effective way to fill a diplomatic meeting with a certain emotion is by choosing the right venue.

Like diplomacy itself, choosing the right venue for a particular purpose is an age-old art. There are countless stories of how diplomats had to shout across rivers or meet in the middle of bridges before diplomatic immunity allowed them to leave their own territories without having to fear violent ends. Once diplomatic travel with significantly reduced risk of being nailed to a tree (as happened to the envoys of Genghis Khan at the hands of the Shah of Khwarazm) or being thrown down a well (as happened to the emissaries of Persia's king Darius at the hands of the Spartans) became possible, the choice of where to meet became an important part of the game. The decision about in whose territory to convene and thus about who received whom or who had to travel longer to get there provided perceived advantages and was thus worth substantial efforts.

It is hard to dispute that creating the right emotions by choosing the right venue can make a difference in whether a diplomatic venture ends up as a success or a failure.

Over the centuries, leaders have gone to great lengths to outdo each other and translate venue choice into diplomatic gains. A story often related is how Stalin insisted on Yalta as location for the February 1945 tri-party talks with the United States and the United Kingdom to underscore the primacy of the Soviet Union in shaping the post-World War II order. Dozens and dozens of counterproposals by UK and US diplomats to meet somewhere different, neutral, or at least in between were thrashed by their Soviet counterparts. Even worse, when Stalin found out that Roosevelt and Churchill had arranged for a preparatory meeting in Malta just before the actual tri-party summit, he sent Roosevelt a famous, rather tense, cable consisting of only five words "I said Yalta, not Malta" to show that he not only disapproved of the bilateral meeting per se but that it was he who had called the shots and pushed through his choice of venue to begin with. If anything, this example shows that the selection of a diplomatic venue is itself important and that it matters (at least to those involved) where one negotiates, not just what and how one negotiates.

While no taxonomy will ever be complete, there are at least three different categories of diplomatic venues with clearly defined purposes that should be distinguished: Venues that impress, venues that remind, and venues that calm.

Venues that impress are the most straightforward category. From the Forbidden City in Beijing to Spain's El Escorial, from the Louvre in Paris to the Apostolic Palace in Rome, princely residences were designed to symbolize the majesty of their owners' power. Their sheer splendor was meant to overwhelm the other party and put its representatives into an unfavorable negotiating position.

The two logics behind venues that remind are equally straightforward. In the first, a venue is chosen because a battle, victory, defeat, or another significant event has taken place there in the past and the organizing party believes that the physical reminder thereof provides it with an advantage or the opposing party with a disadvantage. In the latter case, the venue is often chosen with the clear intent to humiliate the other side or highlight a reversal of fortunes. A good example is the French insistence that the treaty ending the First World War was signed in Versailles, the very place where Prussia's Chancellor Otto von Bismarck had declared unification of the German Empire almost exactly fifty years earlier. To get back at them, Hitler insisted on using the same train carriage (the Compiègne Wagon) for the official capitulation of the French in 1940 that the French had used for the German capitulation in 1918.

In the second, slightly different logic, a place is chosen for its genius loci (Latin for protective spirit of a place), which is a repository of good or bad memories that somehow predetermine or at least influence future developments at the same place. From the natural "Thing" mounds of medieval governing assemblies in the Nordics to the African Baobab tree under which elders met to reach consensus, the history of diplo-

◂ Benedikt Franke at the MSC Core Group Meeting in Cairo in October 2019.

macy is full of such places. A popular example is the choice of Camp David as venue for the negotiations between Ehud Barak and Yasir Arafat in July 2000. The host, US President Bill Clinton, had decided to extend the invitation to his country retreat with the successful negotiations that had taken place between Israel and Egypt at that very venue twenty-two years earlier clearly in mind. He hoped that both opponents would "feel the weight of history" and that their common memories would increase their readiness to reach a compromise or at least a sense of shared responsibility. While Clinton's plan did not work out, there are many other examples of where a genius loci did help to create a conducive atmosphere.

Such atmospheres are also at the heart of the "venues that calm" category. These venues are chosen mainly for the calming effect they have on the participants. Often located in a particularly serene, nature setting, they are supposed to isolate participants from the buzz of more central locations and allow them to concentrate on the important task at hand. Chancellor Merkel's decision to host the 2015 G7 Summit in the secluded Bavarian Retreat Schloss Elmau is a prime example of such reasoning. In a way, neutral venues, such as Geneva for the 2021 Biden-Putin Summit, can be counted in this category, too, as the neutrality removes much of the hassle associated with having to choose a venue and thus helps calm both sides.

Much of the above is highly irrational. Most political decision makers and diplomats should be able to see through venue choices for what they are and factor that into their decision making. At the end of the day, however, it is hard to dispute that creating the right emotions by choosing the right venue can make a difference in whether a diplomatic venture ends up as a success or a failure.

Given all of this, it should not come as a surprise that we at the Munich Security Conference (MSC) try to avoid the nondescript conference halls around the world. Instead, we always attempt to infuse our events with the sparkle of a particular symbolism or genius loci. In Egypt we instrumentalized the unparalleled magic of the Great Pyramids of Giza; in Vienna the glittering splendor of the Palais Liechtenstein; in Iceland the historic aura of Höfði House (where Reagan and Gorbachev met for their famous Reykjavík Summit in 1986); in Washington, DC the rooftop of the Hay Adams with its breathtaking views of the White House directly beneath; in Helsinki the deck of an icebreaker that had just returned from the first successful North-East winter passage; and in Ethiopia the shores of Lake Tana, the source of the Blue Nile. Our venues are always special and always an integral part of what we seek to achieve.

Our home base, the Hotel Bayerischer Hof in the old town of Munich, is another case in point. Every February, its quirky hallways, impossibly small elevators, and dungeon-like cellars get crowded by hundreds of key decisionmakers. Every year we are asked by panicked aides and their exasperated principals when we will finally move the conference to a (seemingly) more suitable venue such as Munich's enormous trade fair or the airport where breathing and meeting space do not come at such a premium. Although they may have a point operationally, they miss another fundamentally. We do want people to bump into each other, we do want them to rub shoulders at the bar, in the elevator, or in the queues for side events or bilats, and we do want them unable to avoid each other for the duration of the weekend. The MSC is all about providing opportunities for exchange. The more engagement points we can create the better, even if that means using some tricks along the way. Or at least that was the plan until the pandemic struck.

COVID-19 forced diplomats, and organizations like the MSC, to reconsider the importance of geography and symbolism. As meetings were moved from conference halls to the internet, the perceived ease, greater inclusivity, and (much) lower costs quickly raised the question of whether virtual summits were the new normal in international diplomacy. There surely are many advantages to holding meetings online rather than having to go through the painstaking process of identifying and agreeing on venues. At the end of the day though, the speedy return to physical meetings in the second half of 2021, including the G7, G20, and NATO Summits or COP26, shows quite clearly that the internet will not replace the need of diplomats to think carefully about their choice of venues in the foreseeable future.

Benedikt Franke is the Chief Executive Officer of the Munich Security Conference. Previously, he worked as Special Assistant to the former Secretary-General of the United Nations Kofi Annan. In his (meager) free time, he serves as Ambassador at Large for the Sovereign Military Order of Malta.

The Leaning Tower, venue of the MSC Energy Security Summit in Norway in 2018. ▸

KVÆRNER

msc

The Mental Maps of Diplomats

Joseph S. Nye

John Maynard Keynes once observed that practical men following their instincts are often the prisoners of some defunct scribblers whose names they have long forgotten. Two schools of thought have provided mental maps for most democratic leaders and diplomats: realism and liberalism. The two are often posed as opposites, but in the best minds and hands they are also complements.

Realists draw a harsh mental map. States operate in a self-help world in which the best way to survive is to be as powerful as possible. In dire situations of survival, consequences justify what appear to be immoral acts. A frequently cited example is Winston Churchill's attack on the French fleet in 1940. He killed some 1,300 of his French allies rather than let the fleet fall into Hitler's hands. Churchill referred to that crisis of British survival as a "supreme emergency," and political theorists such as Michael Walzer have argued that in such rare instances, moral rules can be overridden. Some ethicists have justified Churchill's bombing of German civilian targets in the early days of World War II when Britain's survival was at stake, but they condemn his later support for the fire-bombing of Dresden in February 1945 when victory in Europe was already assured. In the early days of the war, Churchill could claim necessity, but he was wrong to continue to do so in the latter days of the war.

International politics is often called anarchic, but anarchy simply means "without government" and does not necessarily mean chaos. Different mental maps of the world portray anarchy differently, and that affects the way leaders and diplomats frame their policy choices.

In general, such dire straits of supreme emergency are rare and most leaders and diplomats are eclectic in selecting the mental maps with which they navigate the world. Most of international relations and diplomacy is not like lifeboat ethics, but allow a broader range of choices, even though leaders often exaggerate dangers and threats to justify their actions. For example, Donald Trump explained his lack of diplomatic response to the murder and dismemberment of the dissident journalist Jamal Khashoggi in the Saudi consulate in Istanbul on the grounds that "the world is a dangerous place!" Trump was appealing to realism to justify his lack of a diplomatic response like recalling an ambassador or issuing a condemnation from the White House. But realists who describe the world in a way that pretends moral choices do not exist are merely disguising their choice. The murder of Khashoggi was treated like Churchill's dilemma in 1940. Survival comes first, but that is not the end of the list of values that guide foreign policy. Most of international politics is not about survival.

A smart realist also understands that there are different types of power. No one can lead without power, at home or abroad, but power is more than bombs, bullets, or resources. You can get others to do what you want by coercion (sticks), payment (carrots), and attraction (soft power), and a full understanding of power encompasses all three aspects. Because soft power is rarely sufficient by itself and takes longer to accomplish its effects, leaders find the hard power of coercion or payment more tempting. But when wielded alone, hard power can involve higher costs than when it is combined with the soft power of attraction. If you also have soft power, you can economize on carrots and sticks.

The Roman Empire rested not only on its legions, but also on the attraction of Roman culture. The Berlin Wall came down not under an artillery barrage, but from hammers and bulldozers wielded by people who had lost faith in Communism. A nation's soft power rests upon its culture, its values, and its policies when they are seen as legitimate in the eyes of others. It can be reinforced by the narratives that are used in explaining foreign policy. Kennedy and Reagan, for example, framed their policies in ways that attracted support both at home and abroad. Nixon and Trump were less successful in attracting those outside the United States. Trump declared himself a nationalist, but there is a moral difference between a patriotism that includes others and a nativism that excludes others. Promoting broad values such as human rights makes a country's public diplomacy more attractive to others. International polls show that by ignoring such values in favor of a myopic version of realism, Trump squandered American soft power.

International politics is often called anarchic, but anarchy simply means "without government" and does not necessarily mean chaos. Different mental maps of the world portray anarchy differently, and that

◂ Joseph S. Nye at the "Townhall on Diplomacy" at the Munich Security Conference in February 2020.

affects the way leaders and diplomats frame their policy choices. Writing in 1651 after the bloody English Civil War in which the king was decapitated, the realist Thomas Hobbes famously described a state of nature without government as "a war of all against all where life is nasty, brutish, and short." In contrast, writing in a somewhat more peaceful period a few decades later, the liberal John Locke imagined a state of nature as involving social contracts that permitted the successful pursuit of life, liberty, and property. Today, liberals argue that while there is no world government, there is a degree of world governance, and anarchy has limits. Liberals stress the role of institutions, both national and international, in advancing cooperation among sovereign states in managing their interdependence. Liberals argue that rudimentary practices and institutions such as balance of power, international law, norms, and international organizations can create enough order to establish a framework for meaningful moral choices in most cases.

Even in the extreme circumstances of war, law and norms can play a role. The just war doctrine originated in the early Christian church, as Saint Augustine and others wrestled with the paradox that if the good did not fight back, they would perish and the evil would inherit the earth. That doctrine of just self-defense became secularized after the seventeenth century, and today it provides a broad normative structure that considers all three moral dimensions: good intentions represented by a just cause; forceful means that are proportional to the situation and that discriminate between military and civilian targets; and good consequences that emerge from a prudent regard for the probability of success. This just war doctrine is more than theoretical. It is enshrined both in International Humanitarian Law (the Geneva Conventions) and national codes of military justice. Soldiers who violated the laws of armed conflict have been jailed in many countries.

The foreign policy of a democracy always involves trade-offs and trying to get as much of as many values—security, economic, rights—as possible in the circumstances.

The rise of human rights law after World War II, particularly reaction to the horror of genocide, has complicated diplomatic choices. The American public often wants a moral response, but is divided over how much. For example, in retrospect, Bill Clinton himself criticized his failure to respond to the genocide in Rwanda in 1994. Yet had Clinton tried to send American troops he would have encountered stiff resistance in public opinion. Particularly after the death of American soldiers in an earlier humanitarian intervention in Somalia in 1993, the public was not ready for another intervention. Clinton has acknowledged that he could have done more to help the UN and other nations to save some of the lives that were lost in Rwanda.

Human rights issues pose hard questions for leaders and diplomats in a democracy. The public often treats rights as absolute and liberal voices often condemn any policy compromise as hypocrisy. The foreign policy of a democracy always involves trade-offs and trying to get as much of as many values—security, economic, rights—as possible in the circumstances. If a leader has only a human rights policy, he or she does not have a foreign policy. But if the policy ignores human rights, it ignores the importance of soft power in the long term.

Realism is the default position among the mental maps that most leaders and diplomats use to chart their course in foreign policy, and given a world of sovereign states, realism is the best place to start. The problem is that many realists stop where they start rather than realizing that liberalism often has something important to contribute to a successful policy as well. When survival is in jeopardy, realism is a necessary basis for a democratic foreign policy, though not sufficient. The question is one of degree.

Survival and security are not the only important aspects of world politics, and there are other values that citizens in democracies want to see included in their country's foreign policy. For these values, it is important to look beyond realism to liberal mental maps of the world. For example, many citizens have a general sense of a human community and support a refugee policy based not just on international legal obligations, but also upon moral considerations. While foreign aid in general is often not popular, particularly in difficult economic times, public support for international economic and public health assistance is strong enough for Western leaders to consistently maintain such policies. The extent of Good Samaritanism may be limited, but contrary to the skeptics' views, helping others is one of the foreign policy objectives for which democratic leaders have found public support.

Moral crusades do not always enjoy continual support in democracies, and early enthusiasm for interventions such as in Somalia or Afghanistan tend to wane over time. At the same time, respect for the human rights and institutions of other peoples is part of what the great liberal philosopher John Rawls called "the manner in which decent peoples treat each other." Even where basic democratic values are not shared, normal cooperative relations may be possible when authoritarians are not posing a severe threat. Such Rawlsian liberals do not insist on the export of democracy, but they do react to gross violations of human rights—as Bill Clinton found out in Bosnia and Haiti, and Barrack Obama encountered in Libya and Syria.

The difficult debates and moral choices over these issues have often been centered on what means to use. The types and degrees of intervention across borders range from a declaratory policy of critical statements at one end of the spectrum to the large-scale use of military force at the other end. With regard to force, the record is not impressive, with far more failures than successes. As Ronald Reagan once put it, "regimes planted by bayonets do not take root." The failure of the humanitarian intervention in Somalia in 1993 affected Clinton's nonintervention in the genocide in Rwanda six months later. The unsuccessful outcome of the use of air strikes in Libya limited Obama's subsequent willingness to use them in Syria. But as one of his aides observed, Syria became a tragic case of a means-ends gap in which hundreds of thousands of civilians were slaughtered and millions became refugees. By setting maximalist ends and declaring that Assad must go, the United States was unable to achieve its objective.

Leaders and diplomats have to assess how closely a situation fits a Hobbesian or Lockean mental map, and where an action lies on a continuum between security and other important values.

A French official once told me a story (possibly apocryphal) that when George W. Bush called Jacques Chirac about Afghanistan after 9/11, Chirac warned him that some retaliation was necessary, but "don't go in; don't stay if you do; and don't get out if you stay." These problems came back to haunt Joe Biden in 2021. Using a realist analysis, he explained his decision to withdraw the last troops from Afghanistan on the grounds that the United States was not capable of building a democratic nation in Afghanistan and American strategic objectives should be limited to counter terrorism. But his handling of the unexpectedly rapid collapse of the Afghan government produced scenes at the Kabul airport that triggered liberal values for a response to the humanitarian crisis. Democratic leaders must always anticipate events that will be called upon to use both mental maps at the same time.

Since there is never perfect security, the crucial issue is what degree of security must be assured before other values such as welfare, identity, or human rights become part of a foreign policy. Most foreign policy choices involve questions like arms sales to authoritarian allies or criticizing the human rights behavior of another country like China's actions in Xinjiang or Hong Kong. When some realists treat such trade-offs as similar to Churchill's decision to attack the French fleet, they are simply ducking hard choices. It is not enough to utter truisms like "security comes first or "justice presupposes order." Leaders and diplomats have to assess how closely a situation fits a Hobbesian or Lockean mental map, and where an action lies on a continuum between security and other important values. The best diplomats, like Wolfgang Ischinger, wind up as "liberal realists" who understand the complementarity of these mental maps.

Joseph S. Nye is Dean Emeritus of the Harvard Kennedy School of Government and author of *Do Morals Matter? Presidents and Foreign Policy from FDR to Trump.*

Risk Management in Politics and Diplomacy

Nikolaus von Bomhard

Politicians and diplomats suffer from a dramatically increased complexity in performing their duties. Add to this the inevitable human weaknesses in decision-making, institutional malfunction, and significant time pressure. Together, these provide the breeding ground for "bad" decisions in the truest sense of the word. In other words, what makes the difference is good preparation for foreseeable decisions. In this respect, is there anything that politics and—in particular—diplomacy can learn from business?

Today's political and diplomatic leaders are in an unenviable position. One or two generations ago, they had to stand the test in, essentially, a total of only two political fields: domestic economic prosperity, and domestic and international security ("prosperity and peace"). For some decades now, this has been compounded by at least three significant challenges. The first is digitalization, with its fundamental impact on value creation in nearly all industries. The second is the exponential acceleration of climate change, which—like the equally alarming loss of biodiversity—affects the entire planet. The third challenge is a new understanding of "global justice" when it comes to persisting inequalities in prosperity distribution and in corresponding resource consumption. Many of these challenges conflict both with each other and with the objectives of national politics.

For politicians and diplomats, the question is therefore one of how to balance opportunities and risks in a responsible and rational way.

For politicians and diplomats, the question is therefore one of how to balance opportunities and risks in a responsible and rational way. Today's high transparency standards for government action and widespread volatility of public opinion, especially on the various internet platforms, do not make this task any easier. All too often, these preconditions encourage risk-averse behavior both ahead of and during a crisis. In hindsight, and for the sake of exculpation, the crisis is then often described as a "black swan" that no one could possibly have foreseen.

Political and diplomatic decisions are often characterized by a high degree of uncertainty. Good government work—including the work of diplomats—involves seeking to base decisions on evidence, avoiding making bets or decisions too often based on optimistic expectations only. Politics should seek to exert influence, instead of just letting things happen out of an unthinking aversion to risk.

At this point, a comparison with business may be helpful, an arena in which professional risk management has become the norm—spectacular counterexamples notwithstanding. Well-led businesses define their risk appetite; they determine which types of losses are acceptable, up to what level and over what span of time. They have an explicit, formulated risk strategy. With this aim in mind, they identify and evaluate relevant risks, and determine appropriate measures of risk prevention or financing. They establish an early detection system for risks that have not yet been identified as a real or potential risk. The more "diabolical" the imaginative creativity applied, the less surprising an eventual emergency will be. A frequent risk report creates inward and outward transparency regarding the risks and their handling, which is in turn essential for the necessary assignment of responsibilities. Evidence for successful risk management can be easily seen in the way businesses have been shown to successfully deal with crises. The key is to first evaluate each risk separately and to then combine all the results. Only in this fashion can a genuinely comprehensive picture be formed. The fact that, in the final instance, assumptions about the correlations between single risks have to be made on less firm ground does not disqualify this approach.

The risk situation of entire countries—but also of smaller government units—is of a similar type. From the decision-makers' perspective, it is neither more complex nor more dynamic than the situation of businesses in free markets. And because shareholders are no longer the only yardstick of action, business leaders have to adapt to a diverse and confusing mix of stakeholder groups similar to what politicians are facing.

Moreover, risks relevant for political decisions do not, per se, elude indicator-based quantitative assessment. Admittedly, quantitatively assessing the value of soldiers' lives in the context of foreign engagements or the value of domestic social peace is only partly possible, if at all. However, this limitation does not apply to every risk. The costs of the direct and indirect conse-

◂ Nikolaus von Bomhard at the Munich Strategy Forum in Elmau in December 2018.

quences of many important political decisions—for instance, a nuclear phaseout, dealing with a refugee crisis, an international military assignment, or Brexit—are quite specific and measurable.

What does this mean in concrete terms? The approach just described requires an institutional framework—a risk council consisting of experts and led by a national "chief risk officer." This risk council would have to be positioned outside of the executive and the legislative branches in order to ensure its capacity to work independently. It would have the task of providing decision-makers with a comprehensive picture of the entire risk landscape, including proposals for risk appetite and, more importantly, the risk strategy. The key lies in providing an all-encompassing—that is, cross-departmental—view of all risks, including those that have been discussed in public only rarely, or not at all.

In Germany alone, a host of valuable sources of insight—departments, governmental agencies, or non-governmental think tanks—already exist that might serve as the basis of an integrated risk management. These include the Sustainability Report of the Federal Ministry of Finance, which uses model calculations to describe the development of public finances over several decades; the Federal Government White Paper authored by the Defense Ministry, which evaluates the main challenges for security politics; the yearly report of the Council of Experts on economic development; the reports of the Financial Stability Committee; the National Report on Education; the Environmental Report; and many more. Each of these sources identifies and evaluates specific risks and opportunities for future developments. Combined, they already form a valuable basis for risk management. A risk management program of this kind feeds into a full risk report, which would then have to be made public, as long as no significant security interests speak against it.

Agreeing on risk parameters in selected policy areas that are valid and, hopefully, binding for everyone, and deriving from these impulses and guidelines for international cooperation would significantly increase the "value creation" of diplomacy as preparer of political decisions.

This ultimately leads to an obligation to consider and weigh all risks that are connected with a decision and have been made as explicit as possible. The potential consequences of action (and inaction) would be transparent. While the political players' scope of action is not reduced, they are given an indispensable and comprehensible decision-making tool. Expanding this idea beyond national boundaries to international cooperation opens new horizons for diplomacy in particular. Almost every country already has procedures and institutions that support an evidence-based policy from their own national perspective. Agreeing on risk parameters in selected policy areas that are valid and, hopefully, binding for everyone, and deriving from these impulses and guidelines for international cooperation would significantly increase the "value creation" of diplomacy as preparer of political decisions. A common approach that is based on a comprehensible risk management strategy may contribute to substantiating international conflicts and preparing joint decisions relating to challenges that have cross-border implications. This idea is not utopian, as precedents for a risk-oriented international diplomacy exist, with the "Conference of the Parties" (COP) most certainly being the most prominent example: an institution-backed negotiation platform that discusses climate scenarios on the basis of a risk report, defines binding metrics, and agrees on country-specific transformational steps to help to reduce risks.

All too often, the complaint is made that, due to comparatively short legislative periods of typically four or five years, politicians in democratic systems tend to favor short-term policies and to refrain from decisions that would favor sustainable long-term development—decisions that may initially be perceived as negative. A dedicated authority—for example, the proposed national risk council—that makes the long-term "costs" of political decision transparent would help to reveal the deficits of short-term politics and to provide the necessary arguments for a genuinely "sustainable" orientation. This would help—in a desirable and necessary fashion—to strengthen the legitimacy of what is inevitable in the long term, to enhance understanding on the part of citizens, and to noticeably increase the predictability of politics.

Finally, with the right risk management, there would also be fewer black swans.

Nikolaus von Bomhard is the Chairman of the Board of Munich Re and Deutsche Post DHL. He is a member of the Foundation Council of the Munich Security Conference Foundation.

Munich Strategy Forum in Elmau in December 2018. ▸

Munich Security Con

msc

msc
msc
msc

Speak Softly and Carry a Big Book

Tobias Bunde and Benedikt Franke

It is not easy to define diplomacy. What is its essence? Is it an art, a craft, or something in between? What is good diplomacy . . . what isn't? As you will read in this book, there are manifold perspectives on diplomacy—and countless definitions, too. One of the most famous stems from President Theodore Roosevelt, who was known for his "big stick diplomacy" and described his diplomatic maxim by referring to a proverb: "speak softly and carry a big stick; you will go far."[1] For this book, we engaged in what can be called "big book diplomacy" and adopted an only slightly adapted version of Roosevelt's dictum: speak softly and carry a big book. We hope it sticks.

The reason for this book is simple. In April 2021, Wolfgang Ischinger, our long-time boss and mentor at the Munich Security Conference and beyond, turned seventy five. To celebrate him and his lifetime achievements, we decided to compile seventy-five contributions about the art of diplomacy. Neither we—nor he—wanted this to be a book about him. We wanted to edit a book *for* him—and for all the others who, like him, believe in the power of diplomacy. *Ceci n'est pas une Festschrift*—or so we thought.

To end up with seventy-five contributions we decided to write to one hundred of Wolfgang's closest associates and long-standing friends and partners and ask them to send us their favorite instructive anecdotes about the myriad ways in which diplomacy works. What we got back stunned us. For one, not seventy-five, but almost all one hundred immediately agreed to contribute. Second, despite our instructions to the contrary, almost everyone handed in anecdotes that included Wolfgang in one way or another. While we engaged in hefty "editing diplomacy" (try telling a sitting president to rewrite his contribution), it quickly became clear just how important personality and character are to a diplomat's success. Without them, not much is possible. With them, almost everything is. As the many references to him we had to remove testify, Wolfgang Ischinger has both in abundance.

In a way, Wolfgang is the "Forrest Gump" of German diplomacy. Since the early 1980s, he has almost always been where the real action took place. Starting as a young diplomat in the office of then foreign minister Hans-Dietrich Genscher, he witnessed the heated debates about the deployment of Pershing II missiles in Germany and the ensuing détente that allowed the Cold War to end peacefully. At the end of the decade, he was one of the West German diplomats who accompanied the trains with East German refugees who had fled to the German Embassy in Prague. As head of the Political Department in the German embassy in Paris, he witnessed the birth of the Charter of Paris in 1990. As head of Policy Planning and political director of the Federal Foreign Office, he was in the midst of Germany making its first steps as a unified country trying to find its role in a different era. He represented Germany in the Contact Group during the Balkan Wars and was among the negotiators in the Dayton Peace Agreement. He also participated in the negotiation of the NATO-Russia Founding Act, another milestone of diplomacy in the 1990s. As state secretary, he played a key role in the negotiations that led to the creation of Operation Allied Force and the Balkan Stability Pact in 1999. Given this background, it is perhaps not surprising that he was the German ambassador in the United States on September 11, 2001. In fact, it was his first day in office. To this day, his reputation in the US still draws on the very special mark he left during his tenure in Washington, DC.

Following two years as ambassador to the Court of St. James's, including a stint as the representative of the European Union in the Kosovo Troika that tried to find a solution to the status of Kosovo, in 2008 the German government asked Wolfgang to take over as chairman of the Munich Security Conference (MSC). He quickly breathed new life into this venerable organization that was founded by Ewald von Kleist as *Wehrkundetagung* in 1963, and over the years has become an indispensable family gathering for the transatlantic community. What started out as an annual conference, is now a highly efficient private diplomacy service provider and the world's leading platform for the debate of foreign and security policy. Still transatlantic to its core, the MSC regularly hosts the world's top decision makers on its stages around the world and publishes reports to draw attention to particular challenges. Almost all the pictures illustrating this book (in a way adding the art to the diplomacy) have been taken at MSC events over the past decade.

Even while steering the MSC through the last decade, Wolfgang continued to accept special diplomatic missions. For instance he served as the Representative of

◂ Tobias Bunde und Benedikt Franke at the Munich Strategy Retreat in Heiligendamm in October 2021.

the OSCE Chairperson-in-Office for National Dialogue Roundtables in Ukraine and as the chairman of the Panel of Eminent Persons on European Security as a Common Project, as well as in countless track two efforts or expert commissions, trying to find peaceful solutions to difficult problems—from nuclear arms control to cybersecurity. In each of these roles, he could rely on his key strengths, which make him the quintessential diplomat—his readiness to engage, to listen, and to remain open to other views; his ability to adapt to different groups and environments; and his clear moral compass.

Along the way, he built one of the best diplomatic networks in the world. This big book is testament to it. In it, nearly one hundred prominent authors share their personal views behind the scenes of world politics. Almost all of them are masters of diplomacy themselves—many of them spent their careers negotiating difficult agreements or trying to peacefully solve conflicts. Many of them have served as presidents, foreign or defense ministers, heads of international organizations, ambassadors, military leaders, or parliamentarians, while others have influenced the global debate as journalists, scholars, activists, or thought leaders. Each of them offers insights and lessons for diplomacy today and tomorrow.

Of course, this book is not an all-encompassing handbook, discussing every single aspect of diplomacy. Rather, the authors offer their very personal takes on the art of diplomacy. While the charm of the book is the fact that this plethora of views, opinions, and experiences comes relatively unsorted, there is an underlying structure to it all.

The first section of the book deals with some of the key elements of successful diplomacy. Our readers may not be surprised to read about the importance of trust or of personal connections, or to learn about the role of ambassadors and parliamentarians. But they will also learn about the role that tea can play in diplomacy or why diplomacy is, in many ways, like jazz.

The contributions in the second section focus on some of the core challenges for diplomacy today and in the future. Our authors not only reflect on some of the big issues—such as managing great-power competition or defending liberal-democratic values—they also discuss how diplomacy itself, its decision-making structures, its reach, and tools need to be adapted to changing circumstances, including the rise of technology and ever new ways to communicate.

In the third section of the book, our contributors discuss specific episodes of diplomacy in action—some of them very successful, others at least partially helpful, still others complete failures. In many cases, our authors for the first time publicly share their personal stories about these episodes. All these stories provide instructive insights for tomorrow's diplomats.

The final section of the book brings together some more general reflections on diplomacy. Based on their long-time experience, the contributors spell out some of their key diplomatic lessons. Like all the others writing in this volume, they believe that diplomacy has not had its day. If anything, it will become even more important in the future.

Instead of writing a conclusion ourselves, we have asked Wolfgang to distill his career into a number of key takeaways, which you will find at the very end of this book. As we know from experience, his intense diplomatic life has produced a treasure trove of diplomatic insights, hilarious stories, and more-or-less-funny jokes. Many of these stories, especially the jokes, are for a different book, but their essence runs through this one and, in particular, through Wolfgang's epilogue.

We very much hope that you will find the collection of stories about diplomacy both instructive and entertaining. We tried to strike a balance between the serious and the more lighthearted, between the instructive and the descriptive, all in the hope that the overall result provides a valuable glimpse behind the scenes of world politics. The one thing to take away from all the stories is that diplomacy really is an art, best practiced by those who, like Wolfgang, are willing to treat it as such.

Wolfgang Ischinger at the Launch of the Munich Security Report Zeitenwende | Wendezeiten in October 2020. ▸

1 Elements of Diplomacy

www.idausweissysteme.co

A Walk to the Garden

Javier Solana

Diplomacy has changed—no doubt about that. Videoconferences, tweets, and the myriad of policy issues that make their way into diplomatic negotiations have transformed the way state representatives interact with each other. New actors have come to the fore. But this art, which is so dear to Wolfgang Ischinger, remains the same in essence.

The essence of diplomacy is one of timeless simplicity. The big power tensions of the Cold War were on occasion mitigated by a telephone call or a simple promenade, such as Ronald Reagan and Mikhail Gorbachev's 1985 "walk in the woods" in Geneva. Mention of Reagan reminds us of the passing away last February of George Shultz, the US secretary of state for most of his presidency. Shultz was a towering diplomat who left us with many lessons that are worth mentioning.

Let me start with trust, "the coin of the realm." Nothing works without trust, in politics or in life. Shultz was very much aware of its value: "When trust was in the room, whatever room that was—the family room, the schoolroom, the locker room, the office room, the government room or the military room—good things happened. When trust was not in the room, good things did not happen. Everything else is details," he said.

Nothing works without trust, in politics or in life. Diplomacy is about tending relationships—it is done by people, with people.

Without trust, conducting diplomacy becomes an arduous task. Mistrust often prevents actors from taking the initial step and cooperating with each other. Without some degree of trust, formalizing the numerous nuclear arms control agreements between the US and the Soviet Union during the Cold War would have been difficult. Trust is not a given in any kind of relationship, political or personal. It has to be built. As Shultz said, "even our adversaries will have to regain the trust that we can work together to manage global threats to humanity's very existence even when we disagree on other issues." Shultz was especially lucid in suggesting the analogy of diplomacy as tending a garden.

Tending the garden demands patience. Shultz put it in no better terms: "If you plant a garden and you go away for eight months and you come back it is full of weeds. If you tend that garden regularly you get no weeds."

Some may suggest this analogy to be outdated. I believe it still holds true to the core substance of diplomacy. But, perhaps, personal reciprocity is the one thing that the gardening analogy misses. Diplomacy is about tending relationships—it is done by people, with people.

Diplomacy is traditionally a means through which states pursue their grand strategies. But down-to-earth, face-to-face human contact is still its bread and butter. This is where the value of listening, honesty, and loyalty come in.

I will take the liberty of showcasing this with a personal experience. A long series of negotiations preceded the signing of the 1997 Founding Act in Paris between NATO and Russia. Yevgeny Primakov, at the time Russian Foreign Minister, was my counterpart during these negotiations. Primakov's honesty and truthfulness were founding elements of the personal relationship we built, without which a positive political outcome remained dubious. For negotiations, Primakov invited me to a Russian dacha, where our teams met regularly.

We both knew that negotiations would be difficult. He then invited me to walk with him along the snowy woods that surrounded the dacha. After heavily dressing me, we walked and spoke for two hours. The conversation was frank, yet fluid. After that, we knew we would pull it together. That political relationship was underpinned by a latent friendship. We both maintained contact after 1997 and met once again in Russia. Our families took the place of the negotiating teams. The trust was the same.

In a realm where formal negotiations often belittle the value of unstructured conversation, George Shultz's conception of diplomacy is one not to forget. In diplomacy, sometimes all it takes is a walk in the woods. Or should we say, a walk to the garden.

Javier Solana is President of ESADE Center for Global Economy and Geopolitics. After serving as Spanish Foreign Minister and Secretary General of NATO, he was appointed European Union High Representative for Common Foreign and Security Policy, and Secretary-General of the Council of the EU.

◂ Javier Solana (left) with Frank-Walter Steinmeier at the Munich Security Conference in February 2013.

The Test of Trust

Patricia Espinosa

Much of the work devoted to understanding and addressing national security challenges stems from a judicious sense of suspicion, if not outright mistrust. Identifying risks and threats—whether human or natural in origin—and taking measures to avert them is essential to maintaining a stable, secure environment.

National security, however, also depends on mutually beneficial and consistent relationships with other actors—allies, partners, even sympathizers—that are ultimately based on trust. As with so many aspects of international relations, these two opposing attitudes—trust and mistrust—reflect, at the level of national states, pervasive features of social interaction, whether one is talking about human or investment bonds, personal or national security.

As history shows, building trust is more beneficial than managing mistrust. The advantages of collaboration tend to outweigh the benefits of confrontation, provided those involved share some common goals, have a basic sense of respect for each other, and face no irreconcilable differences. This proviso is essential for the statement to hold true and that is why trust has acquired such relevance in today's globalized world. Today, for many global issues, collaboration is the only option that stands any chance of success.

This is especially true in the case of climate change. The global climate agenda is not a single, self-contained issue that can be treated in isolation, but an all-encompassing challenge that affects many aspects of people's lives and calls for sweeping changes in people's lifestyles. Addressing this challenge demands resolute commitments and contributions from every country, every community, and ultimately, every individual.

The critical importance of trust in global efforts against climate change came to the fore at the end of COP15, in Copenhagen. The outcome of that session showed that, even if motivated by the best of intentions, actions that fail to give due consideration to the viewpoints of all countries—regardless of the relative contribution they can or are expected to make to a common endeavor—end up undermining the very goals they seek to achieve. The international regime is predicated on the notion that, as a member of the international community, each nation-state has the same rights and prerogatives as any other. Disregarding this fundamental principle engenders a sense of unfairness and is perceived—rightly or wrongly—as an unequal, heavy-handed treatment.

Instead of feeling confident that a comprehensive and open consultation process was underway, many delegates attending the climate conference in Copenhagen, especially those from developing countries, felt that they were being asked simply to validate a series of resolutions that had been crafted with no regard to their opinions, let alone their contributions. As a result, valuable, sensible proposals prepared in good faith, though perhaps not properly presented and promoted, were brushed aside, and negotiations came to a standstill. It took painstaking, dedicated work over the following twelve months to regain the confidence of parties, observers, and stakeholders. This was ultimately achieved by ensuring that every voice was heard, by holding consultations in an open and inclusive fashion, and by showing consistency between avowed intentions and actual conduct.

The lesson from Copenhagen is not forgotten at the UNFCCC. The commitment to inclusiveness, openness, and transparency must be substantiated in every session and every exchange. This is also central to ongoing efforts toward the success of COP26. There are many complex issues currently under negotiation. Much must be done to reconcile different positions and build common understanding. But the possibility of success in all areas crucially depends on mutual trust, which, in turn, is contingent on the fulfillment of previous pledges. There is no point in undertaking new commitments if those assumed in the past are seen to be disregarded.

Diplomacy has always been based on trust. It is, at the same time, the most readily available means of building the confidence necessary for collaboration among international actors with different, often divergent interests. From the perspective of the intergovernmental process on climate change, the connection between both concepts may be summarized in this way: trust is both a means and an outcome of diplomacy. In international affairs, there can be no successful diplomacy without trust, just as there can be no trust without effective diplomacy.

Patricia Espinosa is the Executive Secretary of the United Nations Framework Convention on Climate Change (UNFCCC). She previously served as Mexican Minister of Foreign Affairs and the Ambassador of Mexico to Germany.

◂ Patricia Espinosa at the Munich Security Conference in February 2020.

The Human Touch

Atifete Jahjaga

Often as heads of states we live in a fast-paced world, moving from one meeting to another, from one bilateral to a conference, to attending the demands of the job at home, to representing our countries to the best of our abilities. In the ever-shifting environment of international relations, we are envisaged by our peers and constituents alike as operators always under pressure to act with prudence, to be clear-eyed, cold-blooded, void of gushing emotions as we reach pragmatic decisions and are held responsible for the failures. We forget that we, too, are products of our lives, the trajectories of our countries, a motley collection of experiences, both personal and professional.

During my mandate as the president of Kosovo, I shared many of the challenges confronting national leaders of these modern times. My challenges were perhaps even more daunting—I was the first woman president of Kosovo, aware that I represented a small, struggling country that was held to a higher standard by its international patrons because of its history and judged even more harshly because it stood as an example of the West's unity to make good on its promise of "never again" to the persecution of innocent people.

We are envisaged by our peers and constituents alike as operators always under pressure to act with prudence, to be clear-eyed, cold-blooded, void of gushing emotions as we reach pragmatic decisions and are held responsible for the failures. We forget that we, too, are products of our lives, the trajectories of our countries, a motley collection of experiences, both personal and professional.

My approach to international relations and diplomacy, thus, became both personal and professional. I never believed that in our "jobs" you could separate the two, for they were inseparable, and the personal outlasts the professional in diplomacy too.

Which brings me to an experience at the end of my tenure in the spring of 2016, when I visited the then US vice president Joe Biden at the White House. By the measure of our mandates, we were both "outgoing" leaders, but the meeting for me was a chance to reiterate to our main ally to stay the course in supporting Kosovo's and the region's integration in the European Union and NATO. It was also a chance to thank Vice President Biden for three decades of active advocacy and honest involvement with the Balkans, which too many people before and after him had written off as too complicated for their time and investment.

As part of the protocol, it's customary for heads of states to give out medals or national honors. But for my generation, Biden's engagement with the Balkans in general and in bringing the 1999 war to an end in Kosovo in particular felt very personal. I literally wouldn't have been standing in his office in the West Wing if it wasn't for the policies that Mr. Biden and a generation of European and US leaders pioneered in the intervention against Serbia's campaign of bloodshed and ethnic cleansing in Kosovo. My gratitude and that of my country had to match that sentiment.

Mr. Biden had just lost his son, Beau, a renowned lawyer. In the office where we met, Beau's pictures featured prominently among the many beautiful family memories shared by the Biden family. My country had a place in those memories: Beau Biden came to Kosovo following the war to help build the rule of law as a trainer of prosecutors. It felt fitting to commemorate his legacy with the naming of the stretch of the highway that links Kosovo's capital Pristina to the US military camp Bondsteel with Beau's name. It would be a token of appreciation for Mr. Biden, but also a symbolic gesture further strengthening the bond between Kosovo and its greatest ally.

As I handed the decree to Mr. Biden, I fought back my tears; my advisers were not as successful. A year later Biden (who was by then out of office as US vice president) and his family came to the inauguration of the highway as we blessed it with Beau's name. He promised that generations of Bidens would come to visit Kosovo and pay their respect to Beau's legacy, now etched in one of the main arteries linking Kosovo to the region and beyond, a dream of one people that he and his father helped turn into reality.

Atifete Jahjaga was President of the Republic of Kosovo from 2011 to 2016. She is the Founder of the Jahjaga Foundation and Chair of its Board of Directors.

◂ Atifete Jahjaga at the Munich Security Conference in February 2013.

Personal Connections

Børge Brende

If, as Otto von Bismarck famously remarked, politics is the "art of the possible," then diplomacy is the art of the personal. In daring to shape a more peaceful and prosperous future, diplomats stretch the boundaries of possibility, bridging divides that seem chasmic and overcoming obstacles that appear impassable. Breakthroughs like the Camp David Accords and the thawing of the Cold War are instances of inspired diplomacy in action—the result of skilled envoys and leaders negotiating challenging contexts to attain historic outcomes.

Underpinning these and other diplomatic feats are personal relationships—ones that have been forged over weeks, months, and even years. President Jimmy Carter was able to encourage the leaders of Egypt and Israel to pursue peace in the late 1970s because of his friendship with President Anwar Sadat. And the trust between President Ronald Reagan and President Mikhail Gorbachev was critical in steering the countries away from nuclear conflict and toward an end to the Cold War.

To be sure, strategic aims, not personal connections, are what ultimately drive diplomatic endeavors. And the success of these endeavors is determined by whether parties can identify where national interests intersect. But it is the person-to-person relationships that can be key to helping sides take risks, work together through logjams, and find pathways forward. These relationships are often born and nurtured not through formal engagements, with their prescribed protocols, but rather through informal interactions in which diplomats can truly get to know—and trust—one another.

Indeed, there is truth in the oft-repeated refrain that much of the work at the World Economic Forum's Annual Meeting in Davos takes place in the hallways. It is the mingling and tête-à-têtes between ministers, CEOs, and other stakeholders that contribute to advancing progress on shared priorities and, as importantly, to cultivating relationships. The wells of trust formed and filled through these interactions can be tapped to advance future diplomatic undertakings.

What happens, though, when opportunities for this essential element of diplomacy—the building and maintenance of personal relationships—appear to be gone? This, of course, is what seemed to happen in the early days of the COVID-19 pandemic. Though formal diplomatic engagements did continue through digital platforms—the G20 met virtually, the United Nations held the opening of the General Assembly via digital means, and, of course, the World Economic Forum and Munich Security Conference convened summits in virtual formats—the personal interactions so necessary to diplomacy felt out of reach. Thankfully, expectations did not fully become reality. Despite the restrictions on physical gatherings, stakeholders were on occasion able to engage in personal ways in virtual settings, and at times in an informal and impromptu manner similar to what would take place in the hallways of physical meetings.

For instance, ahead of each panel that the World Economic Forum convened for its virtual summits, the Forum established a "speakers' room" and encouraged panelists—ministers, CEOs, and leaders of civil society groups—to sign in twenty minutes ahead of the start of the formal dialogue. What was striking was that many public figures and business leaders used the open line to informally meet or catch up with one another, and on a few occasions, offer well-wishes for birthdays or personal milestones. (On more than one occasion, participants ate quick dinners "together.") Though the conversations were often small talk, when they did take place, they yielded a notably more collaborative atmosphere and productive dialogue in the formal portion of the discussions that followed.

The question, then, is, can digital diplomacy replace in-person diplomacy? Here, as any current or former diplomat would offer, is a compromise: there are merits to both. Because, while the virtual meetings enabled personal connections to form and thrive amid an historic public-health challenge and can offer a way for parties to convene when physical interactions are not possible, there is no substitute over the longer term for in-person collaboration.

The roots of diplomacy rest in relationships. And, as many of us experienced during the pandemic, relationships are at their healthiest and thrive when we can see one another in person.

Børge Brende is the President of the World Economic Forum. He served as Norway's Minister of Foreign Affairs from 2013 to 2017, Minister of the Environment from 2001 to 2004, and Minister of Trade and Industry from 2004 to 2005.

◂ Børge Brende at the MSC Core Group Meeting in Washington, DC, in May 2017.

Munich Security Conference
msc
Münchner Sicherheitskonferenz
ORF

The Utility of Ambassadors

Robert Cooper

In the beginning there were princes. But it was dangerous to let them deal directly with each other. Princes grow up in a world in which everyone is their inferior, and their advisers feared that direct dialogue with another sovereign would bring disaster. So, they invented ambassadors, men of protocol and courtesy, who could smooth relations between proud monarchs and aggressive states.

To begin with, they went to foreign courts as temporary guests, to deal with specific problems, or to see whether a prospective bride was suitable for their prince—the camera may not lie, but portraits so often do. Later, endless competition among the Italian city-states of the Renaissance brought the idea of resident ambassadors, who could track the ambitions and plots of rival sovereigns. Or they were sent as courtiers to watch over a royal bride, as Sir Henry Wotton was for Elizabeth of Bohemia, daughter of James I. He is remembered for his ironic definition of an ambassador as an honest gentleman sent to lie abroad for his country; but the poem he wrote for Elizabeth, the winter Queen of Bohemia, shows him to be a man of taste and talent.[1]

Wars in Europe grew more frequent: the need to watch potential enemies and to keep contact with potential friends grew with them. One of the results of the Napoleonic wars and the Congress of Vienna was agreement on a more regular system of diplomatic exchange. The aristocratic tradition of diplomacy continued—countries were still ruled by kings and by courts. But that ended in 1918; and the horrors of war in the twentieth century made diplomacy no less essential.

As the century went on, people began to ask: why do we need these expensive people in their large houses, giving grand dinners? If leaders want to talk to each other, why don't they do it directly? The first intercontinental phone call took place nearly one hundred years ago, in 1926. Since then, people have asked: what's the point of ambassadors when we have telephones?

To answer this question, I offer some stories that friends, mostly from the British diplomatic service, have told me, together with a couple of personal anecdotes from my time with the European Union.

Nick Westcott

Nick Westcott was the British ambassador to a number of African countries. In one a British visitor was taken hostage by one of the various armed groups operating in the countryside. How do you deal with such a problem? Nick went and had a long talk with the president, who was believed to have back-channel contacts with the rebels, not allowing the conversation to end until the president had suggested a concrete way forward that had some prospect of working. The president put him in touch with a man who was generally thought to be the president's "fixer": his channel to the less respectable elements in his country. Then another conversation—this time in a café but also tête-à-tête—between Nick and the fixer. A long silence followed, but a few months later, the hostage was released.

In many countries, perhaps in most, really important business is accomplished face to face. In Africa getting hold of decision makers on their phones or in their offices can in any case be well-nigh impossible. This is why attending funerals is essential diplomatic work. Funerals matter: attendance is an indispensable mark of respect for the departed. In the run up to one particularly hotly contested election, Nick had found it impossible to pin down either the minister or the party boss responsible for the election process. Fraud was widely anticipated. But when, unexpectedly, a cabinet minister died, the whole government and party were present at the funeral. After the (very long) obsequies, Nick was able to get alongside both men and not only praise the late minister, but also to discuss frankly the consequences of blatantly rigging the election. The personal relationships built at the funeral enabled close contact throughout the elections, and eventually helped the government accept that they had lost and should allow a peaceful transfer of power.

Robin Christopher

Robin Christopher became British ambassador to Indonesia in 1997. At that point, President Suharto and the army were still in charge. This was a relatively benign example of military rule: literacy and living standards improved during Suharto's time. The new British foreign secretary, Robin Cook, made a visit to

◂ Robert Cooper (right) with Wolfgang Ischinger at the MSC Core Group Meeting in Vienna in June 2015.

Jakarta shortly after Christopher's arrival—a good event for a new ambassador who wants to get to know the people who matter. The visit went well. Robin was recovering from it on a beach when he received a phone call telling him of the death of Princess Diana in Paris. He opened a book of condolence at the embassy, wondering whether people in Indonesia would be interested. In fact, Diana had visited Indonesia, and left behind a lasting memory. For a week the queues went around the block; Robin greeted and talked to some of those queuing when he could. Then he noticed in the newspaper that the Indonesian Christian Women's Association was holding a memorial service in the cathedral. He and his wife Merril decided to attend, though there had been no invitation. As the service came to an end, the lady in charge announced that the British ambassador would deliver the eulogy. This was a surprise, but the conversations with the people outside the embassy told Robin exactly what to say.

One useful result of the Secretary Cook's visit was that it gave him a feel for the country, its people, and its politics. He also got to know Ambassador Christopher. This helped greatly when the crisis came. Indonesia had two big issues: the financial crash that ended Suharto's dictatorship, and East Timor. These were linked, and the crisis was a dual crisis. The foreign secretary made the policy , but it was the ambassador who proposed each move during a tense period.

Military rule came to an end in 1998. Suharto had been "reelected" in February of that year, with B. J. Habibie as his vice president. Habibie was a brilliant aeronautical engineer with a doctorate from Aachen University. He rose to be vice president of Messerschmitt in Germany. In 1974 Suharto, whose dream was for Indonesia to have its own aerospace industry, persuaded him to return to Indonesia and made him minister for research and technology. Only Suharto thought Habibie would make a good vice president; but at that point, only Suharto's opinion mattered.

The Asian financial crisis began in 1997 and reached its peak in the spring of 1998. Indonesia was its biggest victim. In February Suharto was in full control. By May, a million people were on the streets, and many homes and businesses—especially those owned by Chinese—were in flames. (What do ambassadors do at such times? They help their national communities through the chaos, and in the last resort, organize evacuations—as Robin and his colleagues did.) Suharto held a press conference at which everyone expected him to resign. He didn't, but instead announced a cabinet reshuffle. When every minister refused to serve, he resigned. Habibie had been vice president for just three months, but he took over. The army might have overthrown him but, perhaps in the stability and prosperity of the Suharto years, they had lost the habit. Habibie himself told Robin one evening that the military had surrounded his house the night before and demanded he resign. He had refused and eventually they had gone away. Habibie rode the wave of revolution for a year and saw Indonesia safely to its first free election in a generation.

East Timor had been a Portuguese colony until the collapse of the Portuguese Empire in 1975. With that, Fretelin, a Marxist liberation movement in East Timor, declared independence. In response the Indonesian army moved in from West Timor and began twenty-four years of occupation and atrocities. Only Australia recognized Indonesian sovereignty. Portugal had given its other colonies self-determination, and when it joined the EU in 1985, it kept the EU firmly behind the cause of self-determination for East Timor. One result of this was that no EU head of mission had ever visited East Timor, though it was now the dominant thorn in the side of Indonesia's foreign policy.

When Suharto fell, the UK held the rotating presidency of the EU. Robin led the EU "troika"—which included the previous and following presidency ambassadors—on a fact-finding visit to East Timor. Their reception by crowds of Timorese paved the way for a change of heart by Habibie, now president, who offered East Timor "extensive autonomy" within Indonesia. He recognized that this offer needed to be legitimized and agreed to a referendum, to be organized by the UN. The East Timorese would be asked to vote for or against autonomy, with a clear understanding that a vote against autonomy would be a vote for independence. Robin was one of the international observers at the referendum, which was treated as a kind of festival. A few days later Kofi Annan announced the overwhelming rejection of autonomy. At this point, the Indonesian army again ran amok in East Timor, with arson, rape, murder, and destruction in their wake.

Following the announcement of the result, President Habibie moved the leader of the East Timor independence movement, Xanana Gusmão, from prison to house arrest. Robin had visited him in prison and saw him again on his return from the referendum. Gusmão was to be released soon, but the news from East Timor made clear that he would not be safe there. So, he asked Robin whether, instead, he could stay with him. Robin was able to get an immediate positive response from Robin Cook; the Indonesian government agreed; and the British government provided a protection unit. Gusmão remained at the British embassy for his first two weeks of freedom.

During this time, the UN Security Council sent a team of ambassadors to Indonesia. In Jakarta they met Gusmão at the embassy, and they persuaded the government to let them take General Wiranto, head of the Indonesian army, with them to East Timor. A BBC team was also on board. The BBC interviewed the general in the ruins of Dili, the capital. Wiranto admitted, on camera, that things were not under control and that he was shocked at the destruction wrought by the Indonesian military and its militias. This prepared the way for an eventual UN peacekeeping operation.

Peter Westmacott

Western capitals are less exotic, but they are the site of an endless flow of business. Here the telephone may come into the picture, but if leaders speak to each other directly they still need to be briefed.

Peter Westmacott was the British ambassador in Ankara, Paris, and Washington. One high spot of his mission to Ankara took place not in Ankara but in Brussels: this was the moment in 2004 when a date was finally set for the opening of negotiations with Turkey for membership of the European Union. It came at the end of a period of success for the EU—reform in East and Central Europe that enabled most countries there to join. At that moment, it seemed that Turkey too might follow this path. It had embarked on dramatic reforms to improve its justice system and to integrate its Kurdish minority. The process with Turkey was tense and complicated, and some issues were still open when Prime Minister Erdoğan travelled to Brussels in December 2004. There the European Council was going to take the decision on opening enlargement negotiations with Turkey. Tony Blair asked Peter to be there too . Peter had been alongside Prime Minister Erdoğan and the others in the delegation through the negotiations and knew each of them personally. This continued through the tense climax in Brussels. Afterward, one Turkish newspaper ran a headline "Come quickly, Peter," quoting a text message sent by a member of the delegation at the climax of the negotiations when Erdoğan was about to leave empty-handed in a huff. That message says it all.

The story did not end in success. The EU opened membership negotiations and Turkey remains a vital partner for Europe; but it is also a complicated country, with difficult neighbours. In November 2003, a suicide bomber attacked the British Consulate General in Istanbul, killing twelve of the staff. Then came the war in Iraq—a neighbor of Turkey, with 90 percent of the Turkish people against it. The most destructive shock came when, after years of effort, the Annan plan to reunite Cyprus was accepted by the Turkish community in Cyprus but rejected by the Greek community. When Cyprus then joined the EU, it seemed likely to confirm the division rather than end it.

Another example of what an ambassador can do is from Peter's time in Washington. Getting Iran's agreement to limit its nuclear program was a longstanding British and European objective, dating from the time of the Iraq war. The Obama administration joined, and then took over, the European initiative. It opened a secret back-channel to the Iranians (not a surprise to any ally of Washington). The outcome was what we had wanted all along: an agreement between Iran on the one hand and on the other Britain, France, Germany (plus the EU collectively), the United States, China, and Russia, "the P5 plus 1"[2]. The agreement, a fat document known by the inspiring acronym, "JCPOA"[3], limited Iran's nuclear program and provided for verification by the IAEA. In return, the P5 plus 1 were to remove the economic sanctions they had imposed on Iran.

This was a major success; but in the United States the treaty risked being blocked by Congress. Working for this result was the formidable figure of the Israeli Prime Minister, Benjamin Netanyahu, backed by the American Israeli Public Affairs Committee, the most powerful lobby group in Washington. The President can veto hostile legislation; but a two-thirds majority in the Senate can override his veto. Thus, the administration's target was thirty-four votes in the Senate. Peter and his colleagues thought the agreement with Iran deserved better. He, sometimes on his own, sometimes with colleagues from Germany, France, Russia, and China, talked to dozens of senators and more than a hundred members of the House. The House and the Senate are used to negotiating with the Administration and occasionally to lobbying by foreign governments; but this concerted effort was something new, and it was successful.

Shortly after this, Peter accompanied Philip Hammond, the new UK foreign secretary, to call on the (Republican) chair of the Senate Foreign Relations Committee, Bob Corker. Senator Corker, normally affable and friendly, launched an attack, complaining that the UK had interfered in US internal affairs by lobbying for the JCPOA and saying that he would regard any recurrence as a personal affront. With the foreign secretary unprepared for this, Peter himself replied asking why it was acceptable for the prime minister of Israel to lobby against President Obama's policy, but not for the British ambassador to lobby for a treaty that both Britain and the US had signed.

I end with two stories from my personal experience. Neither involves an ambassador; but each was the man on the spot—which is what an ambassador is.[4]

Peter Sørensen

Technically, Peter Sorensen, a Danish lawyer, soldier, and diplomat, was a third secretary in the Danish embassy in Belgrade. He had served in the Danish contingent in the EU observer mission in Croatia and Bosnia, worked as a legal adviser to Carl Bildt in Sarajevo, and then as the deputy head of the UN mission in Kosovo. Peter is a no-nonsense sort of person, open, friendly, and ready to take risks. With Kosovo preparing to declare itself independent, my boss, Javier Solana, asked Peter to be his personal representative in Belgrade. Copenhagen gave him a position in its embassy; Brussels gave him a telephone.

Peter got to know the Serb politicians who were interested in Kosovo and himself became known around Belgrade. Among others he made friends with the people—mostly about his age—who ran President Boris Tadić's office.

Kosovo declared independence early in 2008. Over the next year, most EU member states recognized Kosovo, but five did not. In the autumn of 2008, Serbia proposed that the UN General Assembly ask the International Court of Justice (ICJ) for an opinion on the legality of Kosovo's declaration of independence. The US and most EU countries resisted, but Serbia won the vote. At the end of that year, President Tadic sent the EU an application for membership. Some member states blocked this, arguing that Serbia should be more constructive on the Kosovo question before the EU took its application forward.

> For almost every country in the world, the person in your government who knows most about that country is your ambassador there. The secret of good foreign policy is simple. Get yourself a good ambassador—and then follow his advice.

In the summer of 2010, the ICJ was about to publish its opinion, and the EU needed to react. We put a draft statement to the EU Political and Security Committee. This was debated at length, with the draft becoming shorter and shorter as the debate went on. At the end of some five or six hours, two member states were holding out—one because of a general allergy to unilateral declarations of independence, the other, partly for the same reason but also because their president was a personal friend of President Tadic.

Throughout the process, we were in touch with Peter by phone. When the committee seemed completely blocked, he said he might be able to help. He called on his friends in Tadic's office, saying that if their president wanted his application to join the EU to go forward, he would need the EU to have an agreed position on Kosovo. That position would not be what Serbia wanted. But if there was no agreed position on Kosovo, the EU would spend its time arguing about Kosovo and would never get round to Serbia's membership application. These were intelligent people and they saw the point. They phoned their opposite numbers in the second state mentioned above, saying that Tadic needed an EU consensus, and he hoped they could join it. They sent new instructions to Brussels. That left one member state isolated, and they agreed to join the consensus.

This was a remarkable piece of diplomacy. Drawing on his imagination, reputation for good sense and honesty, and the trust he built with the key people, Peter pulled it off. Only someone on the ground can do that. The EU statement was a carefully worded piece of bureaucratic prose. But now the EU had a policy. It did not take a position on the legality of Kosovo's declaration of independence (nor did the ICJ) but it did offer to facilitate dialogue between Serbia and Kosovo—at that point, they had no contact with each other. Later, this language became part of a UN General Assembly resolution. The dialogue began a few months later and is still ongoing. It has not solved the problem between Serbia and Kosovo, but it has brought some progress and has helped keep the peace.

Andreas List

My second story is of a tiny episode in a long story. In 2010 Piero Fassino, a distinguished Italian politician, and I visited Myanmar, representing the European Union. This was the first high-level visit for many years. In Myanmar a new government, elected under a new (and flawed) constitution, had surprised the world by releasing Aung San Suu Kyi from house arrest, and was showing signs that it wanted to end their country's pariah status. Mr. Fassino and I brought with us a simple message: If the government did two things the EU would lift all its sanctions, some of which had been in place for more than ten years. What we asked for was first, the release of all political prisoners, and second, that the National League for Democracy (NLD), Aung San Suu Kyi's party, be allowed to participate in national political life.

We were well received. We repeated our message to everyone. The meetings were formal. In the Asian fashion, we sat side by side rather than opposite each other. The Myanmar side usually had a dozen officials supporting their minister. Everyone was polite; everyone listened, nodded, and smiled. No one asked questions or challenged us. Had they understood what we were offering? And what we were asking from them? If the EU dropped sanctions, there was a chance that the US would start down the same road. I worried that we were not getting through.

In this formal setting, there was no chance for a private conversation so after the last official meeting—with the foreign minister—as we left and shook hands, I, the last one in the line, gripped his hand for a long time and told him that we had imposed sanctions because, on our television screens, we had seen the Burmese military shooting monks in the streets. They needed to do something equally dramatic to change their image. For example, if they decided to release political prisoners, as we asked, perhaps they should release them all on one day. That would wake everyone up across the world.

The minister did not reply. He looked puzzled, maybe a little shocked. In the evening, the deputy minister gave a farewell dinner. At the end, he took me aside and told me that his minister had asked if I could repeat to him what I had said earlier in the day. That gave me a chance to explain myself better. I said the point I was trying to make was that we were serious. We meant what we said, and our offer was potentially transformational for Myanmar's relationship with us and with others. The deputy minister listened carefully, but I heard nothing more. I returned to Yangon and was getting ready to leave for the airport when the deputy minister called on a very bad line—telephones were 1950s vintage. He recalled our conversation and asked if we could explain exactly who it was we meant when we talked of "political prisoners." I said we would send him a list the next day. We had been calling for the release of political prisoners for twenty years. This was the first time anyone had asked who we meant.

Where does the ambassador come in? The EU didn't have one in Myanmar; we had a tiny, three-person office. The leader of this small team, Andreas List, was the nearest thing to an ambassador. He had a passion for Myanmar that went back years and had been in and out of the country a number of times. A former Austrian diplomat, he knew the country and its people well.

Before the last meeting, I told him that I worried we were not getting through. Perhaps I might try to shock the Burmese side out of their politeness. I told him what I was thinking of saying and asked what he thought. His reply? "You can't imagine how long I have waited to hear someone suggest something like that." That was what I needed: advice from someone who knew the country. It gave me the confidence to try. I wouldn't have done it without his assent. Nor did his role end there: I told the deputy minister that we would send them a list the following day. In fact, we did not have one. But Andreas called in his friends from the NGO community, and they put together a list of more than a thousand names. This was highly imperfect, but over time, we were able to correct and complete it. Most important, the Myanmar authorities did what we asked—testing the water by releasing first a few, and when that brought positive reactions abroad and at home, in growing numbers. In the end, thousands were freed.

One other small thing Andreas did: the debates in Myanmar's new Parliament were as stiff and stilted as our meetings with them. The fact that a quarter of the seats were reserved for army officers nominated by the commander in chief did not help. Democracy is about debate as well as elections. Andreas organized dinners for MPs while the parliament was in session, so they could debate themes such as the rule of law or trade policy. There was always a lively, open, and serious discussion, usually ending with selfies all round.

Myanmar is now in a new crisis, following yet another military coup, accompanied by terrible acts of violence. Despite this and the COVID-19 crisis, nine months later, resistance to the military still goes on. It is astonishing how nine years of mediocre democracy, under a flawed constitution, has transformed Myanmar. Those involved, who risk their lives and those of their families, deserve all the support we can give them.

A last personal memory: In 1982 my job in the FCO gave me access to almost all incoming cables. When we found ourselves at war with Argentina, normal business stopped. I was reading messages from ambassadors who I had never heard of before, from countries I couldn't find on the map. They were reporting that they had obtained overflight permission, or that they had persuaded a government to delay a shipment of warm clothing for Argentine armed forces. It was a kind of Eureka moment: That's why we had ambassadors in these forgotten places! And they'd been doing a good job.

For almost every country in the world, the person in your government who knows most about that country is your ambassador there. Every country is different: different history, different geography, different hopes and fears, different personalities. The secret of good foreign policy is simple. Get yourself a good ambassador—and then follow his advice.

Robert Cooper was the Director-General for External and Politico-Military Affairs of the Council of the European Union and later served as Counsellor at the European External Action Service. His most recent book, *The Ambassadors. Thinking about Diplomacy from Machiavelli to Modern Times,* was published in 2021.

Khvtisiashvili
Bensouda
Lévy
Lorenz

International Law and Diplomacy

Fatou Bensouda

Many contend that diplomacy and multilateralism are in decline. I don't think that is true, but I do observe with concern that in this new century we increasingly find ourselves confronted with threats to multilateralism and the post-World War II rules-based global order in which the sanctity of sovereignty is misappropriated in the service of exceptionalism and a rejection of international law and the international rule of law.

A Hobbesian world in which every nation must fend for itself in a lawless state of chaos would indeed be nasty and brutish. This is not a theoretical construct, but the reality of the human experience and the lesson of history, and of war and peace, throughout the ages.

These were costly lessons that gave rise to the post-World War II global order, however imperfect, in the hopes of saving future generations from the scourge of destructive great power rivalry, perpetual wars, and mass atrocities. Indeed, these were the same lessons that gave birth to the world's most successful regional integration project to date: the European Union, inspiring many others to follow suit.

Lest we forget that multilateralism as the preferred modus operandi for inter-state relations and cooperation, multilateral institutions, including those that advance the peaceful settlement of disputes and the rule of law, are all hard-earned fruits of our costly experience, our common loss, and indeed, our common awakening and wisdom.

In an increasingly interdependent world, faced with global challenges from global pandemics, climate change, and cross-border terrorism to war and mass atrocities, real success and progress depend on our willingness to acknowledge that it is only through collaboration, diplomatic engagement, and a concerted effort that we can hope to counter the destructive and destabilizing force of these ills. A zero-sum unilateral approach may at best result in short-term gain but is sure to issue in long-term net loss.

In the wake of the World War II, it became clear that international anarchy and the coercion and influence of competing powers could not continue unchecked without catastrophic effect. The only alternative, we had come to accept, was a strong commitment to multilateralism, diplomatic engagement, and the development of a rules-based global order dedicated to mutual respect between nations and the maintenance of international peace and security. The United Nations was hence established, indeed as it has been said, not "to bring us to heaven, but to save us from hell." The world today, irrespective of the many challenges it confronts, is still a less chaotic and safer place because of that innovation.

We must embrace these successes and the forward march of humanity toward a better future in which the outbreak of war is less and less seen as civilized practice but rather the failure of imagination and intellect to do better, to preempt and resolve disputes without resorting to the sword.

Humanity must equip itself with the tools to make war and war making ever more difficult while cultivating and protecting mechanisms and institutions that facilitate dialogue, diplomacy, and the peaceful settlement of disputes. Addressing disputes and violence through international law and legal mechanisms must surely be included in our toolbox.

A zero-sum unilateral approach may at best result in short-term gain but is sure to issue in long-term net loss.

As the former prosecutor of the International Criminal Court (ICC), I sincerely believe that the ICC is a central pillar of a rules-based international system rooted in respect for international law, and the fight against impunity for the world's gravest crimes of concern to the international community.

Over 120 states across the world created the ICC as an independent judicial institution, complementary to national jurisdictions, with the mandate to investigate and prosecute genocide, crimes against humanity, war crimes, and the crime of aggression. The creation of the ICC, against all odds, by itself constitutes a major diplomatic achievement and an important milestone in human history.

This was an achievement of all states that joined the negotiations, but, in particular, small and midsized states. It was due to their relentless effort, often supported by strong civil society actors, that the longtime dream of a permanent ICC became a reality.

◂ Fatou Bensouda at the MSC Core Group Meeting in Doha in October 2019.

With the creation of the ICC, an important normative but also structural and systems-based message was sent globally that the commission of mass atrocities as merely politics by other means will no longer receive a pass, and that perpetrators, irrespective of rank or official status, must answer for their crimes either at the national or international level.

Since its start of operations in 2003, with numerous ups and downs and notwithstanding significant challenges, the court has managed to establish itself as a crucial judicial institution, gradually building its policies, protocols, caseload, and jurisprudence.

The court has been implementing its mandate with full independence and impartiality, while benefiting from the judicial and operational assistance of its states parties.

International criminal justice is necessary if we are to have a less conflict-prone world, or at least, to ensure that the law does not remain silent during otherwise lawless wars. That the victims of atrocity crimes are not forgotten. That they too have a voice. That they too count and have access to justice for the atrocities that have devastated their lives and livelihoods.

International criminal justice is necessary if we are to have a less conflict-prone world, or at least, to ensure that the law does not remain silent during otherwise lawless wars.

Let me emphasize that we cannot accept selective justice and double standards where the reach of justice only extends to some, while others see themselves above the law and take comfort in the belief that "might is right" and that power alone will govern.

It takes the courage and often the sacrifice of millions to finally adopt multilateral institutions that advance the human condition and experience; but it takes only silence and inaction in the face of ill-wishers to lose the progress made.

Although there are still far too many conflicts around the world in which mass atrocities are being committed, during my tenure as ICC prosecutor, I did everything in my power to ensure that the voices of as many victims as possible were heard. That these victims were able to reap the benefits of justice and that justice was applied independently and objectively across the board, irrespective of the nationality of the perpetrator or victim. For our dogged defense of what is right and necessary in the professional discharge of our mandates under the court's founding treaty, I and some of my colleagues paid the price in the form of threats and unprecedented sanctions.

No single advance in human progress has traveled the path of least resistance. In Albert Einstein's timeless words, "Peace is not merely the absence of war, but the presence of justice, of law, and of order."

We must stay the course, even if under strain and the push and pull of Machiavellian politics. Multilateralism and diplomacy have to be the preferred modus operandi for interstate relations and cooperation to advance the human condition, and in the case of international criminal justice, accountability and justice for the victims.

No single advance in human progress has travelled the path of least resistance.

It is my true hope that with unshakable resolve, advocates and agents of peace and stability the world over in this and future generations will commit to ensuring that multilateralism and diplomacy, the international rule of law, and their instruments of practice take humanity to the next eon of civilization.

A world that invests in accountability for atrocity crimes will surely reap its peace dividends.

Fatou Bensouda was Prosecutor of the International Criminal Court from 2012 to 2021. She previously served as Attorney General and Minister of Justice of the Republic of The Gambia and at the UN International Criminal Tribunal for Rwanda, where she worked as a Legal Adviser and Trial Attorney before rising to the position of Senior Legal Advisor and Head of the Legal Advisory Unit.

The Knotted Gun at the United Nations Headquarters in New York City. ▸

Munich Security Conference
msc

Military Power and Diplomacy

James G. Stavridis

I recently published my tenth book, but my first work of fiction. It is entitled 2034: *A Novel of the Next World War*, and is set about a decade from now. The book chronicles how the US and China could stumble into a global conflict that would be in the interests of neither nation. It is an imagined colossal failure of the norms of international law and diplomacy that we all respect and discuss annually at the Munich Security Conference.

People often ask me how I came to write a bestselling novel about a war in the future. The short answer is that I decided to write about the future because I was thinking about the past. I was focused on the rich body of Cold War literature that helped us all imagine how terrible a war between the US and Soviet Union would have been. Movies like *Dr. Strangelove* and *Fail Safe* and novels such as *On the Beach* and *The Third World War* presented doomsday scenarios. I believe they helped deter that war.

But today, the US and China have no such comparative body of literature, either in film or novels. Our collective imagination is failing us, and the nations feel at times as though they are sleepwalking to war. Disputes surrounding Taiwan, the South China Sea, human rights, cybersecurity, 5G networks, trade, and tariffs are all too real. Much as the economies of Europe were intertwined just over a hundred years ago, and the US and Chinese financial systems are highly interconnected today. But that interconnection did not stop an assassin's bullet in Sarajevo in August 1914 from "turning out the lights" in Europe.

Militaries will always prepare for war with great energy and determination. Today, both the US military and the People's Liberation Army are doing so, expending vast amounts of resources to build global navies, hypersonic cruise missiles, military space systems, advanced unmanned vehicles, artificial intelligence capabilities, and elite special forces units. As those militaries come into almost daily contact in the contested waters of the South China Sea, the likelihood for a miscalculation—a twenty-first century version of the assassin's bullet from 1914—is rising inexorably. What I learned as Supreme Allied Commander Europe (SACEUR), is that there must be a coherent linkage between military capability and diplomatic activity. Some of the key tactical elements include ensuring that militaries have active communication and the ability to instantaneously connect over so-called "hotlines"; that there is firm civilian control over the military at the highest level, as well as strong tactical obedience all the way to the ships and aircraft in contact in the field; that objectives and "red lines" are clearly and directly communicated between nations by competent diplomats; and that there are ample opportunities to allow diplomats to do the hard, day-to-day work of meeting and airing differences.

I also learned the high value of alliances. When I led a coalition of more than fifty nations in the International Security Force Afghanistan as the strategic commander, I worked more on international relationships than on anything else. That meant flying to the capital of every nation in the coalition; meeting regularly with the Ambassadors of those nations in Brussels; paying my respects to the military leaders in their home countries; coordinating constantly with the diplomats of NATO, including of course my boss, the Secretary General; and briefing the media in each country. Finally, as I reflect on those days, I realize how important it is to find the balance between hard and soft power. You need *both* if you are going to create real security, because true security does not come solely from the barrel of a gun. Yet soft power alone will not suffice in many situations. Soft power without the ability to apply hard power is essentially no power.

Success requires a balance between hard military power and humanitarian assistance, disaster relief, respect for human rights, economic assistance, infrastructure improvements, and communication—the values of democracy, liberty, and freedom for which NATO stands. Think of it not as an "on and off switch," but rather as a rheostat—you must have hard power, but finding the right balance between hard and soft power is the key. Some have called this "smart power," and I agree with that idea fully.

Diplomats and warriors must work together to achieve lasting security, and if we are going to avoid a war with China, it will require hard efforts by both across the Pacific. That is the crucial lesson I learned in my time as SACEUR. Leadership means warriors and diplomats working together in the cause of peace.

James G. Stavridis, a retired four-star U.S. naval officer, is Vice Chair, Global Affairs, at The Carlyle Group, and Chair of the Board of Trustees at the Rockefeller Foundation. He served as Supreme Allied Commander at NATO from 2009 to 2013 and as Dean of Tuft University's Fletcher School of Law and Diplomacy from 2013 to 2018.

◂ James G. Stavridis as a guest at MSC Events, among others at the Munich Security Conference 2018.

msc
Giesecke+Devrient
msc 2020

The Language of Power

Josep Borrell

October 2019—The Origins of a Fateful Phrase

For good or bad, I suspect that my mandate as EU High Representative will be associated with a phrase I used during my hearing in the European Parliament, namely that Europeans had "to learn to speak the language of power."

I argued then that the origin of the European integration project stemmed from a rejection of power politics among the participating states. Of course, conflicts as such had not been abolished, but the EU had succeeded by turning political problems into technocratic ones and by supplanting power calculations with legal procedures.

In the history of international relations and the continent, this had been a Copernican revolution and a spectacular success, cementing peace and cooperation among previously warring parties. It had created institutions, mental maps, and a certain vocabulary that were unique. Europeans were, rightly, proud of this "escape from history."

In fact, Europe's main problem is not a lack of power per se, but fragmented power.

But this triumph had come at a cost: a reluctance to acknowledge that, outside our post-modern European garden, "the jungle was growing back," as Robert Kagan put it.[1] There had been a rise in power politics with more countries willing to use force, blackmail, and intimidation to get their way.

So, history had not ended, as some argued, but a new chapter had begun. With Europe surrounded by crises and the world marked by great power competition, I argued in October 2019, Europeans had to be realistic and approach the world as it is, not just as they want it to be. They had to learn, or maybe relearn, to think and act in terms of power.

In fact, Europe's main problem is not a lack of power per se, but fragmented power. Europe has plenty of levers—from trade and investment leverage, to our norm- and standard-setting powers (the so-called "Brussels effect" as described by Anu Bradford),[2] to our aid budget, our crisis management operations, our sanctions, and so on. However, policies in these fields proceed according to their own rhythm and logic. Hence, I argued, we must pull these levers together and use them in support of a single political strategy.

The phrase resonated quite well at the time. It was coined when President von der Leyen proclaimed a "Geo-Political Commission"; President Macron was pushing Europeans to defend their "strategic autonomy" or "sovereignty" and Chancellor Merkel had already in 2017 called on Europe "to take its fate into its own hands." The upheavals of the Trump presidency were one big reason for this conceptual convergence, but I am convinced that the drive behind Europe's geopolitical awakening was and is broader and deeper.

What Impact on Policy?

The question is how, two years on, Europe is doing when it comes to putting these phrases and concepts into effect. Giving an answer requires specifying that foreign policy deals with continuous variables, not discrete ones. In other words, diplomacy is a process, not an event. And the verdict is mixed.

There are some areas where we can point to Europe thinking and acting more in terms of the language of power, confidently defending European viewpoints. For example, we are putting into practice our strategy of approaching China along the triptych of "partner, competitor, and rival."

We have taken concrete decisions on investment screening, industrial subsidies, 5G, and procurement, to address the problem of asymmetrical openness, with more measures to come. At the same time, we work with China on climate change or the Iran nuclear deal, as doing so is manifestly in our interest.

There are some areas where we can point to Europe thinking and acting more in terms of the language of power, confidently defending European viewpoints.

I see a similar process around a realistic and robust approach to Russia, along the lines of "push back, constrain, and engage." We have shown our resolve by not only rolling over our sanctions, but adding to them,

◂ Josep Borrell at the Munich Security Conference in February 2020.

despite many who predicted we would split on Russia, as we have done in the past.

We have launched two new CSDP operations: one to enforce the Libyan arms embargo and another to assist Mozambique in addressing the growing terrorist threat. We also launched the Coordinated Maritime Presence concept in the Gulf of Guinea. This shows that Europeans are willing to commit resources to be a security provider.

We have also adopted a global human rights sanctions regime to go after human rights violators, wherever they may be. Even if they reside in China and if our principled stance triggers counter-sanctions. We have also adopted the first-ever sanctions against those who violate basic international norms in the field of cyber, from Russia, China, and North Korea.

If you want dialogue, diplomacy, and multilateralism to succeed, you need to put power behind it. That's the point of "learning the language of power."

There certainly are positive developments. Are they enough? The Taliban takeover in Afghanistan has been a tragedy for the Afghans and a big blow to the West, but also a wake-up call for Europe. We have to enhance our capacity to think, decide, and act in strategic terms, preferably with partners, but alone if needed.

I am convinced that we need to exist as a political union. This will only happen if we have the necessary capabilities, and above all, the will to use them. It is clear that the term "strategic autonomy" is more attractive to some in the EU than others. This often happens with semantic debate in Europe. I believe that what matters is our capacity to act, if need be, on our own. In a hypercompetitive world, Europe has to be able to defend its interests and vision, as others do too. To get serious about this agenda, we must build confidence among us Europeans. We need to invest in understanding each other's security concerns and to take them seriously. And we need to go beyond security and defense. For me strategic autonomy isn't just about a five thousand-strong intervention force—although we need one—but about microchips, supply chains, artificial intelligence, rare earths, and so on. We need to reduce dependencies and maintain our freedom of action in all strategic domains.

How to Do It and Escape the Paralysis of Divisions among Member States

From my European Parliament hearing onward, I have repeatedly stressed that as long as we don't have a common strategic culture and as long as we stick to the unanimity rule, EU foreign policy will suffer. In the past two years, we have seen this when we struggled to take decisions on Hong Kong, the conflict between Israel and Hamas, or sanctions on Belarus.

I have underlined that it is not necessary to consider a move to qualified majority voting across the board, but that we could envisage using qualified majority voting (QMV) or constructive abstention to get around the delays and paralysis of the strict unanimity rule.
It is of course always preferable to have the full backing of all twenty-seven member states. However, at some point the delays and the weakening of positions outweigh these benefits.

The key point is about negotiating dynamics. In the EU, we don't vote very often in fields in which QMV applies. The whole ethos of the council is to keep talking and look for common ground. But because everyone knows that eventually there could be a vote, member states invest in coalition building and converging on compromises. In foreign policy these days, we unfortunately see countries simply sitting on their position. And that makes all the difference.

I believe we need an honest debate about how we make decisions on EU foreign policy. We need to take seriously the different arguments, including the fear of smaller countries or "front line states" being steamrolled by bigger countries. We should experiment with allowing ourselves to escape the paralysis of unanimity, in some elected areas, for instance in human rights statements, civilian operations, and so on.

The best place to have this debate is in the context of the Conference on the Future of Europe. Citizens definitely want a stronger "Europe in the world": around 80 percent support this. They are ahead of governments in sensing that in a world of big threats and uncertainty, we need to go faster and have more impact. That's why I favor a taboo-free discussion on how we can give ourselves the means to do exactly that.

The Language of Power and the Power of Language

I am proud that Europeans continue to favor dialogue over confrontation, diplomacy over force, multilateralism over unilateralism. But if you want dialogue, diplomacy, and multilateralism to succeed, you need to put power behind it. That's the point of "learning the language of power." I think more Europeans agree on this now than ever, and if that's the case, then perhaps it also proves the power of language . . .

We Europeans must use the "language of power," not for narrow purposes, but to defend our legitimate interests and values in a rougher world—and to build larger coalitions for a rules-based international system. Because upholding and reforming that system remains the ultimate goal of European diplomacy.

Josep Borrell is the High Representative of the European Union for Foreign Affairs and Security Policy/Vice-President of the European Commission for a Stronger Europe in the World. He previously served as Spanish Foreign Minister and President of the European Parliament.

Munich Security Confere

msc

The Power of Language

Jasmine M. El-Gamal

In August 2012, US president Barack Obama uttered what would become three of the most consequential words of his presidency: "a red line." In discussing the actions of Syrian president Bashar Al-Assad at the time, President Obama said, "We have been very clear to the Assad regime," he said, "that a red line for us is we start seeing a whole bunch of chemical weapons moving around or being utilized. That would change my calculus."[1]

Many of us working on the Syria portfolio immediately grasped the significance of the president's words and pondered what they would mean in practice should that line be crossed. We would find out soon enough. On August 21, 2013, Assad attacked residents of the Damascus suburb of Ghouta with sarin gas-filled rockets. It was the deadliest use of chemical weapons since the Iran-Iraq War in 1980. In that moment, President Obama's three words loomed larger than he might have ever expected. Depending on how the US responded, those three words could mean a loss of American credibility and deterrence, or another US military engagement in the Middle East. President Obama's advisors, members of Congress, pundits, and activists began churning out arguments for both action and inaction, with each side painting an end-of-the-world scenario if the president made the wrong decision. All the while, images of Ghouta's dead civilians haunted us. President Obama kicked off a diplomatic flurry of activity, calling allies and partners and making the case for a unified stance to send Assad a message that this type of aggression broke the norms of warfare and would not be tolerated. Secretary of State John Kerry was on television making the case to the American public, stating that "we need to hear an appropriate outcry as we think back on those moments of history when large numbers of people have been killed because the world was silent."[2]

The diplomatic push seemed to work. The US had assurances from several countries that they would participate in a response to Assad's actions. The Pentagon drew up response options. Our partners were poised for action. It seemed as if Assad would pay the price for crossing President Obama's red line. Two things happened that would change the course of events. The UK Parliament voted against British participation in any military action and President Obama took a walk with his top advisor, White House Chief of Staff Denis McDonough. The two events put an end to any planned action in Syria, as Obama then announced that he would seek permission from his own legislative branch (which would be denied). America's allies and partners were upset that they were not consulted about the change in plans beforehand and Obama's own secretary of defense at the time, Leon Panetta, would publicly lament the loss of American credibility—both with our friends and our enemies—because of the abrupt about-face.

The lack of military action in the end and the frustration of key partners with President Obama's seeming about-face would go on to undermine a second, critical round of diplomacy, this time with the Russians and Syrians. By the time Secretary Kerry announced a deal with the Russians under which Assad would agree to give up his chemical weapons stockpile, the Americans had lost the leverage they would have needed to ensure that Russia and Syria were engaging in good faith and to act accordingly if they were not. The Russians and the Syrians now had two critical pieces of information: Obama was not willing to engage in military action in Syria and America's friends would likely be wary to join any future coalition should Obama change his mind, given the sting of the previous experience. Obama had lost the levers he needed to enforce Kerry's diplomatic "win." By now, we know how the story ends. While lauded at the time as a positive turn of events, Assad has continued using chemical weapons against the Syrian people, safe in the knowledge that he will bear no consequences for doing so.

So what lessons did we learn from the "red line" crisis? First and foremost, there is power in words and they should therefore be used carefully. Second, keeping one's word is inextricably linked to successful diplomacy. Trust and credibility are at the core of any successful diplomatic initiative and they in turn provide the leverage required to ensure that parties to the diplomatic initiative are acting in good faith—and to marshal collective action when they are not.

Jasmine M. El-Gamal is a Senior Manager for Asia, the Middle East, and Africa at the Institute for Strategic Dialogue. She served at the Pentagon during the Obama presidency and was the head of the Syria team during the "red line" crisis. She was a Munich Young Leader in 2013.

◂ Jasmine M. El-Gamal at the Munich Young Leaders Alumni Meeting in New York City in September 2019.

Tea Diplomacy

Siemtje Möller

In Frisia we drink tea! The Frisian tea ceremony has been celebrated in my electoral district and the north of Germany for centuries. Recently, Frisians were even acknowledged as the world champions of drinking tea, with a consumption of around 300 liters per person per year. The ritual of drinking tea has connected people from all over the world for centuries. Similarly, the art of diplomacy is a way of connecting. Finding commonalities is easier with the help of rituals, and drinking tea can be such a ritual, as it is able to establish a platform for dialogue, to build bridges even when it seems impossible.

When I traveled to Afghanistan as a member of the Defense Committee, I met Shallah Hadid, speaker of the Women's Council of the Balkh province. In one of those typical gatherings of many male interlocutors, we sat in a traditional tent for a meal that included Afghanistan's unofficial national drink: tea. There was no better way to bring together an Afghan and a Frisian woman. The ritual quickly established trust and created an understanding. Sitting down for tea implies that time is taken to enjoy the ceremony. It's not a drink to have on the go. Through the ritual, a channel of communication can open up, just as it did between Shallah Hadid and me. She saw her chance with the German delegation warning of a Taliban rule and violence against women, were the Taliban to return.

Bringing people together and accepting them as coequals is often achieved through rituals. Just like diplomacy, drinking tea is an investment in time.

In 2018 Germany's then foreign minister Sigmar Gabriel sat down with his counterpart Mevlüt Çavuşoğlu from Turkey. The picture this created was obvious, not only for diplomats. Drinking tea at Gabriel's home, the minister served the tea from traditional Turkish tea pots while drinking from traditional German cups. By acknowledging the importance of tea in the Turkish culture, Gabriel set out to create a familiar, comfortable, and welcoming atmosphere, where even tough topics were not off the table. While the event was criticized by many, it was, in the end, a possibility to talk about then detained German journalist Deniz Yücel, who was eventually freed.

◂ Siemtje Möller at the Munich Strategy Retreat in Heiligendamm in October 2021.

Tea in these examples provided a common ground in difficult times. Diplomacy continually relies on such commonalties to find solutions. Drinking tea, after all, is a global affair. To alter Helmut Schmidt's famous quote: "it's better to drink tea for one hundred hours than to shoot for one minute." His take on negotiations remains valid.

When I was elected to the German Parliament in 2017, I made sure to take the grand tradition of drinking tea with me, as my cultural heritage and to ground my parliamentary work in Berlin with my roots in Frisia. Over the past four years, drinking tea in my office has provided an opportunity for conversations and connections, because finding a common denominator takes time, even among members of one's own party, and it is key to getting things done.

Often, patience is required when seeking solutions and compromises, even if not all parties will be completely satisfied with the outcome. Bringing people together and accepting them as coequals is often achieved through rituals. In many countries around the world, people drink tea and celebrate the tradition. Japan, England, and the Middle East come to mind, but many other areas could be added to the list. It is a world-spanning tradition and just like diplomacy, drinking tea is an investment in time. Diplomacy cannot be rushed. It has evolved from official relations between states, to dialogue during summits and conferences conducted on various levels. The Munich Security Conference provides such a venue, proving that there are now many more people involved and able to shape dialogues and discussions, both online and in real life.

My hope and optimism lead me to believe that there will be German-Afghan tea ceremonies once again, maybe even with Shallah Hadid, but the road to this destination is a long one.

Siemtje Möller is Parliamentary State Secretary at the Federal Ministry of Defense. She has been a member of the Bundestag since 2017 and was a Munich Young Leader in 2019.

Jazz and Diplomacy

Sebastian Groth

Richard Holbrooke reportedly said that diplomacy was "like jazz—the improvisation on a theme." Indeed, a whole range of parallels can be observed between the world of diplomacy and the art of jazz. Let me briefly elaborate on three of them.

In no other musical style does improvisation play as crucial a role as in jazz. For instance, the presentation of the main melody—or theme—is typically followed by a run-through of the various instruments, all improvising spontaneously and as creatively as possible on the basis of the harmony sequence of the theme. Each musician has this harmony sequence before his or her inner eye (or on his or her music stand), and communicates with the other ensemble members. Dialogic action, spontaneity, structure and dynamics, and a common understanding of the sound to be created are crucial if the players are to strike the sparks of swing and to groove off each other. In short, success depends on the right balance of structure (key and harmonies) and improvisation (soli). In this context, musical creativity is mainly a matter of communication, responsiveness, and the pursuit of a common goal. Parallels to negotiation situations in diplomacy very readily come to mind. In fact, in any negotiation, a minimum amount of preparation and organization is necessary to implement political guidelines. This requires team play and, above all, a setting that is as productive as possible. Therefore, everything depends on the venue, the agenda, and the composition of the delegations. Once the work of negotiation starts, spontaneous action, perception of subtle interpersonal signals, and a dialogic overall understanding increasingly come to the fore. Over time, a common target corridor develops, making a successful conclusion more likely. On balance, results-oriented diplomacy is fairly similar to the successful performance of jazz, including the risk of (unintentionally) producing dissonances that can only be dissolved by negotiating (or practicing) persistently. Ultimately, both jazz and diplomacy are about creating something lasting, something that will make an impression, out of the current situation—musical or political.

A second parallel between diplomacy and jazz should be familiar to any fan of the Munich Security Conference who has ever visited an international jazz festival: in both cases, there are main stages and side stages, solo performances that thrill the audience (or leave them somewhat perplexed), inspiring conversations in overcrowded hallways, and, let us not forget, all sorts of "jam sessions"—informal ad-hoc events with a variety of players, musicians, or politicians and diplomats entrusted with foreign affairs who would spontaneously step into action. Important factors include not only the somewhat confusing overall atmosphere, but also the individual's staying power ("night owl session" is a key phrase), as people fear to miss out on an epoch-making performance that everyone will be talking about the next day. The MSC has a festival character: it can easily be measured against any leading jazz festival of the world in terms of atmosphere and concentration of "stars" and trendsetters, as well as main and side programs. As with great jazz festivals, the MSC leaves its participants exhausted but content, brimming with ideas, encounters, and inspirations.

Ultimately, both jazz and diplomacy are about creating something lasting, something that will make an impression, out of the current situation—musical or political.

A third important feature of jazz is that, while it is the basis of (almost) any musical development of our time, it frequently absorbs new trends and ideas, translating them into its own musical language. Many of today's jazz ensembles process and assimilate influences from hip hop, rap, or world music. In the realm of foreign affairs and diplomacy, it is equally important to show a generalist's curiosity from time to time, to integrate developments and megatrends into the "mainstream," and to make them tangible and politically relevant to a broader foreign- and security-policy community. Just think of topics such as health and pandemic policy (a topic that the MSC put on the international agenda long before COVID-19 started to keep us busy around the clock), or the crucial future question of the correlation between climate change and a changing security environment. Like the musical trendsetters in jazz, Wolfgang Ischinger has thus made a crucial agenda-setting contribution. Whether we are jazz fans or not, for us, the upcoming generation of diplomats, this has always been fascinating.

Sebastian Groth is Director for Policy Planning at the Federal Foreign Office. He was a Munich Young Leader in 2010.

◂ Sebastian Groth at the Munich Young Leaders Meeting in Madrid in September 2018.

msc

Back-Channel Diplomacy

Karl Kaiser

The back channel is to diplomacy what the axle is to the wheel: It makes the wheel turn while often remaining invisible. One of the grand masters of diplomacy in the twentieth century, Henry Kissinger, developed the back channel to perfection in America's foreign policy—the opening to China being the most prominent case when, in a carefully planned secret mission, he prepared President Nixon's visit and the establishment of diplomatic relations with China. But it is generally overlooked that Germany's Ostpolitik also would not have been possible without a most effective back channel between Washington and Bonn. Would there have been the Helsinki Act, détente, Gorbachev's acceptance of the fall of the Berlin Wall, of Germany's unification and the end of the East-West conflict without Ostpolitik? Hard to imagine.

The Social-Liberal coalition under Willy Brandt and Walter Scheel came into office in 1969 and announced its intention to replace the old policy by a new approach towards the communist world. A pragmatic policy of "small steps" and "change through rapprochement," while focusing first on Moscow, aimed at opening relations with East Germany and Eastern Europe including a recognition of the territorial status quo. At the time, many observers assumed that the Nixon Administration was opposed to Ostpolitik. However, the reality was more complex. True, Richard Nixon, as is well documented, did not like Willy Brandt. But for Henry Kissinger, his chief foreign policy advisor, the main concern relating to Ostpolitik was to ensure that German action did not counteract or hamper his own designs for a new strategy to stabilize the relationship with the Soviet Union and to prevent Bonn from being outmaneuvered by a stronger Russia.

The back channel is to diplomacy what the axle is to the wheel: It makes the wheel turn while often remaining invisible.

In West German domestic politics, the CDU/CSU fiercely opposed Ostpolitik and yearned for some support from the Republican government in Washington. Indeed, a single critical word or gesture from the Nixon Administration could have been fatal to the governing coalition of SPD and FDP, which was near to losing its parliamentary majority as its members deserted to the opposition in protest to Ostpolitik. But Kissinger made sure that no critical word on Ostpolitik whatsoever emanated from the administration. Unknown to the CDU/CSU in Bonn and to the German public, a back channel had been established between the two governments. Egon Bahr, Willy Brandt's intellectual architect of Ostpolitik, his confidant and negotiator, regularly and secretly traveled to Washington, bypassing the state department to discuss with Kissinger all details of the ongoing negotiations with Moscow, thus creating a convergence of views between the White House and the Brandt government on the Eastern treaties. Incidentally, Bahr also established a back channel with the leadership in Moscow that circumvented the notoriously fussy Soviet bureaucracy. Though the ratification by the German Parliament remained controversial to the end, thanks to the work of the back channel, there was no visible dissent from the US government, and the implied concurrence helped to secure their adoption.

What supports this interpretation? More than four decades later, in 2014, on the occasion of establishing a Henry Kissinger Chair at the University of Bonn to honor the former secretary of state on his ninetieth birthday, a number of intellectuals and students protested against this gesture. Egon Bahr felt obliged to intervene in this controversy and firmly supported the creation of this chair, adding: "I am deeply grateful to Henry Kissinger for convincing Nixon to give us green light. Otherwise, there would never have been Ostpolitik."[1]

In a touching testimonial to the relevance of the close personal relationship underpinning the backchannel, Henry Kissinger gave a moving eulogy at a memorial for Egon Bahr, who died in August 2015.[2]

Karl Kaiser is a Senior Fellow at the Project on Europe and the Transatlantic Relationship at the Belfer Center for Science and International Affairs and Adjunct Professor of Public Policy, Emeritus, at Harvard University's John F. Kennedy School of Government. He previously served as Director of the German Council on Foreign Relations from 1973 to 2003 and as advisor to Chancellors Brandt and Schmidt.

◂ Karl Kaiser at the Munich Security Conference in February 2015.

msc
Giesecke+Devrient

Parliamentary Diplomacy

Elmar Brok

Foreign policy is a typical executive activity. Due to international and constitutional law, and for practical reasons, only a government can represent a country to the outside world in binding terms. Only a government commands the necessary resources for planning, analyzing, and negotiating with staff, embassies, and secret services.

Only within a government does the capacity exist for closely coordinating the various goals and responsibilities of foreign, security, defense, trade, energy, economy, finance, currency, infrastructure, and technology policy—if such coordination is desired. At any rate, Europe would be well-advised to finally make a corresponding attempt—all the more so as China, Russia, and, increasingly, the US are each using these factors in an integrated fashion in their strategies to their own benefit.

Germany's tendency to draw a clear line between, for instance, economy and energy policies on the one hand and foreign policy on the other hand is viewed with amusement by Xi, Putin, and Biden and is used against Europeans by all three—albeit with differing motivations and goals.

Since the typical European nation-state lacks the specific weight required to effectively defend its interests within the current global order, the EU must increasingly come to the rescue. However, because these areas are handled differently with respect to responsibilities and decision structures, the EU's capacity for defending interests and ensuring capacity of action is strongly limited—to the detriment of all its member-states.

I hope that the European and national members of Parliament will pay increased attention to this issue in order to achieve enhanced value and synergies. One opportunity to do so is the EU's Conference on the Future of Europe, where a majority of members of Parliament of both levels may—as in the Constitutional Convention—revolt against the inertia of the executive.

The members of Parliament participating in the conference can point to a broad majority of EU citizens who, above all, demand a greater agency for the EU in all opinion polls. Citizens understand that, given the state of the world, this will be the only effective way to protect the EU and its member states, and to turn them into a major player.

Arguments of constitutional law can be overcome. The notion of national sovereignty is being used by change-resistant forces of national government agencies to justify their retention of power, and by populists for other reasons. The great development of the EU single market shows how successfully and responsibly the EU is making use of both majority decisions in the Council of Ministers and the right of codecision on the part of the European Parliament. This positive result has only been possible due to this capacity for action. In this case, what is crucial is, above all, majority decision-making in the council and equal rights for the European Parliament in the legislative procedure.

Since the typical European nation-state lacks the specific weight required to effectively defend its interests within the current global order, the EU must increasingly come to the rescue.

It is not only the fundamental question—which, in parts, affects even EU primary law—that may be subject to dialogue or debate between parliaments and executives. Parliaments and executives may also work towards using parliamentary diplomacy more systematically.

For this to happen within democracies in credible ways, parliaments must have suitably credible tools at their disposal. For instance, a government (or the European Commission) must be elected (or confirmed) by the relevant parliament. It is also desirable that it should be possible to revoke this appointment. This might contribute to the executive's humility and increase its willingness to communicate.

A parliament must also be prepared to make use of budget responsibilities regarding regulations, programs, and human resource development in ministries and external representations. An effective control system for politicians and auditing must also be in place.

Both sides—parliament and executive—must respect each other's rights and use them in a transparent man-

◂ Elmar Brok at the Presentation of a Munich Security Brief in Strasbourg in July 2021

ner. The executive and its diplomatic service shouldn't see this as a permanent fight against "dim-witted" and annoying parliamentarians who have no understanding for the higher art of diplomacy and the necessary confidentiality in international politics.

In fact, a democratic parliament stands for public debate and transparency. In its various roles, it also provides legitimacy to politics in a democratic society. Normally, there is no antagonism between the parliamentary majority and the executive (which builds upon this majority), which means that loyalty should come naturally.

In the democratic systems of the EU and its member states, citizens directly elect only members of Parliament (with the exception of the French president). These are therefore entitled to be taken seriously by the executive, and not only when the budget is being negotiated. And it is simply not true that they are principally "irresponsible." They are as interested in successful politics as the diplomats in the foreign services, who have different party-political and political preferences themselves.

Parliaments and executives may also work towards using parliamentary diplomacy more systematically. With respect to the enforcing of human rights, but also regarding questions of trade, economy, and environment, various clever opportunities for role-playing between the executive and the Parliament exist.

During my thirty-nine years in the European Parliament, I have witnessed more leaks from the Commission and the foreign service than from the European Parliament. This is no less true for the special parliamentary committees responsible for secret services and classified information in the member states and the EU. For more than ten years, I led the relevant EP body—the capacities of which, however, are rather limited due to opposition by some member states. A reason-of-state sense of political responsibility exists not only among civil servants and parliamentarians turned ministers. In addition to serving to legitimize, parliamentary control also prevents abuse of power both on the large and on the small scale.

However, parliaments must also know and accept their limits. Only the executive is able and entitled to represent externally, to act externally, and to conclude agreements and contracts. However, this may also allow for cooperation. The negotiating executive can use its parliament as a "bad guy" who, for instance, defines red lines for ratification, thereby trying to ensure that better negotiation results will be achieved.

From my own activities, I can also name some examples of how, for instance, members of the EP create trust and bring reliability into the relationships by visiting other parliaments, by frequently holding parliamentary meetings, and even by holding joint parliamentary committees with accession candidates and associated countries, thus contributing to the success of the relationships.

Without this type of cooperation between the EP and the US Congress, there would have been no contract negotiations between the EU and the US—which then, however, failed because of Trump. The EP has been the driving force in EU relations with Ukraine, but also with the Georgian Republic and Moldova, for the last twenty years.

I still remember that, prior to the conclusion of the nuclear agreement with Iran, both sides unofficially appealed to the EP's Foreign Affairs Committee to come to Tehran in order to give the Speaker of the Parliament of Iran, Ali Larijani, the opportunity to declare the forthcoming contract worthy of support.

In the Western Balkans, members of the EP have informally and formally—often in consultation with the Commission—carried out valuable and successful negotiation activities to the benefit of all.

With respect to the enforcing of human rights, but also regarding questions of trade, economy, and environment, various clever opportunities for role-playing between the executive and the Parliament exist, which, however, may be leveraged more systematically and with more courage and appreciation for each other's roles.

Elmar Brok was a Member of the European Parliament from 1980 to 2019, where he served as the Chairman of the Foreign Affairs Committee from 1999 to 2007 and from 2012 to 2019. He is a Senior Advisor at the Munich Security Conference.

Wolfgang Ischinger and Dita Charanzová at the presentation of a Munich Security Brief in Strasbourg in July 2021. ▸

Security Brief
msc
Munich Security Conference
Ischinger
Charanzová
Carola
Couper le son

msc

Track Two Diplomacy

Sam Nunn

There are moments when relations between governments are simply stuck, often because of clashes over vital national security concerns. Ironically, breaking communication between nations to demonstrate anger and opposition is often one of the first levers that is pulled in a crisis. This makes governments (like people) feel better, but it is usually counterproductive. Presidents and prime ministers are unable to meet. Ongoing meetings and processes are suspended. Routine exchanges across topics large and small are frozen in place. Because trust is broken, cooperation becomes impossible.

Unfortunately, rather than reduce risks, tensions, and dangers, the suspension of diplomatic, cultural, economic, military, and scientific exchanges almost always accentuates the danger. Our common humanity is buried under the debris of stagnation and stalemate, and the risk of an accident, mistake, or miscalculation leading to broader conflict inevitably increases. In the Euro-Atlantic region, this is the position we have been in for the past several years. Relations between the United States, NATO, the EU, and Russia remain dangerously adversarial. Clashing national interests, insufficient dialogue, eroding arms control agreements, advanced missile systems, and new cyber and hypersonic weapons have come together to destabilize the old equilibrium. This has increased the risk of miscalculation and blunder, including nuclear use.

Fortunately, we have a guide for these moments—track two and track one and-a-half diplomacy, involving former officials and experts who can quietly inform and involve current officials in their work, reach out privately to their leaders, and build support for dialogue. Ideas can be tested, and concrete steps to reduce the risk of conflict and to build a more secure and promising future for all can be advanced.

If you want to experience what these alternative tracks really look like in practice, I invite you to step into the Hotel Bayerischer Hof during the annual Munich Security Conference. Walk the halls, climb the staircases, ride the elevators, enter the conference rooms, sit down for an espresso—and you will see and experience these alternative tracks at work.

In 2012 at an informal breakfast on the opening day of the conference, former and current officials from Europe, Russia, and the United States met to launch a joint effort focused on building bridges and reducing risks in the Euro-Atlantic region. A year later we issued a report entitled "Building Mutual Security."[1] When relations between the West and Russia imploded in 2014, it was again the MSC and the relationships forged and nurtured there that provided a foundation for launching the Euro-Atlantic Security Leadership Group (EASLG).[2] This was a new track one and-a-half initiative that has provided an alternative opportunity for dialogue between individuals and governments throughout the region.

One of the foundations of the EASLG's ongoing work is the opportunity provided by the luncheon held on the Saturday of every Munich Security Conference since then. There, guided by the deliberations of the EASLG, some of the toughest issues—crisis management dialogue, cyber threats to nuclear security and stability, and Ukraine—have been discussed candidly by some of the most powerful people in the world. What is often missed is how difficult it can be to even create these alternative tracks during the crisis. My good friend George Shultz said many times how important it is to "tend the garden" of diplomacy—to focus on the everyday work of building and maintaining relationships and developing trust and confidence. When a crisis arises, there must be a foundation from which to work. We are still a long way from managing instability and building mutual security in the Euro-Atlantic region. In the intervening years and during these turbulent times, we are all fortunate that the MSC provides for, and nurtures, the global garden of diplomacy. Every year, the skillful gardeners at Munich grow and strengthen individual contacts and relationships—including direct exchanges between leaders and governments—that are essential for preventing catastrophe and building mutual security for all.

Sam Nunn served as a United States Senator from Georgia for 24 years (from 1972 to 1996). He is the Co-Founder and Co-Chair of the Nuclear Threat Initiative.

◂ Sam Nunn at the Munich Security Conference in February 2018.

The Younger Generation

Desmond Browne

My colleague Sam Nunn has written wisely about the importance of maintaining track two diplomacy through working with former and current officials and experts to bridge the divide between governments. Perhaps equally if not more important is identifying and engaging with the younger generation as they are beginning their careers in government, education, and business and exposing them to, and involving them in, meaningful discussions about their common future and mutual security.

Following Russia's annexation of Crimea in 2014, it took more than a year to assemble a significant group of "formers" to address the crisis in Euro-Atlantic security. Yet within six months of these events, with colleagues from the European Leadership Network, Nuclear Threat Initiative, and Russian International Affairs Council, we found ourselves walking the streets of Sofia with an extraordinary group of young leaders from across the Euro-Atlantic space, the majority drawn from Ukraine and Russia. That this "younger generation" of leaders—alarmed by an armed conflict at the center of Europe that not only disrupted relations across the continent but had impacted their families and their futures—was willing to meet almost immediately holds a lesson for their elders. For them the stakes were too high to worry about anything else, which is why they agreed to meet without hesitation.

The agenda for the two days of this meeting was simple: for the Ukrainian participants, what kind of future did they want for Ukraine? What would they like their government to do within the next six to eight months? What were the opportunities for and obstacles to realizing their vision of Ukraine? What did they see as the essential problem in Ukraine's relations with Russia, NATO, the EU, and the US? For the Russian, European, and American participants, what was their reaction to the ideas shared by their Ukrainian colleagues? What were the potential problems, and red lines? And importantly, what can be done to help?

It was perhaps unavoidable that the first session, held around a rectangular table, organized itself into "country delegations," Ukrainians next to Ukrainians, Russians next to Russians. Emotions around the table ran high, revealing raw feelings of betrayal and loss. Some of our participants had participated in the events of February 2014 in Ukraine, had seen family and friends injured. Voices and positions were firm and direct, from all sides of the table.

Yet something extraordinary began to happen at the first coffee break. Country delegations began to break, and to mix. Participants who only minutes before were engaged in an intense dialogue between delegations were now standing together reflecting on the conversation just had. There were informal stories being shared, perspectives being underlined, accepted, and understood. This dynamic continued into the evening dinner, and later in the hotel lobby bar, where the vast majority of participants found themselves in the early morning, still debating, still discussing, and perhaps most important: forging personal relationships—relationships of trust. They did not want to stop—and they did not. What started with twenty-five participants in Sofia in 2014 continued through Riga and Sarajevo in 2015, Brussels and Helsinki in 2016, Warsaw and Minsk in 2017, and Berlin in 2018. The "Younger Generation Leaders Network" continues to this day, now hosted by the European Leadership Network, involving close to one-hundred participants.[1]

Throughout these conversations there is one constant: a recognition that if the Euro-Atlantic space is to avoid repeating the tragedies of its past, the answers will need to be informed and shaped by this younger generation. Indeed, it was this insight, conveyed by Wolfgang Ischinger as the spark for initiating this process in 2014, that is perhaps the most compelling and inspiring hope for Europe's future today. I am confident that many of the younger generation in Sofia in 2014 will someday soon be representing their governments—it has already happened, in more than one case. When they meet in those roles and look across the table or break for coffee, at least we can be optimistic that, informed by their experience with each other during some of the darkest days in Europe since the end of the Cold War, they will seek to avoid the mistakes of the past.

Desmond Browne is the Vice Chair of the Nuclear Threat Initiative as well as the Chair of the Board of Trustees and Directors of the European Leadership Network. He is also the former Secretary of State for Defence of the United Kingdom.

◂ Desmond Browne at the Munich Security Conference in February 2013.

Giesecke+Devrient

People’s Diplomacy

Izumi Nakamitsu

One of my great heroes, Dag Hammarskjöld, once described the basis for his belief in a better future. For him, this belief was different from “the fragile faith of generations before us, who thought that everything was arranged for the best in the best of worlds or that physical and psychological development necessarily worked out toward something they called progress.” According to him, it was “a much harder belief—the belief and the faith that the future will be all right because there will always be enough people to fight for a decent future.”[1] I wish to share my brief personal reflections on two aspects of diplomacy that have shaped my own views and experiences with the “art of diplomacy.” First, multilateralism and second, the role of everyday people.

I am not a diplomat by training nor by making. My career has been largely as an international civil servant within the United Nations system—from my early days as a young humanitarian and peacekeeper in the former Yugoslavia, Turkey, and northern Iraq, to my more recent experiences in various leadership roles in disarmament, peace operations, development, migration, and displacement—the prism through which I see diplomacy has always had a strong multilateral underpinning.

More often than not, I have been a witness to, rather than the driver behind, diplomatic outcomes. I have felt the joy and elation in moments of breakthrough and success, where long-standing divisions were overcome to achieve an outcome in the best interest of the international community and humankind. And like most everyone working in the international arena, I have also suffered the sting of disappointment at failed negotiations—sometimes driven by factors of little substantive relationship to the issue at hand.

Since the end of World War II and the founding of the United Nations, the role of multilateralism as a key element within the diplomatic machinery has been simultaneously called into question and proven as invaluable on many occasions. The United Nations was founded by the determination of “we the peoples” with the intent of saving the “succeeding generations from the scourge of war.” These words from the preamble of the UN Charter remain to me the foundation for the diplomacy of today and tomorrow: diplomacy that is driven by and for the people, with an eye toward a more peaceful and prosperous future for all.

To recall, the origin of the word diplomacy—from the Greek *δίπλωμα* (diploma), referring to an object “folded in two,” frequently a travel permit—carries with it the inference of privilege and status of some sort. Indeed, history has given us countless skilled negotiators and diplomats, many of great notoriety. Their work—oftentimes quietly behind the scenes, as well as sometimes vocally in the public arena—has been instrumental in preventing crises, ending wars, and saving lives.

But through my work, I have also had the privilege of seeing a different “art of diplomacy” in action, namely that carried out by “ordinary” people. My long-time mentor and boss at the United Nations Refugee agency, Sadako Ogata, once said to me that you don’t have to be famous to do a meaningful job. Whether in the context of bringing to life new international agreements or in settling a longstanding local dispute, the diplomatic heroes in my experience are often those without notable public profile or status: survivors of armed violence, women’s organizations, community leaders, young people.

I have been lucky to interact and work with people from all these walks of life—and many more. Among them it is the new generation of leaders and champions for multilateralism, peace, and social justice that inspires and motivates me most. Within my current field of disarmament, I get to exchange regularly with, and indeed learn from, youth from across the globe. They are often the most determined and committed to building coalitions; the most creative when it comes to identifying solutions; the savviest at drawing on the broadest possible toolbox to foster dialogue and achieve consensus; and, when given the chance, among the most articulate of speakers on delegations to intergovernmental meetings.

If diplomacy is indeed an “art,” then the most valuable tableau that can be created is perhaps one formed by a collective of “artists” across professions, generations, and cultures. In this vein, let us keep creating our common future together.

Izumi Nakamitsu is the Under-Secretary-General and High Representative for Disarmament Affairs of the United Nations.

◂ Izumi Nakamitsu at the Munich Security Conference in February 2019.

2 Challenges for Diplomacy

Choosing the Right Historical Analogies

Ivan Krastev

Ever since Russia's annexation of Crimea the question that haunts me is: did the fact that the annexation happened in 2014, the year Europe was commemorating the one hundredth anniversary of World War I, define the nature of Western response? Could it be that Americans and Europeans have fallen victim to a wrong historical analogy, and that the flood of books and films produced this year to mark the anniversary of the Great War have made them believe that what we should fear is not inaction but overreaction?

Historical anniversaries are like carpet-bombing. They throw upon us "teachable lessons" in volumes of historical research, novels, conferences, films, and exhibitions, and demand unconditional surrender. These books we all read or at least read about fuel particular fears and make certain future developments look more real than others.[1]

In their classic study, *Thinking in Time*, Richard Neustadt and Ernest May revealed that the choice of the proper historical comparison is at the heart of any crisis decision-making.[2] Policy makers need history to make sense of the present. At the time of the Cuban Missile Crisis, the most important choice that President Kennedy had to make was the choice of proper historical analogy. He had to choose between a Suez, Pearl Harbor, or July Crisis 1914 analogy. The choice predetermined his choice of strategy. Betting on Suez would have meant that Russian missiles were a game of distraction, and the US should be ready for Soviet actions somewhere in Europe. If the Soviets were preparing a Pearl Harbor type of surprise, Americans would have to choose to strike first.

Policy makers need history to make sense of the present. The historical comparison we choose very much depends on the history books we read. And what we read, as we have seen, is predetermined by the historical anniversary that we are currently celebrating.

Kennedy, though, opted to view the crisis in terms of the great-power politics of the summer of 1914 and he was determined not to make the mistakes that were made then. The president clearly explained the logic of his choice and the sources of his decision. It was Barbara Tuchman's popular book *The Guns of August* that shaped his opinion.[3] "I am not going to follow a course," confessed President Kennedy, "which will allow anyone to write a comparable book about this time, 'The Missiles of October.'"[4] Tuchman's book was published in 1962, on the eve of the fifty-year anniversary of the outbreak of World War I. If it was not for the coming anniversary, she could have written a different book and the course of the Cold War could have been different. If not for the imminent anniversary, the president could have decided not to read the book.

When confronted with foreign aggression and the violation of the borders of a sovereign state, European policy makers must choose between two historical comparisons only: July 1914 or Munich 1938. Neither analogy represents history as such; both recall a lesson instead, but different lessons. The story of July 1914 is the story of an accidental war. The popular belief is that the war was caused by misunderstandings, miscommunications, and the lack of trust between the Great Powers. In the collective imagination of Europe, the Great War represents "the collective suicide of Europe." The lesson of July 1914 is a simple one: beware of overreacting and give a chance to diplomacy. Munich 1938 teaches us a different lesson—that capitulating to the demands of a territorially aggressive dictatorship does not bring peace. Although it does avoid a war in the short term, it makes a larger war, on less favorable terms, inevitable later. This analogy warns not against overreaction but against inaction.

But how should we judge if we are back to 1914 or to 1938? How should we decide whether to fear an accidental war or destructive appeasement? The historical comparison we choose very much depends on the history books we read. And what we read, as we have seen, is predetermined by the historical anniversary that we are currently celebrating. To pretend to consult history in 2014 means to go back to the outbreak of the Great War. In this year, any historical comparison other than the reference of World War I did not have a chance to be heard. If Russia had decided to annex Crimea in 2038, the reaction of the West for good or bad could have been very different. So, be aware what kind of books policy makers read or what kind of historical movies they watch and never forget that historical anniversaries very often define what we read or watch.

Ivan Krastev is Chairman of the Centre for Liberal Strategies in Sofia and a Permanent Fellow at the IWM Institute of Human Sciences in Vienna.

◂ Ivan Krastev at the Munich Strategy Forum in Elmau in December 2019.

Learning from Our Experience

John Scarlett

The current state of international relations is marked by rising tensions, mistrust, and misunderstanding, especially, but not only, between the Great Powers. Over the past ten years, in particular, day-to-day dialogue has been in decline; major international agreements, including for arms control, have been revoked. This is occurring at a time of exceptionally rapid technological change, the consequences of which are not fully understood, and growing disinformation through social media. Events move very fast. The potential for confrontation between states is obvious. Even where states have clear common interest, for example in confronting threats from international terrorism and religious extremism, the room for dialogue has been shown to be limited.

There is now a tendency to look back with nostalgia to the Cold War period as a time when some degree of strategic stability was achieved through dialogue, mutual understanding, and recognition of common interests. As someone directly and professionally involved in intelligence and diplomacy during and after the Cold War, this is definitely not how I saw it at the time. We must take care not to fall for the wisdom of hindsight, just because we know that Cold War confrontation was ultimately avoided.

There is now a tendency to look back with nostalgia to the Cold War period as a time when some degree of strategic stability was achieved through dialogue, mutual understanding, and recognition of common interests.

I have a particular memory based on direct personal experience of the nuclear war scare of November 1983. The early 1980s were a time of heightened rhetoric with the use of increasingly extreme language on both sides of the Cold War. In November 1983 it became clear that the Soviet leadership seriously feared the launch of a US nuclear first strike. This was a major misunderstanding of US thinking. But there were serious misunderstandings on the Western side too. Leaders and policy makers had not understood the impact of their rhetoric. Despite the evidence before us, I recall a continuing reluctance to accept that the Soviet fear of a nuclear first strike was genuine. As one of those involved in issuing the warnings, I remember how we were seen by many experts as exaggerating the risk. Fortunately, this was not true for national leaders and the most influential and senior diplomats in the US and the UK—and subsequently the Soviet Union. In 1984 the rhetoric and policy making began to change. Constructive diplomacy came back into action. The risk of confrontation was greatly reduced—a striking example of the interaction of intelligence and diplomacy, and one I witnessed day by day.

This experience makes me think about the situation we face today in our strategic international relationships. To keep it simple, I see four basic lessons to be drawn. First, the importance of mutual comprehension. We must understand the mind of the other side, their thinking, motivation, the lessons they draw from their own history and experience. Second, the importance of objective, honest assessment of information, not distorted by disinformation, propaganda, or wishful thinking. Third, the need for clarity about core values, interests (which must be defended), and areas of basic disagreement, while at the same time seeking to identify areas of common interest. Fourth, regardless of disagreements, the importance of dialogue and keeping open channels of regular communication as the most obvious way to avoid avoidable misunderstanding.

We must take care not to fall for the wisdom of hindsight, just because we know that Cold War confrontation was ultimately avoided.

This will not be easy. Firm defense of core values does not always sit comfortably with meaningful dialogue. The role for effective intelligence and skillful diplomacy is clear. I will not forget my inner emotion and reaction on that day in November 1983 when I understood that the nuclear war risk was real.

Sir John Scarlett served as Chief of the British Secret Intelligence Service (SIS or MI6) from 2004 to 2009.

◂ John Scarlett at the MSC Energy Security Summit in Stavanger in August 2018.

Reviving the Helsinki Spirit

Sauli Niinistö

"Trust, but verify." This quote is often attributed to former US president Ronald Reagan, although its true origin appears to be Russian. Either way, the approach it entails was emblematic for the final decade of the Cold War. Despite the immense disagreements and tensions between the two great powers of that era, Reagan and his Soviet counterpart Mikhail Gorbachev—two world leaders with very different backgrounds, worldviews, and personalities—were able to create an atmosphere of mutual trust. Sure enough, most concretely in the field of arms control, verification was an important part of the equation. Nonetheless, trust was the driving force in the new dynamism of that relationship. As a result, the world became a safer and a more predictable place for all of us. At least for some time.

Now, in the world of the early 2020s, trust seems again to have become a scarce commodity in international politics. As a vicious circle of mistrust coincides with an increasing great-power competition, a more complex landscape of different actors, and the emergence of new technologies, the mix is possibly even more dangerous than during the height of the Cold War. At the same time, we have a growing number of truly global challenges that we can only solve globally, together.

In my view, the most important objective for diplomacy today is to seek ways to shoulder what I like to call our common human responsibilities for the future. How do we make sure that we leave a more peaceful, a more sustainable, and a more affluent planet for the generations to come? As a solution to this conundrum, I have been advocating the revival of the Helsinki Spirit on a global scale.

With that spirit, I refer to the origins of the Helsinki Final Act, signed at the summit of the CSCE in 1975. The letter of that document remains valid to this day, as the essential foundation for cooperative security in Europe and the work of the OSCE. But I believe that the spirit of that meeting holds important lessons for us even more broadly. The ability and willingness of adversaries to come together despite their differences, engage in dialogue to seek at least some common denominators and confidence-building measures, is in high demand today, also beyond the OSCE area.

In a way, Finland has practiced the Helsinki Spirit ever since the 1970s. We have constantly offered our good offices in the service of strategic stability between great powers, even at the highest levels. As a host of such conversations, our main role is to provide circumstances conducive to an atmosphere of trust. That also means absolute confidentiality on our side before, during, and after such meetings. The success or failure ultimately rests in the hands of the parties directly involved, but as a host it is also possible to share one's personal experiences beforehand.

In recent years, I have been worried about the increasing personification of international politics. That brings many risks with it, but also some opportunities. Sometimes deadlocks that have been created by problems between bureaucracies and civil servants can be opened on the highest levels, in direct discussions between leaders. In my ten years as the president of the Republic of Finland, I have been fortunate to be able to build many long-standing relationships with leaders of great powers and smaller states alike. A country like Finland cannot expect to change the course of geopolitics on its own. But when there is trust and respect between individual human beings, in direct and confidential conversations, the likelihood of making the other side listen to and consider our views is far greater than through one-way statements and declarations.

How do we make sure that we leave a more peaceful, a more sustainable, and a more affluent planet for the generations to come? As a solution to this conundrum, I have been advocating the revival of the Helsinki Spirit on a global scale.

In my interactions with leaders from East and West, it is precisely this that has been the important factor: as different as we are as personalities, at the end of the day, we are all human beings. Nothing more, nothing less. Once you reach that kind of a mutual realization, that kind of a trust, in those conversations, positive developments are possible, even when differences and disagreements remain.

As a personal experience, I have never come out of a face-to-face meeting with another head of state or government in a more pessimistic mood than before the meeting. The common challenges of humankind can be solved between human beings. That does not mean that we can afford to be naïve. Verification is always needed. But without at least a minimum of trust, our future will be much darker.

Sauli Niinistö has been President of the Republic of Finland since 2012. He previously served as Chairman of the National Coalition Party, Minister of Justice, Minister of Finance, Deputy Prime Minister, and Speaker of the Parliament of Finland.

◂ Sauli Niinistö at the Munich Security Conference in February 2017.

Securing Fragile Peace

Charles A. Kupchan

Several decades of serving as a professor and policy-maker have led me to form two foundational assumptions about global affairs: one that is sobering, the other more uplifting. The sobering assumption is that we live in a world in which power politics and international rivalry are pervasive. History is littered with wars, both between states and inside them. Europe, for example, has for much of its past been a bloody battleground. The uplifting assumption is that war and rivalry, although pervasive, are escapable. We know that peace can and does break out. The European Union is today a zone of stable peace and many other areas around the world are home to groupings of countries that have left behind rivalry and successfully pursued political and economic integration.

That peace does break out demonstrates the progressive march of history and underscores the momentous successes that effective diplomacy can bring about. But history also makes clear that building stable peace is very difficult and that zones of peace, when they do emerge, are often fragile. The project of European integration has been running for over seven decades—yet is still a work in progress. Seven decades into its own evolution as a federal democracy, the United States fell apart in a bloody civil war. Yugoslavia was a stable multiethnic country for decades, but no longer exists. The United States and Europe today compromise a cohesive community of Atlantic democracies, but it is worth keeping in mind that along the way the United States fought two wars with Britain, one with Spain, and two with Germany.

Our political moment underscores the fragility of history's progressive march toward peace. The Trump era represented a dire threat to American democracy. Britain just defected from the European Union, and illiberal populism is alive and well in many parts of Europe. The political pendulum appears to be swinging back to the moderate center on both sides of the Atlantic. But illiberalism and ethno-nationalism have demonstrated remarkable staying power in democratic societies that were widely deemed to have moved past such political ills.

These observations prompt two main conclusions for the future of diplomacy. First, the top priority for the Atlantic democracies must be to get their own houses in order. Democratic societies need to rebuild their efficacy and their legitimacy in order to safeguard pluralism, liberal values, and multilateral institutions, thereby enabling the Atlantic community to remain a cohesive pillar of the international system. Foreign policy does indeed start at home. Redressing economic inequality, investing in healthcare and infrastructure, mapping out the future of work in the digital age, promoting cohesion and tolerance amid growing social diversity—tackling these and other domestic challenges are central to preserving the zone of peace that spans North America and Europe. The transatlantic partners will be able to deal effectively with external threats only if they succeed in revitalizing their own democratic societies and governing institutions.

Second, even as the Atlantic community focuses on its internal reconstruction, it must confront the reality that the emerging era of global multipolarity and irreversible globalization will bring with it new geopolitical challenges. Multipolarity means more jockeying and rivalry among centers of power. Global cooperation will be harder to come by in a world that is no longer dominated by the West's material and ideological power. At the same time, however, managing and taming globalization requires more global cooperation. Taking on the major challenges of our time, including preserving great-power peace, fighting climate change, combating pandemics and promoting global health, promoting cybersecurity, and managing global flows of finance and trade requires broad and deep international cooperation.

It is here that purposeful diplomacy enters the picture. This is not a moment to call for a defining clash between democracy and autocracy or to draw new geopolitical dividing lines. On the contrary, our predicament necessitates sustained strategic dialogue across ideological dividing lines in order to avert widening geopolitical cleavages. China, Russia, and other non-democracies may not share Western values; indeed, they feel threatened by the liberal values that the Western democracies are so determined to protect. But given the war-proneness of the international system and the irreversible scope of globalization, every effort must be made to deepen and broaden global multilateralism and strategic cooperation. Democracies know how to team up with each other; they have

◂ Charles A. Kupchan at the Munich Strategy Forum in Elmau in December 2018.

been doing so effectively for decades. What we need now is for democracies and non-democracies to learn how to work together more effectively and to address global challenges in a cooperative fashion even as they agree to disagree on issues of values and domestic governance.

The appropriate vehicle for achieving this outcome is a global concert of major powers that would put at the table the players who need to be there regardless of regime type.[1] As the history of the nineteenth-century Concert of Europe demonstrated, a steering group of leading countries can curb the geopolitical and ideological competition that usually accompanies multipolarity. By providing a vehicle for genuine and sustained strategic dialogue, a global concert can realistically mute and manage inescapable geopolitical and ideological differences.

This is not a moment to call for a defining clash between democracy and autocracy or to draw new geopolitical dividing lines.

The members of a twenty-first-century concert could be China, the European Union, India, Japan, Russia, and the United States, collectively representing roughly 70 percent of both global GDP and global military spending. Including these six heavyweights in a global concert's ranks would give it geopolitical clout while protecting it from becoming an unwieldy talk shop.

Concert members would send senior permanent representatives to a standing headquarters in a place determined through mutual agreement. Summits would occur on a regular basis and as needed to deal with crises. Although they would not be formal members, four regional organizations—the African Union, Arab League, Association of Southeast Asian Nations, and Organization of American States—would maintain permanent delegations at the concert's headquarters, giving the body global breadth. When discussing issues affecting these regions, concert members would invite delegates from these bodies as well as other relevant countries to join meetings. For example, were concert members to address a dispute in the Middle East, they could request the participation of the Arab League, its relevant members, and other involved parties, such as Iran, Israel, and Turkey.

A contemporary concert, like its nineteenth-century forebear, would enable continuous strategic dialogue and exhibit two characteristics that would make it particularly well suited to the emerging global landscape: political inclusivity and procedural informality. A concert's inclusivity means that it puts at the table the geopolitically influential and powerful states that need to be there, without regard to regime type. In so doing, it largely separates ideological differences over domestic governance from matters of international cooperation. A concert's informality means that it eschews binding and enforceable procedures and agreements, clearly distinguishing it from the UN Security Council.

A global concert would look to persuasion and compromise to build common ground. The concert would address emerging crises yet ensure that urgent issues would not crowd out important ones. It would build support for collective initiatives while also fashioning new rules of the road and deliberating on reforms to existing norms and institutions. The concert would leave operational oversight to the UN and other existing bodies. It would thus sit atop and backstop, not supplant, the current international architecture and set up decisions that could then be taken and implemented elsewhere.

Establishing a global concert would be no panacea, as bringing the world's heavyweights to the table hardly ensures a consensus among them. Success would entail managing more than eliminating threats to regional and global order. The proposed steering group would accept both liberal and illiberal governments as legitimate and authoritative—effectively abandoning the West's longstanding aspirations of a global liberal order. Restricting membership to the most important and influential actors would sacrifice representation in favor of efficacy, reinforcing hierarchy and inequity in the international system. Concerts lack the certitude, predictability, and enforceability of alliances and other formalized pacts.

But a global concert has one enormous advantage. It offers the best and most realistic way to advance great-power consensus. The Atlantic community must revitalize the socioeconomic foundations of liberal democracy while reaching out across ideological dividing lines to fashion a global concert. That is indeed a tall order—but also a strategic necessity.

Charles A. Kupchan served on the National Security Council under Presidents Bill Clinton and Barack Obama. He is Professor of International Affairs at Georgetown University and Senior Fellow at the Council on Foreign Relations. His most recent book, *Isolationism: A History of America's Efforts to Shield Itself from the World*, was published by Oxford University Press in 2020. The proposal for a global concert draws on Richard N. Haass and Charles A. Kupchan, "The New Concert of Powers," in *Foreign Affairs*.

The Angel of Peace in Munich. ▸

Pursuing Diplomacy in a G-Zero World

Ian Bremmer

The late economist Charles Kindleberger explained that the Great Depression lasted for as long as it did because a declining Britain was unable to underwrite the global economy and a rising America was unwilling to do so.[1] His conclusion often came to mind in the aftermath of the 2008-09 global financial crisis, which sparked impassioned debate about the plausibility and potential of a US-China G2—an arrangement that might, in turn, reenergize the G20 as a vehicle for global cooperation. Little of that discussion, however, focused on the most important number: 0.

Emergency coordination between Washington and Beijing indeed helped to prevent a fast-moving recession from morphing into another depression, but the crisis undermined confidence in US macroeconomic stewardship and underscored a tension in China's development. While seeking acknowledgement as a major power when pursuing greater representation within core international institutions, Beijing simultaneously portrayed itself as a developing country to avoid shouldering greater responsibility for the postwar order's maintenance. On challenges well beyond macroeconomic instability, it was clearer by the day that no country (the United States) or bloc of countries (the G2, the G7, or anything else) had the leverage to drive a global agenda—and that geopolitics would grow more fractious as America's relative heft diminished.

COVID-19 has amplified nationalistic and populistic sentiments that transcend ideology and geography, diminished confidence in the postwar order's core institutions, and, most concerningly, exacerbated great-power tensions.

I coined the term "G-Zero world" in early 2011, looking to capture what would surely prove a transitional dynamic—but with more staying power than any of us would hope.[2] The ensuing years occasionally gave reasons for optimism. The United States and China promised to inaugurate a "new model" of great-power relations in which a preeminent power and its principal challenger could maintain a healthy balance of competition and cooperation.[3] They managed to ink some agreements, especially during the second term of the Obama administration—one on climate change and one on cyberspace—while deepening the interdependence that had anchored their relationship over the previous three and-a-half decades. Washington and Moscow, meanwhile, signed New START and partnered to transport some 1,300 tons of chemical weapons out of Syria after that country's descent into civil war. And there was even a notable instance of trilateral diplomacy: the United States, China, and Russia cooperated to bring about a landmark nuclear deal with Iran.

In retrospect, those accomplishments were less harbingers than aberrations. Indeed, the greatest crisis thus far of this century has tragically affirmed the G-Zero world's persistence: the coronavirus pandemic has claimed over 5.2 million lives as of this essay's writing, and while some countries are contemplating the beginning of its end, vast stretches of humanity across Southeast Asia, sub-Saharan Africa, and Latin America are merely experiencing the end of its beginning; just 7.1 percent of those in low-income countries are even partially inoculated.[4]

COVID-19 has amplified nationalistic and populistic sentiments that transcend ideology and geography, diminished confidence in the postwar order's core institutions, and, most concerningly, exacerbated great-power tensions. As confidently as the United States declares that it is back, its allies and partners question both the stability of its domestic politics and the reliability of its foreign policy. As boldly as China proclaims that it is moving toward national rejuvenation, major powers in and beyond its neighborhood are alarmed by its deepening authoritarianism and uncompromising diplomacy. An increasingly multidimensional confrontation is emerging between the two countries, with a disruptive Russia hitching its coattails to a resurgent China. US-China relations are at their worst since normalization; US-Russia relations are at their worst since the end of the Cold War. Making matters worse, both descents are accelerating while the Sino-Russian entente deepens, meaning that the momentum of strategic competition now overshadows the necessity of cooperation. On balance, the geopolitical fallout from the pandemic has rendered the world less prepared to address systemic crises and stresses.

Less than a month after I submitted the first draft of this essay, a dramatic development underscored the extent to which the G-Zero world has taken hold: on August 15, 2021, the Taliban retook power in Afghani-

◂ Ian Bremmer at the MSC Core Group Meeting in Washington, DC, in May 2017.

stan after a stunning nine-day offensive, facing virtually no resistance from an Afghan army that the US had spent some $88 billion to train. In a humiliating irony, the US could only evacuate its embassy personnel safely after securing a pledge from the Taliban not to attack them as they departed from Hamid Karzai International Airport: 20 years after it had entered Afghanistan and overthrown the regime that had given safe harbor to those who attacked the US homeland on September 11, 2001, the world's lone superpower left at the mercy of its enemy. Shortly after the fall of the Berlin Wall, then-President of Czechoslovakia Václav Havel observed that the world had "literally [had] no time even to be astonished" over how precipitously the Soviet Union was disintegrating.[5] One might say the same of the Taliban's blitzkrieg.

Just two months earlier, the Biden administration had been celebrating a successful diplomatic tour: the G7 and NATO summits seemed to confirm that the United States was back—rallying advanced industrial democracies to pledge hundreds of millions of COVID-19 vaccine doses, announce an ambitious infrastructure plan to rival China's Belt and Road Initiative, and otherwise demonstrate a sense of shared purpose that had seemed so elusive during the Trump administration. As the Taliban crowed over its victory, many of America's friends wondered how the US could so badly have underestimated the speed of the Taliban's resurgence and asked why Washington had not consulted them more closely in implementing its drawdown. For now, Afghanistan tragically appears poised to become the latest posterchild for the G-Zero world. With the US looking to put its ruinous intervention out of mind and rebalance in earnest to the Indo-Pacific, NATO's involvement will also come to an end, and neither China nor Russia has either the resources or the willingness to play the kind of role in Afghanistan that Washington did.

Transatlanticists do themselves no favors by denying the obvious: today's strategic balance is a far cry from the prophesies of post-Cold War triumphalism, which envisioned the ascendance of the West and a convergence around the values it espouses.

The oft-heard conclusion that America's failure in Afghanistan will undermine the credibility of its security commitments in Europe and Asia is overwrought; if anything, the geopolitical fallout will likely compel the Biden administration to shore up those commitments. The US remains indispensable to managing every transnational challenge. And whether one looks at its economic recovery, its military modernization, or its technological investments, it is considerably more powerful than it was before the onset of the pandemic.

But perceptions of US competence continue to suffer, as do beliefs, however misguided they have always been, in its omnipotence. Endless commentaries warn that the ignominious conclusion to America's intervention heralds the end of Pax Americana. The outcome has impressed upon many of America's European allies and partners that they must pursue "strategic autonomy" with greater vigor. And countries around the world—US friends and foes alike—sense that the enthusiastic, even missionary resolve with which Washington set out to promulgate liberal values in the aftermath of the Cold War has weakened.

But the story extends far beyond the United States: democracies are simply not as preponderant as they once were (the G7's share of the global economy declined from 67 percent in 1989 to 45 percent in 2019).[6] And their critiques of authoritarian governance have grown less potent as their own domestic underperformance has grown more pronounced. Most of them are struggling with growing nationalism, ideological tribalism, and income inequality—not to mention public disillusionment with elites who promised that the unfettered globalization of the halcyon 1990s would lift all boats.

Democracies combined, of course, are still vastly more capable, economically and militarily, than China and Russia. And speculations that an ideological axis will emerge between the two are overstated; we should take care not to confuse democratic malaise with authoritarian ascendance. Still, transatlanticists do themselves no favors by denying the obvious: today's strategic balance is a far cry from the prophesies of post-Cold War triumphalism, which envisioned the ascendance of the West and a convergence around the values it espouses. Few observers would have imagined that just three decades after US President George H. W. Bush had declared "a new world order" to be attainable, the Munich Security Conference would publish a report on the theme of "Westlessness"; Wolfgang lamented in the foreword that "the West as we know it is contested both from within and from without."[7] It could not have been easy for him to pen that conclusion. He has, after all, dedicated his storied career to strengthening ties between the United States and Europe and advocating for their enduring importance. But the greatest friends of the transatlantic project are not those who call for restoring it to the position it once occupied, but those who urge it to adapt to the world that is emerging.

Policymakers and pundits often traffic in binary formulations; if a predominant frame of the late 2000s and early 2010s was "the West versus the rest," today it is "democracies versus autocracies." But no matter which metric one considers, the West accounts for a declining share of global power. Two of the world's three great powers, China and Russia, are nondemocratic, and while each confronts numerous internal vulnerabilities, the United States and the European Union would be remiss to underestimate their resilience (I long ago lost count of how many times government and business friends in Washington and Brussels have predicted their impending disintegration since I founded Eurasia Group in 1998). Challenging those two will only go so far in bringing about a renewed sense of Western cohesion, for the United States and even its closest European allies diverge sharply in their approaches. They will be unable to narrow that gap and adopt a more cohesive approach toward Beijing and Moscow, in any event, unless they first achieve greater consensus among themselves over the transatlantic project's aims in the early decades of this century. Finally, it is—and will remain—impossible to address any global challenge without involving Beijing.

The greatest friends of the transatlantic project are not those who call for restoring it to the position it once occupied, but those who urge it to adapt to the world that is emerging.

The entrenchment of the G-Zero world increases the urgency of great-power diplomacy, as Wolfgang explains in his book *World in Danger*: "If foreign policy meant working only with those we like, many challenges could not be approached at all. And if we only deal with real democracies, we would have to ignore most of humanity. Besides, diplomacy is the art of dealing with your adversaries."[8] So self-evident a conclusion should scarcely need to be articulated, let alone defended. But ideological polarization in the United States means that lawmakers increasingly deride the conduct of diplomacy as a display of weakness rather than an exercise of necessity. They compete over who is "tougher" on China and Russia, as though the United States could better advance its national interests through autarky than negotiations.

But this depiction is ahistorical. The United States and the Soviet Union, after all, cooperated not only to constrain nuclear proliferation, but also to develop a vaccine for smallpox. They did so not out of altruism, but of self-interest. If two nuclear-armed antagonists that regarded one another as existential threats were capable of finding common ground, Washington, Beijing, and Moscow should surely be capable of doing so. And they must try—not only to avoid a great-power war that would inflict inconceivable damage, but also to give the world a fighting chance of slowing climate change, enhancing resilience against future pandemics, and addressing the other global challenges that exist now and will surely emerge. The risks of silence outweigh the difficulties of dialogue.

Some observers contend that only the destruction wrought by war can birth a new order. Accepting that conclusion in today's age could imperil the survival of the human species. Nor should one hope, though, that enlightened calculations will enable the United States, China, and Russia to conclude grand bargains over the postwar order's evolution. The journey to strategic stability—and, in due course, competitive coexistence—will be slow, fraught, and meandering. The role of diplomacy is to find a middle ground between fatalism and idealism, appreciating that leaders are the authors of history, not its prisoners.

Ian Bremmer is the founder and president of Eurasia Group and GZERO Media.

Preparing for a World without Order

Klaus Naumann

Diplomacy is one of the oldest ways for states to deal with one another. It requires finding and applying methods and tools to solve problems, resolve conflicts, and settle disputes peacefully. Diplomacy assumes that a state is willing to achieve its goals, and that it is prepared to use any tool available including, at the extreme, legitimate force. Only then can diplomats act and achieve results that serve the state. Diplomacy, therefore, presupposes well-functioning states and an international network of agreed-upon rules and institutions. This rules-based order—enabling the interaction between today's states, but also being the source of conflicts—developed over centuries since the first city-states formed thousands of years ago. After the Peace of Westphalia in 1648, it grew into an ever-denser network of institutions, contracts, agreements, and conventions. Within this set of rules, diplomacy takes place to the benefit of the world of states. Diplomacy as we know it today originated in the Northern Italian city-states at the beginning of the Modern Age and developed into a network of national and international missions, in which ambassadors pursue the interests of their respective state—or group of states.

Today, in a world in turmoil—which may be facing the beginning of a new systemic conflict between democracy and autocracy—the question facing us is what diplomacy should look like in the future if we are to achieve the unvaryingly essential goals of any form of human cohabitation: protecting citizens, avoiding conflicts, and maintaining peace. How can we expect the world to change in the coming years, and what are the consequences for diplomacy and the way states will be dealing with each other?

A Changing World

Looking at tomorrow starts with looking at today. The coronavirus pandemic has deeply wounded the world, changing it fundamentally—and often for good. It will be possible neither to return to the familiar globalized world of the last two decades, which has brought us so many conveniences—and problems—nor to the multilateral order based on agreed-upon rules. As old problems persist, new ones will arise, and we will certainly have to renounce many a cherished amenity. Even without the pandemic, however, the world of 2021 would be completely different from the world we knew.

Here are just four examples. First, by denouncing multilateral bonds and contracts, the United States—still the world's only truly global power—has further weakened a vulnerable European Union suffering from the debilitating effects of Brexit and growing nationalism. This remains valid even after the renewal of commitments by the US under President Biden, given that there has been no resolute answer on the part of the EU. Additionally, the US and its allies have forfeited their credibility thoroughly and for some time to come through their precipitated withdrawal from Afghanistan. At the same time, an autocratic China announced the provision of a new and better system for the world, while an ultimately weak Russia threw its weight around—with a ruinous nuclear over-armament and a conspicuous demonstration of power in the Middle East, Ukraine, and the Caucasus.

Second, a global confrontation between the US and China seems to be about to set in, initiated by Trump's shortsighted canceling of the Trans-Pacific Partnership (TPP), and capitalized on by China's three-components strategy: the New Silk Road, which includes the development of a military projection capability, the "China 2025" technology concept, and the offer of a new world order determined by China, which leaves no space for the freedom of the individual, subordinating individuals' rights and international law to the interests of the Beijing-led community. At the beginning of November 2020, the next step toward implementing this strategy took place: the establishment of what is probably the most powerful economic grouping, the Regional Comprehensive Economic Partnership (RCEP). Fifteen states of the Asian-Pacific world, including democracies like Australia and Japan, have joined forces under China's lead, representing 2.2 billion people and 30 percent of global trade. Nobody will be able to bypass the RCEP. This includes both the United States and the European Union, which—after years of tolerating China's outreach to critical infrastructure and crucial technology and the "17+1 declaration" with its potential to undermine unanimity amongst EU member states—has now become almost marginal. Precipitously signed in December 2020, the EU investment agreement with China does not alter this fact, as it demands little from China but does impede the development of a common China strategy on the part of the EU, the US, and the United Kingdom.

◂ Klaus Naumann (third from left) at the Munich Strategy Forum in Elmau in November 2015.

Third, the fatigued Americans have just renounced their role as the world's policemen. It may be a lasting decision, as a majority of citizens of America's deeply split society are no longer prepared to bear the risks of others—and to bear them alone. What's more, American democracy increasingly weakened itself during Donald Trump's reign. With the storming of the Capitol on January 6, 2021, it finally ceased to be a role model. It is thus fair to say that the power that has protected the values of the West is in the process of resigning that responsibility—at a time when the confidence in the power of the law is diminishing and fear of the power of the strongest is on the increase. It was Trump who, at the very end of his term in power, initiated the US's shameful departure from its leading role as a democratic world power, thereby strengthening the authoritarian models of China and even Russia. The internal division of the US may now grow into a chasm, as millions of irrational, nationalist Trumpists who are prone to violence—even at risk of civil war—are opposing any form of international commitment by the US.

Fourth, Europe is finally recognizing that, in the world of the future, security must always be understood in global terms. There will be barely any future crisis that can be handled in a purely regional context or exclusively by using military force. Modern resources—the full spectrum from social media to artificial intelligence—will make it possible to solve conflicts prior to the use of arms. The threat thus becomes more diffuse, while response times shrink to zero and deterrence becomes nearly impossible.

The liberal values of the West are increasingly challenged by China's claim to be able to offer a new and more attractive set of values.

In conclusion, this means that China is now the global challenger in the struggle for predominance in the world. Being too weak to prevent this development, Europe must recognize that a clearer positioning—and preferably the revitalization of the transatlantic partnership—will be the price for the indispensable asset of American protection. The usual empty phrases—and, in particular, German vagueness—will no longer be enough.

As for the future, here are the points that we must remember. First, what will determine the future of the transatlantic relationship is Europe's approach to China, although the US itself would be well-advised to maintain a certain—albeit reduced—level of cooperation with China. The argument concerning Europe's military commitments will continue, and these commitments will ultimately have to be fulfilled. This is especially applicable to Germany, a nation which, despite its trade surplus, has jeopardized its reputation as a reliable ally—a controversy that, however, is of secondary importance compared to the question of whether Europe will stand at the side of the US when it comes to China.

Second, the US of the future will be more Pacific and less European—as has been the case since Obama. This is also evidenced by the demographic development in the US, as a majority of US citizens will soon have Asian, Latin American, or African roots. All of this is confirmed by the report authored by of NATO's reflection group, published on November 25, 2020. The report demands ensuring Europe's capability to defend itself and will serve as the basis for working out NATO's long-awaited new strategic concept. While the alliance remains responsible for the security of the Euro-Atlantic region, this concept must take into account the truly global changes—as well as future forms of conflict, that can be described as a no-holds-barred fight for information superiority, accelerated by automation. In succeeding stages, what will have to be discussed is NATO's future, its strategy in the new forms of conflict, and certainly also the relation between response and prevention and the options for gaining the conflict-stopping initiative.

However, there will be an overarching systemic conflict: the liberal values of the West are increasingly challenged by China's claim to be able to offer a new and more attractive set of values. NATO's member states must meet this challenge by fostering the resilience of its democracies by proving NATO's capacity to reliably protect the liberal constitutional democracies of the alliance. This strategy can only succeed if the EU member states, the United Kingdom, Canada, and the US jointly decide whether an alliance of the democracies, with NATO as its core, represents the right way forward.

So much for the near future, but what do we know about the way the world will change beyond 2030?

The World beyond 2030

Forecasts are always difficult—especially in an era of change. However, some general developments can be discerned, and one thing is certain: After 2030, there will still be a small number of states that will have the power to destroy the world with nuclear weapons. This gives them a special status and responsibility, uniting them with the goal of preventing the proliferation of these weapons.

There are essentially four drivers of change. First, the development of a world with many regional centers of power but without an uncontroversial central power is likely to continue. In this world, the US will initially remain the only power capable of acting in all power categories—even though confidence in the US and the multilateral order has considerably suffered. While the US can be expected to increasingly turn inward, it will not turn away from the world, and it will be prepared to respond to the challenge of China.

China is likely to still be the challenger in 2030, despite its efforts to gain supra-regional—including military—agency. China will probably not achieve full global agency before mid-century. Its great advantage in this rivalry is that it will implement its coherent and long-term strategy in a step-by-step fashion. However, China has significant domestic weaknesses, as evidenced by its treatment of Hong Kong and the Uyghur people. Achilles heels—including demography—limit China's scope for action and can be used against it.

Second, the world will be increasingly urbanized, with huge, hardly governable cities, in which new, easily applicable technologies and artificial intelligence are likely to be increasingly used by internationally cooperating criminals—which may eventually cause the states' monopoly on the use of force to collapse. Domestic conflicts may increase, and more states are likely to become ungovernable, ultimately falling apart. This may also lead to conflicts between states.

Third, it seems conceivable that we will see the forming of huge industrial cartels that still have their headquarters in one country but produce globally and evade any political influence on the part of their country of origin. They may become more powerful than any government. They will only follow the laws of the market and their own interests—without democratic legitimacy, but with greater financial power than the world of states.

Fourth, we equally cannot rule out a world in which the familiar orders of states and societies are at risk of breaking up. If the liberal, law-governed states prove themselves unable to deal with the increasingly complex questions of safeguarding the future and continue to use up wealth as they follow a comfortable, business-as-usual approach, the resilience of the democracies may run into danger, or even dissolve altogether.

However, what is of primary importance—although it cannot be seen with certainty—is the impact of global climate change and of demographics. Climate change can still be influenced by the actions of the world of states, even though the extent and the prospects are still open. While demographic development can be calculated up to the midpoint of the century, it may be exacerbated by climate change to such a degree that it may affect the security situation.

On the doorsteps of Europe, which is dependent on free sea access, lies one of the areas of the world that will be most affected by the climate change—the Arctic Ocean. Within the next twenty years, it may become ice-free—throughout the year, or, at least, for most of the year. There will be new mining opportunities, given that 15 percent of the world's oil reserves and 25 percent of its gas reserves are believed to lie here, and there will be new sea routes to Asia that are 5,000 nautical miles shorter than the existing ones. This is equivalent to one week less transit time and will pose new challenges in terms of controlling a huge, thus far barely monitored sea area. All European nations depend upon using the high seas. With access denied, the survival of all NATO and EU states is at risk.

While the US can be expected to increasingly turn inward, it will not turn away from the world, and it will be prepared to respond to the challenge of China.

However, the consequences of climate change will be most dramatic when it comes to drinking water supply and food production. If the glaciers of the Himalayas continue to melt, the drinking water supply of about two billion people will be at risk, potentially forcing them to leave their homeland. The interaction of climate change and demographies can produce migratory pressures leading to conflicts that may escalate into climate wars, such as occurred in the Darfur region of Sudan.

Combined, these four factors may lead to a world without world order and without commonly held values, in which the old causes of conflict, such as territorial claims, ethnic problems, and religious tensions still exist, but to which would be added demographic shifts, resource scarcity, and the effects of technical and economic disparities.

Europe, for instance, with its aging and shrinking societies—not unlike Russia—needs to maintain cohesion, wealth, and a certain level of social security, while simultaneously dealing with the migratory pressure from Africa, which will intensify—with or without climate change. The African population is likely to reach the level of two billion by 2050. The population of the Middle East will also become larger and younger. Driven by thirst and hunger, millions of refugees from southern Africa may set out for the north. Reducing migratory pressure by providing aid and incentives to stay may well become a question of survival for the European states—if they do not do this, there will be no security.

By 2050 humankind—by then around nine to ten billion people—will have a demand for food that is 30 percent higher than today. The productivity of agriculture must be increased by 60 percent, and the exorbitant waste of food—with currently 50 percent being dumped—will have to stop. Already 800 million people are starving. The problem will be to shelter and feed humankind in 2050. A huge drinking water problem adds to this. Lack of water may become a cause for conflict. Today, 870 million people—including 300 million Chinese people—are without access to safe drinking water. Every day, about 1,000 people die after drinking dirty water. Dam projects worsen the situation. The sources of the Mekong in Tibet are one example: for China, this dam is about drinking and irrigation water, but it would lead to Vietnam being deprived of the silt that makes the Mekong delta the rice bowl of Indochina. The impact of China's Brahmaputra project may be even worse, as it could mean that China, the nuclear power, would be turning off the tap for India, another nuclear power.

However, there will also be disputes over other resources—not primarily over oil and gas. For large parts of Europe, the biggest problem may consist in the lack of metals and rare earths, since significant segments of industrial production and the energy revolution (which has become quite a damp squib in Germany) depend upon their availability. Future distribution and access conflicts cannot be ruled out—not least because of the raw materials colonialism of the People's Republic of China.

New Forms of Conflict

In this future world, there will be no shortage of causes of conflict, and these conflicts will be easier to wage. They will be quite different from the wars between states as we know them. Future conflicts between states will be waged in five dimensions: land, air, sea, space, and cyber. They will make use of technologies such as quantum computers, artificial intelligence, and robotics. They will be unbelievably fast, possibly providing ways to make an adversary defenseless even before the attack has been recognized. The possibility of paralyzing a nuclear weapons arsenal by cyberattacks also cannot be ruled out. Because a scenario of this kind would be extremely destabilizing, trying to prevent it through agreements will be crucial.

A transitional form is constituted by hybrid forms of conflict in which non-governmental parties have access to states' potential for violence: these have already been recognized and are being used. Moreover, most types of weapons are available on the market, with international criminal cartels commanding enormous amounts of money. They may obtain access to any means of power, and the world's connectedness would allow them to move around in no time. Controlled by non-governmental and governmental actors, future conflicts may start in the guise of domestic conflicts. They may be waged—wholly or partially—by actors such as terrorists, organized criminals, mercenaries, pirates, and—in the distant future—even by robotic forces. They are difficult to discern and can often scarcely be attributed to one actor. An additional risk lies in the fact that the proliferation of weapons of mass destruction—including biological weapons as well as guided missiles and even hypersonic weapons—may continue. Warfare will be revolutionized, approaching the threshold of autonomous systems. In line with Industry 4.0, there will be Military 4.0, which will soon be followed by Military 5.0—including new technologies such as quantum computers, robotics, nanotechnology, biochemical substances, and maybe even androids—which will use 5G, and soon enough also 6G. Attackers may acquire the option of making an adversary defenseless through purely preemptive action, and without the use of kinetic or destructive force. More than 2,500 years ago, Sunzi already deemed this the best form of warfare. As early as 2030, very large states may be capable of blackmailing smaller states, and of partially or even totally disabling them electronically, without revealing themselves as attackers.

Does Diplomacy Have a Future in This World?

To answer this question, one must first examine whether today's world of states will be able to survive the challenges of the world of 2030 and beyond, and how this world may change.

Is the multilateral, rules-based order fit for such a future? We may doubt this, as multinational cooperating entities of various types—from industrial cartels to organized, globally operating criminals—may use modern technology to become more capable of acting than any state. Organizations of this type may be capable of challenging states and even of defeating them in conflicts, as they can act faster and command unlimited financial means, while not being bound by laws. Against this background, the multilateral, rules-based order of the world will only have a chance of survival if both competing global powers, the US and China, see such an order as a surplus value. Indeed, optimism seems justified, as—especially in view of the global competition of systems—a remnant of order is better than the law of the strongest, which would inevitably lead to a ruinous arms race and a high risk of conflict—something that neither of the competitors wish for. For the time being, today's umbrella organizations of the multilateral world order, the United Nations and the Security Council, are therefore likely to persist (with a reform of the Security Council currently appearing unlikely).

It seems equally likely that international organizations such as NATO, the European Union, the African Union, and the ASEAN will persist. However, they will need to significantly change their behavior. In particular, the principle of unanimity has to be given up for the sake of being able to cope with the terrifically fast course of events.

The way states are organized must significantly change in order to make them faster and leaner. Predictions are not yet possible. It is an open question whether the three traditional separate pillars of a state—legislative, executive, and judiciary—will persist. Even in Europe, attempts to put the judiciary under the control of the executive can be observed. Add to this the dwindling of confidence in the elected representatives in democratic states due to their tendency to shun responsibility, which ultimately benefits the autocrats—in the context of a global competition between democracy and autocracy, at that. Add also, the as-yet-unmet challenge of effectively applying all available political tools in a coordinated fashion—domestically and internationally. Currently, none of the existing government agencies and international organizations is in a position to fill this role, even if we are only talking about dealing with governmental actors as opposed to non-governmental global actors. How the latter could be brought to enter into negotiations and to stick to commitments is another unsolved question. The unbelievable acceleration of the courses of action we can expect to see due to artificial intelligence and new technologies must also be taken into account. Often, it will be necessary to act preemptively rather than react. In the future, relying on the principle of unanimity in decision making will be equivalent to being unable to act.

Will diplomacy, as we understand it today, still be needed in a world of international action as outlined above? Will embassies still play a role? Very slimmed-down, staffed representations will probably still be necessary, because, from time to time, problems may arise that can only be solved through personal contacts. However, the embassies of the future will be quite different from those of today. Only a small number of people will be present on site, helped by a lot of artificial intelligence and other types of machine support.

There will also be no lengthy struggles for unanimity in international bodies. It will even be necessary to delegate execution of agreed-upon joint action—including steps taking in military defense—to operational bodies beforehand. The crises of the future will require the coordinated use of all political means available to a state, which necessitates certain skills and, most importantly, the political will to act in a decisive manner. In the future, the world of states will still not be able to resolve conflicts exclusively through means of action; however, there will also rarely be a conflict allowing for out-of-hand foreclosure of the use of any of those means. Seen in this way, the two statements about crises that can be most frequently heard in this part of the world—namely, that, first, there is no military solution, and second, that a diplomatic solution must be found—will be as wrong tomorrow as they are today. A mindset of this kind ultimately puts the weak at the mercy of the ruthless.

In this future world, there will be no shortage of causes of conflict, and these conflicts will be easier to wage. They will be quite different from the wars between states as we know them.

Crisis response, the masterpiece of diplomacy, can be described as a room endowed with many doors leading out of it, where the adversary is present. There is only one door that you must allow your adversary to take on their way out if you want to achieve your goal. Diplomacy helps you obstruct any option other than the one the adversary must choose in order for you to reach your goal.

Reaching one's own goal has always been—and will always be—the epitome of diplomacy. It is thus guaranteed that diplomacy will persist even in the uncertain world of the future—something that cannot be said with equal certainty about international organizations and today's multilateral, rules-based order.

Klaus Naumann is a retired German general who served as Chief of Staff of the Bundeswehr from 1991 to 1996, and as Chairman of the NATO Military Committee from 1996 to 1999.

Munich Security Conference
Münchner Sicherheitskon
EUROPE
INTEGRATION
FOREIGN AFFAIRS
FEDERAL MINISTRY
REPUBLIC OF AUSTRIA

Dealing with Difficult Partners in Central Europe

Wolfgang Schüssel

"Central Europe": what a magical term it once was. How we marveled at the heroes of the turnaround of 1989—Václav Havel, József Antall, Lech Wałęsa. Each of them was excited about European reunification and a continent breathing again with both lungs (copyright by Pope John Paul II). Today, many, especially in the Brussels community, see the four "Visegrád countries"—Poland, Hungary, the Czech Republic, and Slovakia—as problematic. These countries, they say, disturb the mainstream and endanger the rule of law and the working of the institutions. The European Parliament has opened proceedings under Article 7. Occasionally, exclusions from the families of parties have been called for.

How has it come to this? The people cannot be blamed. Opinion polls show much higher rates of approval of the European Union in these countries, with Poland and Hungary showing the highest rates. Economically, there is likewise hardly any reason for concern. Three-quarters of Poles and two-thirds of Czechs are happy with their economic situation. After the turnaround, there was quite a downturn—Poland lost about 20 percent of GDP, Slovakia 15 percent, and Hungary and the Czech Republic 12 percent. Recovery, however, was quick. Today, these countries' economic power amounts to more than 1 trillion euros, which is more than the combined GDP of Sweden, Finland, and the three Baltic countries. Growth rates are three times as high as in the Euro zone. The industrial supply chains to Germany and Austria are absolutely intact. The Czechs have the highest prosperity level of the region; Poland has made the biggest leap forward. Polish GDP, which, back in 2004 was at 19 percent of the German level, is now at nearly 60 percent, with Hungary keeping pace. Since their accession in 2004, Poland, Slovakia, and the Czech Republic have caught up by 20 percent apiece. The Visegrád Four's political weight has also increased considerably. Their total population approximately equals that of Britain; their voting weight in the Council (Poland: 27, Hungary: 12, the Czech Republic: 12, and Slovakia: 7) is significant.

Is it because of the political color scale? Hardly. Slovakia has been governed by social democrats, the Czech Republic by a liberal prime minister, Poland by conservatives, and Hungary by Fidesz. In each of these four countries, civil society is highly active. Remember the mass protests after the assassination of Slovakian journalist Jan Kuciak and his fiancée in February 2018, which led to political resignations and the electoral defeat of the Social Democrats in March 2020; the demonstrations in Poland against the judicial reforms; the victory of the united opposition in several Hungarian cities; and the ongoing protests against the economic entanglements of the head of government in Prague. Might the (still to be reappraised) decades of communist dominance and misdeeds have played a role? Many of the former leaders have retained their influential positions in the administrative and judicial branches, or have taken refuge in cultural or economic institutions. We can observe quite inconsiderate ways of dealing with the rule of law, a lack of respect for different opinions and minorities, and an ominous level of corruption (to which, admittedly, other countries aren't immune either).

For us Austrians, these countries are valued neighbors, with whom we are deeply connected through centuries of common history, as well as numerous cultural, economic, and family ties. Hungary is the country in which the first piece was broken out from the Iron Curtain—and hence from the Berlin Wall. This is why Austria has always championed a speedy integration of these countries into the EU. I therefore believe that there is a strong case against the quest by some European Parliament members to strengthen the bonds within EU party families by way of excluding certain member parties. In difficult times in particular, it is important to encourage—rather than stifle—dialogue. Helmut Kohl, who wanted the expansion, and whose name is invoked by many EPP members, knew very well that expansion would mean that the party families would need to change and broaden. This applies not only to the EPP, but also to the Liberals and the Social Democrats. Speaking openly and critically with partners, rather than scolding them, is the only way to keep Europe together, instead of breaking it up.

Wolfgang Schüssel was the Federal Chancellor of Austria from 2000 to 2007. Among his other roles, he has previously served as Minister for Economic Affairs and as Minister for Foreign Affairs. This text is reprinted from his 2020 book *Was. Mut. Macht.: Bemerkungen und Bemerkenswertes* in a slightly edited form, with the permission of Ecowin Verlag.

◂ Wolfgang Schüssel at the MSC Core Group Meeting in Vienna in June 2015.

Core Group Meeting Vienna
June 16–17, 2015
Munich Security Conference msc Münchner Sicherheitskonferenz
EUROPE INTEGRATION FOREIGN AFFAIRS FEDERAL MINISTRY REPUBLIC OF AUSTRIA
Solana

ch Security Conference msc

Putting Ourselves in Others' Shoes

Sigmar Gabriel

The Hotel Bayerischer Hof looks back on a proud history of nearly two hundred years. Empress Elisabeth of Austria, Enrico Caruso, and Sigmund Freud were frequent guests there. The architect Friedrich von Gärtner devised this luxury hotel in the center of Munich as an oasis of peace. It was back in 1918 that the Bayerische Hof first became a venue of difficult negotiations. Later that year, the founding documents of the Bavarian Soviet Republic were signed in the Königssaal. A few months after that, the first republican premier of Bavaria, a social democrat named Kurt Eisner, was assassinated in the hotel's immediate neighborhood.

Hardly anyone could have imagined that this place would one day become the venue for an event like the Munich Security Conference (MSC), where—in a microcosm of world politics—people would discuss, negotiate, and, often enough, get into a row about world politics. With an eye to Germany's cautious foreign and security policy, I have frequently compared the country to a vegetarian in a world of carnivores. To extend the metaphor, we might say that the MSC sees the world paying a visit to vegetarians—who then, sure enough, dish up proper Bavarian food. These occasions bring together more than five hundred decision makers who would normally rarely interact on equal terms. Everyone is gathered together in one place: Iranian intelligence officials and Israeli diplomats, Russian military staff and American think-tank members, Saudi sheiks and Chinese businessmen. Most importantly, they can talk directly with political leaders from all around the world.

When dealing with difficult partners, it is particularly important to use plain language and to identify differences, but also to try to build reliable and robust communication channels and to reopen those that have been blocked.

I believe that, when dealing with difficult partners, it is particularly important to use plain language and to identify differences, but also to try to build reliable and robust communication channels and to reopen those that have been blocked. Where conflicts are on the rise and periodically threatening to escalate, people must talk and—at least on a personal level—create trust in order for the guns to fall silent.

This requires personal encounters. After all, "you can't 'Zoom' trust."[1] At the Munich Security Conference, people cannot help encountering each other: in the breakfast room in the Dachgarten Lounge, in the piano bar, or in the much-too-slow lift. In the bustle that prevails year after year in the Bayerischer Hof, people literally cannot keep out of each other's way. The hotel is actually much too small for a global conference of this type. Year after year, the people of Munich sigh at the traffic chaos in the center of the city caused by the necessary security measures. This compression, however, hugely contributes to the compact atmosphere that makes the MSC so legendary and effective. People are outspoken. They get to know each other. There is even some mutual understanding. The real art is in being able to understand opposing positions while making the case for one's own standpoint.

It was the resistance fighter Ewald-Heinrich von Kleist-Schmenzin—a member of the Stauffenberg circle—who, after the war, laid the foundations for what was then known as the Internationale Wehrkunde-Begegnung. Among others, he invited Henry Kissinger and Helmut Schmidt to make their contribution to military de-escalation. This "encounter" (*Begegnung*) eventually became the Munich Security Conference (more than once named as the world's "Best Think Tank Conference" by the University of Pennsylvania).[2] A major German newspaper once commented that Wolfgang Ischinger handled world politics there with the experience of a diplomat and the charm of the skiing instructor he had been in his younger years.[3] This aptly describes his character, and also reflects a lesson I have learned in foreign politics: diplomacy is about being firm in the matter, but soft with people. As hard interests increasingly gain priority over "soft" values and conventions in the world of the twenty-first century, Munich lets us see how geopolitical and geoeconomic interests intertwine—as no other place in the world could. Quite a few of its participants can be expected to attach greater importance to the Munich Security Conference than to the World Economic Forum's Davos summit.

Long before German and European political circles had come to fully appreciate the global shifts in the world's economic, political, and military power axes, the Munich Security Conference had already become a place where you could not only hear this but feel it in the way the various participants appeared "on stage."

◂ Sigmar Gabriel at the Munich Security Conference in February 2018.

The dense program and the sheer physical closeness made it easy for participants to have confidential talks, while making it nearly impossible for them to avoid running into political opponents—whenever they tried, there was a good chance that Wolfgang Ischinger would step in to successfully facilitate personal encounters and confidential conversations.

After the ending of the Cold War, the US Army War College coined the term "VUCA world," with VUCA referring to volatility, uncertainty, complexity, and ambiguity.[4] It is my impression that the world has now become even more volatile, insecure, complex, and ambiguous than it was thirty years ago, leading to a loss of forecasting capability, as Wolfgang Ischinger has described. In his hugely readable book *World in Danger*, he mentions examples including the Maidan movement and its consequences, Brexit, and the emergence of ISIS.[5] To illustrate this, Wolfgang describes a meeting he had with the Saudi minister of foreign affairs and me in the summer of 2017. At that time, neither of the three of us was able to foresee the major crisis that was about to rock the Middle East—with outright war between Saudi Arabia and Qatar a possibility according to some analysts. Presumably not even the Saudi minister knew of the confrontation between the Gulf states, which was, to a significant degree, led by the Saudi head of government. Conflicts are escalating with increasing speed, and the escalation point can rarely be anticipated with accuracy. Conflict prevention thus becomes more difficult. And, in a VUCA world, conflict pacification becomes even more difficult than conflict prevention.

Long before German and European political circles had come to fully appreciate the global shifts in the world's economic, political, and military power axes, the Munich Security Conference had already become a place where you could not only hear this but feel it in the way the various participants appeared "on stage."

To this day, the Allied victories over Japan and Germany in World War II remain the only truly convincing examples of regimes of criminals being defeated by military means and their countries then being permanently pacified, democratized, and turned into partners. All interventions of the more recent past—notably in Iraq and Afghanistan—have produced sobering results. In the former Yugoslavia, the West intervened far too late. In the Balkans, the international community acted only half-heartedly or not at all as it saw the horrors of the wars of the 1990s unfold. In the Bosnian War alone, 100,000 people died—8,000 of them during the Srebrenica massacre. Mass rape and other war crimes left behind a scarred society. The numerous UN peacekeepers who watched the homicide without doing anything about it provided no basis for international mediation efforts. Only when NATO established a rapid reaction force to create a credible threat of force and began to launch air strikes was it possible to enforce negotiations, leading to the Dayton Accords peace agreement, which provided a sufficient level of stability. Subsequently, in Kosovo, NATO acted in a more timely and committed fashion, so that, at the end of the Balkan wars, it appears justified to speak of successful interventions.

The military operations in the aftermath of September 11, 2001, must be judged differently. Bush's Iraqi campaign has certainly not led to security and freedom, but to new bloody conflicts with Islamist terror. And the US and Europe's haphazard and sudden withdrawal from Afghanistan, letting down thousands of local employees who loyally stood by us for years, has cost the West much credibility. The US administration puts the costs of the wars in Iraq and Afghanistan alone at about one trillion dollars—an astronomical number (twelve zeros) that does not even include additional costs, such as for war invalids and refugees, as well as the contributions of allied states. More than 300,000 people have lost their lives in these two wars, including 4,804 allied troops in Iraq and 3,449 NATO troops (59 of which were members of the Bundeswehr). In the Hindu Kush, twenty years of deaths and expensive reconstruction attempts have resulted in a state that, after a few weeks of being left on its own, collapsed and, showing almost no resistance, once again fell prey to the Taliban. Former German Social Democratic Party (SPD) Chairman Kurt Beck was once derided for suggesting that we should negotiate with the moderate Taliban. Today, it has become the only option left.

Our action in enabling the Kurds and Yazidis to stand up to the terror of ISIS by providing training and weapons can be seen as a—admittedly rather small—step in the right direction. This case example may show how, in the future, a contribution to stability and peace can be made using limited means, but with a clear goal. Costly interventions with unrealistic and unclear goals—like the campaigns in Iraq and Afghanistan—will increasingly become a thing of the past.

We should take the time to learn lessons from the foreign assignments of the Bundeswehr, without going from one extreme to the other. A commission of inquiry of the German Bundestag may be the appropriate setting. The way the withdrawal from Afghanistan was carried out has raised fundamental questions, and there is a risk that it will completely destroy the political support for military operations of this kind. Western values—notably human rights, freedoms, and democracy—will continue to determine our approach to foreign policy. However, it is questionable to say the least whether we have the right and the ability to force these values upon others by means of military intervention. After the Afghanistan debacle, the use of military force will increasingly refocus on national interests. In the future, combat operations will serve the purpose of either self-protection or protection of friendly nations, but not the enforcement of values. This means that we must dare to deal in realpolitik.

It is clear that NATO will continue to be the essential pillar of our security, and this territorial defense alliance has not been questioned. However, the era in which NATO participated in operations aiming to do more than stop war or terror is over.

It is equally clear that we must expand our shared European capabilities. If something happens in the Persian Gulf, as Europeans we are not even capable of conducting a joint monitoring mission. We shouldn't, of course, start with the most difficult tasks; instead, we should focus on settling the obvious and the solvable in close collaboration with other nations. Metaphorically speaking, European politics wants to participate in every Masters golf tournament when it doesn't even succeed at miniature golf. Wolfgang Ischinger is right when he writes that, for diplomacy to be credible, it must be undergirded by military means. As Frederick the Great said, "diplomacy without weapons is like an orchestra without instruments."

Diplomacy—the art of negotiating conflicting interests—has its natural constraints. When dialogue is denied or even an encounter between conflicting parties is considered by them to threaten their positions, diplomacy has a tough job. However, the history of diplomacy abounds with examples of the human factor being leveraged to improve the relationship between nations.

Without the close relationship of Willy Brandt and Leonid Brezhnev, the Ostverträge (from the 1970 Treaty of Moscow to the 1973 Treaty of Prague) would certainly not have been achieved so quickly. When Egyptian President Anwar as-Sadat philosophized with Helmut Schmidt about Islam and Christianity till late at night on their legendary boat ride on the Nile in 1977, they also laid a resilient foundation for diplomatic breakthroughs. Only in this way was it possible to foster a sense of mutual understanding between Germany and Israel's key strategic neighbor. Germany's close partnership with its former "hereditary enemy" France would not have developed as well as it did if it wasn't for the friendly relationships between Adenauer and de Gaulle, between Schmidt and Giscard d'Estaing, between Kohl and Mitterrand, and between Schröder and Chirac.

More than once, I have personally experienced the importance of human closeness in the realm of diplomacy. During a phase of harrowing public confrontation between the Federal Republic and Turkey in 2017, when Germany vetoed election campaign appearances of Turkish politicians in the Federal Republic and Turkish politicians were comparing the Federal Republic with Nazi Germany, I had a first encounter with my Turkish counterpart, Mevlüt Çavuşoğlu, in Berlin.

German-Turkish relations had not been so strained in a long time. According to the protocol, my Turkish colleague should have visited me at my official residence, but I specifically wished to see him first in his Berlin hotel for breakfast.
In Turkey, to visit one's elders rather than expecting them to attend on you is a well-received gesture of respect. As a present, I brought him an old mining sign highlighting the dangers of working underground—in both the German and Turkish languages. The text on the sign was: "High voltage! Attention! Risk of death!" Çavuşoğlu immediately got the point, and our first encounter started in a highly humorous mood.

When dialogue is denied or even an encounter between conflicting parties is considered by them to threaten their positions, diplomacy has a tough job.

This culminated, at the following year's Munich Security Conference, with the release of the human rights activist Peter Steudter and the German journalist Denis Yücel after 367 days in Turkish custody. The time in between was filled with many joint meetings and private visits, from which a close personal relationship and friendship arose. Our mutual trust ultimately enabled us to overcome severe political frictions between both of our countries. The 2018 Munich Security Conference represented the concluding harmony to this duet. I used the occasion to suggest that we make continued use of all forms of dialogue with Turkey and said: "There is no other way. You have to use good moments to get to better ones."

Wolfgang Ischinger can certainly tell many similar stories from his personal experience as a diplomat and as the chairman of the Munich Security Conference. Direct, personal encounters and endeavors do not always produce happy endings, and this is another of the lessons to be learned from international diplomacy. Vladimir Putin's 2001 speech to the German Bundestag, with which he reached out his hand to us, gave rise to hopes for a lasting cooperation with our powerful neighbor in the East.[6] Six years later, however, he announced his departure from it at the 2007 Munich Security Conference when he said: "The format of the conference gives me the opportunity to elude the 'exaggerated politeness' of having to talk in polished and pleasant-to-the-ear, but ultimately empty diplomatic phrases. The format of the conference allows me to say what I really think about the problems of international security."[7] Dialogue with the Kremlin is one of the greatest challenges facing German diplomacy. This makes it all-the-more important to have the MSC as a high-caliber format where we can meet and talk on equal terms and with respect, but also with unambiguous clarity.

My friend Wolfgang Niedecken of the Kölschrock band BAP once asked me about my favorite song, to which I answered: "Sympathy For The Devil." Its sound is pure rock. But aside from the song's disturbing lyrics, my moody answer was also meant as a reference to the fact that democratic politics—and diplomacy in particular—must never succumb to complacency.

We must develop the ability to "put ourselves in others' shoes"—even if those are rather uncomfortable shoes. Only if we understand why our dialogue partners not uncommonly have mindsets that are so completely different from ours can we go and seek peaceful solutions to conflicts. My take is that "Sympathy For The Devil" would make quite a suitable soundtrack for the Munich Security Conference.

We must develop the ability to "put ourselves in others' shoes"—even if those are rather uncomfortable shoes. Only if we understand why our dialogue partners not uncommonly have mindsets that are so completely different from ours can we go and seek peaceful solutions to conflicts.

Sigmar Gabriel is a former German Minister for Foreign Affairs. He was the Chairman of the Social Democratic Party (SPD) of Germany from 2009 to 2017. He also served as the Minister for the Environment and as the Minister for Economic Affairs and Energy. He is the Chairman of Atlantik-Brücke ("Atlantic Bridge") non-profit association.

Mevlüt Çavuşoğlu (left) and Sergey Lavrov at the Munich Security Conference in February 2018. ▸

Müller

Keeping Communication Channels Open

Nora Müller

"To jaw-jaw is always better than to war-war."[1] With this quote from 1954 published in *The New York Times*, Winston Churchill rendered an immortal service not only to every speechwriter, but also to every practitioner of international dialogue. Sharp-witted as usual, the British prime minister summed up his way of dealing with communist Cold-War adversaries: better keep talking than risk an incalculable escalation of tensions. Nearly seventy years later, dialogue with challenging actors" such as China or Russia is still both indispensable and difficult. However, the conditions for this dialogue have dramatically changed. China and the US are competing for geopolitical, technological, and economic supremacy. The West is meandering between self-assertion and self-destruction. Between the poles of rival superpowers, the rules-based international order becomes increasingly brittle. In this climate, aren't conversations with Beijing, Moscow, and other autocracies inevitably turning into "alibi events"? Or, even worse, aren't they giving rise to—more or less conspicuously—a state of throwing accusations at each other, as was the case with the US-China talks in Anchorage?[2]

In the current political climate, postulating dialogue for the sake of dialogue would be naïve. However, simply discarding dialogue as a means of international politics would be equally foolish. As the Finnish president Sauli Niinistö rightly reminds us, "we need dialogue most with those we agree the least with." Therefore, the question is how to turn this dialogue into more than a show, despite the difficult conditions. Looking back at history isn't much help, since, as *Die Zeit* journalist Michael Thumann writes, "it is hard to imagine how yesterday's Ostpolitik could serve as a useful blueprint for dealing with the Russian and Chinese governments in the future."[3]

The following four rules are thus to be understood as guiding principles rather than an ultimate how-to for successful dialogue.

First, acknowledge clashes of values and interests. A sober view of China and Russia—and of other states with an anti-West orientation such as Iran—shows that an increased economic interdependence (or the prospect of it) hasn't developed the transformative power envisaged by concepts such as "change through trade" or "modernization partnership." Instead of the hoped-for convergence, clashes of values and interests have increasingly been brought to the fore. Acknowledging this strategic reality and stating it in clear terms better paves the way for focused, outcome-oriented conversations than hiding behind empty phrases such as "win-win cooperation" or "strategic partnership." It presupposes everyone's readiness to spell out their own core interests, to make them transparent, and to consistently demand their fulfillment. If this doesn't happen, the resulting imbalance may easily become a burden for the conversations. For instance, in its relationship to China, which itself is fond of drawing red lines and defending them tooth and nail, the EU still has to learn how to clearly communicate its own core interests—compliance with international law, respect for human and civil rights, and fairness in business and trade—and how to firmly respond to their not being respected.

Second, set realistic expectations and goals. "I did what I came to do . . . identify areas of practical work our two countries can do to advance our mutual interests . . ." With these words, US president Joe Biden matter-of-factly and pragmatically summarized the first meeting with his Russian counterpart Vladimir Putin in Geneva.[4] At a time when China and Russia are increasingly challenging the West (I may be forgiven for this oversimplification) and relations are characterized by mutual mistrust, he used these words to indicate a "dialogue paradigm" that is better suited to the strategic realities: dialogue as a means for aligning mutual interests—no more and no less. By this logic, conversations are particularly productive when they focus on interests and pursue limited goals. Or if the aim of conducting such conversations is, as the American political scientist Thomas Wright put it, "to avoid unintentional provocations and to facilitate transactional cooperation on shared interests."[5]

> In international relations, trust is as crucially important as in every other area of human interaction.

And what about the much-praised "trust factor"? "The difference between war and peace can be a matter of trust," says the American political scientist Andrew H. Kydd.[6] In international relations, trust is as crucially important as in every other area of human interaction. However, the assumption that the other side will keep

◂ Nora Müller at the MSC Core Group Meeting in Beijing in April 2016.

its promises and abide by agreed-upon rules—that is, that it is literally "trustworthy"—isn't something that simply drops out of the sky. In the best case, it develops during a process of dialogue and negotiation, and is strengthened by cooperation projects in certain areas—so-called confidence-building measures. Therefore, trust can be, at best, the outcome of conversations, but not their precondition—especially with a view to the "dialogue with challenging players."

Third, invest in personal relationships. What seems contradictory at first sight makes sense from the perspective of "practical diplomacy": the higher the tensions and the mistrust between the countries or players, the more an investment in personal relationships becomes important—on all levels of the system. Adenauer and de Gaulle, Kissinger and Zhou Enlai, Kohl and Gorbachev: the personal chemistry—occasionally even friendship—between the acting players proved a significant success factor in diplomatic efforts. Anne-Marie Slaughter and Samm Sacks are right: "foreign policy—like politics more broadly—is based on relationships created not only at the negotiating table, but also after hours, unwinding over an informal meal and finding common interests and identities."[7] When we consider this, we must not underestimate the influence of the location—what has been called, since Roman antiquity, genius loci—on the mood and atmosphere of a diplomatic meeting. The so-called "miracle of the Caucasus"—Mikhail Gorbachev's consent to the NATO membership of a reunified Germany—can be attributed to a number of factors, one of which is certainly the casually relaxed atmosphere that the Soviet president's guest house in his North Caucasian homeland offered for the "cardigan diplomacy" between the German chancellor and his Soviet counterpart.

The COVID-19 pandemic, with its contact and travel limitations, has undeniably led to a significant "dialogue deficit," as even the most professional Zoom meeting can never entirely replace the complexity of face-to-face encounters. In the digital media, it is simply not possible to take a dialogue partner to the side for a confidential tête-à-tête in a coffee break. And when conversations get stuck, simply pushing the "leave meeting" button is significantly easier in a virtual meeting than standing up from a real negotiation table is.[8]

Fourth, include various stakeholders. Complex international challenges can be met more effectively if not only government officials, but also stakeholders from other areas—business, science, and civil society—have their say. The best example of this is the management of the COVID-19 crisis. This is also valid for the dialogue with challenging players. It is hardly surprising that, with regard to the currently highly strained US-Chinese relations, Anne-Marie Slaughter and Samm Sacks advocate "a much broader dialogue" that includes stakeholders from a variety of political areas.[9] This type of broader dialogue must also involve younger people—a credo that the Munich Young Leaders, a joint project of the Munich Security Conference and the Körber Foundation, has been following for more than ten years.[10]

> The higher the tensions and the mistrust between the countries or players, the more an investment in personal relationships becomes important—on all levels of the system.

Dialogue needs principles and rules. Especially in the complex world of the twenty-first century, in which the international order is increasingly coming under pressure, "talking with, not about each other" is more important than ever. And so, we can still say "it is better to jaw-jaw than to war-war."

Nora Müller is Executive Director International Affairs at the Körber-Stiftung.

Mohammad Javad Zarif at the MSC Core Group Meeting in Doha in 2019. ▸

Core Group Meeting Doha | اجتماع المجموعة الأساسية - الدوحة
October 29, 2019
Munich Security Conference msc
Münchner Sicherheitskonferenz
12

Promoting Mutual Understanding between China and the West

Fu Ying

While serving as head of European Affairs in the Chinese Ministry of Foreign Affairs during the 2010s, I often visited European countries and attended conferences, and I became familiar with the Munich Security Conference (MSC).

Attending the MSC for the First Time

I was invited to the MSC for the first time at its fiftieth conference, which was convened on January 31, 2014. That happened to be the first day of the Chinese New Year. I led a small team of assistants and flew to Munich on the Chinese New Year's Eve. The focal points at MSC 2014 included the transatlantic security landscape, emerging countries and global governance, the European debt crisis and the future of the European Union, situations in Mali and Syria, and Iran's nuclear issue. However, the hottest topic that attracted attention was the internal development in Ukraine.

I was invited to speak at the plenary panel discussion on global power and regional stability themed "Europe, America, and Asia." The other panelists included Ivo Josipović, then president of the Republic of Croatia; US Senator Lindsey Graham; Shivshankar Menon, national security advisor to the Indian prime minister; and retired US Navy Admiral James G. Stavridis as our moderator. It was obvious that the panelists came from very different backgrounds and were concerned about different matters. Before the discussion started, I wondered what the common topic of interest could be for the four of us.

The moderator Admiral Stavridis had no difficulty finding his focal point. He opened the panel by saying that "there are five panelists here today, and four of us are from democratic countries."[1] It was not difficult to understand that he was implying that I was the only one whose country stood for different political beliefs. I also realized that most European countries shared this view of China, if not the whole Western world. They saw China as "a non-democratic country with a wrong political system." The Western countries typically believe that the Cold War against the Soviet Union, which lasted nearly half a century, ended with communism being finally defeated, signifying "the end of history." They have difficulty understanding that China, under the leadership of its Communist Party (CPC), had not only survived but became increasingly successful.

Topics for the panel had little to do with China's political system, and therefore Stavridis' words received no response from the other panelists as they made their presentations. When it was my turn to speak, I thought I needed to say something to respond to the moderator's provocation. However, since the panel was not an appropriate occasion to debate specific political disagreements, my focus needed to be on the theme and on presenting China's opinion on the topic.

With an easy smile, I said: "Yesterday was the first day of the Chinese New Year. For this most important festival, the Chinese people, wherever they are, make every effort to return home before New Year's Eve to enjoy a family reunion dinner. At such a moment, my colleagues and I have flown nine hours to come to Munich. Why did we do that? Because we want to promote mutual understanding with you."

When I said that, I could hear gentle chuckles from the audience and I saw Dr. Kissinger, who was sitting in the first row, nodding slightly, expressing his consent. My words were not aggressive, but the audience obviously picked up the hint. I sensed that I had gained some appreciation and could now make my points, so I went on, "Of course, mutual respect is a prerequisite of mutual understanding, including respecting the right of people in other countries to find their path and establish their political systems based on their own history and cultural experience. China has been carrying out reform and opening up for more than thirty years and has achieved enormous success in economic growth and social progress, which speaks for the success of China's political system."

The MSC is a mature international platform where rich opinions and information converge. The participants and journalists eagerly collected the various views and wasted no time in disseminating them to the world. I received many questions that day and was impressed by the wide interest in China.

After the panel ended, Ambassador Wolfgang Ischinger walked onto the stage to offer his congratulations to the panelists. He expressed appreciation for my participation and expressed his hope of seeing me more often at

◂ Fu Ying with Javier Solana at the Munich Strategy Forum in Elmau in December 2017.

the MSC. He believed that China needed to be represented at the MSC and that China's voice should be heard when debating international security issues.

This was the beginning of my bond with the MSC. In 2017 I became a member of the MSC Advisory Council and have attended the MSC as long as circumstances have permitted me.

Participating in the MSC during the Pandemic

On February 13, 2020, I arrived in Munich to attend the 56th MSC, together with a group of scholars and assistants. By this time, the COVID-19 pandemic was already raging in China. The World Health Organization (WHO) and the International Committee of the Red Cross (ICRC) sent participants to the conference who helped to broaden awareness of what was happening in China and the enormous efforts and sacrifices the Chinese people had made in combating the virus. They called on the international community to see the danger, extend help, and fight the pandemic in a concerted effort.

The WHO experts highly commended China's effective response in containing the outbreak and called upon other countries to join efforts with China in developing vaccines and treatments. They pointed out that the world had to be prepared for further spread of the virus and that it would be valuable for the international community to learn from China's experience and use it as a template should the need arise.

To create a relationship of cooperation and coordination, there needs to be a foundation built with some level of trust. Building trust is therefore an important subject that China must work on as it moves closer to the center of the international stage.

Wang Yi, state councillor and minister of foreign affairs of China; and Qin Gang, vice minister of foreign affairs, attended the MSC's plenary session and some of the events. They shared how the Chinese people led by the CPC and the Chinese government went all out to fight the spread of the virus. Their speeches were well received.

At the MSC in 2020, China became a hot topic and was the center of discussion in eleven subforums under such topics as "Taming the Dragon: How the West Must Confront and Engage the China Challenge"; "Partner, Competitor, or Rival? Transatlantic Relations and the China Conundrum"; "How Should Europe Deal with Rising China?"; "What If... Russia and China Become Allies?"; and "The Future of China's Participation in Arms Control Regimes." Many other panels touched on issues related to China, resulting in China being mentioned in almost every discussion.

I led a small team of Chinese participants, which included Mr. Wu Shicun, president of the National Institute for South China Sea Studies, Mr. Wang Huiyao, president of the Center for China and Globalization (CCG), and Tang Bei, associate professor at Shanghai International Studies University. We tried to attend as many side events as possible to present a Chinese perspective on the issues of general concern, and we responded to questions about China. From my observations, when there was a Chinese voice, people would pay attention and wanted to know what people in China thought and wanted. For example, a German scholar came to my speech at a luncheon and said that "listening to you talking about China face to face makes me feel that we can trust each other. But on many occasions, the Chinese voice is absent, and we seldom hear China's opinions directly or get convincing explanations to many issues concerning China."

Indeed, international relations are like interpersonal relations. To create a relationship of cooperation and coordination, there needs to be a foundation built with some level of trust. Building trust is therefore an important subject that China must work on as it moves closer to the center of the international stage. At MSC, although my team and I tried to reach out as much as possible to meet the need for Chinese voices, we found it impossible to appear on every panel and side event that concerned China, as there were so many. We did our best to present, on as many occasions as possible, China's case in fighting COVID-19—telling the stories of families hit by the virus, people's fear and distress, the brave medical personnel and healthcare workers, the selfless volunteers, and strong leaders and members of the CPC. Although biases against China still exist, there were many voices expressing sympathy and support for China. Some European businessmen asked me what specific assistance was needed to combat the virus, indicating that they wanted to offer support.

Wolfgang mentioned it when introducing State Councillor and Minister of Foreign Affairs Wang Yi: "China has undertaken a huge, truly huge effort to fight what has become a huge medical challenge that now, of course, goes beyond China. And I think China deserves a little bit of compassion and cooperation and expressions of support and encouragement, rather than only criticism."[2]

During off-record talks, some European scholars pointed out that many countries had restricted contact and suspended flights with China. This may result in a kind of isolation. If countries start to disconnect, it will certainly cause adverse economic and political consequences for the world and must be corrected in one way or another. There were also scholars who noted that the COVID-19 pandemic might lead to the US "decoupling" from China, which could cause systematic decoupling if not carefully handled. These forward-looking thoughts in early February 2020 proved to be true soon after.

In the months that followed, some US government officials and senators criticized China for "disguising" the pandemic. However, as I remember, many senior Americans, including the officials and senators attending the MSC, showed little interest in the information about the pandemic from the Chinese attendees. They paid little attention to the outbreaks as revealed by the WHO experts or how China was fighting the virus, discussed during many of the MSC panels. They did bring up the topic of China a lot, but mostly as a security threat to the West.

Back at the beginning of 2020, no one could have foreseen what kind of drastic change the COVID-19 pandemic would bring to the world. Now we are in the second half of 2021, and the pandemic is still raging worldwide, causing profound impacts on the life of people the world over. The performance of each government in pandemic control and prevention varies and the results are clear for people to see.

Raising a Question to US House Speaker Nancy Pelosi about 5G

There was an interesting episode at the 56th MSC in 2020—one that drew broad publicity here in China. It was a question I raised to Mrs. Nancy Pelosi, speaker of the US House of Representatives, during a plenary panel discussion on the subject of "the State of Democracy in the West."

Wolfgang Schäuble, president of the German Bundestag, was also a panelist, and the moderator was Ivan Krastev, chairman of the Centre for Liberal Strategies in Bulgaria.

Pelosi was eloquent and talked at length, from collective security of American alignment to climate change and from NATO to the G20. Her emphasis was on how the European allies should work closely with the US in responding to the "common challenges." Then she raised the topic of 5G and cybersecurity. Looking serious, she started by saying, "I'm going to say something that may not be agreeable to many of you here, but you've invited candor—no lecture, but candor—and that is the subject of 5G and cybersecurity."[3]

"China is seeking to export its digital autocracy through its telecommunication giant, Huawei, threatening economic retaliation against those who do not adopt their technologies. The United States has recognized Huawei as a national security threat by putting it on our entity list restricting engagement with US companies."[4]

She urged European countries to steer clear of Huawei. "Nations cannot cede telecommunication infrastructure to China for financial expediency," she said.[5] She saw the Huawei issue into a stance upon values and said: "allowing the Sinification of 5G would be to choose autocracy over democracy." She suggested that "we must instead move to an internationalization—I know Europe is working hard on this, Europeanization—an internationalization of digital infrastructure that does not enable an autocracy. Not an American or European model—if we can't come together—but an international model."[6]

If countries start to disconnect, it will certainly cause adverse economic and political consequences for the world and must be corrected in one way or another.

After Pelosi spoke, Schäuble was invited to speak. He called for "strengthening European cooperation, not to be against anyone, but aim to be relevant. Otherwise, we cannot be a reliable partner, neither for the United States, nor for stabilizing the global world."[7]

When it came to the Q&A session, people in the hall started to ask questions. I also raised my hand, and the moderator, Mr. Krastev saw me and invited me to ask my question.

"Technology is a tool," I said, "China, since its reform started forty years ago, has introduced all kinds of

Western technologies—Microsoft, IBM, Amazon—they are all active in China. Since we started with 1G, 2G, 3G, and 4G, all the technology had come from Western countries, from the developed world, and China has maintained its political system. The system led by the Communist Party of China has been successful and these technologies do not threaten it. So how, if Huawei's technology with 5G is introduced into Western countries, will it threaten the political system? Do you really think that the democratic system is so fragile that it could be threatened by this single high-tech company of Huawei?"

Though I spoke in a soft tone and in a friendly manner, my question pointed out a flaw in her drawn-out speech, which was not logically consistent. As I finished, there was even some applause from the audience, and people looked amused. Obviously, my question had struck a chord. Failing to find a focus for her response, Pelosi mumbled about China's domestic affairs and avoided the question on whether Western democracy was fragile. Looking flustered, she continued to insist that taking Huawei's 5G technology is choosing to become an "autocracy" like China.

Although her answer was evasive and aggressive, she still managed to show some degree of friendliness toward China by saying something nice. She said, "China is on the forefront of doing many great things on climate issues . . . We work together in that regard."[8]

But she did not want to conclude on such a friendly tone and reemphasized, "If you want a free flow of information, if you want to build a collective conscience of values and respect for human rights and the rest, don't go near Huawei."[9]

President Schäuble also picked up the topic and commented: "To secure freedom, we need diversity. And we have to fight against monopolies, and even a duopoly is not what I like."[10]

The panel discussion was rich in content, and participants raised questions about cross-Atlantic relations and populism. My impression was that Europeans have their own concerns and doubts. Graham Allison, professor at Harvard University, mentioned a few interesting pieces of survey data during his subsequent speech at a side event. According to a poll from the Pew Research Center in 2019, 49 percent of French and German respondents considered the US as the biggest threat, while 40 percent and 33 percent, respectively, saw China as the biggest threat. This research may reflect the evolution of the Europeans' perception of world security.

My impression was that many European participants wanted to see better communication between China and the US. They also hoped that China could address certain concrete issues in its relations with European countries and the EU—which would add some certainty to the current international relations.

Personally, I see being able to raise the question to Pelosi as a valuable opportunity to communicate face to face with a senior American politician. And I hope that the question gave people something to think about.

A Few Impressions about the MSC 2020

My impression from the 56th MSC was that the US was trying to pull together a united front against China, whereas European countries were reconsidering their own international roles and seeking to enhance their influence as a third party. China should increase its voice at international platforms.

The Americans value the role of the MSC and regard it as an important platform for sharing policy ideas and promoting coordination of transatlantic positions. The American participants from the two political parties seemed to have coordinated their stances and focused on the same mission: to cope with the rise of China and the "China threat" with the ultimate objective of preventing European countries from using Huawei's 5G technology.

US Secretary of State Mike Pompeo did not give a long speech, but one-third of his time was dedicated to lambasting China. He accused China of being coercive in maritime matters, that Huawei was a "Trojan horse" for Chinese intelligence, and that China used military and diplomatic efforts to provoke others. He urged Europe to take sides with the US to face "an increasingly aggressive Chinese Communist Party." US Secretary of Defense Mark Esper stated that Huawei was the poster child for China's "nefarious activity." He claimed that it was not too late for the British to rescind their decision of permitting Huawei to participate in part of its 5G development.

What was the reaction to the Americans being so fixated on China and being obsessed with launching verbal attacks? From my observations, some people agreed with this argument from the perspective of the Cold War days when the US and the Soviet Union were in a verbal tug-of-war and echoed the American attacks on China's domestic and foreign policies. While others kept a cool approach in observing the China-US wrangling, they seemed to prefer to learn more about the facts and wanted to make decisions that could best serve their own interests.

Against the backdrop of deteriorating China-US relations, European countries could not stay detached. But most people did not like the idea of a return to power polarization and the collapse of the current international order due to vicious competition between China and the US. They did not want to see a decoupling of science and technology, which would impede the progress of humanity. The choice many in Europe saw was to reinforce their own strength and make a bigger contribution to world affairs.

"Westlessness," the title of the Munich Security Report 2020, mirrored a prevailing anxiety within Western society, which worries that the West is losing its dominance in a rapidly changing world.[11] Concerns that the once unified European-American position was being eroded due to the emerging divergence in their aspirations and interests; fears that the West-dominated world system might be subject to "revision" by so-called authoritarian forces.

The idea of Westlessness comes mainly from two perceptions. One is the acknowledgment of China's rise, with mixed feelings of recognition and concern. More and more insightful Europeans have come to realize that a rising China has become an inevitable development and that Europe and other Western countries must find ways to peacefully coexist with China despite the difference in political systems. The other is the recognition that the protectionism, isolationism, and unilateralism upheld by US conservatives has deviated from the fundamental principles that underpin the liberal international order. Hence, the feeling has grown that Europe has to formulate its own strategy and find its own way.

Europe's reflection is multifaceted. On the one hand, it sees that a "systematic crisis" is taking place, but on the other, it believes that the Western consciousness is still strong and will not end. It feels uncomfortable about the emerging forces' integration into the West-dominated international order and their expanding role but remain open-minded to preserving the system's integrity and maintaining coexistence through adjustment and coordination. So, as some in the media have commented, Europe was not singing a funeral dirge for the West. Instead, Europe wants to reconstruct the system at the level of strategy and values. Europeans are worried because they recognize a danger looming that the world could become divided and slide into a fierce competition between the US, China, and Russia. Instead, they want to find a new position and play a more constructive role. Therefore, they stress "transcendence," namely, internally rising above differences in interests and values, enhancing the capacity for collective action, while externally going beyond the dependence on existing paths and developing a more diversified, balanced, and pragmatic global strategy.

Europeans are worried because they recognize a danger looming that the world could become divided and slide into a fierce competition between the US, China, and Russia. Instead, they want to find a new position and play a more constructive role.

Recent years have seen an increasing number of topics about China discussed at the MSC. As the world experiences rapid changes, China has been confronted with growing, complex challenges in its international role and status. China needs to send prominent figures to speak at international forums such as the MSC. There should also be more Chinese scholars and members of congress participating in the discussions. Otherwise, it will be difficult for China to be understood and therefore harder for China to seek cooperation on issues of common interest.

I hope and believe there will be more Chinese officials and scholars invited to the MSC to not only share Chinese thinking through frank conversations and communications but also to help China understand the concerns of other countries across the world.

Fu Ying is the former Vice Foreign Minister of China. She is also a member of the Advisory Council of the Munich Security Conference.

Giesecke & Devrient
msc
Giesecke & Devrient

Managing U.S.-China Strategic Competition

Kevin Rudd

What is the art of diplomacy? Diplomats have many roles managing the numerous day-to-day formalities, cordial communications, and minor disputes that come with relations between states. But they have one calling above all others: to serve on the front line in the preservation of peace—to prove, as Winston Churchill put it, that "meeting jaw to jaw is better than war."

Despite the "long peace" that has persisted since the end of the great wars that wracked the world in the twentieth century, we should be under no illusions about the critical need for diplomacy to continue to serve this role today. The reality is that we are now entering a decade of living dangerously, in which the relationship between two superpowers, the United States and China, may determine whether that peace is maintained or shattered, with unimaginable consequences for the world.

The contest between these two countries will enter a decisive phase in the 2020s. The Chinese Communist Party is increasingly confident that, by decade's end, China's economy will finally surpass that of the United States. Western elites may dismiss the significance of that milestone; the CCP does not. Taking the top slot will turbocharge Beijing's confidence, assertiveness, and leverage in its dealings with Washington and its allies—including on the issue of singular importance to Xi Jinping and the rest of China's leadership: the reunification of Taiwan with the mainland.

Washington must decide how to respond strategically to Beijing's assertive agenda—and quickly. If it were to opt for open strategic confrontation and economic decoupling, every country in the world would be forced to take sides, and the risk of escalation would only grow. No matter what stratagems the two sides pursue or what events unfold, the tension between the United States and China will grow, and competition will intensify—it is inevitable. War, however, is not. It is still possible for bold and artful diplomacy to navigate this challenge.

The two countries can put in place guardrails to prevent disaster: a joint framework for what I call "managed strategic competition" that would reduce the risk of competition escalating into open conflict. While many now doubt that their leaders can find their way to a framework to manage their diplomatic relations, the two countries must consider something akin to the procedures that the United States and the Soviet Union put in place to govern their relations after the Cuban missile crisis—but in this case, without first going through the near-death experience of a barely avoided war.

Managed strategic competition would involve establishing certain hard limits on each country's security policies and conduct, but would allow for full and open competition in the technological, economic, and ideological realms. It would also make it possible for Washington and Beijing to cooperate in certain areas, bilaterally and multilaterally.

The idea of managed strategic competition is anchored in a deeply realist view of the global order. It accepts that states will continue to seek security by building a balance of power in their favor. But even amid escalating competition, there will still be political space for cooperation on critical global challenges. Aside from collaborating on climate change, the two countries could conduct nuclear arms control negotiations, or work toward an agreement on acceptable military applications of artificial intelligence. They could coordinate disaster-response and humanitarian relief. They could work together to improve global financial stability in the wake of the pandemic.

This list is far from exhaustive. But the strategic rationale should be clear: it is better for both countries to operate within a joint framework of managed competition than to have no rules at all. There will be many who will criticize this approach as naive. Their responsibility, however, is to come up with something better. Short of crisis, conflict, and war.

Although such a framework would be difficult to construct, doing so is still possible. The hard truth is that no relationship can ever be managed unless there is a basic agreement between the parties on the terms of that management. And, in the end, only the art of diplomacy can make that possible.

Kevin Rudd is President and Chief Executive Officer of the Asia Society and president of the Asia Society Policy Institute. He previously served as Australia's Prime Minister from 2007 to 2010, as Foreign Minister from 2010 to 2012, and again as Prime Minister in 2013.

◂ Kevin Rudd at the Munich Young Leaders Alumni Meeting in New York City in September 2019.

Munich Security Conference
msc
Münchner Sicherheitskonferenz

Standing Up to China

Kenneth Roth

The Chinese government presents one of today's most difficult diplomatic challenges. As it crushes basic rights and freedoms at home and seeks to undermine international human rights institutions, Beijing threatens anyone who criticizes it, using its global surveillance tools, baseless prosecution of foreigners, and economic retaliation. In just one example, it imposed substantial tariffs on many Australian exports to China because the Australian government had the audacity to promote an independent investigation into the origins of the COVID-19 pandemic, challenging the Chinese government's cover-up and lies.

It has not been easy for Germany—or any government—to navigate such difficult terrain. On the one hand, Germany's voice on human rights is important, both in its own right and as a key member of the European Union. On the other hand, Germany's economy depends on exports, and China is one of its largest customers. Despite an occasional misstep, the German government has shown that it is possible to confront Beijing's severe repression.

In human rights terms, people across China are enduring the worst state repression since the murderous 1989 Tiananmen crackdown. Although President Xi Jinping presents himself as a strong, confident leader, he has gone to extraordinary lengths to ensure that the people of China cannot participate in unapproved public life or mobilize any challenge to Chinese Communist Party rule.

The Chinese government presents one of today's most difficult diplomatic challenges.

The persecution has been especially severe in Xinjiang, where Beijing has arbitrarily detained a million Uyghur and other Turkic Muslims, placing them in a program of forced indoctrination designed to compel them to abandon their religion, culture, and language. The Chinese government has installed a highly intrusive surveillance state in Xinjiang to help determine whom to detain. In many cases, these detainees have done nothing more than grow a beard, attend a mosque, or contact family abroad.

Some Turkic Muslims are placed in a program of forced labor. This potentially infects any export from Xinjiang, which is known foremost for its cotton, tomatoes, and polysilicon used for solar panels. These serious human rights violations, committed as part of a widespread and systemic attack on the population, amount to crimes against humanity—so far committed with utter impunity.

Other ethnic minorities, notably in Tibet and inner Mongolia, have also faced intense repression, and the crackdown extends throughout China, with the internet and social media strictly censored, independent voices silenced, civil society suppressed, and the rule of law—to the extent it ever existed—erased. The Chinese government claims that the people support its rule. But when many people in Hong Kong—one part of China where people had been free to voice their dissent—took part in large protests against the Chinese Communist Party's dictatorship, Beijing responded by effectively ripping up the "one country, two systems" agreement and crushing Hong Kong's freedoms.

It is not simple to know how to effectively respond to such repression, but the system's weakness suggests one fruitful avenue. Because the Chinese Communist Party refuses to submit to free and fair elections to establish its legitimacy and seeks to avoid any international accountability for its actions, it values international endorsements of its rule—and works vigorously to avoid international condemnation. That dual purpose—promoting state-to-state friendships and silencing critics—is a major motivation behind Xi Jinping's trillion-dollar Belt and Road Initiative.

That background suggests that international efforts to hold the Chinese government accountable for its serious human rights violations, by depriving Xi Jinping of the impunity he expects, can play a significant role in pressuring Beijing to curb its repression. But who would risk such an effort if it yields economic retaliation of the sort experienced by Australia? This is where German leadership has been impressive.

Beginning in 2019 several Western governments including Germany started organizing periodic joint statements at the United Nations decrying abuses in Xinjiang, during sessions of either the Human Rights Council in Geneva or the General Assembly in New York. The idea was that a combined voice would be more powerful than states speaking individually—and

◂ Kenneth Roth at the Munich Security Conference in February 2018.

that there would be safety in numbers against Beijing's retaliation.

At first the fear was palpable: during the initial effort in Geneva, twenty-five countries including Germany agreed to sign such a statement, but no one dared to read it out loud at the Human Rights Council, as is traditional for such joint statements. Over time, however, that began to change—with Germany playing a key part. When China's rights record came up for review at the Human Rights Council (as part of a periodic review of all UN member states), Germany was one of five governments backing an event, led by the United States, to shine a spotlight on Beijing's abuses in Xinjiang. In October 2020 Germany's ambassador to the United Nations in New York, Christoph Heusgen, played a central role in rallying an unprecedented (at the time) thirty-nine governments to speak out against the severe repression in Xinjiang, Tibet, and Hong Kong. In June 2021 a Canadian-led effort in Geneva, which Germany actively supported, secured forty-four signatories.

Beijing predictably would respond to each group condemnation with a counterstatement, but the human rights record of many signatories—the autocrats of the world—undermined the statement's credibility. There have also been questions about whether all the "signatories" had actually agreed to sign the Chinese statements. In 2019 one country asked China to remove it from the list of supporters because it had never pledged to sign. In some cases Beijing would not even reveal the names behind the declared number of signatories.

As the number of governments condemning Beijing's repression and calling for UN access to Xinjiang mounts, and as those willing to defend Beijing diminishes support for a formal UN resolution on the Chinese government's repression is growing.

As the number of governments condemning Beijing's repression and calling for UN access to Xinjiang mounts, and as those willing to defend Beijing diminishes—especially among Muslim-majority nations that are unhappy with the crushing of Islam in Xinjiang—support for a formal UN resolution on the Chinese government's repression is growing.

There is other evidence of Beijing's diminishing influence within the international human rights system. The Chinese government in October 2020 sought a seat on the UN Human Rights Council. The previous time it ran, four years earlier, it received the most votes of any country running from the Asia-Pacific region. This time, however, it received the fewest votes of any such government that secured a seat. Only Saudi Arabia received fewer votes and was denied a seat. When it came to electing the president of the UN Human Rights Council in January 2021, it was the turn of the Asia-Pacific region. The Chinese government, along with Russia and Saudi Arabia, favored a diplomat from abusive Bahrain, but that candidate lost overwhelmingly to Fiji's highly respected ambassador in Geneva.

In the UN Security Council, where Germany most recently occupied a seat in 2019–2020, Berlin repeatedly challenged Russian and Chinese vetoes on vital resolutions to advance and protect rights, including in Syria. While China, as a permanent member of the Council, would have vetoed any effort to take it to task for its own violations, Germany played a central role in organizing a separate virtual event on Xinjiang in May 2021.

The Chinese government clearly felt the reputational sting of the event, as illustrated by its extraordinary step of issuing "disinvitations"—perhaps better understood as threats against those who might join the event. Nonetheless, an extraordinary fifty-one states showed up at the ambassadorial level. So did a Chinese diplomat, who insisted on speaking and, when given the microphone, could only bluster, revealing how little Beijing had to say in defense of its extraordinary mistreatment of Turkic Muslims.

Germany had become such a relentless and principled voice for the Turkic communities of Xinjiang, as well as other victims of Beijing's repression, that at the end of Germany's two-year Security Council term, a Chinese diplomat announced, "Good riddance!" My view was, "Good work!"

Outside of the United Nations, however, German policy toward China sometimes has fallen short. There have been positive steps: In 2018 Chancellor Angela Merkel gained the release from China of Liu Xia, the widow of the Nobel Laureate Liu Xiaobo. But in December 2020 at the end of Germany's presidency of the European Union, Merkel was so eager to secure a European Union investment deal with China—as were French President Emmanuel Macron and European Commission President Ursula von der Leyen—that Berlin settled for a ploy to ignore the enormous problem of forced labor in Xinjiang. Rather than insist on an end to this illegal and abusive practice as a condition of a deal, the German government, representing EU leaders, settled for a pledge from Beijing to consider acceding to the International Labor Organization treaty on forced labor. Beijing didn't pledge to ratify the treaty, or to comply with it, but only to think about accepting the treaty.

Still, the deal was stymied. In 2021 the European Union, the United States, the United Kingdom, and Canada responded to Beijing's grave violations in Xinjiang by jointly imposing targeted sanctions on various Chinese officials and entities. The Chinese government responded by sanctioning EU ambassadors, European lawmakers, and European organizations. In turn the European Parliament made clear that it rejected the forced-labor subterfuge on which the proposed EU-China investment deal was based. So, for now, the deal is dead.

Raising the price for serious human rights violations, ranging from carrying out investigations to targeted sanctions, from providing sanctuary for survivors of Beijing's repression to international leadership in countering it, will be critical. Germany has recently shown the way.

Looking ahead, a new German government should take the next logical step, based on the growing number of governments willing to challenge Chinese repression, and rally its EU partners to seek a resolution at the Human Rights Council to establish a UN inquiry into Beijing's continued crimes against humanity in Xinjiang, as well as the ruthless crackdown on rights and freedoms in Hong Kong, and the persecution of dissenters across China.

The new government should press German companies to recognize the gravity of abuses in Xinjiang, including forced labor. The new German Parliament could initiate an inquiry into the issue, while pointing out companies' responsibilities under international guidelines and German law, despite the reluctance of some to accept them, not to become complicit in serious human rights violations through their direct business activities and supply chains. Given the opacity of Chinese supply chains—and Beijing's refusal to allow unfettered monitoring—any import from Xinjiang at least should be assumed to be tainted unless proven otherwise.

Concerted imposition of additional targeted sanctions against Chinese officials and entities responsible for serious abuses should also be advanced.

At a time when Beijing rebuts German criticism by pointing out the country's past history of mass killings, mere rhetoric—even from the highest levels of the new government—is unlikely to compel change in China. Raising the price for serious human rights violations, ranging from carrying out investigations to targeted sanctions, from providing sanctuary for survivors of Beijing's repression to international leadership in countering it, will be critical. Germany has recently shown the way. One hopes the new government will deepen those efforts.

As more governments gain courage to confront Chinese repression, Beijing faces the prospect of increasing opprobrium. That cannot be a pleasant prospect for China's leadership. As it discovers that its threats and enticements are not working to diminish the growing coalition of nations willing to challenge Xi Jinping's dictatorial rule—a coalition that German diplomats have played a central role in organizing—it will be the best chance we have of moving Beijing in a more rights-respecting direction.

Kenneth Roth is Executive Director of Human Rights Watch.

Munich Security Conference
msc
Münchner Sicherheitskonferenz
McKinsey&
McKi
lschinger
Giesecke & Devrient
Thor

Protecting Liberal-Democratic Values

Nathalie Tocci

Democracy has made a comeback in international relations. With the confrontation between the US and China, as well as Russia—reinterpreted as one between political systems and ideologies—democracy and authoritarianism have again become dominant signifiers of international relations. What does it mean for foreign policy?

Both during and especially after the end of the Cold War, values were at the forefront of US and European foreign policy. The US portrayed itself as a force for good in the world, with soft power as an indispensable complement to its unmatched military capabilities. Europe prided itself as a civilian and normative power in global affairs. Those were the days of the liberal international order and the end of history.

By the 2010s, values started exiting the scene. The global financial crisis and the return of geostrategic rivalry saw the rise of powers that either openly defied liberal democratic values or just rejected the hegemony of the West. The wars in Afghanistan and Iraq, followed by the burial of the "responsibility to protect" in Libya, eroded Western support for military interventions. The poor outcomes of the color revolutions in Eastern Europe, not to mention the Arab uprisings, pointed to an entrenchment of authoritarianism. And the surge of nationalist populism in the West spoke of a crisis of democracy and the sidelining of liberal values in Western foreign policy.

Now democracy is back in foreign affairs. Under President Biden, the strategic rivalry with China is no longer framed in transactional Trumpian terms. Today, tensions over tariffs, 5G, maritime security, and cyber or arms control are grouped together under a common ideational umbrella. The political overtone that the US-China confrontation is acquiring does not exclude the existence of other power centers, of which the EU and Russia are two. But these, while claiming their autonomous "right to choose," will be drawn to one side or the other because of the values they represent. The growing transatlantic convergence that is centered on the reassertion of liberal democratic values indicates the direction of travel.

A return of values to the forefront of international relations does not signal a return to the past, however. Rather than the promotion of such values at the height of the liberal international order, these days liberal democracies are concerned foremost with their protection. This is where two apparently disconnected concepts find common cause: when President Biden talks about a "foreign policy for the middle class" and Europeans talk about "strategic autonomy," deep down they have similar concerns in mind. Both goals belong to an international context in which external players that stand for different values seek to undermine liberal democratic ones in the West. Whether through traditional military means or, far more often, through hybrid security tactics and the weaponization of the economy, liberal democracies have to protect themselves from external interference. Failing to do so would hamper the security, rights, and welfare of their citizens, and this would feed illiberal, undemocratic, and nationalist forces in the West. There is an implicit link between the rise of authoritarianism worldwide and the appeal of illiberal and undemocratic forces at home.

The protection agenda inherent in European strategic autonomy and a US foreign policy for the middle class starts at home. It means strengthening human rights and the rule of law; addressing inequalities; investing in research, innovation, and industrial capabilities; and ensuring the security of citizens. It means proving that liberal democracy delivers. On the flip side of the coin, it requires deterring and assertively constraining all those external attempts at interference and destabilization.

As the West develops a protection agenda based on rights, equality, and prosperity, diplomacy's tough task is that of preventing this from lapsing into protectionism and closure. It must rethink how to promote values in undemocratic countries as well. With military means being set aside as instruments to promote democratic values, diplomacy must develop new avenues to exert influence through economic and other means. In doing so it must blend principle and pragmatism, while making the case at home that the protection and promotion of values are two sides of the same coin.

Nathalie Tocci is Director of the Istituto Affari Internazionali in Rome and Honorary Professor at the University of Tübingen. She is Special Advisor to EU High Representative and Vice President of the Commission Josep Borrell Fontelles. As Special Advisor to HRVP Federica Mogherini, she wrote the European Global Strategy and worked on its implementation.

◂ Nathalie Tocci with Wolfgang Ischinger at the MSC European Defense Roundtable in Berlin in November 2017.

Sustaining Liberal Democracy

Ana Palacio

Winston Churchill famously said, "never waste a good crisis." By this measure, despite our fair share of solid opportunities, most notably the 2008 financial crisis and the ongoing pandemic, Western democracies seem to be spectacularly failing. The West is no longer sure of itself or its purpose. Horizons have been cut and a sense of foreboding, rather than hope, has descended over our visions of the future. Yet, maintaining the present course of navel-gazing will not do.

It behooves us to be clear-eyed about these new realities and to react accordingly by adapting the indispensable institutions and "gatekeepers" of democracy. To accomplish this would require more than traditional diplomacy or lofty rhetoric. It will demand bold action in reviving the very notion of responsible citizenship and genuine civic discourse, which forms the bedrock of our system. Doing so would benefit not just those of us in the West, but all who cherish and aspire to the values of dignity, liberty, and the pursuit of happiness.

Our values and very way of life are being challenged, like never before. As great power competition returns, the very pillars of our system emerge stale and fractured. The material efficiency of "state capitalism" is being peddled as an attractive alternative to the liberal democratic system. It is sobering news for those of us who have dedicated our life's work to enhancing democracy's reach and depth.

However, we can hardly afford the luxury of complacency or hand wringing. We cannot look the other way as authoritarians trample international norms or construct alternative institutions, appropriating the frame of traditional international institutions that are falsely portrayed as hostile to the legitimate aspiration of the non-Western world. Underpinning this philosophy is the notion that collective interests, defined by the powers in place, trump individual rights, liberties, or interests.

What are we to make of all of this? What is certainly at play is the very real change occurring to the world beneath our feet. We are witnessing a great unsettling: governments, progressively unable to meet the commitments of social contracts signed decades ago, struggle to connect with an increasingly fragmented and frustrated citizenry that has come to appreciate and measure democracy's effectiveness solely by the economic prosperity it delivers. The European Union is learning this the hard way. Part of it surely reflects our failure, in the words of Emmanuel Macron, to effectively protect the people "from the major shocks of the modern world." These have taken numerous forms, from the effects of unchecked globalization, the blows of the financial crisis, or the unrelenting waves of migration.

Most critically, however, the tools we have traditionally used to sustain the social fabric and democracy—religious institutions and faith groups, education and the media, civic engagement and political parties—are being challenged and undermined. Our social edifice bears the stresses of identity politics and the excesses of the cancel culture. The traditional left and right seem deflated, feeding into a populist rejection of the political establishment. Cultural wars keep tearing at the fabric of our societies, leaving abundant space for radicals such as Le Pen and Orbán to expropriate universal values and to pose as agents of meaningful change. Yet, populism and nationalism, where they prevailed, have failed to deliver, and often made things manifestly worse. Bolsonaro's Brazil offers a vivid testament to that end.

All of this makes it imperative to reinforce our institutions in a way that can nurture our fragile democracies and encourage true dialogue and civic discourse. But it is also crucial to reimagine the very notion of citizenship away from the one-way street of entitlement that has gradually developed. At the same time, it will take a robust effort to set expectations as we embark upon reforms, such as climate neutrality, that are likely to exact economic pain.

By now it has become clichéd to say that the present is a pivotal moment. Yet, it truly is. Circumstance will never allow us time for quiet reflection on the future. It is therefore essential, as we tackle the challenges of the day, to chart a feasible yet ambitious long-term course for our societies. And most of all, we need to chart a unified path ahead. Getting there will be neither straightforward nor painless. However, the alternative would be worse.

Ana Palacio was Foreign Minister of Spain from 2002 to 2004 and a Member of the European Parliament from 1994 to 2002. She also served as Senior Vice-President and General Counsel of the World Bank and is a Visiting Professor at the Edmund E. Walsh School of Foreign Service at Georgetown University.

◂ Ana Palacio with former United Nations Secretary-General Kofi Annan during a meeting of the UN Security Council in July 2003.

Munich Security Conference msc
Münchner Sicherheitskonferenz

Not Giving Up on Democracy and Equality in the Middle East

Tawakkol Karman

Some believe that the Middle East will remain an exception in terms of its adherence to democracy and its respect for human rights. The proponents of this perspective point to the stumbling democratic transition in the Arab Spring countries. The last country in which political measures were taken that contributed to the undermining of democracy was Tunisia. Tunisian President Kais Saied, following an emergency meeting with military and security leaders on July 25, 2012, relieved the prime minister of his post, suspended the functions and powers of Parliament, and assumed executive power, in clear violation of his country's constitution.

Egypt had witnessed a similar scenario. The Egyptian army carried out a coup d'état on July 3, 2013, against the first elected civilian president, President Mohamed Morsi, who was arrested and tried on trumped-up charges. In Yemen and Libya, armed militias were used to carry out bloody coups, which led to devastating civil wars. Syria remains a very cruel model, where one family controls the government's affairs and the country's economic resources. However, what is unfair in this particular case is that Syria's Assad family enjoys the support and backing of many influential governments in the region, such as Russia and China, in addition to the leniency of many governments that help to keep al-Assad as president of Syria—despite the horrific violations that he is committing.

This brief article seeks to discuss three hypotheses related to democracy in the Middle East: 1) there is an aversion by the prevailing cultures in the Middle East to democracy; 2) democracy contributes to instability, extremism, and terrorism as a result of the rise to power of so-called political Islamist groups; and 3) the obstacles to democracy are local obstacles, and Western governments seek to support rather than obstruct the democratic transition.

Democracy and Middle Eastern Cultures

Some views trace the lack of democracy in the Middle East to the prevailing cultures in the Middle East—cultures in which religion, customs, and traditions play a major role. More precisely, there are many theorists, both in the West and in the East, who embrace the idea that Islam, the most espoused religion in the Middle East and the most influential, includes a set of teachings and principles that are not conducive to the existence of true democracy.

This perception has turned the facts upside down. Instead of blaming authoritarian regimes—which often do not pay any attention to religion except to the extent that gives them the power to control society—religion is blamed, as if the teachings of religion are the goal that those regimes seek to achieve. And with more reflection, it can be said that religions, and Islam in particular, cannot be interpreted according to the desires of a particular group. The reading of a religious text remains a human reading that is subject to development and change, so it is not appropriate to assert that religion is contrary to democracy.

The reading of a religious text remains a human reading that is subject to development and change, so it is not appropriate to assert that religion is contrary to democracy.

As for Islam, there is no credible reason that makes it an opponent of democracy. On the contrary, many texts and practices call for establishing justice and opposing injustice and tyranny. The ordeals that Islamists have been exposed to recently in more than one Arab country have contributed to emphasizing the importance of democracy for a large segment of them. On the other hand, repressive regimes in the Middle East that are keen to portray themselves as secular or modern tend to establish special relations with Salafist groups that are characterized by religious extremism simply because they believe in the sanctity of the ruler, regardless of religious infractions or political mistakes.

In addition to religion, the perspective that considers culture in the Middle East to be a deterrent to democratic development sees cultural heritage, social structure, customs, and traditions as factors that lead to the consolidation of a dictatorship. In this regard, it has been widely argued that tyranny suits the East, and the Arabs in particular.

Women and Democracy: One Battle

In the context of this narrow-minded view that sees a contradiction between Middle Eastern cultures and democracy, the issue of women's inclusion in political

◂ Tawakkol Karman as a guest at MSC Events, among others at the MSC Core Group Meeting in Doha in 2019.

work and the recognition of their economic and social rights emerges as an element that casts doubt on the goals of democracy. The proponents of this view believe that adopting equitable policies for women is evidence that there are colonial tendencies to sabotage the cohesion of Arab and Islamic societies, and they imagine that democracy will eventually lead to endless waves of moral corruption and sexual decay.

These irrational perceptions have been accompanied in many Middle Eastern countries by well-established policies that marginalize women. These policies have led to the impoverishment of society and to the undermining of development plans, as women—who comprise a significant portion of the population—represent important leverage for development and real renaissance. This has directly contributed to weakening the role and status of civil society forces. On the contrary, it can be said that where women are present and active, civil society has shown itself capable of taking initiative and being proactive. In Yemen, where armed militias control power using force, brutality, and extrajudicial killings, the performance of political parties and civil society organizations has declined during the war that erupted at the end of March 2015, except for that of the Abductees' Mothers Association, which proved its firmness in challenging the militia authorities in the north and south.

Where women are present and active, civil society has shown itself capable of taking initiative and being proactive.

Despite the positive role played by this women's organization as the only human rights voice in the country, none of the UN envoys dared to meet with its founders, whether in the north or the south, although UN envoys were keen to meet with parties not directly involved in the war.

The United Nations and governments that are interested in establishing the principles of peace and freedom in the world must learn to benefit from the important presence of women in the diplomatic domain, whether in the context of supporting peace efforts in countries experiencing armed conflicts or in the context of contributing to a successful democratic transition. Many events have proven that women are a great force who can contribute to achieving diplomatic breakthroughs, especially in countries that suffer from turmoil and instability. Communication with women and with women's organizations is an issue of some importance, and often with fruitful results.

Attention must also be paid to the issue of women's exploitation by dictatorial regimes, many of which appoint women in the diplomatic corps and the government just to say that they are politically mature regimes with modern visions. In 2011 I met the under-secretary-general of the United Nations and the director of the United Nations Development Program, Helen Clark, during her visit to Sana'a a few days before the peaceful February revolution. She invited me to discuss the issue of women's political participation and ways to enable them to occupy senior posts in government. I expressed my viewpoint that there is no way for men to participate in politics, let alone women, under these tyrannical, failed, and corrupt political systems.

Many events have proven that women are a great force who can contribute to achieving diplomatic breakthroughs, especially in countries that suffer from turmoil and instability.

Democracy, the Growth of Terrorism, and the Role of Foreign Countries

It is increasingly noted that the repressive Arab regime-controlled media links the expansion of terrorism in the Middle East to the existence of democracy. Followers of these channels have always heard phrases such as "Human rights may go to hell; security is the most important thing." Arab officials, of course, often stress the danger that democracy represents to stability. This misconception has not been limited to the regimes of the Middle East. Rather, it is the same perception adopted by a major country—the United States of America, which has great influence in the Middle East. US Secretary of State Condoleezza Rice admitted in her 2005 speech in Cairo that her country shared the same view about democracy and stability by saying: "For sixty years, my country, the United States, pursued stability at the expense of democracy in this region here in the Middle East—and we achieved neither."[1]

In tandem with Ahtisaari, Chernomyrdin saved many Serbians' lives by forcing Milošević to give up on the war that he had started more than a decade ago.

Contrary to these allegations, there is increasing evidence of interworking between the Arab regimes in the Middle East and extremist and fanatic groups, where each side has an interest in the existence of the other. This exploitation and interworking are clear, for example, in Yemen, Syria, and Egypt. There is a perception that the persistence of terrorism gives Arab regimes a license to renew their legitimacy without success in developing or improving the economy.

There is a common saying in the Arab world that Western governments have no interest in having democracy in the Middle East—whether for colonial or economic reasons—and therefore those governments prefer to deal with authoritarian regimes over others. Regardless of the validity of this opinion, there are many reservations about the Western position toward the revolutions of the Arab Spring and support for the counterrevolution. It seems that the goal of many Western governments is to have governments in the region that include an acceptable degree of authoritarianism.

Western governments have violated their long-promoted principles by disregarding the coups that occurred in many Arab countries after 2011, which may indicate a Western abandonment of support for democracy and human rights in the Arab region. Western governments that prioritize human rights and democracy issues or emphasize them in their foreign policy agenda should reduce cooperation with those repressive regimes and exert serious pressure to bring about change. It is important to stress that these pressures do not include military action, which has proven to be a failure by producing extremely bad conditions and political, economic, and social disasters, as has been the case in Iraq and Syria.

Western diplomacy failed the Arab Spring test and seemed complicit with the dictatorial regimes in the region.

In total, between 1974 and 2005, more than forty countries transitioned to democracy, and, as a result, the number of democracies jumped from forty to eighty-nine countries. The Arab world did not contribute to this increase. However, with the outbreak of the Arab Spring revolutions in 2011, there were signs that democracy might take hold—until externally supported coups disrupted the process of democracy. It is necessary that we learn from this, try to correct our mistakes, and make the building of democracy an essential rule that governs relationships between democratic countries and countries that pursue authoritarian rule.

Western diplomacy failed the Arab Spring test and seemed complicit with the dictatorial regimes in the region. This must be corrected, and, driven by a courage born of strong conviction, diplomacy must become the most important key to consolidating democracy and peace in the Middle East, a place that has been in flames for centuries.

Tawakkol Karman is the leader and cofounder of the human rights group Women Journalists Without Chains. She is the corecipient of the 2011 Nobel Peace Prize.

Independence to Statehood
EARLY

EXIT
Stairs to
Tours
Library Shop
Exit
Elevators
2

Building a Global Alliance of Democracies

Anders Fogh Rasmussen

What is the first responsibility of our diplomats? To promote their country's interests, or their country's values? In a world of global interdependency in which autocrats are willing to weaponize economic ties, that dilemma will only grow.

Weaponizing our freedoms and turning our greatest strengths against us is a common trait for autocracies. Free speech, for example, underpins our democratic way of life. Yet autocracies have weaponized our free speech to spread disinformation and polarizing narratives that undermine the legitimacy of our democracies. Too often, this creation of parallel realities that plagues our democratic discourse has been aided and abetted by domestic politicians seeking electoral advantage.

Weaponizing our freedoms and turning our greatest strengths against us is a common trait for autocracies.

Likewise, globally interconnected supply chains should be a strength for the global economy. Yet, they are now being used and abused by autocracies, especially China, to silence criticism and force the free world to bend to Beijing's will.

The building blocks for Chinese economic coercion were laid a decade ago. China used the Eurozone crisis to go on a shopping spree of distressed assets around the Mediterranean. But with this investment also came strings attached. For example, in June 2017, Greece blocked an EU statement at the UN that criticized China's human rights record only months after the acquisition of the Port of Piraeus by China's COSCO.

More recently we have seen that pressure increase. Sometimes industries are caught in the crossfire between governments. For example, Australian wine producers have been subjected to Chinese tariffs (China was their biggest market) after the Australian government criticized Beijing's human rights record and called for an inquiry into the origins of COVID-19.

Other times individual businesses themselves are directly targeted with boycotts, for example when they make statements that they will not use materials that could be linked to forced labor in Xinjiang. The list of companies goes beyond clothing; China insisted the Taiwanese flag on Tom Cruise's jacket in the new Top Gun movie be removed. In 2018 the Marriott hotel chain had its website shut down by authorities for a week after a customer form listed Taiwan, Tibet, and Hong Kong as separate countries.

The problem is that, often, this tactic works for China. After all, its market is just too big to ignore. Other autocracies, notably Russia, are also building similar economic client states such as in Africa, investing heavily in its minerals sector, expanding arms exports, and using mercenary forces to prop up beleaguered governments.

This presents diplomats with a challenge. In the past their role was to seek foreign direct investment from all comers. Likewise, businesses were actively encouraged to build global supply chains, even if that meant working with undemocratic regimes. However, we must be more self-aware and strategic in our thinking. Global business and geopolitics can no longer be placed in separate baskets.

COVID-19 has triggered much soul searching in the Western world about our level of strategic dependence on non-democratic states. The challenge of technology transfer has been exacerbated by the global semiconductor shortage and China's efforts to purchase its own industry from the West.

From the EU's project of "strategic autonomy" to the G7's work on building economic resilience, the free world is trying to find a formula to become more self-dependent, but without becoming protectionist. Therefore, the democratic community needs to develop tools to collectively push back against economic coercion. Just as NATO has Article 5 to provoke a collective response whenever an ally is attacked, the free world now needs an economic Article 5 to counter economic coercion.

Global business and geopolitics can no longer be placed in separate baskets.

The premise should be simple. A country could ask its allies to impose retaliatory measures against the offending state. Or it could include a global credit facility that could be called upon to cushion the losses and redirect supply chains. If economic coercion stops being a successful weapon, autocrats will stop using it.

◂ Anders Fogh Rasmussen at the Munich Security Conference in February 2018.

Such initiatives should become some of the early building blocks of a new alliance of democracies, an initiative I promote through my Alliance of Democracies Foundation. Last year we adopted the Copenhagen Charter with ideas to push back on authoritarianism, make technology work for democracy, and stand up for those on the frontlines between democracy and autocracy.

Ultimately, this closer coordination between the democracies is the best answer we have to the values-vs.-interests dilemma. Diplomats from democratic countries should be empowered to address their host capitals from a position of relative strength, not fearing damaged interests for speaking out.

> The free world needs to decide what is more important: petty interests or setting the global rules for the twenty-first century in our own image.

Such an alliance would not come at the expense of multilateralism. On the contrary. It would strengthen our ailing multilateral structures on the basis of the democratic principles of openness, reciprocity, and a rules-based international order.

The world's rulebook is being rewritten. The free world needs to decide what is more important: petty interests or setting the global rules for the twenty-first century in our own image. Only through the latter can we continue to pursue our mutual interests without sacrificing the core values that have made the world relatively richer, freer, and more peaceful.

Anders Fogh Rasmussen served as Secretary General of NATO, Prime Minister of Denmark, Danish Minister of Economic Affairs, and a leading Danish parliamentarian. He is the founder of the Alliance of Democracies Foundation and CEO of Rasmussen Global.

MSC Townhall at the Munich Security Conference in February 2019. ▸

msc TOWNHALL

Körber Stiftung
msc

Rethinking the Transatlantic Community

Anne-Marie Slaughter

It is 2038. The Munich Security Conference is celebrating its seventy-fifth anniversary. The host meeting is still at the Hotel Bayerischer Hof in Munich, but participants are joining from around the world, including from various regional hubs in West Africa, the Middle East, and North and South America.

The annual photo of the participants is strikingly different from the picture of the first small meeting of Western defense professionals in 1963.[1] To modern eyes, all those white men in dark suits, as illustrious and dedicated as they were, look almost indistinguishable from one another. Part of the history of the MSC has been steady diversification, both in people and in the issues addressed. As the MSC website explained back in 2022, the audience had steadily expanded geographically, to include government officials and experts from China, Brazil, India, the Middle East, and parts of Africa, but the focus remained transatlantic. At the same time, the group expanded to include many people other than military leaders, including "CEOs, human rights activists, environmentalists, and other leaders representing global civil society." The inclusion of this broader cross-section of participants "mirror[ed] the broader understanding of security itself."[2] Today, one of the striking changes is that between one third and one half of the military and business leaders are women, as is the Chairperson of the MSC itself.

The biggest change, however, is that the enduring "transatlantic core" of the MSC now extends to the South as well as the North Atlantic. So too does NATO, which was renamed the "New Atlantic Treaty Organization" in 2030. The idea of expanding and adapting the old NATO was the theme of the MSC in 2025, based on a speech given by the German Defense Minister at the sixtieth anniversary celebration in 2023. The changing nature of global security needs in light of climate change, massive migration, continuing threats to global health through pandemics, and the digitization of everything from work to war, meant that it was imperative to engage the Atlantic hemisphere from North to South as well as East to West.

Both Europe and the United States and Canada were also looking at their demography, recognizing, in the case of the United States, that Americans with historic and cultural roots in the Caribbean, Central, and South America, would be the largest plurality group after white Americans by the 2040s. An entire new generation of African-Americans descended from Africans who had immigrated in the twentieth century rather than from enslaved ancestors had also developed strong commercial and cultural ties with various West African countries. The Canadian shift was much more to the Pacific, given that over half of Canadian immigrants in a rapidly growing population hailed from Asia,[3] but Canadian defense thinkers also saw the advantage in an expanded transatlantic community to match an expanded transpacific group.

The shifts in European populations have been less dramatic, but a growing number of French, Spanish, Belgian, German, and Italian citizens with Middle Eastern and North African roots have made themselves felt. Europe as a whole has also realized the great economic value of strengthening ties between their newer immigrants and the markets in their "old countries."[4] Over the course of many MSC working group meetings, European Union leaders also began to explore the concept of having a "multiple geometry" NATO, modeled on the different circles of membership in various economic and social communities within the EU.

As they look forward twenty-five more years, to the one hundredth anniversary in 2063, the leaders and planners of the MSC can already see the ways in which that gathering will have evolved from a Cold War "family meeting" to a hub of planetary politics.

As they look forward twenty-five more years, to the one hundredth anniversary in 2063, the leaders and planners of the MSC can already see the ways in which that gathering will have evolved from a Cold War "family meeting" to a hub of planetary politics. But they also know how to adapt, following the wisdom of those leaders who know that their continued value and relevance depends upon it.

Anne-Marie Slaughter is the CEO of New America and the Bert G. Kerstetter '66 University Professor Emerita of Politics and International Affairs at Princeton University. From 2009 to 2011, she served as the Director of Policy Planning for the United States Department of State.

◂ Anne-Marie Slaughter at the Munich Young Leaders Alumni Meeting in New York City in September 2019.

Giesecke+Devrient

Recalibrating Western Ambition

Thomas Kleine-Brockhoff

As the Western world wallows in despondency, the Afghanistan debacle being only the latest cause, defeatism and retreatism appear to be the only alternative to turning to cold-blooded realpolitik. There is a self-flagellating mood all around, finding culprits here and there and everywhere; and if no one to be accused can be found nearby, there is always the United States to blame. In periods like this, it is paramount not to fall prey to the seductive power of cultural pessimism. Decades ago, historian Fritz Stern warned not to get ensnared in fatalistic jeremiads about the downfall of one's own country, one's own continent, or the whole idea of the West.[1] For cultural pessimism can easily revert into cultural despair—a destructive political force.

Yes, it is true, the West needs to reconsider, rethink, and regroup. A look into the rearview mirror is necessary to figure out what went wrong; not to assign blame, but as a precondition to a revised approach. The goal should be to recalibrate Western ambition and thus help diplomacy to adjust to the new multi-order world.

Only in retrospect has it become clear that, post-1990, Western countries had settled into an exaggerated optimism about the future. It was commonly expected that the triumph in the Cold War would translate into the triumph of the Western model of organizing society. Such optimism quickly morphed into determinism. Hope was replaced by certainty. Democratic peace would inevitably ensue. Others would enthusiastically follow. Therefore, the means needed for such a global transformation would be limited. An often-missionary brand of Western liberalism emerged. In its center-left variant, it aimed to mutualize ever-more policy areas under the umbrella of global governance, thus placing the latest version of Western principles beyond the reach of skeptical (smaller) nation states. In its center-right variety, it wanted to introduce democracy at gunpoint if all else failed. It was the age of expansive democracy promotion and military interventionism. With the painful exposure of Western overreach and the glaring gap between ends and means, some see the end of the West nearing. But recalibrating an ambition is not simply retreating. Rightsizing is not capitulating. The end of liberal interventionism is not isolationism.

Recalibrating an ambition is not simply retreating. Rightsizing is not capitulating. The end of liberal interventionism is not isolationism.

The alternative is for friends of the free world to revive democratic liberalism in a way that is more in tune with the times: most certainly willing to defend itself, but more skeptical, more aware of liberalism's limitations. This brand of moderate yet robust liberalism continues to stand up for universal principles, human rights in particular, but drops the missionary zeal. It is cautious and defensive, not strident and offensive; it leads by example, not by intervention. This version of liberalism does not seek a perfect world, a summum bonum. It is content to prevent a summum malum, a great evil (like genocide).

This is not an easy task during an age of democratic recession and authoritarian revival. It requires diplomacy to develop a posture that does not allow for restraint to be misunderstood as disregard of principle. And it asks Western democracies to follow their own rules. Otherwise, leading by example is a hopeless task. It also demands that democracies confront those who are trying to undermine and infect them by importing authoritarian habits like corruption, money laundering, and transnational persecution of dissidents. Such a defense of liberal principals at home requires democracies to band together to defend against the forces of autocracy promotion.

Some may call this systemic competition. Whatever the term, there is a lot to be learned from the intellectuals of the Cold War era (like Raymond Aron, Hannah Arendt, Isaiah Berlin, and Dolf Sternberger) whose posture of principled moderation offers an intellectual blueprint to decide when to confront, when to cooperate, and when to stand down. Their position of stern temperance allowed to uphold Western values and confront dangerous regimes while still coexisting with them. During a time of unparalleled interdependence, a modicum of cooperation will doubtlessly be called for to jointly address climate change, cyber war, and biodiversity challenges.

To look at a glass half full: rethinking and renewal of Western liberalism and the necessary recalibration of ends and means have begun.

Thomas Kleine-Brockhoff is a former advisor to German Federal President Joachim Gauck. He serves as a Vice President of the German Marshall Fund of the US.

◂ Thomas Kleine-Brockhoff at the MSC Conversations in the framework of the Munich Security Conference in February 2020.

ort 2020
Westlessness
Munich Security Conference msc Münchner Sicherheitskonferenz
Bayerische Vertretung in Berlin

Overcoming Westlessness

Tobias Bunde

Everyone who has had the chance to attend the Munich Security Conference knows that the main conference hall of the Bayerischer Hof is a rather small venue for a high-level international conference. What looks like a big conference hall on television is in fact a venue not bigger than a basketball court—just packed with heads of state and government, ministers, generals, journalists, CEOs, activists, think tankers, and academics. When the big shots speak, participants often sit on the stairs leading from the ground floor to the gallery. This intimate atmosphere is part of the special aura of the conference.[1]

Yet, in February 2019, the small venue was large enough to fit two completely different worlds. Within half an hour, Vice President Mike Pence and Chancellor Angela Merkel had given speeches that highlighted just how different the worldviews of two key players in the Western world had become. It was hard to see any common ground beneath a litany of quite fundamental disagreements.

For sure, the Munich Security Conference had seen quite emotional transatlantic family spats before. Transatlantic leaders regularly disagreed about specific policies—and some of the debates in Munich were heated and emotional, as family meetings sometimes are. But the speeches and debates at the Munich Security Conference in 2019 were different. This was a deeper crisis, as the leaders not only disagreed about policies. It felt as if they were not sure anymore if they were still part of a family, of the same community based on shared values. The world around us was in turmoil. Yet, key representatives of the West seemed unable to understand each other, let alone chart a common agenda.

"Westlessness" meant to capture the sense of anxiety and restlessness in Western societies against the backdrop of a world that was rapidly becoming less Western and a West that was becoming less Western, too.

I remember that, sitting on the upper gallery in the main hall and taking a bird's-eye perspective, I really worried about what all of this meant for the future of the transatlantic family and the West in general. Apparently, I was not the only one who sensed that the conference demonstrated—very much in a nutshell—that we were witnessing a more profound crisis in the West. Writing in *The New York Times*, Roger Cohen even described the 2019 conference as a "requiem for the West."[2]

In the months after the conference, the sense of a deeper crisis hardened. After Donald Trump tried to withdraw from the joint G7 summit communiqué on his flight home the year before, the French hosts of the 2019 summit recognized early on that a joint substantial communiqué would not be possible. The one-page final statement of the Biarritz summit contained just over 250 empty words, highlighting that there was not much the key Western powers could still agree on.[3] When the US pulled out of Syria at the end of the year, apparently without coordinating with its NATO allies who also had forces on the ground, French President Emmanuel Macron spoke of "the brain death of NATO."[4] In short, it was hard to identify "the West" as a meaningful entity anymore, causing an obvious nervousness in the public debate.

While preparing for the conference in 2020, we decided to tackle this widespread sense of uneasiness head-on. After all, Munich is the venue for open and frank discussions, not for transatlantic window dressing. The Munich Security Report 2020, our scene-setter traditionally published just a few days before the conference, coined the term "Westlessness." It meant to capture the "sense of anxiety and restlessness" in Western societies against the backdrop of a world that was rapidly becoming less Western and a West that was becoming less Western, too.[5]

Westlessness was meant as a provocation, and it worked. The term was immediately picked up by politicians, analysts, and the media, as it seemed to hit a nerve and to adequately capture the zeitgeist, putting a name to a diffuse but widely shared sentiment. As German president Frank-Walter Steinmeier noted when opening the conference, "the 'we' of 'the West' that was once a given is clearly no longer something that can be taken entirely for granted. This is true both within our societies, but also in relation to the existential issues of foreign and security policy on which this conference focuses."[6]

For some, however, speaking of Westlessness, even turning it into the unofficial motto of the conference, was defeatism, perhaps even heresy, coming from the MSC

◂ Tobias Bunde at the Presentation of the Munich Security Report "Westlessness" in Berlin in February 2020.

as the traditional transatlantic family meeting. At a time when the West was under pressure, the critics held, it was wrong and irresponsible to talk it down or highlight the fissures. Mike Pompeo, the US secretary of state, was said to be furious about this choice of motto and decided to adapt his speech accordingly. "The West," he proclaimed in Munich, "is winning. We are collectively winning." The reaction in the room, though, was stone-cold silence. For the audience in the Bayerischer Hof, Pompeo's insistence that everything was fine if America's allies just "accepted reality," seemed out of touch—as the headline of David E. Sanger and Steven Erlanger's report from Munich brilliantly put it: "'The West Is Winning,' Pompeo Said. The West Wasn't Buying It."[7]

Others, in contrast, felt that Westlessness exemplified a backward-looking perspective, in which the old, traditional West saw itself as the navel of the world. From this point of view, we should stop talking about the West because it was unnecessarily counterproductive and antagonistic. In today's world, in which the transatlantic partners had to reach out to new partners beyond the traditional West, focusing on a term that comes with historical baggage was seen as unhelpful. As Kang Kyung-wha, the South Korean minister of foreign affairs at the time, put it at the conference, "the values that have underpinned multilateralism are no longer the preserve of the West. . . . Perhaps the better framing when we discuss the future of multilateralism is not necessarily to tie it down to the West, not necessarily tie it down to any geographical distinctions for that matter, [but] throw the discussion open wide to the larger globe."[8]

How do we define the West today and in the future? Can we return to an era of "Westfulness," as some put it? And even if we could, should we?

In a sense, these two strands of criticism the report provoked only drive home the very point of Westlessness and the questions it tried to raise. For we need to have an honest and open debate about the future of the West. How do we define the West today and in the future? Can we return to an era of "Westfulness," as some put it? And even if we could, should we?[9] What is the best way to organize, legitimize, and communicate cooperation among liberal democracies today?

Beyond Westlessness?

Since the MSC in 2020, one of the key questions informing our work has thus been how to move beyond Westlessness and think about how those who believe in the strength of liberal-democratic values and international cooperation—wherever they are located—can work together to protect these principles in a world in which powerful forces at home and abroad are attacking them. It is perhaps one of the key challenges for the traditional audience of the MSC in particular—and for Western diplomacy in general.[10]

From this perspective, it was good to see that the term Westlessness did not immediately disappear after the conference ended but "sparked a discussion across the North Atlantic policy elites and the pages of international broadsheets."[11] After all, encouraging open debate about key security challenges is one of the main goals of the MSC. Yet, the fact that many observers feel that our diagnosis has been vindicated is no cause for joy. Rather, it underlines the dimension of the challenge liberal democrats in the world must tackle.

Indeed, the past two years have not alleviated our concerns. As some observers have pointed out, the symptom we described has become even more severe: "Everything since that report has borne out the danger, because the rate at which the world is becoming Westless—and, therefore, restless—keeps accelerating."[12] Against this background, it is difficult to claim that the West is winning.

Certainly, critics might ask what exactly "less Western" is supposed to mean. After all, despite its widespread use as a shorthand for a community of mostly North American and European liberal democracies as well as a normative project, the "West" is a concept that is not always easy to pin down. The West has never been a monolithic concept but rather an amalgam of different traditions, the mix of which changed over time.[13] After all, the proponents of the "illiberal counterrevolution" also claim to speak on behalf of the West, which they define based on ethnic, cultural, or religious criteria.[14]

Yet, for the past decades, the answer to the question what it was that kept the West together was straightforward: a commitment to liberal democracy and human rights, to a market-based economy, and to international cooperation in international institutions. After the fall of the Berlin Wall and the dissolution of the Soviet Union, these principles seemed to conquer the globe. In this sense, the post-Cold War era was not just defined by the "unipolar moment." It was also, and perhaps most importantly, a Western or liberal moment. This moment, defined by the dominance of liberal-democratic ideas, has clearly come to an end—not just on the global level, but also within the West itself. Today, the defenders of an open and liberal West appear on the defensive.

To begin with, Westlessness in our own societies remains a major—perhaps the most important—concern. After all, you cannot fight Westlessness in the world while ignoring Westlessness at home. If anything, attacks on some of the core norms of the liberal-democratic West have become more severe. While US voters did not grant Donald Trump a second term, the storming of the US Capitol on January 6, 2021, Trump's claim he had been cheated out of reelection, and the subsequent failure of almost the complete Republican establishment to condemn these attempts to overturn the election only demonstrate the degree to which the most basic liberal-democratic norms are now contested in the United States. As Robert Kagan warns, the United States is facing "its greatest political and constitutional crisis since the Civil War."[15] According to data from our Munich Security Index, only four in ten Americans think that democracy is safe in their country.[16] There is good reason for President Biden to keep stressing the importance of working for democratic renewal and showing that "democracies can still deliver for our people in this changed world."[17]

In Europe, several governments have tried to control public broadcast, stifle civil society organizations, and undermine the independence of the judiciary. In many countries, the electorate does not have much of a choice anymore as voters who believe in core principles such as the rule of law or the freedom of the press must rally behind one candidate to fend off a radical who runs on a platform questioning them. For years the European Union has been unable to address the developments in Hungary, as the first EU member state ranked "partly free" by Freedom House.[18] Most recently, the ruling of the Polish Constitutional Court that questioned the primacy of European law, a core principle of the European Union, has put the future of the EU as a legal community in doubt. What is more, many of the countries that see themselves as the cradle of the Enlightenment are witnessing the rise of modern anti-scientism and a plethora of conspiracy narratives, only exacerbated by the rise of the pandemic. For many critics, the "incompetent responses of Western governments" during the pandemic are further proof of their relative decline.[19]

Westlessness abroad, though, is no less concerning. For years, analysts have described the detrimental effects of Western absence from key conflicts and the increasing involvement of other players. As a result, concerns about "human security" or the "responsibility to protect" have too often been gleefully neglected. According to Anne Applebaum, the "crisis of Western values" at home has "a bloodier, more violent face" abroad.[20] China and Russia have not only repeatedly prevented the UN Security Council from speaking out against the atrocities committed by the Assad regime in Syria but also limited humanitarian access, thus directly contributing to the human plight just to support the regime and make the point that the conflict was an internal matter. Russian forces have even participated in bombing raids on hospitals and schools in Syria.[21] Against the background of Western "intervention fatigue," they have become the key enablers of what David Miliband calls an "age of impunity."[22]

China, Russia, and other opponents of a human-rights-based interpretation of international law now openly try to walk back some of the liberal progress made in recent decades, trying to bring back what Wolfgang Ischinger referred to as international law for the protection of dictators and what some scholars see as the potential emergence of an "authoritarian international law."[23] Indeed, we are witnessing increasingly open attempts to reinterpret the core principles of the international order—to the detriment of human rights and liberal-democratic principles.

Westlessness in our own societies remains a major—perhaps the most important—concern. After all, you cannot fight Westlessness in the world while ignoring Westlessness at home.

One could have expected that these increasing threats to what the Western world believes to be universal values would have galvanized a concerted response from the defenders of the liberal international order. Yet, recent years have seen the continued deterioration of the West as a meaningful collective actor in the world. On too many issues, key Western countries have been at loggerheads, displaying the narcissism of minor differences despite much bigger common challenges that need to be addressed.

When the financial and economic crisis hit more than a decade ago, transatlantic leaders were quick to closely coordinate their fiscal and political measures. But when the pandemic began to spread across the globe last year, such coordination was almost completely absent. As Ian Bremmer put it at an MSC Digital Conversation in April 2020, "you could not have a better example of 'Westlessness' than the response we are not seeing globally, from the US and Europe, to the largest crisis we have had since World War II."[24] The Brexit saga has become a seemingly endless story of unnecessary self-harm that continues to plague both the UK and the EU, preventing future cooperation on crucial security challenges. With the Americans, but mostly among themselves, the Europeans are discussing what the real meaning of "strategic autonomy" or "European sovereignty" could be—as if the world was waiting for their deliberations.

For all those who believed that Westlessness just described the various crises triggered by Donald Trump, it should be clear by now that Trump was surely a catalyst for the trends described here, but certainly not the only cause, nor one whose removal would singlehandedly reinvigorate the West. For sure, the election of Joe Biden as US president was met with relief in the democratic world. After years of transatlantic tension, President Biden's virtual speech at the MSC Special Edition on February 21, 2021, and the joint appearance with Angela Merkel and Emmanuel Macron was described as a "beautiful love fest of the old West."[25] Yet, listening carefully to the speeches, one could not help realizing that the transatlantic partners are still far from agreeing on a joint strategy to tackle the challenges of today and tomorrow. While there is now a shared understanding that the world's liberal democracies are facing an "inflection point," as Biden put it, defined by the struggle between the supporters of liberal democracy and their autocratic competitors,[26] a truly common agenda or even a joint strategy seem elusive.

> Recent years have seen the continued deterioration of the West as a meaningful collective actor in the world. On too many issues, key Western countries have been at loggerheads, displaying the narcissism of minor differences despite much bigger common challenges that need to be addressed.

Perhaps the Europeans have taken Biden's message from the MSC Special Edition— "America is back!"—too literally. Yet, as has become all too obvious in recent months, a return to the transatlantic status quo ante is not in the cards. The Europeans, absorbed with their own challenges at home, have largely failed to bring something to the table that would have signaled a new transatlantic beginning and allowed them to look, as Biden suggested, forward together. Now, the Biden administration is moving forward, clearly focusing on the strategic competition with China. "But where is Europe?" seems to be the appropriate follow-up question that is still without an answer.

Even before the Biden administration came into office, the EU decided to conclude the Comprehensive Agreement on Investment with China, an unfortunate signal causing irritation in Washington, where the incoming administration had hoped for a new common transatlantic approach toward China.[27] At the same time, the Biden administration does not seem keen on waiting for their European partners to make up their mind about the China challenge, as it pushes forward with new multilateral frameworks in the Indo-Pacific such as the "Quad" and the new trilateral security partnership with Australia and the United Kingdom, called AUKUS. As the latter also included the termination of a huge submarine deal between Australia and France, new transatlantic tensions broke out, casting into doubt transatlantic cooperation on the region in general. Finally, the disastrous end of the twenty-year Afghanistan mission was perceived by many in Europe as a "degradation of the Western alliance and everything it is supposed to stand for in the world."[28] For many European leaders, the developments seem to call for a reassessment of Europe's dependence on the United States. As the President of the European Council, Charles Michel, put it, "This Afghan crisis imposes on us a full-scale exercise in strategic autonomy."[29]

And while the liberal democracies in the West appear weak, exhausted, uncoordinated, or even at odds with each other, their autocratic challengers seem convinced that they are on a winning streak. In Moscow and Beijing, the ruling elites have concluded that "the West is declining, and the East is rising."[30]

Reinvigorating the West by Renewing Cooperation among Democracies?

Arguably, the world's liberal democracies are only at the beginning of an overdue debate on the key strategic question of our time. How can we preserve an international order based on liberal principles and defend our way of life in a world in which the West is less powerful?

It is against this background that the idea of enhanced cooperation among like-minded liberal democracies on a global scale is gaining ground. It is a precondition for a "renaissance of democracies," one of the five scenarios—and by far the most positive one from a Western point of view—envisaged by the most recent Global Trends Report prepared by the US National Intelligence Council.[31] While the transatlantic democracies have lost economic power in relative terms, together with democratic states in other parts of the world, they still are by far the most powerful group of countries. It makes no sense anymore for cooperation among democratic countries to be confined to specific regions if they all grapple with the same challenges. Given the growing recognition that there is a new systemic competition, various political leaders have made proposals to reinvigorate global, values-based cooperation.

During the US presidential campaign, Joe Biden announced that his administration would "organize and host a global Summit for Democracy to renew the spirit and shared purpose of the nations of the free world."[32] At the MSC Special Edition, both President Biden and UK Prime Minister Boris Johnson called for values-based cooperation among the "free world," and NATO Secretary General Jens Stoltenberg stressed that the Alliance should strengthen partnerships with like-minded partners and build new ones around the world.[33] Several former European leaders, including Carl Bildt, Toomas Ilves, and Anders Fogh Rasmussen, have made proposals for a democratic alliance dealing with technology and cyber threats.[34] Johnson also called for using the D10, an informal grouping of the ten leading democracies, to coordinate telecommunications policies and develop a joint response to the ongoing debate about 5G and the security of networks.[35] Even in Germany, long among the most cautious Western countries and reluctant to push back against autocratic assertiveness, the debate has changed. In a first brief paper summarizing some key positions of the potential new coalition partners, the parties underline the importance of "multilateral cooperation in the world, especially in close connection with those states that share our democratic values. This also involves systemic competition with authoritarian states and dictatorships." In particular, they stress that they "support and strengthen initiatives such as the Alliance of Democracies."

How can we preserve an international order based on liberal principles and defend our way of life in a world in which the West is less powerful?

For some, a new organization bringing together liberal democracies would be "just the type of body the world needs: a group of capable, committed, and cohesive democracies that could muster political will and real resources."[37] Yet, all these proposals for exclusive cooperation among liberal-democratic countries lack important details. Skeptics have warned of the practical hurdles that a "Summit for Democracy" would have to clear, as it would be hard to draw the line for the guest list.[38] Others wonder whether the US should play the role of host, considering that its role as a symbol for democratic freedoms has been severely damaged.[39] And it is far from clear how the various initiatives relate to each other. For instance, is the Summit for Democracy a complement to the Franco-German initiative of an "Alliance for Multilateralism"? Would it be better to cooperate informally in issue-specific coalitions of the willing, or is a more institutionalized platform or even a new formal international organization needed?

At the very least, however, these proposals demonstrate increasing support for the idea that the world's democracies need to better coordinate to prevail in a new ideological struggle. In this context, it is important to avoid a major misunderstanding. Unlike the neoconservatives of the past, today's proponents of increased cooperation among the world's liberal democracies are no zealots. They neither pursue an offensive mission to spread democracy nor do they have any illusions about remaking the world in their image. Rather, today's mission is defensive—and rightly so. In this sense, G. John Ikenberry offers a different reading of Woodrow Wilson's famous call to make the world safe for democracy. To him "making the world safe for democracy" today should "be read literally, as a plea for safety. Rather than an idealist appeal, it is a call to reform the postwar international order so as to allow Western liberal democracy to survive."[40]

In a similar vein, Hal Brands and Charles Edel have made the case for a "grand strategy of democratic solidarity." According to them, such a grand strategy should "comprise efforts to shield the world's democracies from authoritarian pressure, while enabling them to exert selective counterpressures of their own."[41] Perhaps most importantly, solidarity among democracies will help to resist divide-and-conquer strategies that punish or reward individual countries for their behavior.

Still, some key leaders continue to warn that talking up a dichotomy between democracies and autocracies may become a self-fulfilling prophecy, cementing the kind of global bifurcation it anticipates. For example, numerous European politicians have warned of pushing Russia into China's camp. French President Emmanuel Macron has argued that "pushing Russia away from Europe is a major strategic error, because we are pushing it either toward isolation, which heightens tensions, or toward alliances with other great powers such as China, which would not at all be in our interest."[42] In a similar vein, Macron has also warned of building a united front against China, which he described as "a scenario of the highest possible conflictuality."[43] Angela Merkel has also publicly expressed her agreement with Chinese President Xi, who warned of the building of new blocs.[44] For them, too strong a focus on cooperation among the world's liberal democracies will cement competition with other states and damage global cooperation in general.

Some scholars share these concerns and warn of taking "a manifestly ideological approach to the global agenda."[45] The question is, though, whether this is still a choice and whether trying to ignore the systemic competition that already takes place will produce more positive results. Others argue that a certain degree of "othering" illiberal and authoritarian countries—stressing the differences between different types of regimes to strengthen democratic solidarity—may even be necessary to defend key achievements of the liberal international order.[46] From this point of view, the transatlantic partners should jointly reach out to like-minded democracies in other parts of the world. Moreover, stressing the commonalities between liberal democracies as part of a defensive agenda does not exclude cooperation with non-democracies on issues of common concern. After all, "democracies alone cannot address the world's most pressing transnational issues. But by stressing democratic unity from the outset, they can secure action on more favorable terms."[47]

Perhaps it is time to move beyond the notion of the West if we want to overcome a world of Westlessness.

The question for the world's liberal democracies today is thus how to strike a balance between strengthening cooperation among like-minded countries to push back against competitors and preserve core elements of the liberal international order on the one hand, and and avoiding to turn the competition with autocratic states into outright confrontation on the other hand—in which case there would not be much space for necessary cooperation.

Overcoming Westlessness, Moving beyond "the West"?

Perhaps it is time to move beyond the notion of the West if we want to overcome a world of Westlessness. Even if most supporters of the idea of the West today argue that it is a political concept based on liberal-democratic values rather than a position on the map, the term still conveys geographical, civilizational, or even colonial baggage.

Some therefore prefer not to talk about the West anymore. Instead, they suggest we talk about building a coalition of those willing to strengthen the rules-based international order. Notwithstanding the fact that any order will be based on rules (the important question being, which kind of rules), this proposal is not exactly a campaign slogan. Just like the Alliance for Multilateralism, shepherded by France and Germany, it sounds technical and abstract. "Take back control" or "America first" are powerful slogans. "Defend the rules-based international order" or "make multilateralism great again" are not. Can we agree on the "Alliance of Democracies"—or is this framing already too militaristic and antagonizing, as some fear?

These questions are no minor issues. An essential part of politics—and of diplomacy—is, after all, identity building and storytelling. Successful leaders often are excellent storytellers, making sense of the world around them and offering their constituencies an inspiring perspective. How the relevant "we" is described and defined often makes a major difference. Are we talking about the nation-state, Europe, the transatlantic partnership, the West, or a global alliance of democracies? Who is the "we" that is supposed to act together? What makes us hang together—our geographical position, our history, or our shared values and convictions? How much distancing from those who do not share our values do we need, how much "othering" do we have to accept to bring about the necessary cohesion among liberal democracies to defend key liberal-democratic norms? How can we avoid turning this endeavor into a new dangerous confrontation? And how we can we make sure that we can continue to work with others on issues of common concern?

These are just some of the questions that do not have easy answers. Only one thing is certain: the West, if it is to remain a meaningful political force, will need to adapt. It will have to look different than in previous decades and become more diverse, bringing in more perspectives from beyond the transatlantic world. It will need to function differently, with more equitable burden-sharing and co-leadership exerted by many. Perhaps it will also have to adopt a different name. If the essential mission underlying it—enabling value-based cooperation among liberal democracies—can be preserved, this, however, would be the least of the problems.

Tobias Bunde is Director of Research and Policy at the Munich Security Conference and the lead author of its annual Munich Security Report. He is also a member of the Board of Directors of the Munich Security Conference Foundation and a postdoctoral researcher at the Hertie School's Centre for International Security in Berlin.

Frank-Walter Steinmeier at the Munich Security Conference in February 2020. ▸

Munich Security Conference msc
Münchner Sicherheitskonferenz
Munich Security Conference msc

msc
msc
msc
msc
msc
msc
msc

msc
SC
Edition

#MSC20
Munich Security Conference
msc
Münchner Sicherheitskonferenz

Developing a Weltpolitikfähigkeits-verlustvermeidungsstrategie

Timothy Garton Ash

One of the minor peculiarities of German editorial practice is that instructions for the length of an article or chapter are often expressed as a number of characters rather than a number of words. Thus, for this volume, we were invited to make contributions of up to 4,550 characters. So the last word in my title, having 61 characters, is already more than 1% of that.

I launched this enormous German compound noun—Weltpolitikfähigkeitsverlustvermeidungsstrategie—in my introductory remarks at the Berlin kickoff event for the Munich Security Conference in February 2019.[1] It enjoyed some temporary fame, or notoriety, not least because Wolfgang Ischinger repeated it several times, including to the audience at the main Munich event shortly thereafter. It is, of course, a joke—but a joke with a serious point. Translated into English, it means something like "a strategy to avoid the loss of the capacity to shape world affairs," and I would argue quite seriously that this is precisely what Europe needs.

Deploying the power of language is an important part of the art of diplomacy, but also of the art of promoting a particular line of foreign policy to public opinion.

Deploying the power of language is an important part of the art of diplomacy, but also of the art of promoting a particular line of foreign policy to public opinion. Those two arts require different ways with words. In diplomacy it is often about finding an elegant formula to paper over irreducible differences, or—to put it in plain English—to fudge. In the politics of foreign policy, by contrast, it is about finding a short, vivid, compelling formulation to capture and promote the essence of what you are about. If the former is the art of dilution, the latter is the art of concentration.

Nothing is more powerfully concentrated than a good German compound noun. Weltanschauung. Weltschmerz. Erfolgserlebnis. Schadenfreude. And, indeed, #Weltpolitikfähigkeit, which actually exists as a hashtag on Twitter. For the capacity to shape world affairs is more vital than ever for Europe—indeed for the whole of the West, in a world increasingly shaped by non-European and non-Western powers. And that capacity is now very much in doubt. Wolfgang Ischinger and the MSC have pursued the linguistic-political exercise in a rather unusual way, coining and promoting the term #Westlessness,[2] which is a kind of German compound noun in English. It has had considerable success, since it captures the essence of the thought in a single word.

Nonetheless, we must always recall Thomas Hobbes' warning: "Words are wise men's counters . . . but they are the money of fools." All too often, especially in the field of foreign policy, Europe has had a surfeit of words and a deficit of action. No fine formula like "strategic autonomy" or "European sovereignty" could do anything for the fact that, when the US president decided unilaterally and precipitately to withdraw from Afghanistan, European forces simply did not have the capabilities to stay a little longer and prevent the resulting debacle—even if their countries had had the political will to do so. The lack of will and the lack of capabilities are, of course, closely connected. Important as is the power of language, its essential complement is the language of power. Only the two together will give Europe a true, effective Weltpolitikfähigkeitsverlustvermeidungsstrategie.

Timothy Garton Ash is Professor of European Studies at the University of Oxford; Isaiah Berlin Professorial Fellow at St Antony's College, Oxford; and a Senior Fellow at the Hoover Institution, Stanford University.

◂ Timothy Garton Ash at the Kick-off Event for the Munich Security Conference in February 2019.

Demonstrating Courage and Determination

Markus Söder

Each February, Munich becomes the global capital of diplomacy—as has now been the case for nearly sixty years. In the jostling of the Bayerischer Hof and during the nights in the Munich Residenz, the diplomatic wires run hot. In no other big city could an event like this take place, and this shows the characteristic power of Munich and Bavaria. They are dynamic, but they also rest in themselves; they are globally connected, but firmly rooted; they are highly developed, but embedded in a generous nature; and—as is demanded by the high positions of the numerous international guests—they are a secure haven.

In the context of Europe's history, Bavaria has always been a power of its own kind, situated at the lively center between Paris and Vienna, Berlin and Rome. The fact that Bavaria today marks the geographic center of unified Europe is a fortunate coincidence and the result of an unwavering policy of unity, freedom, peace, and prosperity.

This is the great legacy of the twentieth century. The answers to the big questions of the twenty-first century must also come from Europe. In order to present itself as a credible player on the international stage, Europe must show determination and courage in embracing change. The founding principle of European security policy must not be the ideal of a perfect world, but sound analysis of the causes, backgrounds, and consequences of international crises. When it comes to foreign policy, Europe must show its colors. What are our interests? What are our values? And how can we combine both to form one firm and unified stance?

When it comes to foreign policy, Europe must show its colors. What are our interests? What are our values? And how can we combine both to form one firm and unified stance?

Consequently, the EU must do more than merely manage the foreign-policy interests of Germany, France, and other member states. European decision processes have to be redefined and accelerated in order for the EU to be able to respond to current crises in a timelier and more flexible fashion.

In addition to the acceleration of decision processes, our defense structures will play a crucial role. There will be no alternative to strengthening our military capabilities. The goal is not to become independent from the US; indeed, we must persuade the US to remain committed to the security and freedom of Europe. The transatlantic collaboration with the US and Britain within NATO forms the basis for talking to China, Russia, and other competitors on equal terms. The European members of NATO—Germany in particular—must commit to a significant stepping up of their defense efforts, with the two-percent target defining the baseline. The collaboration between our national defense forces must also be intensified significantly.

The global competition of systems does not stop at Europe's borders—or at Germany's. Europe must therefore maintain a dialogue even with countries that do not share the Western value system. As uncomfortable as it may seem, sanctions are no replacement for political dialogue. Channels of communication must be kept open. Without collaboration with Russia (to which Bavaria historically has strong links) as well as China and other challenging partners, global crises cannot be defused. This also applies to the resolving of armed conflicts, to the fight against pandemics, and to the challenge of dealing with climate change.

In the future, there will continue to be no shortage of good reasons for dialogue. The invitation to Munich still stands.

Markus Söder is the Minister-President of Bavaria and the Chairman of the Christian Social Union (CSU).

◂ Markus Söder at the Kleist-Award Ceremony in the framework of the Munich Security Conference in February 2020.

Forging a Common European Strategic Culture

Franziska Brantner

Ever since the 2020 Munich Security Conference, the notion of "Westlessness" has been on everyone's lips—meaning that a global shift in power coupled with rapid technological change has led to a world that is less "Western." Even the West is now less Western than in the past.[1]

In this context, Western is to be understood as a normative rather than geographical category. So, has the West lost its relevance as a normative model? After the disastrous ending of the twenty-year Afghanistan mission in particular, this question has become louder and louder. Europe clearly needs to redefine its role in the world and within the transatlantic relationship.

The good news is that few people today would deny that the European Union needs more capacity for action, more sovereignty, and more "competence in world politics." The bad news is that there has been little tangible progress in this respect. Back in 2017, Angela Merkel announced in a Munich beer tent that "we Europeans must take our fate into our own hands."[2] However, little has happened since.

The good news is that few people today would deny that the European Union needs more capacity for action, more sovereignty, and more "competence in world politics." The bad news is that there has been little tangible progress in this respect.

Specifically, there are two ways of enhancing the European capacity for action, both of which must be pursued simultaneously. First, there is a need for institutional reforms, such as implementing qualified majority voting in those policy areas that still require unanimity—especially votes regarding the common foreign and security policy. This would allow the EU to act faster and more credibly and effectively on the world stage.

Second, member states must converge "culturally" by developing a common strategic culture and a common understanding of security within the EU. In the same year in which Angela Merkel suggested that Europe needed to take its fate into its own hands, French president Emmanuel Macron said that "what today's Europe . . . lacks most is a common strategic culture."[3]

The road to a common culture of this type is bumpy. It requires diplomatic sensitivity, plus spaces where such convergence can take place.

The Franco-German Parliamentary Assembly provides just such a space. Since 2019 fifty members of the Bundestag and fifty members of the Assemblée nationale have met twice a year. This includes the "Foreign and Security Policy" working group, whose objective is to determine how "common strategic modes of thinking and acting on the field of security and defense policy can be developed."[4] During the brief time for which it has existed, the working group has laid a solid foundation. However, more attention and political capital is needed in order to give the results more weight. As a further step, the results and experiences gained should be introduced to the European Strategic Compass, which is the place where Franco-German analyses are brought together with those from the rest of Europe.

Another space in which such Franco-German, European, and transatlantic convergence can take place is the Munich Security Conference. In 2018 the then federal defense minister Ursula von der Leyen advocated a common European strategic culture. Over the following years, there have been "strategy retreats" and "nightcap" events dedicated to the subject; these focused on advancing the debate constructively and in cooperation with EU member states, the United Kingdom, the United States, and other democratic partners.

These places of diplomacy and convergence represent an important contribution to a common strategic culture in Europe. Therefore, they also form a building block for a constructive opposition to "Westlessness." They must be supported, cultivated, and appreciated.

Franziska Brantner is Parliamentary State Secretary at the Ministry for Economic Affairs and Climate Action. She has been a member of the Bundestag since 2013 and served as Parliamentary Secretary of the Bündnis90/Die Grünen parliamentary group and as its spokesperson for European policy.

◂ Franziska Brantner at the Launch of the Munich Security Report "Zeitenwende | Wendezeiten" in Berlin in October 2020.

51st Munich Security
Conference
51. Münchner Sicherhe
Februa
6. - 8.

Making the Case for Defense

Frederick "Ben" Hodges

In a 2019 interview with *The Economist*, when asked if he believed that NATO's commitment to Article 5 of NATO's founding treaty was still functional, French President Emmanuel Macron replied: "I don't know."

I do know, and the answer is a resounding "yes!" I served five times in NATO. In my last assignment in the army, from 2014 until the end of 2017, I served as commanding general of US Army Europe, in Wiesbaden, Germany. During these years of service with our allies, I never doubted that NATO would respond to an armed attack on one of its members.

But I became alarmed by statements from President Macron, the very damaging public statements by former US president Donald Trump, and other challenges to NATO's cohesion. I felt it was my duty, as a senior US army officer with responsibilities for deterrence and defense in Europe, to protect the cohesion of NATO and the relationship between the US and our essential ally, Germany. I embarked on a campaign on both sides of the Atlantic, explaining the threats to our collective security, looking for innovative ways to encourage Germany to increase its defense spending, and educating American media, leaders, and members of Congress about why Germany is so important to NATO and to the United States. I felt that I had the credibility to speak more openly in public about these issues and work closely with diplomats and parliamentarians from allied nations, while respecting the civilian authority over the military and taking care to not get in front of US government policy.

President Macron's statement that NATO was "brain dead" was widely criticized by most NATO member states, including Germany. Nonetheless, it generated serious discussion and it put additional pressure on the German government. France, after all, has nuclear weapons and a permanent seat on the UN Security Council. It can talk, to a certain extent, about "strategic autonomy." Germany has neither nuclear weapons nor a permanent seat on the council, which is why successive German governments regarded NATO as one of its central strategic pillars. If NATO is "brain dead," Germany has much to lose. But if NATO is vital to Germany's security, why doesn't Germany do all it can to ensure the alliance's continued strength? Germany needs to fulfill its obligations within NATO, to make it impossible for an American or French President to even consider leaving.

Instead, there is a strategic inertia in Berlin, a reluctance to have a serious public debate about Germany's strategic role in the world. One of the most visible manifestations of this inertia is Germany's failure to invest more in its own defense. Most NATO allies are expected to achieve the target of 2 percent of GDP by 2024. Germany is not one of them. Germans complained that President Trump was "destroying NATO." While that was too strong, it was indeed unhelpful when he cast doubt on American commitment to NATO and our European allies. Yet it's also damaging to the cohesion of the alliance when one of its most prosperous members fails to fulfill its defense investment obligation. Failing to invest prevents Germany from maintaining an appropriate level of readiness, cyber defense of critical infrastructure, or adequate missile defense.

This current situation is the result of political decisions that were made a decade ago. It will take time and money to fix it. Bundeswehr leadership is working hard to make improvements as resources become available. They deserve more support from the German public and political leadership, as German Defense Minister Annegret Kramp-Karrenbauer recently said in her speech in Hamburg.

I often hear the excuse for why Germany doesn't lead: "our history." This excuse is not worthy of a nation that has for seventy years demonstrated that it is a liberal democracy with high moral standards, while building Europe's largest economy. Germans need to regain trust in themselves. If Germany owes anything because of its history, it is that it should live up to the responsibilities it has as a strong state within the community of democratic nations. Germany has benefited from the security provided by NATO. It's time for Germany to step forward, lead by example, and fulfill its defense-spending obligation. On the occasion of German reunification in 1990, US President George H. W. Bush expressed hope that the US and Germany would be "partners in leadership." Thirty-one years later, fulfilling that wish remains essential for our collective security and prosperity.

Frederick "Ben" Hodges is a retired United States Army officer who served as commanding general of the United States Army Europe. He is currently the Pershing Chair in Strategic Studies at the Center for European Policy Analysis.

◂ Frederick "Ben" Hodges at the Munich Security Conference in February 2015.

msc

Securing Public Support

Norbert Röttgen

After the disaster of the withdrawal from Afghanistan, it is clear that Germany and Europe must redefine their foreign policies. As the priorities of the US administration shift, so does the role of the US in the world. The Middle East is no longer of major significance to the US, but it remains central to our stability and security in Europe. We cannot simply ignore this region, because crises will impact our own societies through terror and streams of refugees. For us the withdrawal of the US therefore amounts to an existential challenge: we must develop an idea of who we want to be in this world, and what role we want to play in a transitional era between a vanishing old and a budding new order. Do we seek to stand our own ground, or will we remain weak and powerless without the US at our side? As a society, we haven't yet answered this fundamental identity question. It must be decided now, or else our foreign policy and related diplomacy will continue to lack orientation.

An identity-forming process must be established, because, without societal backing, we will be unable to assume the international responsibility that we have been talking about for many years now, but which is reflected neither in our political will to act, nor in our military capabilities.

Herein lies the crucial role of the parliament. An identity-forming process must be established, because, without societal backing, we will be unable to assume the international responsibility that we have been talking about for many years now, but which is reflected neither in our political will to act, nor in our military capabilities. It is this societal backing that has been lacking in Germany. This is quite surprising, given that many people today are experiencing foreign policy very directly, as questions of domestic and foreign policy increasingly intermingle. Refugee crisis or climate change—each of these problems has global implications, while also impacting our life here in Germany in specific ways and sometimes with dramatic consequences. People are seeing this. They are experiencing a world around them that is radically changing, and they want to understand these changes. It is our responsibility, as members of Parliament, to explain these changes to the people.

The necessary identity-forming process must take place not only inwardly, but also between states. Who we are and who we want to be is something we experience not only by reflecting on it ourselves, but also by arguing and debating with others—as can be observed on the government level, but increasingly also between parliaments. This became particularly obvious during the Donald Trump presidency when US-German relations were plunged into a crisis. Donald Trump saw Germany as more of an adversary than a close partner. The parliamentary and civil contacts that were left to fill this void became all the more important. Memorably, when Donald Trump refused to take part in the Munich Security Conference, the largest delegation ever of the US Congress came to Munich in his stead.

Interaction and collaboration between the chairpersons of the committees on foreign affairs have also significantly increased in recent years. Through our constant personal exchange, we are frequently able to express ourselves in a more timely manner than the ministries. Prior to this year's G7 summit, for instance, nearly seventy members of Parliament from all the G7 states published a joint declaration on dealing with China. In various configurations, we frequently offer joint declarations on subjects of transatlantic and European interest.

It is of existential significance to us in Germany—and as Western democracies—to determine for ourselves who we want to be in this world of disorder, and what we are willing to do. This understanding does not come from nowhere, but needs to be developed.

Norbert Röttgen has been a member of the Bundestag since 1994. He was the Federal Minister of Environment, Nature Conservation and Nuclear Safety from 2009 to 2012 and Chairperson of the Committee on Foreign Affairs of the Bundestag from 2014 to 2021.

◂ Norbert Röttgen as a guest at MSC Events, among others at the MSC Core Group Meeting in Washington, DC in May 2017.

SC

Reforming Germany's National Security Architecture

Boris Ruge

In 1998 Wolfgang Ischinger was appointed state secretary of the German Foreign Office. Along with Michael Steiner, foreign policy adviser to Chancellor Gerhard Schröder, Ischinger produced a proposal for a new decision-making setup for national security issues, ensuring closer coordination. As the story goes, Foreign Minister Joschka Fischer did not approve and the paper disappeared—never to be seen again.[1]

Since 1998, despite the unceremonious dismissal of the Ischinger-Steiner paper, practitioners and analysts have continued to debate the pros and cons of a national security council. The limiting factors have always been clear: German governments are based on coalitions of several parties, and cabinet ministers have a constitutionally guaranteed level of autonomy in running their ministries.

Proponents of the status quo have argued that an NSC-type structure would be problematic both in political and constitutional terms. Some have taken the view that the system works well enough and there is no need for increased coordination to begin with. Others maintain that Germany must do better, but that better foreign policy is a matter of political will rather than a function of better institutions.

By contrast those calling for change have pointed to the increasing complexity of national security issues, now including energy, climate change, migration, and tech, and the need to coordinate an increasing number of government agencies above and beyond the ministries traditionally engaged on these matters. They have highlighted that new threats are shrinking time frames for crisis response, and also point to challenges experienced during the COVID-19 pandemic, the deadly European floods of July 2021, and the August 2021 events in Afghanistan.

In its 2016 White Paper, the government announced that the (existing but underutilized) Federal Security Council would in the future address strategic issues "more consistently."[2] In practice, this has not happened. Instead, the status quo in Berlin is marked by contradictions: Important portfolios have gravitated to the Federal Chancellery (as in the case of China and Russia policy). At the same time, coalition politics, the principle of ministerial autonomy, and bureaucratic silos have gotten in the way of coherent policy-making and effective crisis management.

Over the years, Germany's allies have learned to navigate the system, but not without frustration. In 2019 Julie Smith (herself an alumna of the White House NSC) observed that Germany was "missing in action at a time of transformative change and disruption" and that this was partly due to the lack of a "body for strategic debates, prioritization, and coordination."[3]

In October 2020, the MSC laid out the case for change identifying a more systematic use of the Federal Security Council supported by additional personnel and the creation of an entirely new coordination structure as options.[4]

At the time of writing, in early September 2021, we don't know what Germany's next government coalition will look like. It is noteworthy that, in their respective election platforms, the CDU/CSU and FDP specifically call for the creation of a national security council while the Greens propose a "national council for peace, sustainability, and human rights" (the platform of the SPD is silent on the matter but calls for overcoming "silo thinking" between ministries). Whether a future coalition can agree on a new setup remains to be seen. Judging from the polls, it seems clear that one or several parties arguing in favor of new structures will be at the negotiating table.

One additional element may come into play after the elections: the post-mortem of the August 2021 evacuation operation from Kabul. We cannot know whether an NSC-type structure would have delivered a better result. But by bringing key cabinet members to the table, an NSC would have provided for greater transparency within the government and hence accountability. Across party lines, members of the Bundestag may come to see this as a key argument in favor of change.

Twenty years after Wolfgang Ischinger got the ball rolling, the German debate on its national security architecture is coming to a head. Whatever the outcome, it will tell us a great deal about Berlin's level of ambition for German and European foreign policy in the twenty-first century.

Boris Ruge is Vice Chairman of the Munich Security Conference. He is a German career diplomat and previously served as Director Middle East/North Africa at the Foreign Office in Berlin, as German Ambassador to Saudi Arabia, and as Deputy Ambassador in the US.

◂ Boris Ruge at the Launch of the Munich Security Report Special Edition "Zeitenwende | Wendezeiten" in Berlin in October 2020.

Giesecke+Devrient
msc
msc

Navigating Propaganda and Social Media

Steven Erlanger

In the prolegomena to the war that began in Iraq in 2003, I had a long interview with Gerhard Schröder in his Hanover home. This was the start of my page one story in early September 2002:

> Gerhard Schröder, the German chancellor, believes that the Bush administration is making a terrible mistake in planning a war against Iraq, and he is not afraid to say so. A new war in the Middle East, he says bluntly, would put at risk all that has been gained so far in the unfinished battle against Al Qaeda.[1]

Schröder was running for reelection, and he told me that his first goal was to reinspire his own Social Democratic Party. But he was also correct. Wolfgang Ischinger was Germany's ambassador to Washington. After the interview appeared, he called. "Steve," he asked with some chagrin, "what are you doing to me?"

I describe this anecdote because the relationship between the United States and Germany remains both strong and ambivalent, awkward and necessary. It is a relationship that has helped define our lives—my own first visit to Germany was to East Berlin in 1981, the summer of Solidarność. The gratitude Germans felt to a United States that enabled reunification was real—I still remember the flowers strangers sent to my office in Berlin after September 11, 2001. Schröder and his coalition strongly supported NATO's response in Afghanistan. But neither the United States nor Germany are what they were. Our relationship is drifting into rocky shallows. If Schröder, Joschka Fischer, and Jacques Chirac were right to oppose Bush over Iraq, too many Germans now see opposition to Washington as a moral requirement.

All that has made me wonder more about the role of journalism and diplomacy in the age of social media, of Twitter and Facebook and Instagram, and hot takes on every topic. It is speculation, of course, but what would have happened had the Schröder warning gone out on Twitter? How would the White House have responded, and how quickly? How would the French have reacted? Or Saddam Hussein? Let alone the passionate, often rabid Twittersphere?

I think of Richard Holbrooke, one of my country's most creative diplomats, who was expert at using the media as a tool of diplomacy. Would his skills have transferred to social media or would they have been undermined by it and the fierce competition it engenders?

Debate around sensitive diplomatic issues can also be guided and manipulated by social media—two recent examples are the collapse of the Afghan government and the Australian-American-British alliance that so enraged France.

On Afghanistan, the Americans have used social media to push the inevitability of it all; European critics, the supposed lack of consultation; non-governmental organizations, the danger to the rights of women and minorities and the risk of famine without continued aid to the very group they fear, the Taliban. And the Taliban, to be sure, have been pushing their putative new moderation. And all of this with little context or moderation by editors or reporters or Western diplomats, who are few on the ground and highly constrained in what they can see and where they can go. Hence, governments must try to make policy in the dark, while being pushed and shoved by highly emotive and evocative social media posts uploaded by partisans.

So too with AUKUS and France's fury over its betrayal by close allies. Twitter went nuclear, as it were, with screeds about everything from the technicalities of nuclear propulsion and French policy in the Indo-Pacific to ugly insults aimed at China and all the countries involved. How does diplomacy, which depends on trust and secrecy, manage to function in such a raging hothouse?

I'm also struck by the use governments are making of social media for announcements and propaganda, too. And here I don't just mean the Russian Embassy in London, known for its cynicism and even wit, but the way Ursula von der Leyen, to use just one example, tries to control her image and her message by using social media created by her own PR team to avoid those tricky press conferences, where the unpredictable media can ask awkward questions.

Of course, for many leaders, Zoom was heaven-sent. Follow-up questions are almost impossible and it is the spokesperson or press secretary who controls access to the microphone.

The world turns, and we spin in circles with it. A new generation of Ischingers has a serious task ahead, to somehow slow us down and allow a form of responsible discussion to surface from the chaos, so diplomacy can continue to manage the deep fissures among our nations.

Steven Erlanger is the chief diplomatic correspondent in Europe for *The New York Times*, a position he assumed in 2017.

◂ Steven Erlanger at the Munich Security Conference in February 2020.

Tiilikainen

Mitigating Hybrid Threats

Teija Tiilikainen

Hybridity refers to something that does not conform to established concepts, conventions, or forms of behavior. By representing something unconventional, hybridity usually requires new approaches, including rules and practices, to accommodate it as a part of social life.

Difficulties start when hybridity is purposefully used as an instrument against other people or states. This is the simple philosophy behind current hybrid threat activity—including phenomena called hybrid interference and hybrid warfare—which plays a key role in international politics. This activity is usually linked with the use of unconventional means such as critical infrastructure disturbances or manipulation of domestic information spaces as tools in power projection. But there are reasons to perceive this phenomenon of hybridity on a larger scale—targeting the very cornerstones of the current international order with its basic norms, conventions, and structures.

This contribution focuses on the phenomenon of hybrid threats and the question of how to mitigate them. Is there any room for international mediation or confidence-building measures to mitigate hybrid threats or does deterrence provide the only useful tool in the current international environment? Does traditional diplomacy play a role in preventing hybrid threats?

The Context of Hybrid Threats

We are living in an era of many simultaneous transitions taking place in the global system of power. The most visible of them deals with changes in the balance of power among states. The well-known argument about a gradual weakening of the role of Western powers, including the transatlantic unity, and a corresponding strengthening of China, Russia, and many regional hegemons, seems uncontroversial. For a longer time, another trend called diffusion of state power has made itself obvious.[1] It refers to the strengthening of a variety of non-state actors—from intergovernmental organizations and multinational companies to terrorist groups and even powerful individuals—at the expense of state power. Both of these trends have led to a gradual dissolution of the post-war international order with its norms and institutions as both the value base and the question of subjects have turned controversial. An international order based on cooperation and mutual trust has been developing to a direction where a pure balance of power between the leading actors is replacing cooperation with mutual distrust and unpredictability.

Such an environment of transition and disorder provides a fertile ground for unconventional instruments of power. These "hybrid means" are partly linked with the conflict of values in the current international system and the efforts of non-democratic states to take advantage of vulnerabilities within the political and societal systems of their democratic counterparts.[2] But they can equally be linked with a power asymmetry and the efforts of weaker actors to balance shortcomings in their power arsenal.[3] This threat environment also nourishes an emergence of unconventional allies between states and non-state actors in promotion of shared interests. Unconventional power instruments such as disinformation campaigns, cyberattacks, disturbance of critical infrastructure, election interference, instrumentalized migration, or even different forms of hybrid warfare are cost-efficient in comparison with more conventional forms of power politics. They are also much more difficult to attribute, which lowers the risks for effective countermeasures such as economic or political sanctions.

Unconventional power instruments such as disinformation campaigns, cyberattacks, disturbance of critical infrastructure, election interference, instrumentalized migration, or even different forms of hybrid warfare are cost-efficient in comparison with more conventional forms of power politics.

The Ideology and Strategy of Hybrid Threats

The hybridity of hybrid threats originates in its ideological approach. In general terms, this approach is that of the total state giving priority to the state above law or individual rights.[4] The justification for the total state is anchored in cultural and political nationalism or, in some cases, religious extremism.

This total state ideology is veiled in different political doctrines for the various authoritarian states. For Russia it is the doctrine of political war according to which Russia is in a constant war with the West that threatens

◂ Teija Tiilikainen at the MSC Arctic Security Roundtable in Stavanger in August 2018.

its political system and culture.[5] Russia is thus claimed to need to use the whole range of instruments to protect itself. Also the enemy is presented in a comprehensive light consisting of the whole post-war international order in which the hegemony of the US power is seen to be embedded. The whole unique Russian civilization being threatened justifies a solid response and demands the unity of the population to support it.

Chinese thinking revolves around similar doctrines with the ideas of a united front and indirect warfare as its core.[6] A nationalist understanding of cultural superiority characterizes Chinese political thinking, legitimizing its hostile approach to the West that is perceived to have humiliated it and is seen to constantly undermine and threaten it.[7] China thus must use its superior skills to defeat the enemy and this implies the use of "indirect warfare" referring to creative non-military and preemptive means. This again requires a united front of actors—governmental as well as non-governmental—to protect Chinese political and cultural unity.

There are similarities between the total state idea and the approaches of actors such as Iran or Islamist movements, which base their attack on the West on religious doctrines. Also they find the justification for their use of tools from the understanding of a comprehensive cultural and religious war that is seen to take place with the Western world.[8]

Covert Means and Manipulation as the Hybrid Threat Strategy

Hybrid threat activity is ultimately revisionist, even if the scale and time horizon of this revisionism tend to differ. The general goal of hybrid threat activity is to change international power structures to the benefit of the actor in question. This may take place by targeted means, such as by affecting another state's decision-making or by affecting the physical or normative foundations for those power structures. The Russian long-term hybrid threat activity against Ukraine is an example of both of them (short term and long term), while the massive Chinese investments in critical infrastructures globally include a strong potential for the latter.

To strengthen their position and minimize costs, covert activity, undetectability, as well as different forms of manipulation belong to the strategic approach of hybrid threat actors. By hiding their responsibility, the actors try, first of all, to avoid countermeasures both from the target state and its possible allies as well as from the larger international community. Therefore, acting below the threshold of armed conflict, using proxy actors, or manipulating the situational awareness of the target and deceiving it to take decisions in support of the adversary are typical forms of action. Countermeasures are thus complicated when hostile activities cannot be attributed or when their goals and logic remain highly unclear. There are plenty of recent examples where this tactic has been used, from interference in the 2016 US presidential elections where the final proof of Russian responsibility only came much later or the external political funding for European extremist parties, which also took time to be detected and thus delayed a change in the EU's internal norms.[9]

Another strategic approach of hybrid threat operations deals with the way target states' vulnerabilities are used as an asset. By identifying different kinds of weaknesses from gaps in societal protection to political disunity and polarization or problems in economic and financial sustainability, hybrid threat actors mitigate a negative power asymmetry to their own benefit. Concerning their origin, vulnerabilities can be divided between technological, political, economic, or legal vulnerabilities with the measures to repair them differing.

Functional interdependencies built in a society's networks of critical infrastructures provide good examples of technological vulnerabilities as they can be used to cause harm and political instability to modern technology-driven societies.[10] Technological vulnerabilities cut across societies and affect equally the military sector with direct consequences to the conventional defense apparatus.

Economic vulnerabilities enhance a state's dependence of external sources and might make it an alluring target for geoeconomic power projection. Foreign investments in critical infrastructures provide an optimal instrument for this purpose as well as foreign loans. Economic vulnerabilities and instability again form fertile ground for political dissatisfaction and instability, which can be amplified by various forms of foreign interference. Corruption and shortcomings in rule of law structures furthermore increase possibilities of hybrid influencing.

Finally, legal vulnerabilities have become a widely used tool for hybrid threat activities both at the national and the international level. Legal vulnerabilities in a broad sense refer both to gaps in existing normative frameworks and to the use of law for strategic purposes, that is, "lawfare." The former can take the form of underregulated cyberspace or the inability to prevent weaponized migration due to the existing framework of international law. The latter might imply that a law is used against its original purpose to justify malicious activity.[11]

Preventing Hybrid Threats: Diplomacy or Deterrence?

The starting points for any broader international mechanisms being established for the prevention of hybrid threats are not encouraging. With the overall interpretations of the main reasons for the international confrontation diverging vastly, there is not much common ground for international conflict resolution or prevention mechanisms. The revisionism of Russia and China implies that a large part of those international norms and structures that Western actors perceive as products of common international norms are considered unjust.[12] Hybrid threat actors thus consider their activities as legitimate efforts to balance or—as they interestingly describe—'democratize' the international system. As long as maintenance of political instability in Ukraine forms a key tool for Russia in preventing the country from accessing the Western institutions, the EU, and NATO, the joint conflict resolution efforts remain highly symbolic.

A majority of the international community, however, considers existing rules and norms of international law to form a system of compulsory law whose letter and spirit shall be complied with even when conflicting with major national interests. The significance of majority opinion reflects itself in the efforts of hybrid threat actors to present their activities as lawful to the last. As pointed out earlier, with this strategy, the actors attempt to escape possible countermeasures. Russia and China, however, made a joint resolution on international law in 2016, which enshrines a narrow interpretation of international law delineating it basically to the UN and its Security Council.[13]

> The resilience toolbox aims to enable a state to adapt to exceptional conditions and to absorb and recover from a shock. It does this by providing everything from political and legislative tools to instruments raising public awareness of risks related to hybrid threats and tackling the challenge of disinformation.

On the other hand, an inability to create new international norms for emerging policy fields such as the cyberspace or space, may ultimately serve similar needs in relation to hybrid threat activity and a willingness to balance asymmetric power relations.[14]

The strengthened use of hybrid threat operations together with their rationale lower the threshold for international conflicts. First, the cost efficiency of these tools encourages actors to use them more easily and with less political consideration than traditional instruments of power projection. But second, missing instruments and platforms for conflict-prevention and settlement may also drive the target countries to react with unexpected means in the absence of clear plans and forms of both national preparedness and credible international means for conflict resolution.[15] The risk for accidents and unmanaged escalation thus characterizes the current environment of amplified hybrid threat activity.

Countering Hybrid Threats: Resilience and Deterrence as an Approach

With a broader international confrontation and lack of trust prevailing, instruments for the mitigation of hybrid threat activities are mainly sought in national frameworks or among democratic countries in the EU or NATO context. The policies on enhancing a broad societal resilience and creating a policy of credible deterrence against hybrid threats form the core of these instruments. Both toolboxes require new approaches, such as more long-term strategic planning to decrease vulnerabilities for external interference. Another instrument relates to affecting the cost calculus of actors exerting hybrid threat activity and involvement of broad societal actors to create tools for resilience. The resilience toolbox aims to enable a state to adapt to exceptional conditions and to absorb and recover from a shock. It does this by providing everything from political and legislative tools to instruments raising public awareness of risks related to hybrid threats and tackling the challenge of disinformation.

Along with their member states, both the EU and NATO have strengthened their policies and preparedness vis-à-vis hybrid threats during the past few years. As complex institutional entities, they share the same vulnerabilities as regards their functioning and integrity. Furthermore, their tasks and mandates require them to act in support of their member states in this field.

The EU and NATO have thus consolidated their efforts in responding to hybrid threats and enhancing the resilience of their member states through different policy instruments and new institutional structures and practices, including better coordination and sharing of good practices. The EU and NATO have both been active in cyber security and critical infrastructure protection. For the EU's part, enhancing resilience takes the form of legislative projects and mapping vulnerabilities in major fields of critical infrastructure protection. NATO approaches this issue through its policies on civil preparedness, which has been gaining new momentum recently. Both organizations are focusing on the challenge posed by cyber security, recognizing the vulnerabilities of their own functions, and those of their member states. NATO thus declared cyber defense another field for collective defense and recognized cyberspace as a domain of operations in which NATO must defend itself as effectively as in any other domain. Apart from its strengthened legislative measures, the EU has established cyber defense projects within the framework of Permanent Structured Cooperation (PESCO) and taken into use sanctions against cyberattacks constituting a threat to the union or its member states.

Hybrid threats form an integral part of the current transition in the post-Cold War international order. As an instrument of authoritarian powers, they are deeply rooted in the inability of these powers to guarantee regime legitimacy through a democratic process.

Countering hybrid threats became one of the topics for the new strategic partnership between the EU and NATO, on which the organizations agreed in 2016. In their joint declaration, the two actors decided to boost their activity to counter hybrid threats by working together on analysis, prevention, and early detection, through timely information sharing and cooperating on strategic communication and response.[16] As a part of the implementation of the joint declaration, EU and NATO encouraged the member states of both organizations to participate in the European Centre of Excellence for Countering Hybrid Threats (CoE), established in 2017. In 2021 Hybrid CoE has enlarged to cover a membership of thirty-one participating states with its capacity-building efforts being enhanced through joint projects and exercises both with a growing number of practitioners and external experts.

Democracies Have to Stand United

Hybrid threats form an integral part of the current transition in the post-Cold War international order. As an instrument of authoritarian powers, they are deeply rooted in the inability of these powers to guarantee regime legitimacy through a democratic process. These states make a comprehensive effort to change the rules and practices of the international order to their own benefit. Hybrid threats consist of measures that function on a short to a very long perspective. As they build on ambiguity, surprise, and covert activity, applying international conflict prevention mechanisms to them is in contradiction with their rationale, if seen from the perpetrators' perspective. The potential for hybrid threat activity therefore seems rather to be growing than decreasing.

Hybrid threats require new thinking and measures from the democratic societies that they are mainly targeted against. Measures have to be diverse and involve a broad range of actors, from international organizations and bodies to private actors and NGOs. Democracies have to stand united behind their values and communicate their willingness to do so both domestically and internationally. When rules and agreements are violated—or proxy actors are used to cover the tracks of state actors—responsibilities must be made visible to the whole international community. The long-term goal must be to bring respect and trust back to international law and conventional practices of the international community.

Teija Tiilikainen is the Director of the European Centre of Excellence for Countering Hybrid Threats. Previously, she was the Director of the Finnish Institute of International Affairs from 2010 to 2019 and the Director of the Network of European Studies at the University of Helsinki from 2003 to 2009. She also served as Secretary of State at the Ministry for Foreign Affairs of Finland from 2007 to 2008.

Yuval Diskin (left) at the MSC Cyber Security Summit in Tel Aviv in June 2017. ▸

Giesecke & Devrient
Giesecke & Devrient
msc

Understanding the Digitization of War

Toomas Hendrik Ilves

What is security? Most basically, it provides some kind of assurance of the continuance of one's own life as well as one's offspring. If your genes do not continue, you go extinct, and as Richard Dawkins has so effectively argued in *The Selfish Gene*, we can understand much of animal behavior by thinking of the basic unit of evolution as the gene. Behaviorally, this means fundamentally that you seek nourishment, and in higher animals, phylogenetically from vertebrates on up, you protect your young until they reach reproductive age.

For most of the history of civilization and long before that, as long as there have been social apes, pre-human hominids, and the modern humans we have been for several hundred thousand years, we also have had war. Bands of apes, hominids, Neanderthals, and Cro-Magnon social biped males (generally) have used killing their own kind for their own benefit, and attacked each other to get food, females, and property/territory. I stress the social, because non-social animals may kill their own kind, but it requires social behavior and organization to carry out war: groups of a species attacking groups from the same species, distinguishing between your own group and another.

From simple hand-to-hand conflict to rocks to weapons of stone leading to bronze spears to iron, technological developments give an advantage to those who possess them.

Beginning with British philosopher Thomas Hobbes—who was really the first to develop the social contract theory of the state in his *Leviathan* (1651)—theorists of the state have argued in one way or another that war is the beginning of the state. Hobbes characterized life in the state of nature as *Bellum omnium contra omnes*, a war of all against all. It took the state to control, to harness, and focus this. This in turn required social organization: warriors to defend and attack, others to supply food, leading to a division of labor, and from that, taxes and a bureaucracy.

For our purposes, it's enough merely to say, war and the need for security has been part of life since our evolutionary ancestors. In other words, other than food and procreation, security is one of life's fundamental needs. When we talk about security in this context, we can leave out the newer concepts of security—food security, climate security, water security—that have come into the discourse on security from climate change to pandemics. These threats, of course, can quite effectively eliminate the prospects of survival for much of mankind, but for this essay's purposes, I will stick to the traditional concept of security we associate with war.

Technology and War

War, be it between tribes, nations, or nation-states, has always been a matter of numerical and technological advantage. If you want to win, there have to be more of you or you need better weapons, which effectively increase one side's numerical advantage. Or you need, as in the case of the Soviet Union fighting Nazi Germany or Finland, to be willing to have enough of your own die simply to swamp the technologically superior adversary with numbers.

Technology changes conflict, war, and so too obviously, security. From simple hand-to-hand conflict to rocks to weapons of stone leading to bronze spears to iron, technological developments give an advantage to those who possess them. The bow, the English longbow, stirrups, armor, gun powder—all have changed the nature of conflict. A stone thrown or attached to a stick as a spear, a knife, or an axe gave you more mass or increased distance. A bow and an arrow gave you increased velocity and distance.

To put it briefly, the primary unit of war has been force, the definition of which we learned in high school as Newton's Second Law: force = mass times acceleration.

$$F = M x A$$

Where acceleration—A—is the change in velocity over time.

$$F = M x s x v/t$$

Which reduces to:

$$F = M x ds/dt x t$$

In physics we know this as kinetic force. All use of force from pre-history until the end of the second millennium exclusively has been kinetic. You can increase

◂ Toomas Hendrik Ilves at the MSC Cyber Security Summit in Tallinn in May 2018.

force through a greater mass (a bigger rock, a bigger bomb) or through increased velocity (a better spear-throwing arm, a bow, a trebuchet, or missile).

The problem is that roughly since the beginning of the millennium, we have seen the increasing use of *digital* force. Digital force has no mass and within the confines of earth, distance and time are reduced to trivial figures. The implications of this change are the subject of this article.

The Rise of Non-kinetic Weapons in the Twenty-First Century

The technology of war up to the end the twentieth century was essentially kinetic. True, in the twentieth century, we saw the use of chemical weapons in World War I and more recently in Syria. The problem with these weapons is that they can't be targeted. The wind can change and blow back, they can linger and affect others. They are indiscriminate weapons of mass destruction and as such are forbidden by international treaties, though as we have seen with the use by Russia of the Novichok nerve agent against Alexei Navalni and the Skripals, they continue to be developed and used to this day. Yet, these are outlier cases. The true change has been the digitization of war.

The Digitization of War

The nature of war changed dramatically with the development of the computer and its use as a weapon, a profound change that alters the most fundamental assumptions of security and warfare from the previous several million years. This is not to say that kinetic warfare has disappeared, as any number of current low-level conflicts shows, yet the use of digital technologies in state-on-state warfare adds a new dimension to security policy that requires us to alter our understanding of aggression, alliances, defense, and responses.

> The technology of war up to the end the twentieth century was essentially kinetic. The nature of war changed dramatically with the development of the computer and its use as a weapon, a profound change that alters the most fundamental assumptions of security and warfare from the previous several million years.

Most importantly, given the power of digital weaponry, we can already assume that any serious state-on-state conflict will begin not with a kinetic attack, but through creating paralysis in—and indeed shutting down—the state attacked. Electricity grids will be shut down, traffic lights turned red, water supplies and gas shut off. Essentially, all unprotected infrastructure will be shut down. This will occur before any kinetic attack even begins. If it even does.

Any kinetic military infrastructure that is left functional after an initial digital shutdown will be subjected to digital/electronic attacks ranging from electromagnetic pulses (EMPs) that disable all electronics, to the ghosting of GPS on ships and airplanes and guided missiles, as we have already seen with US ships in the Black Sea. Digital systems that survive these attacks will also be targeted. These changes are only beginning to be played out in security policy thinking.

All of this, in the history of warfare, is only as old as the twenty-first century and thus has come only recently into security policy thinking. The first panel ever held on cyber issues at the Munich Security Conference took place in February 2011. Doctrine is even slower to come onto the scene.

Developments in the Past Twenty-One Years

Nonetheless, there has been no absence of different types of digital warfare in these twenty years. We can distinguish several broad categories or attack vectors of digital warfare. They differ in many ways where the only common element is the use of digital technology.

There is cyber warfare: hacking, spying, and the use of logic bombs against other computers and computer-run systems. As we have seen from the last several years of ransomware, data also can simply be locked and made inaccessible. DDOS or Digital Denial of Service attacks shut down servers, rendering access impossible to those who depend on them, be they banks, newspapers, or any other needed service.

There is also information warfare, waged at much higher levels of cognition. Information warfare is aimed at political disruption via social media with false news, artificial social media groups, and disinformation-based conspiracy theories. Moreover, these can be used in hybrid form as was the case in 2016 and 2017 when Hillary Clinton's server was hacked by a Russian (seemingly intelligence service affiliated) hacking group and then Russia supplied its contents to Wikileaks, which subsequently released them. The following year before the French presidential election, Emmanuel Macron's servers were hacked, with little effect as election staff had "seeded" the server with obvious fakes that obviated any political effects. The new threats of the digital era are often confounded by policy makers, leading to thinking that occasionally resembles Donald Trump's "the cyber."

Espionage/Hacking

The computer was first and foremost and remains a tool of espionage. One can penetrate another nation's computer systems innermost sanctums, find their deepest secrets, and no one might ever know. The first big publicly known nation-to-nation hack was Moonlight Maze, the US name given to Russian penetration of the US Department of Defense in 1999. Since then, we have seen countless more hacks carried out by most major state actors, either directly or through proxies. Among the best known are the (presumably) Chinese hack of the OPM, the US government's Office of Personnel Management in 2015, stealing 23 million personal records of US federal employees (including, among other things, the psychological profiles of CIA officers; the hack of Hillary Clinton's emails by the Russians in 2016, which arguably altered the course of the US elections; the SolarWinds hack discovered in December of 2020, in which the Russians gained access, it is thought, to large swaths of US digital infrastructure, as well as private companies, including defense contractors.

We can distinguish several broad categories or attack vectors of digital warfare. They differ in many ways where the only common element is the use of digital technology.

More broadly, just two Russian hacking groups, in American nomenclature, APT 28 and APT 29, for *Advanced Persistent Threat*, have penetrated the German Bundestag, leading German think tanks, the US Congress, the US State Department, the Italian and Dutch foreign ministries, and the World Anti-Doping Agency.

Undoubtedly, they have penetrated far more Western governments—agencies as well as international and non-governmental organizations—but few have admitted to a breach, and some may not even know their data has been stolen. Western governments, moreover, are loath to consider hacking attacks and penetrations as aggression, primarily because Western nations presumably do the same to their adversaries, but the latter don't admit they have been penetrated. More importantly and as we saw in the case of the 2020 SolarWinds hack, governments will not respond with aggressive counteraction if the hack was simply a matter of theft, with no discernible damage.

Logic Bombs, or Weaponized Hacks

A step up from mere espionage are logic bombs. These are digital forms of sabotage, not merely exfiltration of data, and thus rise to the threshold of war. The three best known as of this writing are the Iranian Shamoon virus, which disabled large swaths of the Saudi Arabian Oil company Aramco's computer system, requiring all affected computers to be replaced; the attacks on Ukraine's electrical grid by Russia in 2014, which blanked out entire sections of Ukraine's electrical grid; and the American-Israeli Stuxnet virus, which took down the Iranian nuclear enrichment plant in a so-called SCADA (Systems Control and Data Acquisition) attack, manipulating feedback information from the centrifuges used to make enriched plutonium for Iran's nuclear weapons program.

These are nation-state actions. Yet as with hacks, these can be performed by smaller groups. In 2006 in Los Angeles, two employees of the city's traffic authority in a labor dispute accessed the Automated Traffic Surveillance Center and shut down the system at key intersections in the car-overpopulated city. One could imagine that instead of disabling a few intersections, a skilled hostile could turn all the city's traffic lights green. The number of accidents and casualties would be incalculable.

Distributed Denial of Service (DDoS)

Estonians tend to glorify the most minor of our international achievements, as is to be expected and as we see on the part of all small countries.

What we fail to recognize, though, is that since 2007 we have been known as the place where state-on-state cyber war occurred for the first time. Yes, we had seen hacks and other occasional tricks and nuisance operations, but if we take Carl von Clausewitz' classical definition of war as "the continuation of policy by other means," this was truly the first time that digital means were used as a form of debilitating aggression by one nation-state. This was Russia's response to the government moving a Soviet statue that had become the focal point of civil disturbances. Estonia was not invaded; it was not attacked kinetically. No one was killed, but Russia managed effectively to shut down the entire country. Media, banks, and the government could barely function. Estonia had to digitally cut itself off from the rest of the world. Being first, when we went to the EU and NATO, they did not understand what we were talking about.

DDoS stands for Distributed Denial of Service. It refers to the bombardment and overloading of servers with so many messages that they simply stop responding. Any server so targeted will shut down. There are many ways to do this, using hijacked computers that have been turned into robot messengers called bots. One computer is not enough, so mafia gangs that use bots create networks called botnets that send these overloading messages for a fee. Primarily they are used for spam, which was a big problem in the 2000s. These days, DDoS attacks are more likely to use internet devices—routers for example—or closed-circuit TVs that have been hijacked by someone.

DDoS attacks also are a form of hybrid war, in this case using criminal gangs in the service of a nation state. But even individuals can perform them, as was the case with the largest DDoS attack ever, the Myrai attack in 2016. A single graduate student at Rutgers University in New Jersey created a self-perpetuating DDoS botnet of closed-circuit TVs and routers and blacked out servers on the East coast of the US as well as Western Europe.

In a strict sense, each of these cyberattacks differs from kinetic attacks in one other critical way: attribution or the ability to assign responsibility.

The Attribution Issue

A fundamental security and defense issue with cyberattacks—one that distinguishes digital use of force from kinetic—is attribution, more specifically, its difficulty. In a kinetic attack, the source of the attack is almost immediately clear, often even before any kinetic damage occurs. Often you can see it coming, and, if not, can easily determine where it came from.

Attribution with cyberattacks is difficult and laborious. Although using digital forensics as well HUMINT or human intelligence (as apparently was the case with North Korea's attack on Sony), it is possible with reasonable assurance ultimately to know the source of a digital attack, attribution takes time. An immediate response is rarely possible. A state also needs to be sure an attack was not a "false flag" operation to avoid the possibility of a counterattack on the wrong party. Moreover, even with a high level of confidence in the source of an attack, in twenty years, no identified attackers have yet to admit to committing a cyberattack.

Equally problematic is outsourcing by states to non-governmental hackers, adding to deniability of responsibility. This is the digital form of military subcontracting, as used by the Kremlin in the kinetic world with the "Wagner group" in Syria, Ukraine, the Central African Republic, and elsewhere. Is a "rogue hacking group" genuinely rogue? How does a subcontracting group of hackers differ from one consisting of GRU or PLA officers?

Information Warfare and Disinformation

Attacks on our cyber security have evolved, and the scope and extent of the threat is ever increasing. One of the greatest cyberattack threats is posed by disinformation. Many have heard of the so-called *Internet Research Agency*, the St. Petersburg troll farm that has spread disinformation around the liberal democratic West.

Disinformation is nothing new. In written literature, it goes back to *The Aeneid* and the story of the Trojan horse. And we have seen massive disinformation campaigns throughout the twentieth century, most famously the KGB-manufactured story that the CIA created the HIV virus that causes AIDS. This was planted in a provincial communist party newspaper, *The Patriot*, in India in 1983 and eventually made its way into mainstream European and American newspapers. Contrast that with the ten or so variant stories about the shooting down of Malaysian Airliner MH17 by the Russians in July of 2014. Within hours of the accident, social as well as mainstream media was filled with disinformation.

Prior to the widespread availability of the iPhone and Android phones, relatively few people had access to computers. Even in the most internet-connected country, the US, only one-third of households had computers at home and a smaller number had reliable internet access. Elsewhere, the number was far smaller and in developing countries such as in the Arab World and Russia, far fewer. The smartphone changed all that. Everyone could access the World Wide Web.

Facebook was the first major social media company and remains preeminent with over 2.3 billion users. But the huge leap took place with the smartphone app. Previously, you could access the internet on the phone via a URL (and signing in with your passport), but with the app on the phone, all it took was a mere push of the finger and you were on. Today in much of the world, where for almost all people the smart phone is the sole connection to the internet, large numbers of people think Facebook is the internet.

Arab Spring

The first major case of the smart phone plus social media as a major political tool took place in 2011 in the so-called Arab Spring, when large masses of people revolted, posting smartphone videos and pictures of brutality and regime crimes on Facebook and other platforms, reaching tens if not hundreds of thousands of people across the Arab world as well as the world at large—images that soon spread also to television.

The Arab Spring began in Tunisia, and spread to Libya, Egypt, Yemen, Syria, and Bahrain, and led to the authoritarian leaders of Tunisia, Libya, and Egypt being deposed. The war in Syria and Yemen is still going on. These happened in rapid succession, where pictures of protests and police crackdown spread in minutes via Facebook. At this point, Facebook and many pro-democracy activists and social scientists proclaimed the beginning of a new era, in which civil society would bring down despotic governments merely with the help of social media and the smart phone.

You no longer need a kinetic war to change policy by other means.

Unfortunately, it didn't turn out that way. Leaving aside that there are brutal civil wars still going on in Libya, Yemen, and Syria, the real lesson that came out of this was the power of social media. Authoritarian governments, and for the purpose of European security, Russia, concluded that if civil society with no government or government resources behind it can overthrow governments via mass protests enabled by social media, imagine how much more powerful this could be if the full power and finances of the state were behind a social media campaign. And on top of that, imagine if instead of just spreading news, you spread lies.

As we know from numerous studies, false, exaggerated, and sensationalist stories are shared or retweeted far more often than news that nothing happened. We saw this first during the Ukraine crisis of 2014 when the Russians spread the news that Ukrainians had crucified a three-year-old boy. This was a completely false story. Yet it spread like wildfire. Ukraine turned out to be the testing ground for using social media to spread false and misleading news.

The next time it was successfully used in the West was in 2015 during the association agreement referendum for Ukraine and the EU in the Netherlands, which began as a social media-inspired petition for a referendum. (There had never been an association agreement referendum. It's a minor treaty, a free trade agreement really, which Estonia signed in 1995, almost ten years before finally acceding to the EU.) The next time the Russians tried an active campaign, again successfully, was for the Brexit referendum. Of course, domestic forces played a role, as they generally do, but you accomplish your goal merely by changing political opinion.

Since 2016 we have seen an explosion of fake news. In 2016, as I mentioned, Russia mounted a frontal assault on Hillary Clinton in the US using hacked materials, highly targeted advertising, and fake newspapers with fake news. And, as some scholars argue, through targeting key states, they changed the results enough to allow Donald Trump to win. This is because in the US you win in the electoral college. In the popular vote—which does not directly count—Hilary won by three million votes.

What Does This Mean for Security?

First and foremost, this means that you no longer need a kinetic war to change policy by other means. Before the Digital Era, physical possession of territory was—other than buying off the leadership of a country—the only way to win. War is expensive; it is an enormous, potentially ruinous drain on resources. Many of your own population are killed, GDP plummets, post-war economies are in tatters, and of course, you run the risk, in the case of attacking NATO, of a nuclear war that will destroy your own country. If you win in a conventional, non-nuclear war, you will have to pay forever for the costs of occupation of a hostile, resentful population, as both Nazi Germany and the USSR discovered.

Instead of invading a NATO country and risking via Article 5 a war with the forces of NATO, an adversary nation instead changes a government using finances, disinformation, and hacking confidential information to alter a democratic election to elect an anti-NATO, anti-EU party or presidential candidate.

We have seen this a number of times since Russia adopted social media disinformation as a tool of political manipulation. In 2015, for the first time ever, an EU country held a referendum on an association agreement. Using a low threshold for holding referenda in the Netherlands, the country held a plebiscite on Ukraine's association agreement. Social media sites spread disinformation about Ukraine, Russians pretending to be Ukrainians held disruptive false-flag demonstrations.

In 2016, as has been extensively described, Russia interfered massively in the US presidential elections using both hacking and social media. In 2020 the UK Parliament's Intelligence and Security Committee issued a long-delayed report on Russian interference in the UK elections. Meanwhile Russian interference in the Brexit referendum was not reported since the government had declined to investigate. In the run-up to the French presidential election, Russia loaned Marine Le Pen, the anti-NATO candidate, 9 million Euros for her campaign, actively spread disinformation about Emmanuel Macron, and hacked his server—this last undertaking fell flat because, after the Hillary Clinton hack, the French prepared by seeding their server with their own disinformation. Most recently, Russia went all out with a disinformation campaign to discredit the German Green Party and its leader, Annalena Baerbock.

Что делать?

. . . Or as Lenin asked, "What is to be done?" What is important to realize is that security is no longer just a matter of a strong kinetic military. Yes, that is necessary—you can't fight an invading army with memes, but when adversaries come to rely on different weapons, you do need a greatly expanded notion of what security is. Currently, we face a number of problems in dealing with these threats.

The most significant problem is a lack of understanding among policy makers of the importance of digital threats. True, at least when it comes to hacking, there is now some awareness on the part of militaries and at least some companies.

We face two broad problems in this regard: we lack interdisciplinary, inter-agency cooperation and we have national silos that effect feeble international and multilateral information sharing. Clearly, when foreign ministries, parliaments, think tanks, candidates in elections, and even the World Anti-Doping Agency are all attacked by one of the Russian hacking groups (APT 28 and 29), Europe and NATO do not share information sufficiently.

In part this is explained by the SIGINT background of those who deal with hacking. Signal intelligence is a form of espionage, a realm with a tradition of holding information close to the vest. The sole information-sharing SIGINT group is the Five Eyes alliance, consisting of the US, UK, Canada, New Zealand, and Australia. That includes no other NATO allies (though two non-allies) and no EU member states. However, adversary groups—whether APT 28 or 29 or the infamous troll and disinformation farm, the Internet Research Agency—do not base their activities on who belongs to which multilateral group. Borders mean nothing in cyberspace and social media.

The most significant problem is a lack of understanding among policy makers of the importance of digital threats. We face two broad problems in this regard: we lack interdisciplinary, inter-agency cooperation and we have national silos that effect feeble international and multilateral information sharing.

Indeed, the truly dramatic change the Digital Era has brought to security is that geography no longer matters. NATO after all is the *North Atlantic* Treaty Organization not because the North Atlantic represents a unique group of liberal democracies. Nor are Japan, South Korea, Australia, and New Zealand excluded from NATO for a failure to adhere to liberal democracy. NATO was and is an organization not to a small degree based on bomber range, jet fighter refueling capabilities, troop and tank transport, and equipment logistics. With all the considerable planning and infrastructure development through its seven decades, cyber did not come into planning until only recently, and even there to a limited degree. Two of some eighty NATO Centres of Excellence, one for cyber issues based in

Tallinn and a second to assess disinformation in Riga, are largely hampered by their mandates: they can report on attacks on NATO, the organization, but have limited authority to assess and report attacks on individual member states—essentially limiting already limited defense with proscriptions. Neither has any operational authority. I do understand that cooperation has improved since a little more than a decade ago when Estonia reported to NATO that it had found a Russian worm in its military network and the response was "Oh, you too." For an organization that requires strong common standards and interoperability of weapons systems, the attention paid to cyber and disinformation attacks is woefully weak.

In the European Union, a focus on PESCO (Permanent Structured Cooperation) as a kind of parallel NATO structure doesn't quite fit the bill either. While ENISA (The European Union Agency for Cybersecurity) was created to deal with these issues, it simply does not carry the heft and weight to be able to respond. Similarly, a recent op-ed by Wolfgang Ischinger, chairman of the West's premier security forum, the Munich Security Conference, laments the complete lack of a security dimension in EU legislation.[2] New digital era competition regulations that do not take into account digital security, as if all platforms and devices are playing on a level playing field show how little the EU's policies have been concerned with the new threats the digital era poses to privacy and security. As Ulrike Franke and Jose Ignacio Torreblanca wrote in a recent paper for the ECFR, ". . . the EU, for all its pathbreaking work on regulation, does not appear to have fully recognized just how geopolitical technology can be—or how geopolitical the current generation of emerging, primarily digital, technologies has become."[3]

Today, neither of the West's premier international institutions has come to grips with the complete transformation of the security environment, where Tallinn, Toronto, and Tokyo are spatially and temporally equidistant in a potential attack from an adversary; indeed, one major economic and political democracy isn't even in the loop because of dated, geographically based security arrangements. Nor does this piece even delve into another whole aspect of security, artificial intelligence, with respect to which, since the departure of the UK from the EU, Europe has ceased to be a player.

Any serious approach to security of liberal democracies, moreover, will have to go beyond current institutional limitations. Why in the Digital Era would we leave out Japan, South Korea, New Zealand, Australia, and—given its crucial role in chip production—Taiwan? Moreover, why stop there? If we want liberal democracies to be secure in the Digital Era, why not include Switzerland, Israel, Uruguay, Chile, and Costa Rica—all digitally advanced nations?

Today, however, when the European Commission's primary mission seems to be reining in GAFA, the Five Eyes do not even talk to Europe, and a number of critical potential allies are not on our radar screens at all, we need to begin to rethink what security means in the Digital Era.

Technology changes conflict, war, and so too obviously, security. From weapons of stone to bronze to iron, technological developments give an advantage to those who have them. Stirrups and gun powder too, changed the nature of conflict. The first made the cavalry far more versatile, and the second rendered medieval castles useless.

Today, the West as a whole continues to build or at least plans to build castles that are more in the air than grounded in reality, while our adversaries are busy producing ever-better gunpowder.

Toomas Hendrik Ilves is a former President and Foreign Minister of Estonia and the originator in 1995 of Estonia's Tiger Leap program to digitize public services in his country. Currently, he is a Visiting Professor of Democratic Digital Governance at Tartu University.

Mastering the Art of Deniability

Thomas Rid

The first twenty years of the twenty-first century were marked by a full-blown revolution in intelligence.[1] That revolution is of historic proportions, ongoing, yet often ignored. Several elements drive this sea change in how information is collected in secret or put to effect under cover, ranging from the technical to the cultural, from the political to the historical, from tradecraft to diplomacy. I will focus here on the most visible and most antagonistic aspect: the remarkable return and expansion of covert action.

Examples of events that have all the trappings of covert intelligence activity abound. A full a list of recent cases would include the following entries: the 2007 distributed-denial-of-service attacks against Estonia; the late 2000s campaign known as Stuxnet; various wiping attacks against Iranian targets in 2011; the 2012 attack against Saudi Aramco and Rasgas; the neglected 2013 Britam Defence leak; the 2014 Sony Entertainment breach-and-leak; two remarkable blackouts in Kiev in 2015 and 2016, as well numerous other operations in Ukraine; the series of breach-and-leak operations against the US election in 2016; the mysterious series of Shadow Brokers leaks; the destructive attacks known as Wannacry and NotPetya in 2017; and many more, some of them subtle, others as yet not publicly discussed.

The apparent proliferation and prevalence of remotely executed, computer-enabled, hands-only-on-keyboard cases raise a curious question: has the rise of the internet enabled an entirely new class of covert action?

Traditional covert action of course persists, for instance the covert support for militias or media organizations in contested places, or temporarily covert assassinations. Yet the apparent proliferation and prevalence of remotely executed, computer-enabled, hands-only-on-keyboard cases raise a curious question: has the rise of the internet enabled an entirely new class of covert action? What characterizes these new operations? And do these operations require an equally innovative approach to operations and diplomacy to counter them?

Digital covert action, this short essay argues, can only be understood in conjunction with—and in juxtaposition to—another new and partly related trend in twenty-first-century intelligence operations: the reemergence of public attribution of intelligence operations that go beyond classical espionage, including adversarial covert action. The majority of large, network-enabled covert actions in the past two decades has been attributed, but not always by governments, to other government-linked entities. These attributions were made with varying levels of confidence and certainty, from low confidence to full certainty—yet attributed they were, in most cases. One intelligence activity, in short, cannot be understood without the other. The two practices are sharply different yet closely intertwined; they form the core of an intricate escalation in intelligence competition, albeit an asymmetric escalation. Asymmetric because at closer inspection it is closed societies and authoritarian regimes that tend to focus on covert action and neglect public counterintelligence—while the reverse tends to be the case for open societies and liberal democracies, although there are exceptions on either side.

The argument, in short, is this: the internet itself has enabled a set of surprisingly sharp, dialectic interactions between computer-enabled covert action and computer-enabled counterintelligence, in ways that probably have no historical precedent. At the core of this dialectic is *deniability*. Covert action and public counterintelligence compete for deniability—the goal of the former is to take it and keep it, the goal of the latter is to take it away.

Five mutually reinforcing interactions, or *Wechselwirkungen*, spring from this basic observation, in Clausewitzian terms.

Deniability

First, conceptual clarity is needed. *Digital covert action* is the art and science of crafting and administering effects that are enabled, at least in part, by some form of computer network operation—for example, breaching victims or victim networks, exfiltrating files, and then leaking the stolen material through the use of deceptive assets. Or by orchestrating an influence campaign that uses deceptive assets yet amplifies actual, existing grievances and cleavages in the target society. One central purpose of such operations is the provision of deniability. Covert action, then and now, tends to have a wide range of targets across an adversarial country's political system or wider society.

◂ Thomas Rid at the MSC Cyber Security Summit in Silicon Valley in September 2016.

Digital counterintelligence is the art and science of finding, identifying, clustering, exposing, and possibly attributing adversarial intelligence operations, with the goal of countering such activity. Often but not always digital counterintelligence involves a public, or partly public, exposure of adversary operations, infrastructure, or other indicators. The counterintelligence action may counter both espionage or covert action. Such activity may have multiple overlapping goals, for instance to "burn" infrastructure on a tactical level or to deter an adversary on a strategic level. One core purpose, in nearly all cases, is the removal of deniability. Here it is important to note that per definition, counterintelligence has a narrow set of targets: spy agencies, their proxies, and their political masters.

A short but important historical caveat is also in order. The practice of public counterintelligence, notably, is not new, but simply reemerging, if in force and in new ways. The US intelligence community started publicly countering Soviet covert action, specifically a subset then known as "active measures." On June 2, 1961, Richard Helms, who had overseen the CIA's own covert operations as Deputy Director for Plans, presented a wide range of artifacts and evidence to Congress, in a hearing that exposed dozens of Eastern bloc covert measures against the United States and its allies. The CIA put an extraordinary amount of attention into preparing the documentation for this hearing, and authorized the publication of multiple appendixes with artifacts, 127 pages in total.[2] Indeed, the hearing itself was a form of public counterintelligence. In later hearings in the 1980s, the agency went even further. The CIA revealed some of its investigative techniques, even having its own investigators and analysts testify on how the CIA built its attributive capabilities.

Deniability itself offers the first interaction. Deniability is different from denial. Denial is the explicit refusal to claim responsibility for an action. One prominent example is the Kremlin's persistent practice of denying that Russian entities were behind the attempted interference in the 2016 election. Deniability, by contrast, is a more subtle, more abstract, and more dynamic property.

At first glance, deniability may appear as a diminishing asset. An actor may continue to deny yet lose deniability in relation to a specific action. A prominent example is the French government's initial denial of the sinking of the *Rainbow Warrior,* a Greenpeace ship, in New Zealand, in July 1985. Only two months later, the evidence implicating the French government was so overwhelming that the French prime minister admitted to a covert DGSE operation to sink the ship. *Deniability*, in simple terms, is determined by the structure of an action, by the intelligence that has become available on the action, and by the credibility of the actor in question. Deniability may quickly erode in response to new information becoming available. Deniability is also a non-binary property that in some cases may diminish but not be entirely reduced to zero. Even in the face of overwhelming evidence that entirely exposes a perpetrator, that perpetrator's denial may still retain some appeal for specific groups or individuals in the target country, for political or psychological reasons. The most prominent example was Donald Trump's apparent inability to admit that Russian intelligence had attempted to interfere in the election that he won.

If the deniability of an action is either too low or too high, then deniability may disappear entirely and—counterintuitively—lose its value for the perpetrators either way. Diminished deniability implies a higher risk of consequences, for instance economic sanctions or international arrest warrants or diplomatic isolation. Excess deniability, on the other side, means an operation has no clear symbolic, strategic, or political value (beyond a potential tactical value), perhaps comparable to a natural event like a provably accidental explosion in a munitions factory, a lightning-caused fire, or a traffic accident. One example is the infamous "Saudi Cables" leak, sourced from an advanced network breach at the Saudi Foreign Ministry, published on a mysterious website, wikisaleaks.com,[3] and adopted as a Wikileaks leak—no noteworthy public attribution was ever achieved in this case.

Events with excess deniability may have direct effects, including intended effects, but no sufficiently clear political messages or threats attached to them as an indirect effect (although private messaging to targets should not be excluded, sometimes even on public channels). Public counterintelligence may therefore sometimes work, counterintuitively, in favor of the perpetrators, by keeping an operation's deniability in a productive range—not too high, and not too low.

Speed

The second interaction is related to speed. *The faster that a covert action is countered by contesting its deniability, the more effective the response will be.* Yet an immediate tension will emerge. Investigating in detail what actually happened will take time, including for instance the sifting of large volumes of log files and images, follow-on research into the full range of infrastructure used, the targeted analysis of large volumes of intelligence data, issuing subpoenas and awaiting responses, and even follow-on intelligence tasking to shed light an operation through targeted intelligence collection. In short, speed favors covert action—patience favors counterintelligence.

Yet there is a counteracting dynamic at work. *The more successful an operation, the harder it will be to keep it covert in the long term.* Deniability has a half-life, and the covert aspect of covert action is almost always temporary. Yet the half-life of an operation's secrecy is not a given constant like the half-life of a radioactive isotope; it is a function of the resources that are invested in solving a case. These resources, in turn, are a function of the political stakes at play.

Active measures and covert action operators tend to be pragmatists, not perfectionists. They tend to understand that an action may not remain covert for extended periods of time, for several reasons: first, its effects, by definition, are visible to the target, even if the target cannot immediately explain what is happening. An example is Iranian enrichment centrifuges in Natanz no longer spinning at the speeds for which they were programmed, and the engineers struggling to understand what is going on, let alone to appreciate that they were the target of a sabotage campaign. Second, digital covert measures—and even digital clandestine intelligence operations—leave behind a host of digital forensic artifacts, from malware samples, on disk or in memory, to log files and command-and-control infrastructure. It is likely that investigators, often in the private sector, will notice such traces and act on them in one fashion or the other, for example by updating security products so they can detect the newly discovered, mysterious threat, or by sharing the new-found indicators with partners, thus making full exposure more likely in the long run. Third, especially large operations of historic proportion, especially when considered successful, will tempt the operators, organizations, and political leaders to make information public after the fact, even if anonymously. Here again, Stuxnet is a useful example. US government sources anonymously gave information on the operation to investigative journalists, and engineers would hint at their roles on the sidelines of some technical conferences.

Deniability has a half-life, and the covert aspect of covert action is almost always temporary.

The most potent, and probably still the most common form of disclosure, in the long term, is to have the perpetrators speak for themselves. Intelligence agencies and intelligence officers speak for themselves in three principal ways: first by opening their archives, in most cases only decades after the fact. Archival sources are some of the most detailed and most reliable artifacts we have to describe covert action and active measures across their full lifecycle, from proposal to termination. The second way in which intelligence officers speak for themselves is by writing or talking about their work. Such disclosures tend to be more detailed and revealing if the officers in question either defected to another country, where they can be debriefed more formally, or if their former employers no longer exist, for instance in the case of former Eastern bloc intelligence organizations. Finally, there is the less common unauthorized disclosure of intelligence documents by leaks. The Snowden leaks, for instance, enabled the detailed attribution of a range of Five Eyes intelligence operations that would have remained undiscovered and unattributed otherwise.

Visibility

The third interaction is related to the public aspect of both types of operations. *The public counterintelligence response to a covert action will affect the countered action; the defense interacts with the offense.* Put differently, the response to a covert action should neither fall significantly behind the visibility and impact of an offensive operation nor should it exceed the offensive act in visibility and impact. In the case of imbalance, in either direction, the offense likely has the advantage.

The textbook case for a covert action overshadowing the target's reaction is offered by Operations Plan 10-1. In the early 1960s, the KGB successfully penetrated the US Army Forces Courier Center at Orly Field, Paris, with a spy. The spy handed a large volume of photographs of top-secret US military documents to Moscow. Once he was exposed, the KGB decided to recycle some of the material in a series of leaks, amplified by forgeries. The highly controversial documents revealed US nuclear targeting in Western Europe, including in West Germany, as well as aggressive unconventional war plans for special forces to fight behind enemy lines in the case of a Red Army invasion of Western Europe. The US State Department counted twenty surfacings of these highly damaging leaks across Europe—yet failed to respond to the operation, arguably making it more effective as a result.[4]

The response to a covert action should neither fall significantly behind the visibility and impact of an offensive operation nor should it exceed the offensive act in visibility and impact. In the case of imbalance, in either direction, the offense likely has the advantage.

A more recent illustration is The Shadow Brokers incident—tactically one of the most destructive and costly leaks in intelligence history. Yet the US government, at all levels, has studiously avoided acknowledging the incident or shedding any light on it, thus giving rise to the theory that the Shadow Brokers were perhaps one of the most sophisticated and effective covert actions ever to target the NSA.

A covert action—or the outputs of a covert action—can be highly visible and likely impactful, or it may lack impact, or alternatively be detected at an early stage before even any meaningful impact could be achieved. This problem is exacerbated by a new dynamic. The internet has lowered the risk threshold for covert action. Remote on-keyboard action is far less risky than traveling into foreign territory and planning or executing an operation on the ground, even a simple one. The result is a higher prevalence of low-quality, low-impact attempts at covert action. This situation offers unique difficulties for investigators ahead of a revelation or "takedown," as the practice is known in social media companies. The takedown would often receive significant press coverage and attention on social media, and thus risk having a bigger effect, and more public visibility, than the revealed, takedown campaign itself. Several Facebook takedowns from 2018 to 2020 illustrate this asymmetry, especially in cases in which Facebook removed campaigns in early stages—in some cases, the removal or dozens of fake accounts and pages with low numbers of followers or impressions in turn created hundreds of press stories with high numbers of readers and impressions, thus creating an inevitable second-order effect that vastly outperformed the first-order effect.[5] Press interest in the subject of disinformation, paradoxically, resulted in more visibility for disinformation in the exposure stage.

Effects

Attribution doesn't stop with the *who*, it includes the *why* and the *so-what*. Identifying perpetrators, such as governments, agencies, units, or individuals, is one important step in public counterintelligence. Identifying intentions and goals that go into an operation, and the effectiveness in reaching these goals, is as least as important—and it is harder. The so-called cyber kill chain is a seven-step conceptual model to analyze network intrusions from reconnaissance all the way to action-on-target; what is missing in the model, however, and what cannot be gleaned from network forensics, is phase zero (planning) and phase eight (assessment). Attributing phase zero and phase eight is hard but crucial. For without doing so it is much more difficult to gauge an appropriate public counterintelligence response.

This specific attribution problem brings into sharp relief another counterintuitive interaction: *the effect that is easiest to determine and to measure is the counterintelligence effect.*

Both covert action and counterintelligence operate in a zone of epistemological ambiguity when it comes to assessing their effectiveness—and both offenders and defenders deal with this baked-in uncertainty. Assessing the effectiveness of the GRU operation to interfere in the US general election of 2016, for example, is inherently difficult for both the victim and for adversarial intelligence agencies. This lack of a "measurement device," as one Soviet bloc active measures defector put it to me in an interview, is a feature of disinformation operations, for example, as they attempt to exploit existing social or political divisions that would have continued to develop independent of an operation anyway. Assessing the effectiveness of the US public counterintelligence response is equally ambiguous for the US government—but not for the GRU.

Any public attribution claim with a counterintelligence purpose has two fundamentally different modes of communication that are, by definition, wrapped into one act, for instance the publication of a government press release or a law enforcement document such as an indictment. Those two modes of communication address two fundamentally different audiences: the perpetrators and third-party audiences.

The third-party audiences are primarily a domestic audience, and only then an international audience of stakeholders, including third party governments, third party network defenders, and other actual and potential victims.

The prime target audience for any public attribution claim is the adversary in question. But the adversary, crucially, does not need to be convinced of the validity of the attribution claim—the perpetrators and their superiors already know the fact that they committed an operation that is now publicly revealed, albeit in a partly deniable way. For the adversary, the question is how much of a campaign is revealed, how thoroughly and how accurately, how the revelation affects active assets still in use, and what the negative and positive aspects of the disclosure are.

The irony, of course, is that the recipients of successful counterintelligence measures will, in turn, try to keep that effect secret or deny it.

Open versus Closed

The final interaction is political and related to the constitutional form of the governments engaged in either intelligence activity.

Deniable covert action, at the core, is an undemocratic tactic that is incompatible with core values of accountability, openness, and transparency. The more ambitious an operation is in its goals, the harder it will be for a democratically accountable intelligence agency to succeed in planning, funding, authorizing, and executing covert operations that rely, often to a significant extent, on deniability. The risk of subsequent exposure of successful covert operations is also significantly higher in an open democracy.

The main ethical and ultimately political problem is the wide target set of many on-keyboard covert operations, which often resemble what used to be called active measures. Such operations may target entire political communities or subcultures, for instance by attempting to widen existing racial or cultural or political divisions. But once the target set is narrowed to individual intelligence agencies—again counterintuitively—some covert action tactics become attractive for public counterintelligence tactics deployed by an increasing number of liberal democracies.

The critical context here is the proliferation of entities and actors that take part in the public attribution process. By the early twenties, it has become possible to reveal details about adversarial intelligence operations in creative ways, by using the help—witting and unwitting—of an entire investigative counterintelligence community that has developed in the first two decades of this century.[6] Public attribution is enabled, in creative ways, by non-governmental entities, first and foremost by cutting-edge cybersecurity companies, but also by educators, non-profit investigators, activists, and even hobbyists. Perhaps ironically, it has become possible to feed investigative leads into this community in ways that are covert and, if necessary, deniable.

The rise of what effectively is a cross-cutting counterintelligence community presents unprecedented challenges to diplomacy. Three stand out. First, career diplomats, often trained as generalists, frequently lack the subject-matter focus and the skills to appreciate the nuances of what can be rather technical case studies and debates. Governments that historically had a close working relationship between diplomacy and intelligence may therefore have an advantage in countering covert action in the twenty-first century, notably the United Kingdom and, to a lesser extent, the United States. A second challenge for diplomacy follows from the sharp contrast between open and closed systems. Diplomats from aggressive authoritarian countries will follow a very different rulebook and ethical standards when compared with diplomats that represent open societies. It will be in the interest of open societies to emphasize and broadcast this ethical asymmetry in diplomacy—and thus to defend their own credibility against persistent attempted portrayals of moral equivalency. Western diplomats, as a consequence, should strictly refrain from attempting to craft norms of attribution in forums that include non-democratic states. Finally, foreign service offices in liberal democracies will have to react to digital covert action, disinformation, hacks and leaks, and other dirty tricks—almost always—on the basis of incomplete and unsatisfactory knowledge of the evidence and the facts. In those moments, these Western diplomats may find reassurance in the historically informed observation that the foreign service officers in the authoritarian governments accused of perpetrating covert action in many cases are not read into details, and will have even less of an idea what really happened.

The rise of what effectively is a cross-cutting counterintelligence community presents unprecedented challenges to diplomacy.

Thomas Rid is Professor of Strategic Studies and Founding Director of the Alperovitch Institute for Cybersecurity Studies at Johns Hopkins University's School of Advanced International Studies (SAIS) in Washington, DC. His most recent book, *Active Measures: The Secret History of Disinformation and Political Warfare,* was published in 2020.

Cyber Security
September 19 – 20, 201

Treating Cyber Problems as Geopolitical Problems

Dmitri Alperovitch

In September of 2015, President Barack Obama stood next to Chinese President Xi Jinping in the White House Rose Garden to announce that the United States and the People's Republic of China (PRC) had reached a historic deal to curb cyber-related economic espionage. In the universe of cyber-related threats, the scope of the two leaders' agreement was fairly modest: to prevent their respective governments from engaging in state-sponsored cyber intrusions to steal private intellectual property and trade secrets with the intent of providing a competitive advantage to domestic commercial sectors. The agreement was an easy commitment for the US side, since it has long had a prohibition on intelligence services conducting economic espionage for the benefit of private companies, but it was an important and groundbreaking pledge to receive from China. Shortly after the Rose Garden press conference, China announced a similar agreement with the United Kingdom, and in November of 2015, China joined Germany, France, Russia, and other members of the Group of Twenty in recognizing a norm against conducting cyber-enabled economic espionage.

The vast majority of cyberattacks targeting the US and its allies emanate from the four countries that also pose the greatest risk to the allies in conventional space: Russia, China, Iran, and North Korea. We do not have a cyber problem; we have a Russia, China, Iran, and North Korea problem.

The US-China agreement was noteworthy not only for what it hoped to achieve but also for how it hoped to do it. For the first time in the history of America's handling of cyber espionage, President Obama threatened to impose sanctions on Chinese companies and citizens who continued to target US companies or continued to benefit from stolen intellectual property. "What I've said to President Xi and what I say to the American people is the question now is, are words followed by actions?" President Obama said in his remarks announcing the agreement. "We will be watching carefully to make an assessment as to whether progress has been made in this area."[1]

The success of the Obama-Xi agreement was short-lived. Although the agreement led to a brief pause of cyber-enabled economic espionage originating from China, the détente came to an end by 2018, after the Trump administration imposed initial tariffs on $34 billion of Chinese imports in response to its findings that the PRC had systematically stolen US intellectual property. The tariffs sparked a trade war that undercut the economic leverage that implicitly underpinned the 2015 agreement, rendering it functionally moot. By 2018 the National Security Agency had publicly accused the Chinese of violating the agreement, and the US declined to impose sanctions in response.

Its long-term failure notwithstanding, the Obama-Xi agreement should serve as a model for allied action on cyber in both the bilateral and multilateral forums. The fundamental strength of the agreement was that it treated cyber-enabled economic espionage not as a narrow cyber problem but as part of a broader geopolitical competition. The Obama administration correctly understood that China's relentless pursuit of American intellectual property and trade secrets was part of its long-term effort to overtake the United States both economically and militarily, and that cyber-enabled economic espionage was only one part of that effort. Its response—the threat of economic sanction—was calibrated to undermine not the cyber activity itself but China's broader geopolitical goal.

Much has changed since 2015, both in terms of China's place in the world and the global cyber threat landscape. Nevertheless, the insight embodied in the Obama-Xi agreement remains more important than ever: cyber problems are at their core geopolitical problems, which have been exacerbated by the asymmetric capabilities brought on by cyber offense. Solving these challenges requires an understanding of the root geopolitical causes that create and stoke cyber conflict and a deft use of diplomatic tools to mitigate it.

The vast majority of cyberattacks targeting the US and its allies emanate from the four countries that also pose the greatest risk to the allies in conventional space: Russia, China, Iran, and North Korea. As I have been saying for the past half decade, we do not have a cyber problem; we have a Russia, China, Iran, and North Korea problem.

Each country's actions in cyberspace mirror its broader geopolitical goals. The PRC, which had made no secret of its ambition to leapfrog the United States

◂ Dmitri Alperovitch at the MSC Cyber Security Summit in Silicon Valley in September 2016.

as the world's leading economic and military superpower, has engaged in extensive economic espionage for the purpose of funneling stolen intellectual property and trade secrets to its domestic industries. Unsurprisingly, China's cyber espionage has been particularly aggressive in areas that it deems critical to its economic and national security objectives, such as semiconductors, 5G, and defense technology.

Russia, the other one of the allies' most prominent cyber adversaries, has engaged in some targeted economic and traditional espionage, but the bulk of its cyber activity seeks to advance its primary geopolitical goal: to preserve its status as global power by undermining the United States' global reputation and frustrating its international ambitions, especially in the region that Russia views as its exclusive sphere of influence. Russia's penchant for destructive attacks, its unapologetic interference in democratic elections, and its tolerance for ransomware criminals operating within its borders are all responses to its enduring suspicion that the US and its allies are seeking to undermine Russia's control over its near-abroad region and undercut its ruling elite at home.

There is no silver bullet, technological or otherwise, for resolving cyber threats. In the long term, the allies will not be able to solve the cyber challenges that they face without making progress on the broader geopolitical conflicts that manifest in these threats.

North Korea and Iran have similarly used cyber tools to advance their domestic and international goals. North Korea has used cybercrime to accumulate tens of millions of dollars in illicit gains to finance its regime, while Iran has used cyber-enabled economic espionage to circumvent Western sanctions on the acquisition of strategic technologies. In the regional context, both nations have used cyberattacks to target their regional opponents, with North Korea launching attacks against South Korea and Iran targeting Saudi Arabia and Israel.

The lesson to be drawn from this analysis is this: there is no silver bullet, technological or otherwise, for resolving cyber threats. Defensive measures are important but will be insufficient on their own to address these threats. In the long term, the allies will not be able to solve the cyber challenges that they face without making progress on the broader geopolitical conflicts that manifest in these threats.

To address China's cyber intrusions, the allies will have to convince China's leaders to make significant legal and practical reforms to address forced technology transfer, IP theft, and market-distorting industrial subsidies in exchange for a de-escalation of the ongoing trade war. If allied democracies want to make progress with Russia on election interference campaigns, disruptive attacks, and ransomware, they will have to devise the right combination of carrots and sticks that will resolve Russia's concerns about US interference in their domestic and foreign affairs while also raising the cost of their tolerance for ransomware criminals to the point that the cost of inaction outweighs the benefits. Meaningful progress on cyberattacks originating from Iran and North Korea is unlikely so long as the allies' most critical concerns about those nation's respective nuclear weapons programs remain unresolved.

This might seem like a case for gloomy fatalism about the prospect of resolving cyber issues, but it is, in fact, the precise opposite. Like any complex geopolitical challenge, cyber conflicts can be solved using the right combination of incentives, disincentives, and compromises, deployed either in bilateral or multilateral settings. The question for the allies then becomes whether they will be willing to prioritize progress on cyber over other geopolitical objectives—and what they are willing to give up for the sake of that progress.

Dmitri Alperovitch is the Executive Chairman at Silverado Policy Accelerator. He is also Cofounder and Former Chief Technology Officer of CrowdStrike Inc.

MSC Cyber Security Summit in Berlin in November 2019. ►

Maintaining the Negotiating Edge in the Age of Tech-Geopolitics

Sorin Ducaru

The technological accelerations and disruptions of our times are influencing or changing the conduct and enhancing the scope of diplomacy. First, technology is giving rise to important changes in the way diplomacy is being conducted. It offers a great opportunity to enhance the "toolbox" of diplomacy through new, efficient ways of having access to much-needed and relevant information, new and modern ways of fast communication and influencing, message amplifications, and so on. At the same time, these technological opportunities in the conduct of diplomacy also generate some particular challenges, or vulnerabilities related to the security and reliability of the different platforms or technology infrastructures used in the modern conduct of diplomacy. The age of so-called digital or e-diplomacy is not without controversies and challenges. It indeed has an impact upon the methods and tools employed in diplomacy. But I am clearly among those who would challenge the notion that it fundamentally changes the essence of what diplomacy is all about, its "purity" or the unique value and role of the diplomatic vocation.

Second, technology changes the complexity of the diplomatic démarche due to the important changes the new age of technological acceleration is projecting upon the subject matter of diplomatic endeavors, namely the international landscape and the conduct of international relations. The unprecedented impact of these technological accelerations upon the geopolitical landscape is determining the development of novel concepts or areas of conceptual study, coined as: geopolitics of technology, tech-geopolitics, or geotechnology. This development has geostrategic significance and is consequently expanding the area of application of the diplomatic démarche, which implies some specific requirements related to the need to study and comprehend megatrends in technological developments and their impact upon global power dynamics and international relations.

Technology is giving rise to important changes in the way diplomacy is being conducted. It offers a great opportunity to enhance the "toolbox" of diplomacy through new, efficient ways of having access to much-needed and relevant information, new and modern ways of fast communication and influencing, message amplifications, and so on.

Both paths of change are relevant and interesting to study and comprehend in order to adapt modern diplomatic focus, action, and methods to these major tech-enabled changes, with their associated opportunities and challenges.

The Munich Security Conference and its leadership were quite quick to include on the agenda some of the relevant technology-induced game changes for the international landscape, such as cybersecurity or the new space technological race. Being personally involved in these domains in my jobs at NATO and the EU, I am personally grateful to be offered the MSC "stage" by Wolfgang Ischinger and the MSC team and to take part in some of most relevant international debates about cyber-defense or the strategic impact of key technology development trends upon international politics and security. For too long now, these themes have been just on the agenda of side events and fringe debates. I, for one, would clearly propose that the game-changing and accelerated technology megatrends are placed on the front stage of geopolitics and high-level diplomatic action.

Some Conceptual Clarifications in an Evolving Geopolitical Landscape

"Diplomacy" is not a term that should require too many explanations. It is widely used as a "brand"—function, profession, or vocation with a key role in the conduct of international relations. In his book on the history of diplomacy, Sir Harold Nicolson describes diplomacy as the management of international relations by means of negotiations or the art of implementing foreign policy by negotiation.[1]

In more detailed terms, diplomacy is considered as the art, method, or process of influencing the decisions and behavior of foreign governments and peoples through dialogue, negotiation, and other measures short of war or violence. Therefore, diplomacy is employed as the main substitute for the use of force in statecraft. It is about the way national power is applied to peaceful adjustment of differences between states. It is therefore clear that, in essence, diplomacy is about a method based on negotiation and non-violent influencing of states, the main actors in international relations. It is many times coined as an area of special vocation or "art" given the complex mix of comprehensive knowledge, talent, training, skills, access to continuously updated information, etc.,

◂ Sorin Ducaru at the MSC Cyber Security Roundtable in Brussels in November 2017.

required for the efficient conduct of diplomacy.

While the essential scope and method of diplomacy have remained the same, its "toolbox," conduct, complexity of deployment, as well as outreach vectors toward an enhanced number of relevant actors, have evolved tremendously.

The term "geopolitics" was coined by Swedish political scientist Rudolf Kjellén, at the beginning of the last century, as the analysis of the geographic influences on power relationships in international relations.[2]

Strategic considerations about the political effects of geography, topography, land, climate, and access to the sea have appeared in political thought since ancient times. Such considerations appear in the work of ancient philosophers like Plato and Aristotle or, later, in the work of political thinkers, such as Machiavelli and Montesquieu.

However, the best-known body of geopolitical writings is the extensive literature of the late nineteenth and early twentieth centuries, much of which focused on the impact on world politics of the new technologies of the Industrial Revolution. The link between technological breakthrough and geopolitics was evident in the conceptual development of the discipline. Geopoliticians have consistently sought to understand how the new industrial capabilities of transportation, communication, and destruction (most notably railroads, steamships, airplanes, telegraphy, and new explosives) interacting with the largest-scale geographic features of the earth would shape the balance of power in the emerging global international system.

Artificial intelligence (AI), 5G, cybersecurity, robotics, semiconductors, and space technologies are domains with unprecedented global impact. All these accelerated technological developments are now deeply affecting all human activities and, by extension, international relations.

In recent decades, geopolitics has been widely employed, in the political and academic discourse, as a loose synonym for international or global politics. Geopolitics is therefore widely accepted as the study of global politics, taking into consideration not just the geographic but all the key strategic determinants of global power relationships.

With the acceleration of technological developments, their impact upon geopolitics is gaining a prominent role more than ever. The recent studies regarding the impact of modern technological developments upon the power manifestations in global politics are coined in different studies as: geopolitics of technology, tech-geopolitics, or geotechnology (although the last term might be confused with a different and more narrow meaning, namely the application of science and technology in order to utilize the earth's natural resources).

An increasing number of academic studies or programs on the geopolitics of technology aim to analyze the redistribution of power in international relations caused by new technologies, particularly digital, military, and dual-use innovations. Artificial intelligence (AI), 5G, cybersecurity, robotics, semiconductors, and space technologies are domains with unprecedented global impact. All these accelerated technological developments are now deeply affecting all human activities and, by extension, international relations.

Today's Disruptive Technologies and Their Impact upon Geopolitics

Throughout history, technology has not only transformed economies and societies but has also been a major redistributor of power among states and a significant force shaping and reshaping international relations. New technologies can massively boost a country's economy and, therefore, global influence. The standards that tech products disseminate are determined by those who manufacture them. Furthermore, groundbreaking technologies can enable capabilities that provide a country with military advantages or even dominance.

While technology as a great enabler or disruptor has had an impact upon geopolitics since the very inception of the concept, there are some differences in the way the major technological accelerations shape the geopolitical environment today, compared to the past. Most of the key specificities of the impact of today's technology developments upon geopolitics are reflected by the speed, scale, diversity, and complexity of these technological changes, by the blurring between civilian and military use and by the multiplication of the actors involved.

Technological breakthroughs in the past, especially those with military applications, were mainly driven and financed by governments. From the harnessing of nuclear power to satellites or the internet, the major technological achievements were state-sponsored and state-controlled, thereby maintaining tech-induced geopolitical influence at the state level. In recent years, due to the lower entry barriers in terms of investments for key technological innovation, some private big-tech actors have emerged with meaningful geopolitical influence.

Since innovation today is mainly driven by the private sector at a highly accelerated pace, governments have difficulty catching up with the assessment of the potentially negative impact of some innovations and therefore keeping pace with the relevant regulatory framework related to safety and security.

Recent technological developments with potential dual (civ-mil) use have concerning "weaponization" tendencies, which are widely spread for civilian use, therefore allowing engagement of both military and non-military actors in technology-enabled attacks aimed at civilians.

The increased dependency of our institutional and social organization, economies, and militaries upon technological developments means that every vulnerability in the employed technology increases the attack surface that can be exploited by attackers. Technological developments have created new domains of confrontation, such as cyberspace, info-space, or outer-space, thus increasing the multi-domain complexity of international confrontation.

The increased US-China technological competition will accelerate the development of a global technological bipolarity. This process will be driven by the promotion and dissemination of quite different technological standards (for example, 5G, quantum computing, and biotech) and regulations (for the benefit of the citizens and the authorities, respectively). This phenomenon will even manifest by conditioning political relations with other states regarding the adoption of specific standards, technologies, and products, or by excluding the technologies of the competitor. As a result, this will also generate a competition for markets and for the power to influence big decisions on technology standards in developing countries.

There are significant global discrepancies regarding the ethical and human-centric employment of technology. We are indeed at a point of inflection from this point of view. I see two development trends: 1) the employment of new technologies based on a state-centric approach, without much concern for people security and human rights or values—putting citizens under the pressure of surveillance and control; and 2) the more people-centric approach in democratic countries with regard to tech development. These two evolving trends also seem to lead to a new ideological divide determined by the approach vis-à-vis the human-centric application of technological innovations.

A new "technological arms race," with revolutionary outcomes and radical implications for international security, is already palpable. It highlights the need for a rapid and rigorous adaptation of the arms control and non-proliferation regime. The dynamics of technological developments have a significant impact in the military field too. There is an increased use of remote-controlled military platforms—so-called air, land, sea, or submarine drones. Artificial intelligence enhances the accelerated development of autonomous combat systems. The robotization of battle systems is becoming a reality. There is increased concern for the proliferation of anti-satellite technologies. Cyberspace and extra-atmospheric space are already recognized and addressed as military operational domains. Against this background, the international arms control, nuclear, and technological non-proliferation regimes need substantial upgrading.

Technological developments have created new domains of confrontation, such as cyberspace, info-space, or outer-space, thus increasing the multi-domain complexity of international confrontation.

Embracing the Attributes of Modern Diplomacy in the Age of Tech-Geopolitics

The profound and accelerated tech-induced changes upon all aspects of human life and the international strategic landscape, the multiplication of influential actors in the conduct of international relations, the expansion of domain areas subject to diplomatic action, as well as the so-called "diplomatic toolbox," invite the following question: How does all this change the meaning and understanding we have of the vocation of diplomacy? What is the meaning of concepts such as tech-diplomacy, digital-diplomacy, e-diplomacy, etc., and how do they relate to the essence of the diplomatic function and tradition? Is the "purity" of the diplomatic vocation lost, obsolete, or fundamentally transformed in the age of technological accelerations?

My response to this is that the need and essential function of diplomacy as the art and vocation of implementing foreign policy through negotiations is now as relevant as ever, but is actually extended and amplified in the age of tech-geopolitics. The essential attributes of diplomacy and diplomats continue to matter and need to be further cultivated. Modern diplomacy also involves an increasing complexity, diversity, and area of coverage. The meaning of diplomatic professional excellence and sophistication is amplified!

At the same time, modern diplomacy cannot and should not ignore the huge opportunities offered by technology to enhance its "toolbox," diversify its approach, amplify its messages, and therefore increase the efficiency and effectiveness of the diplomatic démarche. "Geek-skills" training should be considered not just a nice-to-have advantage, but a must have for the maximization of a modern diplomat's success. It would actually imply a double value. First, such modern diplomatic training offers new enabling skills for the enhanced efficiency and impact of diplomatic actions. Second, it can also offer potential defense skills or a shield in the face of tech-enabled distortive and disruptive actions (such as cyberattacks, information manipulation, and so on) against diplomatic actions and diplomats.

How does all this change the meaning and understanding we have of the vocation of diplomacy? Is the "purity" of the diplomatic vocation lost, obsolete, or fundamentally transformed in the age of technological accelerations?

An increased level of so called "tech-literacy" with strategic ramifications is key not just to master modern tools or methods to support diplomacy, but, more importantly, for a better understanding of the subject matter of diplomatic endeavors, namely the international landscape and the conduct of international relations in the era of tech-geopolitics. Indeed, the key to understanding modern geopolitical trends is in gaining a keen understanding of the development of disruptive technologies—such as artificial intelligence and autonomous systems, quantum computing, 5G and 6G communications, etc. And, more specifically, to understand their potential applications (including malign ones), the standards-setting approach and regulatory framework, and the preparation and conduct of diplomatic actions and negotiations.

Technological developments with a strategic impact will continue to determine certain tech-induced areas of diplomatic conduct or specialization, such as cyber-diplomacy, space diplomacy, or more general tech-diplomacy.

Tech-geopolitics and associated diplomatic action will have a significant impact upon the need to update, modernize, and enhance the international regulatory framework, stability regimes, and relevant international institutional frameworks. One cannot imagine a modern effective arms control and non-proliferation regime without skillful negotiations based on an understanding of how the new technologies impact security and stability. Post-Cold War deterrence and defense concepts and stability frameworks are seriously challenged by the straightforward defense and security impact, as well as the geostrategic implications of accelerated and disruptive technology developments.

Different standards and approaches in different countries related to the employment of new technologies while preserving—or not preserving—essential human rights, freedoms, or values, tend to point toward a new bipolarity at the international level. A tech-induced bipolarity. It derives from the difference between the people-centric versus the state-centric approach related to the standard of employment of key technologies.

With the multiplication and diversification of key actors with geopolitical relevance, including big-tech private actors, modern diplomacy will need to embrace more of a so-called multi-stakeholder approach, which will be important for the smooth conduct and problem-solving approach on many strategic international issues. Since the private sector "owns" about 80 percent of the digital infrastructure or cyberspace, it is hardly conceivable that we could develop an international framework or regime for cybersecurity and stability without involvement of the private sector. In the cyber domain in particular, private sector activism has manifested some geopolitical resonance through initiatives such as the establishment of the Cybersecurity Tech Accord or the CyberPeace Institute. Furthermore, the 2018 "Paris Call for Trust and Security in Cyberspace,"[3] signed by a large number of governments, private sector representatives, and academic or think-tank entities is a telling result of multi-stakeholder diplomacy, applied to a new domain generated by digital technology.

Finally, to support modern diplomacy endeavors, it is important to acknowledge technology megatrends with a strategic impact and place them on the front stage of geopolitics. This is important at conceptual, academic, and think-tank levels and even more so at the high level of political and diplomatic action.

Conclusions

Technological development, at accelerated scale, is, more than ever, affecting all human activities and, consequently, the current international landscape. The resulting political, strategic, economic, and social issues manifest themselves at multiple political scales involving states, international organizations, and private companies. The dynamics of international competition and cooperation are transformed at an unprecedented scale, thereby changing the stakes of international security and stability, and affecting the conduct of international relations and diplomacy.

Diplomacy remains essential in the age of tech-geopolitics. In fact, its unique role, complexity, and value will probably be amplified and enhanced.

Diplomacy remains essential in the age of tech-geopolitics. In fact, its unique role, complexity, and value will probably be amplified and enhanced. Diplomacy is one of the professions, or better said, vocations, that cannot be outsourced to robots or algorithms (although the application of sound algorithms could be useful in context analysis, potential development simulations, or scenarios). The top skills and talent-enabled, human interaction, engagement, debate, and negotiation should and will remain at the core of the diplomatic démarche. Indeed, we need to preserve this element of diplomatic "purity," or else we cannot speak of diplomacy. Therefore, modern diplomacy in the age of tech-geopolitics should not deviate from the core vocation of diplomacy: that of managing international relations through the art of peaceful and skillful negotiations.

The art of skillfully negotiated dealmaking will remain at the core of diplomacy. One could therefore say that diplomacy will remain very essentially the same with regard to its negotiations-based function and method. But modern diplomacy should, at the same time, accept and aspire to be different and adapt to the requirements and increased complexity of the international environment.

Modern diplomacy implies the recognition and understanding of the profound impact of today's technological accelerations upon the subject matter of diplomacy, namely the so-called geopolitics of technology. It is essential to understand how truly geopolitical the current generation of emerging technologies has become.

In modern diplomacy, we should embrace new attributes and skills and stimulate them to evolve. It means embracing and taking on board both the conceptual developments reflecting the impact of disruptive technologies upon the geostrategic landscape, and the enhanced tech-enabled diplomatic toolbox for the conduct of modern diplomacy in a strategically complex twenty-first century.

Sorin Ducaru is the Director of the European Union Satellite Centre. He previously served as NATO Assistant Secretary General for Emerging Security Challenges and as Romania's ambassador to the United Nations, the United States of America, and NATO.

CASAMÉRICA
Körber Stiftung
msc

Deploying an Effective Technology Diplomacy

Manuel Muñiz Villa

Technology is radically changing the world. From the way information is generated, transmitted, and processed, to how companies operate and compete, to how economies develop. There is almost no field of policy that is today unaffected by the pace and depth of technological change. And the pace of change is increasing.

It is estimated that more data was generated by our societies in the last two years than in the past twenty thousand. That increase in volume was accompanied by an incredible growth in the capacity to share it. During the last fifteen years, the global population with access to the internet went from one billion to close to five. In 2005 the first *Youtube* video was uploaded to the internet. Today more than five hundred hours of content are uploaded to that platform every sixty seconds. That is just *Youtube*. And this is only one example of rapid change. The deployment of 5G networks will also have a significant impact on how companies operate, as well as having major security implications. As will the use of advanced AI systems in everything from domestic surveillance to cyber offense. The combination of advancements in fields like data analytics, AI, neuroscience, and behavioral sciences is opening questions about privacy, and even individual agency. Growingly, actors, both private and public, are developing the capacity not just to have knowledge of how individuals are behaving in real time but also to shape that behavior in ways that are beneficial to them.

A New Domain for Foreign Policy

From a foreign policy point of view, technological change is becoming a pervasive force altering fundamental features of the international order. It is rapidly changing the nature and distribution of power, as well as the structure of the global economy, or as indicated above, how individual rights and freedoms are exercised or infringed upon. To put it simply: the governance of technology is becoming a new domain for foreign policy.

When looking at how technology governance is tackled globally today, one is reminded of the origins of climate change or global health governance. In their origins these were considered preeminently technical matters and, in many ways, subordinated to other areas of policy, be it energy policy, national health policy, or others. So, when addressed at international forums, if at all, they were tackled by technical experts coming mostly from sectoral ministries. Over time, however, climate and global health came to be understood as spaces where strategic interests were addressed and in need of international cooperation. Or to put it differently: areas in need of diplomacy. This prompted the emergence of entire governance structures around them; from international accords to supervisory bodies, to specialized groups of experts at foreign ministries working on those subject matters full time. Something similar is starting to occur in the field of emerging technologies.

From a foreign policy point of view, technological change is becoming a pervasive force altering fundamental features of the international order.

There is an evident need, for example, for the development of growingly detailed agreements on data collection, usage, and sharing. Or, one could argue, even for a broader international agreement on digital rights. Some countries like Spain have now, in fact, produced national bills of digital rights. These almost naturally call for broader frameworks to be built across borders. One could also foresee attempts at limiting the use of AI in certain scenarios or in cooperation around cybersecurity. Agreements on international taxation of digital activities, or on the management and use of cryptocurrencies could now also be seen as strategic for countries and not just a byproduct of economic policy. The list of areas in which international cooperation on the governance of emerging technologies is conceivable is, indeed, long. Some have begun to feature more prominently in gatherings like the Munich Security Conference, in a sign that the field is slowly gaining strategic depth.

Drawing the Perimeter of Technology Diplomacy

What the field of technology diplomacy lacks at this stage is structure. Technology is everything and anything. It is unclear what its boundaries are. During my time at Spain's Foreign Ministry, we worked with various categories of technologies according to their stage of development, the way they were being deployed, or the estimated impact they might have on our strategic

◂ Manuel Muñiz Villa (second from right) at the Munich Young Leaders Meeting in Madrid in September 2018.

interests. In particular, we used the following five categories: traditional, combined, emerging, disruptive, and critical technologies. I will use these terms interchangeably although there are slight differences between them. The "critical" category is perhaps the most relevant as it captured those technologies whose impact on our strategic interests was expected to be significant. We identified three as the most important: 5G networks, advanced computing—with edge and quantum as its main two components—and artificial intelligence. There are, of course, many others and one has to be ready to update these categories as technologies evolve over time. But some basic framing is a fundamental step in charting a path forward.

What the field of technology diplomacy lacks at this stage is structure. Technology is everything and anything. It is unclear what its boundaries are.

What remains particularly challenging, however, is to describe how diplomacy should address this subject matter. Most analysis on this topic uses the digital lens, with a tendency to confuse emerging technologies with the much-narrower batch of information technologies. Technology diplomacy is not just about attempting to regulate social media or fighting disinformation. This is a normal misconception that stems from a lack of structured analysis of the field. In fact, the greatest source of confusion in this area comes from equating technology diplomacy to digital diplomacy. Digital diplomacy is about equipping foreign ministries with digital tools. At its core it is about developing digital capabilities for more effective action on the ground and about communicating better, both internally and externally. Digital diplomacy is, hence, about the instruments of diplomacy. Technology diplomacy should be about the substance of policy. Confusing the two is analogous to equating climate diplomacy to the carbon footprint reduction measures at foreign ministries.

A possible framework for understanding the scale and scope of technology diplomacy could be built around the core areas of impact of emerging technologies on global politics. We could call it the 3 Ps framework, and these might be its components: 1) Power, 2) Prosperity, and 3) Principles & Political Systems. This framework was the cornerstone of the first drafts of the National Strategy on Technology and Global Order, a document aimed at launching Spanish technology diplomacy. Let's look at each of the Ps individually.

Power: The Geopolitics of Technology

Emerging technologies change the nature and the distribution of power in the international order. They have created new domains of strategic competition like cyberspace or outer space, and have added new offensive and defensive capabilities to the arsenal that both state and non-state actors have. A clear example of the latter would be AI-powered offensive and defensive systems, but also new capabilities in the fields of robotics, UAVs, and others. The full development of a quantum computer would also have severe security implications, rendering, for example, most past forms of encryption obsolete. The centrality of these new technologies to our security and defense has also meant that the materials needed for their deployment become critical. So much so, in fact, that states now look at access to critical raw materials (or CRMs) like lithium, graphite, and cobalt as a matter of national security importance. Additionally, technology is changing the distribution of power across and within states, by reducing the cost of access to powerful offensive tools or shifting the centrality of the development process from the public to the private sector.

If foreign policy is the business of protecting the strategic interests of a country, then quite clearly it should consider the effects of technology and innovation on global security and on power distribution. This is not new to diplomacy. Historically, our diplomats have had to deal with technological change that led to shifts in power. Today, however, this seems to be more pervasive and multifaceted. We are bombarded by change. It is not just one technology, like the invention of flight or the development of nuclear weapons, that is changing the landscape. Today, one might identify over a dozen technologies with very severe implications for national security. An effective technology diplomacy might entail putting forward initiatives to establish ethical frameworks for the use of certain weapons, or seeking a broad and effective regulation of activities in outer space, or enhancing cyber defense capabilities as well as setting up cooperation frameworks with other countries. Not understanding that these issues are connected and that they should be part of a wholistic diplomatic strategy aimed at governing the effects of technological change will hinder our efforts and make them less effective.

Emerging technologies change the nature and the distribution of power in the international order.

Prosperity: Economics in the Tech Era

Emerging technologies are also changing our economies. This is true when speaking about how and where innovation takes place and, hence, where prosperity is concentrated. Indeed, one feature of the knowledge economy seems to be the concentration of innovation, of transfer, and of entrepreneurship in very specific geographic locations. These hubs of innovation are the places where growth is occurring. Beyond the clear implications for domestic politics of these trends, with the "periphery" being left behind when it comes to economic growth, they have severe global implications. The knowledge economy, counter to what was expected, appears to be more zero sum and to pivot on a strong competition for talent. Something similar, and perhaps even more consequential, seems to be occurring in the space of productivity growth. Productivity is concentrating on a very reduced number of firms, what the OECD calls "frontier companies," which are the ones capable of deploying technologies quickly. This is leading to a bifurcated global economy with a few winners and many losers that are falling behind on competitiveness. There are clear oligopolistic if not outright monopolistic forces in the digital economy. This again configures a global economy in which competition is fiercer, and in which dominance in talent, and in technology deployment leads to enormous market benefits and growth.

> If we are unable to deploy effective diplomatic action in this field, we will not be able to forward our economic interests.

What does this mean for how diplomacy is configured? On the one hand, it means that our diplomatic action should be geared toward helping our economies occupy the technological frontier. This might entail guaranteeing a regular and secure supply of critical raw materials, attracting the right kinds of investment or talent, joining international initiatives in specific areas like quantum computing, green technologies, or AI; or, for Europeans, completing the digital single market, so that our start-ups have the capacity to scale up like they would if they were operating in the US or China. This all equates to bringing together our economic and technology diplomacies.

On the other hand, it also means addressing the negative externalities of the changes to our economic structure brought about by technological change. From establishing new competition and antitrust rules that prevent undue market concentration, to fighting tax avoidance by technology giants whose activities span the globe and are hard to pin down to one specific jurisdiction, to regulating cybercurrencies. These are not minor or haphazard issues. If we are unable to deploy effective diplomatic action in this field, we will not be able to forward our economic interests. Not doing so might mean attaining less economic growth, not creating the right type of employment, particularly high value-added jobs in the technology sector, having less competitive firms, seeing a reduction in our states' capacity to tax economic activity, and, hence, fund basic public services and others.

Principles and Political Systems: Technological Humanism and Liberal Democracy

Lastly, but perhaps most importantly, emerging technologies can have a significant impact on individual rights and freedoms and on the sustainability of democratic societies. There are at least two ways in which technology is impacting fundamental rights. The first is through the rapid spread of disinformation. The deepening of cyberspace and the extensive use of social media platforms have opened a new flank for liberal democracies. Foreign actors can now access and impact our public debate in ways that were unthinkable in the past. And they are doing so with growing frequency and intensity. The goals pursued by these campaigns vary greatly but if there is one common goal it is this: spreading the notion that democratic institutions are ineffective. At a deeper level, the message being conveyed is that the system is rigged, incapable of structuring a healthy public debate, and that collective truths are impossible to arrive at. Hence, disinformation is highly subversive, revolutionary, and in many respects, anti-enlightened as it seeks to upend citizens' faith in their institutions and their political systems, and to erode the very meaning of truth. It is a significant threat to liberal and deliberative democracies that depend for their existence on a healthy public debate, and on the willingness of citizens to cede representation and power to intermediation institutions.

Another way in which technology is impacting rights and freedoms is through the capacity it unleashes to collect and process data on individuals. This capacity enables surveillance at a scale not seen until today. Minorities and dissent groups around the world are being monitored and repressed with growing sophistication. Some have argued that this system of data collection and processing could even substitute the role of individual agency that is so central to democratic models. Instead of getting to know citizens' preferences through their exercise of individual rights, such as the right to vote or the right to speak freely, some argue that governments could now simply infer preferences from surveilled behavior. There would therefore be no need for individual agency. In fact, a political system built on surveillance could be more effective at tending to peoples' needs as it could be more nuanced, faster, and even anticipatory. What this line of argumentation obviates is that, with our expanding knowledge of neuroscience and of behavioral sciences, the frontier separating surveillance from outright manipulation is growing thinner. Governments around the world could soon have the capacity not just to coerce dissidents into certain forms of behavior but also to nudge the rest of the population into specific actions. So, what lies at the bottom of the rapid and extensive deployment of surveillance capabilities is a normatively different form of governance, based on techno-authoritarianism and the attack on individual freedom.

What lies at the bottom of the rapid and extensive deployment of surveillance capabilities is a normatively different form of governance, based on techno-authoritarianism and the attack on individual freedom.

Our diplomacy should be fully aware of the depth and implications of these developments. This knowledge should shape the measures we implement to control the sale of dual-use technology, or the way we respond to states that systematically use technology to impinge on peoples' rights and freedoms. Democratic countries around the world should have a clear and shared interest in fighting disinformation and in building an international framework for the protection of digital rights, for example. All in all, this should amount to an international agenda that puts technological humanism at the center.

Tools and Capabilities: A True Technology Diplomacy

Drawing the intellectual and political perimeter of this new form of diplomacy is important. It is likely that in the following years, we will see attempts at that coming from countries around the world. The framework delineated previously might be of use to some. Others will pursue a different path, perhaps narrowing the scope of the agenda or linking it more tightly to economic diplomacy. What is certain, however, is that if this field is ever going to consolidate, it will require the creation of specific capabilities and structures within foreign ministries. These would be offices and teams that have a sole focus on the subject matter of technology governance. In some instances, it might crystalize in the creation of a dedicated directorate general, in others it might be an ambassador-at-large or even a state secretariat (or an undersecretary in the US case). These units within foreign ministries would be the ones responsible for the execution of technology diplomacy strategies, liaising with similar teams in other countries, and coordinating national actions across relevant national ministries. The government of Denmark has been one of the first in Europe to move in this direction with the establishment of a technology ambassador and two small teams working out of Silicon Valley and Beijing.

In fact, the idea of having dedicated diplomatic personnel in key locations around the world seems like a necessity in this field. A large portion of the technology diplomacy agenda is developed through contacts on the ground, and by being able to have a fluid dialogue with the key actors driving change. A perfect example of this is the Swissnex network deployed by Switzerland with the motto "Connecting Tomorrow" and the goal of building and maintaining relations with third countries in the areas of education, research, and innovation.

The creation of such structures in foreign ministries will necessitate the development of the right kind of human capital in diplomatic corps. And the key will be interdisciplinarity and being able to navigate between two worlds: technology and international politics. Three models seem to exist in this space. First, training diplomats on the fundamentals of science and technology. Second, training individuals with a technical background on diplomacy. And third, incorporating into ministries "translators" or individuals who can understand the technical aspects of a dossier and convey them in a digestible manner to others with experience in negotiation, mediation, and international agreement setting. In most cases it would be wise to pursue all three routes in order to have a mix of profiles.

Be this as it may, the curricula at diplomatic academies will need to be tweaked and updated so as to incorporate courses and content on technology and innovation. Additionally, new educational products will need to be developed—products that are more modular, shorter, and faster to deliver. With the growth in the velocity of change, comes a shortening of the life expectancy of knowledge acquired through formal training. The problem of knowledge and skill obsolescence can only be addressed through lifelong learning strategies and an agile educational offering.

Lastly, technology diplomacy calls for a deep and structured public-private dialogue. So much of the change in this area of policy is produced by private innovation, and so much of the success in this field is dependent on private actors benefiting from the results of public policy that a constant dialogue between government and business is fundamental. Start-ups, large technology companies, established players, and our diplomats need to be engaged in a permanent conversation about challenges, opportunities, and potential lines of action. Given the pace of change, they should also be engaged in a shared exercise of foresight and in drawing shared scenarios. One example of an institution that fulfils these goals is the Geneva Science Diplomacy Accelerator (GESDA), a Swiss private-public foundation that brings together diplomats and key actors in the technology and innovation space with the aim of anticipating "scientific and technological advancements and . . . (developing) inclusive and global solutions for a sustainable future."

Foreign ministries that do not address the structure and capacity issues delineated previously will struggle to deploy an effective technology diplomacy. This will raise an additional challenge: that of disintermediation as other parts of government seek to execute global policy in the field of technology. Sectoral ministries, like those of science and innovation, or energy, or finance, will have to step in and execute decisions at international organizations or establish bilateral agreements with third countries. The need for governance in this space will simply not allow for there to be a vacuum. And if this work is done individually by sectoral ministries, it will be done less effectively, with less resources abroad, and with a lack of alignment with broader foreign policy goals.

If the field of technology diplomacy is ever going to consolidate, it will require the creating of specific capabilities and structures within foreign ministries."

The Opportunity for Diplomacy to Step Up

Our diplomacies have the opportunity to step up and both make the most of the technology revolution as well as address the challenges it raises. This will require adaptation and change. A potential model for this has been outlined here. Each of the Ps described previously capture areas of societal transformation driven by technology. Each deserves more extensive analysis, but they serve as a starting point to the spaces where technology diplomacy could concentrate time and effort. Work in this field will almost inevitably remain unfinished for some time to come as the landscape itself changes and countries around the world slowly build both analytical and material capacity to deal with the subject matter. Technology diplomacy will be, however, an important area of policy to continue to study, explore, and develop.

Manuel Muñiz Villa is Provost of IE University in Madrid and a former State Secretary in Spain's Ministry of Foreign Affairs, European Union and Cooperation, where, among other things, he led the Strategy and Foresight team.

Kersti Kaljulaid
President of Estonia

Paving the Way for a Free and Democratic Digital Future

Kersti Kaljulaid

At the Tallinn Digital Summit on September 7, 2021, high-level representatives from Estonia, the United States, Australia, Poland, the European Council, the European Commission, the Organization for Economic Co-operation and Development, among others, called for a unifying framework—Trusted Connectivity—to optimize coordination across democratic countries with a view to ensuring that our digital future be built upon democratic values and that it reaffirm the international rules-based order. This collective concern gave rise to the Tallinn Consensus on Trusted Connectivity.[1]

It is a welcome and hitherto the most consequential acknowledgment by Western democracies that connectivity— that is, the full spectrum of digital and physical infrastructure—plays a pivotal role in twenty-first-century power politics, both in the developed and in the developing world. Indeed, amidst the seemingly incessant fusillade of cyber operations on everything from government databases[2] to oil pipelines[3] and given that authoritarian regimes such as China and Russia are ramping up their efforts to expand their geopolitical and economic influence through connectivity, it was high time the West issue a resolute response and commit itself to harnessing the power of the market economy to counter the malign and anti-democratic influence of certain national and subnational actors. What remains is to put the ambitious agenda of Trusted Connectivity into practice.

The West needs to make full use of its policy toolbox to prevail in the ongoing tug-of-war between democratic and autocratic forces in the realm of connectivity. The Three Seas Initiative serves as an example of how the Trusted Connectivity framework boosts sustainable economic growth, interstate cohesion, and regional security.

Instrumental to the success of such an endeavor is to build trust in connectivity and in new technologies. This is of particular import when trust in public and private institutions persists on a downward trajectory.[4] To drive public and private investments into large-scale, cross-border infrastructure projects, governments must devise a lucid and robust legal and political framework that ensures data and cyber security and facilitates the free flow of data between countries. In constructing such frameworks, governments need to actively engage both private and public stakeholders and resolve to be fully transparent in the eventual implementation of its policies. Couched in and buttressed by an overarching fidelity among Western countries to their "shared values of democracy, freedom, equality, the rule of law and respect for human rights," as stated in the G7's joint communiqué from June 2021 and as articulated by the Trusted Connectivity framework, garnering public trust in and through connectivity is very much feasible.[5]

The principles of Trusted Connectivity—democratic values and high standards—foster an environment in which private entrepreneurship may excel, as it propels genuine and sustainable economic growth, especially as we strive to finally emerge from the economic and social devastation wrought by the COVID-19 pandemic. Now it is up to the governments to design fit-for-purpose incentive structures and then watch free markets work their magic.

Trusted Connectivity envelops the myriad connectivity initiatives among democratic countries and aims to bind them together. It provides an umbrella for various preexisting regional and global connectivity initiatives, among them the European Union's Global Gateway connectivity strategy, the United States' Build Back Better World (B3W), and Australia's Infrastructure Financing Facility for the Pacific.[6]

Of particular note is the Blue Dot Network (BDN), spearheaded by the US, Japan, and Australia, and officially launched in June 2021 at the Organization for Economic Cooperation and Development (OECD).[7] In responding to the needs and demands of investors and citizens alike, the BDN is poised to be the first quality-control mechanism to adopt a wide array of strategies and guidelines on investment—including the G20 Principles for Quality Infrastructure Investment, the OECD Policy Framework for Investment, and the Equator Principles—to ensure that future infrastructure projects will be environmentally friendly and resilient, and that their financing will be guided by openness, transparency, and inclusiveness.[8] The BDN is a testament to the need for streamlining international infrastructure standards. The BDN and other potential certification mechanisms can attest that a particular connectivity project is in keeping with the principles of Trusted Connectivity. In other words,

◂ Kersti Kaljulaid as a guest at MSC Events, among others at the MSC Cyber Security Summit in Tallinn in May 2018.

provide a branding tool for the brand of Trusted Connectivity.

The actual viability of the undertakings outlined above will manifest itself when the rubber meets the road. Fortunately, there already exists a lodestar in Central and Eastern Europe for the world's democracies to emulate, proving that the principles of Trusted Connectivity can be and have been put to use successfully—the Three Seas Initiative (3SI).[9] The 3SI, established in 2015 by twelve European nations spanning from the Baltic Sea south to the Adriatic and the Black Sea, utilizes the Trusted Connectivity framework and transparent financing to promote the development of digital, energy, and other forms of infrastructure across the region. These countries form the land bridge between Europe and Asia; thus, they possess tremendous geopolitical significance and are indispensable to transcontinental connectivity projects. Likewise, their relative geographical proximity to Russia and China has cemented their adherence to creating trust in connectivity and in new technologies to counterbalance the influence of those countries in their region. Furthermore, the 3SI includes some of the fastest-growing economies in Europe, as well as countries that are global leaders in the use of digital technology in which their citizens have high confidence.

Given that connectivity lies at the nexus of geopolitics, sustainable economic growth, and the digital transformation, it is incumbent on democratic countries to offer values- and market-based alternatives to investments into connectivity projects by malign actors.

To finance infrastructure projects, the 3SI countries established the 3SI Investment Fund, a novel kind of public-private partnership that is managed according to commercial business principles and that selects projects to finance based on their profitability. The fund has secured over $1.2 billion in capital, some of which has already been allocated to projects such as the Greenergy Data Centers, a data center platform in Estonia that will establish in the region a network of data centers that are both green and energy efficient. Potential future investments may include many of the some ninety priority projects among the 3SI countries.[10]

Given that connectivity lies at the nexus of geopolitics, sustainable economic growth, and the digital transformation, it is incumbent on democratic countries to offer values- and market-based alternatives to investments into connectivity projects by malign actors. Initiatives such as Global Gateway and B3W, encompassed and amplified by the Trusted Connectivity framework, are welcome first steps. Democratic countries, by marshaling their resources and redoubling their efforts, should endorse the Trusted Connectivity framework to enable us to successfully navigate the digital and green transformations toward a future more free, prosperous, inclusive, and sustainable.

Kersti Kaljulaid served as the President of Estonia from 2016 to 2021.

MSC Cyber Security Summit in Tallinn in May 2018. ▸

msc
msc

Balancing the Geopolitical Power of Tech Companies

Marietje Schaake

Not long ago, "digital diplomacy" seemed to be where foreign policy and technology intersected. Men in pressed suits who spent their days in meetings at long mahogany tables with little flags in front of them had to learn how to tweet about their activities to represent their governments in the digital era. However, between the iconic "Senator, we run ads" quip at Zuckerberg's congressional hearing to Richard Blumenthal's awkwardly phrased question to Instagram, there is still much that needs to adjust in government and policy circles.[1] What's more is that today it is not only diplomacy but the core functions of the state that tech companies are disrupting. Democratic governments must adjust to survive.

Spyware companies are building sophisticated hacking tools, making systems comparable to intelligence-grade software available to whomever can afford it. Private software companies are at the frontlines of defending the homeland as they engage in offensive and defensive cyber operations. All kinds of key functions that were previously the exclusive domain of nation states are now built and run by tech companies. As they deploy undersea cables or build the digital infrastructure to operate energy pipelines, it is frequently unclear who can and should keep these sophisticated systems safe. We are only as secure as our weakest digital defenses, but when something goes wrong, where do you turn for accountability? To paraphrase Henry Kissinger: if you need to speak to Silicon Valley, who do you call?

Today it is not only diplomacy but the core functions of the state that tech companies are disrupting.

President Biden went as far as remarking that a majority of US critical infrastructure is now in the hands of private companies, and that the government alone is not capable of ensuring cybersecurity. The US president is of course correct in his analysis but accelerating and deepening private governance is not a solution. Outsourcing more capacity, agency, and oversight will not lead to levels of accountability we need. Instead of outsourcing geopolitics to tech companies, diplomats and public authorities of democracies should regain adequate skills and knowledge, meaningful agency, and the ability to hold these new geopolitical players to account.

Beyond the risks of outsourcing critical functions and the lack of accountability, there is no clear alignment between democratic principles and the behavior of tech companies, even if they were born and raised within democratic societies. While democracies call for the defense of press freedom, journalists are traced with spyware. And while decoupling between the US and China is underway, polling by Brookings shows that US CEOs do not seem interested in aligning with either the US or China.[2] Despite their rhetoric, we should not assume that tech companies necessarily favor openness and democratic principles. Market and profit opportunities continue to be the strongest drivers, even if their roles are increasingly geopolitical.

Instead of outsourcing geopolitics to tech companies, diplomats and public authorities of democracies should regain adequate skills and knowledge, meaningful agency, and the ability to hold these new geopolitical players to account.

Some tech executives are now representing their companies in diplomatic circles; Microsoft has even opened a mission to the United Nations. Others only show up when they are summoned by the US Congress or the European Parliament—though even that is not a guarantee.[3] The new geopolitical powers are certainly no diplomats. What is certain is that systematic accountability mechanisms are lacking: tech companies are operating in similar forums as politicians and diplomats, but with far fewer constraints. Put differently, the geopolitical power of tech companies is not balanced with proportionate countervailing powers.

Marietje Schaake is the International Policy Director at Stanford University's Cyber Policy Center and International Policy Fellow at Stanford's Institute for Human-Centered Artificial Intelligence. She was named President of the Cyber Peace Institute. Previously, Schaake served as a Member of European Parliament for the Dutch liberal democratic party, where she focused on trade, foreign affairs, and technology policies. She was a Munich Young Leader in 2013.

◂ Marietje Schaake at the MSC Cyber Security Summit in Berlin in November 2019.

POLIZEI
BY
1321
msc
msc
msc TOWNHALL
msc
NATO
OTAN
Atlantic Cou

Reversing the Tide of Impunity

David Miliband

Diplomacy is not an end in itself. One of its key purposes is to defend the idea of a rules-based international order and strengthen the accountability of power in international as well as national affairs. Tomorrow's diplomats must halt the trend toward what today is emerging as a new age of impunity.

The argument for codifying some set of agreed-upon rules and norms in the international system—as a check on the abuse of power—is ultimately pragmatic and realistic, not just idealistic. Throughout history the most dangerous and destructive periods in international affairs have always been those in which the restraints on power have been weakest and the only rule in effect is "might makes right." Nowhere is that more important than in protection for the most vulnerable.

Over the past century, the modern rules-based international order has codified the protection of civilians and humanitarian access in conflict zones. From the Hague and Geneva Conventions to the Universal Declaration of Human Rights and the Responsibility to Protect doctrine, the rights of civilians represent the most basic pillar of a rules-based order and a critical signal that power has responsibilities and limits.

Today, I see from my work with the International Rescue Committee, that basic notion is under threat from an emerging "age of impunity." In conflict zones around the world today, impunity is on the march. Whether it is the Saudi-led coalition bombing a bus carrying Yemeni schoolchildren or President Bashar al-Assad and his allies targeting health facilities in Syria, governments and rebel groups in conflict zones around the world increasingly violate international laws and norms without being punished or held to account.

Far from adhering to the laws of war, combatants increasingly proclaim that the law is for suckers. That sentiment is a dangerous one, not just for civilians, but for the entire international project. The law-breaking and norm-breaking that we are seeing in the world's war zones are only the most visible evidence of the rise of impunity in areas of public and private life, where laws are less clear and rights less well demarcated. And if rights are not defended and their abuse called out in areas where they are clear, then they will be far harder to defend in areas where they are not.

◂ David Miliband as a guest at MSC Events, among others at the Munich Security Conference 2020.

As a result of the rise of impunity, civilian death and displacement are on the rise. An average of 37,000 civilians were killed in conflict each year between 2016 and 2020, according to the Armed Conflict Location and Event Data Project. That is two and-a-half times as many civilian fatalities as in the previous five-year period and nearly ten times as many as in the period from 2005 to 2009. Around the world, a record 79.5 million people have been forced to flee their homes, primarily as a result of conflict. Attacks on health facilities have also increased. Since the UN Security Council passed a resolution condemning attacks on hospitals in May 2016, there have been over 2,000 attacks on health facilities worldwide. Even during the COVID-19 pandemic, more health workers and patients were killed in 2020 than in 2019. Meanwhile, ethnic cleansing and killings of aid workers have accelerated as well.

Reestablishing the rules of a rules-based order will demand more than "quoting laws to men with swords." Diplomats, generals, politicians, activists, businesses, and civil society must come together to serve as a "countervailing power"—to borrow a phrase from the American economist John Kenneth Galbraith—to the forces of impunity. Where impunity thrives on secrecy, countervailing power should demand transparency. Where impunity seeks to hide, countervailing power should seek to expose. Where impunity dismisses calls for accountability as foreign meddling, countervailing power should point to the UN Charter and the laws associated with it and demand that they be honored.

Combatants in conflict all too often feel free to disregard the rights of civilians in war because they face few political, economic, or legal costs for doing so. Changing their calculus, in order to change their behavior, will require establishing costs. This should be the animating principle behind a new generation of diplomats—and politicians, businesspeople, civil society activists—to build and defend a rules-based international order.

David Miliband is the President and Chief Executive Officer of the International Rescue Committee and a former Foreign Secretary of the United Kingdom.

Understanding Security Comprehensively

Achim Steiner

In earlier times, it was called the Wehrkundetagung, and was essentially limited to a small circle of generals and military officers. Today, the Munich Security Conference is a big international event—the "place to be" at the beginning of each year (or rather, it was so in non-coronavirus times). Not only for security politicians in the narrower sense, but also for representatives from the United Nations, development institutions, environment groups, and non-governmental organizations, as well as scientists, managers, and media representatives—in short, for anyone seeking to minimize risks and maximize progress in our world.

Today, if we look at the attendee and contribution lists of the Munich Security Conference, the message is clear: security has to be understood not merely in military terms, but far more broadly. If the goal of a decent existence for every human being is to transcend mere rhetoric, the notion of security must also include economic, ecological, and social dimensions. Wolfgang Ischinger has repeatedly made this clear in recent years, in more or less this form of words, and I can only agree.

Topics like climate change, loss of biodiversity, water shortage, and overfishing—challenges even skeptics can no longer deny—make the importance of this paradigm shift obvious. In myriad ways, mankind is reaching its limits and placing itself in a fragile situation that cannot be understood in military terms or solved by military means. That is why, in its yearly ranking, the World Economic Forum now primarily lists non-military risks among those it considers most threatening—including, of course, COVID-19, as well as environmental and cyber-driven dangers.

The bad news, however, is that this comprehensive notion of security, while being on everyone's lips, has not yet found its way into reality—especially when it comes to crises and conflicts in the global South. In my experience, developmental cooperation and, consequently, developmental expertise are, frequently, still not seen as priorities. To this day, many leaders from around the globe regard military operations (sometimes applied in a knee-jerk fashion) and, where necessary, humanitarian aid for immediate relief as the instruments of choice.

This is a mistake, not only because there is ultimately no alternative to lengthy—but ultimately sustainable—development processes, but also because this type of politics is expensive. In 2020 global military spending amounted to 2 trillion US dollars, according to calculations conducted by the SIPRI institute. In the same year, funding for development cooperation totaled 160 billion US dollars, according to OECD calculations—less than one-tenth of the global military spend (though this, by itself, is historically a record sum).

Almost all crises of at least the past thirty years (since the end of the Cold War) have indeed been multidimensional, each possessing a whole array of causes. Only rarely could a crisis of the past decades be resolved solely by military means. This applies still more to future crises—not least because their nature will continue to change due to increasing environmental problems and growing social inequality. We won't be able to make the world any more secure by means of power politics and unbridled competition alone.

In order for a generalized notion of security to take effect, we must patiently and persistently work on the development issue, rather than dismissing it as "nice to have." There is no way around the hard work that leads to better health systems, more education, cleaner electricity for everyone, a functioning statehood, and making our economies more sustainable, to name just a few objectives.

In order for a generalized notion of security to take effect, we must patiently and persistently work on the development issue, rather than dismissing it as "nice to have."

This changed understanding of security and the interplay of the many foreign policy, security policy, and development policy instruments has certainly been partly responsible for prompting Wolfgang Ischinger to call for a "three-percent criterion."[1] This proposal aimed to allot at least three percent of the gross domestic product (GDP) to crisis prevention, development cooperation, diplomacy, and defense. Bundling international expenses in this way would help to highlight the importance of considering these areas in combination, including in applied terms. Only if we live this out in practice can we move toward comprehensive security—which we need so much more than ever before.

Achim Steiner has served as the Administrator of the United Nations Development Program (UNDP) since 2017. He is UN Under-Secretary-General, and the highest-ranking German serving with the United Nations.

◂ Achim Steiner at the Munich Strategy Forum in Elmau in November 2015.

MSC2

Charting a Path to Lasting Food Security and Peace

David Beasley

In May 2018, the United Nations Security Council made a historic decision when it endorsed Resolution 2417, which condemned the starvation of civilians as a method of warfare, as well as the unlawful denial of humanitarian access to civilian populations. Adopted unanimously by the council's fifteen member states, this landmark resolution was a triumph of international diplomacy.

For the first time, our political leaders explicitly acknowledged the links between armed conflict, food insecurity, and the threat of famine, and condemned the suffering it inflicts upon civilian populations. Resolution 2417 called on all parties to armed conflict to comply with their obligations under international humanitarian law to protect civilians and to guarantee the safe and unimpeded access of humanitarian personnel to civilians in armed conflicts. Importantly, it also paved the way for the adoption of sanctions—where appropriate and in line with existing practices—that would apply to those obstructing the delivery or distribution of humanitarian assistance, such as food to civilians in need.

For all of us in the humanitarian community who have seen for ourselves the immense human cost of conflict paid by innocent civilians, Resolution 2417 was a watershed moment. It publicly acknowledged an important truth that we all know: conflict and instability drive hunger, and hunger drives conflict and instability.

As executive director of the world's largest organization dedicated to eradicating hunger, I have witnessed the devastating impact of this vicious cycle for myself, time after time. On visits to Yemen, the Democratic Republic of the Congo, and South Sudan, for example, I have met families and children who are literally starving because they are caught in the crosshairs.

The facts speak for themselves and tell a heartbreaking story. Ten of the thirteen largest hunger crises in the world today are fueled primarily by armed violence. Roughly sixty percent of the planet's 811 million chronically hungry people live in conflict zones. And around 80 percent of resources raised by humanitarian appeals in recent years have been spent in conflict zones. The link between hunger and conflict is beyond doubt—the question is how do we use diplomacy to break it, once and for all?

We must start with recognizing, as Resolution 2417 does, that starvation and famine are not natural disasters—they are overwhelmingly man-made. Instability and conflict combine with economic crisis to destroy the systems that produce, manage, and distribute food to civilian populations. The result is both tragic and predictable. To change this, we need to take a three-pronged approach.
First, we need concerted diplomatic action by the international community to end the rising number of conflicts around the world. Resolution 2417 provides a framework to find political solutions to many of the forgotten conflicts that fester across the world. But political leaders must seize the opportunity it creates and live up to the values it enshrines.

Second, we have to make the right investments, at the right time. In the short term, this means tackling the rising tide of global hunger being powered by a toxic combination of conflict, extreme weather, and, most recently, the COVID-19 pandemic. It is unacceptable that in the twenty-first century, tens of millions of people are just one step away from starvation. The world must act to avoid this hunger crisis spinning out of control.

Longer term, we must also invest in health, education, and sustainable livelihood programs, which are the best way to offer vulnerable communities the chance to build resilience and stand on their own two feet. This is critical to help lay the foundations for peace and sustainable economic development.

And third, we need to work with governments to strengthen national food systems and social safety net programs to ensure that all communities—no matter who they are or where they live—have equal access to nutritious foods. This is fundamental to reduce social tensions and support long-term stability.

This is an ambitious diplomatic agenda, but I remain hopeful that if the international community invests wisely and works in genuine partnership, we can help vulnerable communities find a pathway out of poverty and hunger toward a more peaceful and prosperous future.

Resolution 2417 was the starting point for our journey. Now it is time to harness the spirit of goodwill and diplomatic cooperation it symbolizes and work together to finally get the job done.

David Beasley is the Executive Director of the United Nations World Food Programme.

◂ David Beasley at the Munich Security Conference in February 2020.

00:00:58
Munich Security
Conference
msc

Investing in Pandemic Preparedness

Tedros Adhanom Ghebreyesus

History will judge us based not on the catastrophes that strike us, but how we react to them. The story of the COVID-19 pandemic is still being written, but we do know that it has been the cause of much preventable suffering and death, as well as social, economic, and political turmoil. It is not too late to correct course. Several clear lessons in leadership and diplomacy have already emerged.

Shared threats require a shared response. No single organization and no single nation can prepare for and respond to pandemics and other global threats alone. There are many recent examples of cooperation: in 2015 the world came together to adopt the Sustainable Development Goals, the Paris Agreement, and the Addis Ababa Action Agenda on Financing for Development. At the United Nations General Assembly in 2019, just a few months before the pandemic started, UN member states endorsed the high-level political declaration on universal health coverage.

But geopolitical divisions have been exacerbated by COVID-19. Misguided nationalism and isolationism have eroded that sense of common purpose. The global vaccine equity crisis illustrates the consequences of these trends. At the time of writing, almost half of the world's population is fully vaccinated against COVID-19, but only 8 percent of people in Africa are. Countries with the most financial and geopolitical muscle have taken control of the global supply of vaccines, effectively excluding dozens of countries and billions of people from the global vaccine marketplace.

Vaccine equity is a litmus test for solidarity and global health diplomacy. While every government has the responsibility to protect its own people, the lack of global solidarity and sharing—of information, biological samples, resources, and tools—has deprived governments in low- and lower-middle income countries of the opportunity to fulfill that responsibility.

Even when the COVID-19 pandemic is subdued, we will still be left with many of the same vulnerabilities we had before it started. There is no vaccine for poverty, hunger, racism, gender equality, or climate change. The pandemic exposed and exploited the inequalities in our societies, and frayed trust in public institutions. It has laid bare our fragility, and exposed the gaps in national, regional, and global preparedness and response systems, and the weaknesses of the international health architecture.

In December 2021, WHO's member states agreed to negotiate a new convention, agreement or other international instrument on pandemic prevention, preparedness and response. Such an accord will provide a vital overarching framework for strengthening the governance, financing, and systems and tools needed to bolster global health security, including by giving additional high-level political support to the International Health Regulations (IHR), the legal framework that governs the global response to pandemics and other health emergencies. The IHR has its roots in the International Sanitary Conferences in Paris that began in 1851. That's when countries first came together to discuss cooperating to combat shared public health threats like cholera and plague, which not only had devastating health effects, but also severely disrupted trade and economies. Countries realized that it was in their interests to work together.

The IHR has been revised several times since then, often in the wake of crises—the last time in 2005, after SARS. The pandemic has shown not only why the IHR is an important tool but has also shown its limitations. In its current form, the IHR depends upon each country's compliance, but the mechanisms to promote compliance are limited, including by the fact that WHO has no direct enforcement authority.

A treaty on pandemic preparedness and response could lay out mutually agreed principles, priorities, and targets for keeping the world safer. These could include building resilience to pandemics and other global health emergencies, with robust national preparedness and response systems built on a foundation of strong national public health systems; supporting sustainable funding and capacity for prevention, detection, and responses to outbreaks; and ensuring equitable access to pandemic countermeasures.

The world cannot afford to wait until the pandemic is over to start planning for the next global health emergency. We cannot do things the way we have done them before and expect a different result. It is time to break the cycle of panic and neglect. We need to reimagine leadership, built on mutual trust and mutual accountability—to end the pandemic and address the fundamental inequalities that lie at the root of so many of the world's problems.

Tedros Adhanom Ghebreyesus is the Director-General of the World Health Organization. He previously served as Minister of Health and Minister of Foreign Affairs of Ethiopia.

◂ Tedros Adhanom Ghebreyesus at the Munich Security Conference in February 2020.

SC CONVERSATIONS
#MSC2020

Making Sense of the Quantum World

Armen Sarkissian

A new world order is taking shape. But not in the way you think.

Many geopolitical events are taking place to catalyze the repositioning of the chess pieces: the United States' strategic shift to focus on the Asia-Pacific (compounded by the gradual decline of their soft power since the consequences of 9/11); the continued uncertainty and indecision of the EU as it searches for its most efficient structure and geopolitical future coupled with fragmented values across its member states; Russia's strategy to consolidate and restore its historic influence globally, which it lost after the collapse of the Soviet Union; and China's rapid expansion and influence across all corners and industries of the globe. Concurrently, the international system (dominated by US hegemony for the last three decades) is encountering the rise of the "middle powers," such as India, Turkey, Iran, Brazil, and others. These changes are provoking largely dormant regional conflicts to spark up again, establishing new areas of conflict in trade, cyber, and technology, and creating more instability in the international rules-based system that the post-World War II generations had become accustomed to.

Yet at the same time, a smaller, quieter but more dramatic change has been taking place since the beginning of this century. The world has become hyperconnected through the internet and smart devices; technology is evolving at a rapid pace (far beyond any regulation or state oversight); information has become overabundant to the point where fact and fiction have become purely subjective; and the way in which humans are interacting and engaging with each other, our institutions, and the state has become completely different as compared to the previous century. What does this all mean?

This fast-changing political and social landscape is something humans have not experienced before. It is the harbinger of a new era. An era of *quantum politics*.

How do these two very distinct concepts of politics and quantum theory overlap with each other to explain where our world and international system is heading? In the early 2000s, it became clear that the world was not only becoming more globalized and connected, but also more sensitive, whereby small, localized events were gaining increasingly asymmetric outcomes due to the changing ways in which business, politics, and social constructs were interacting; in some cases, merging with each other or together with other fields such as entertainment and gaming. This was because people did not anticipate the power of quantum mechanics and how it shaped the rapid evolution of technology and how such technologies would come to not only dominate our lives, but shape how we behave as individuals as well as groups of individuals.

How do these two very distinct concepts of politics and quantum theory overlap with each other to explain where our world and international system is heading?

I began speaking about this phenomenon in the early 2000s at the World Economic Forum and other platforms, as something I termed *quantum politics,* to explain how politics and politicians will no longer behave or be as they have been in the past, and the same will happen with the business world. At the beginning of each talk, I would make sure that the audience understood that the term quantum politics (*or a quantum world*) does not mean that the rules of quantum physics or mechanics should be directly applied to politics, people, or society, but rather that it is the most relevant metaphor to discuss this new state of politics and the world. It does not indicate that a politician has the same properties as an elementary particle, but it does explain how our concepts and relationships have drastically changed because of how we interact and communicate with each other and with our institutions. Therefore, the term quantum used herein should be read both as a metaphor and as an actual change taking place in our lives. The intention here is not to compare, prescribe, or enforce the rules of quantum physics and mechanics to politics or other aspects of our lives, but to use such frameworks practically and metaphorically to help make a little bit more sense of our increasingly complex and unpredictable world.

We are rapidly evolving from having used only classical mechanics for centuries to using, more and more—as a global species—quantum mechanics as the basis of our new technologies, communications systems, and ways of interaction. Yet it wasn't until the 2020 pandemic forced us to change our own frameworks

◂ Armen Sarkissian at the Munich Security Conference in February 2020.

(whether we wanted to or not)—how we behave, how we live, and how we design our institutions. Crises are always an opportunity to see the world differently and make big changes, which may have been impossible before.

To commence our journey using these new concepts of quantum politics and a quantum world, we must start with a simple observation:

The human race has always been a species evolving at a non-natural pace: the technologies we create are a part of our evolutionary story and are increasingly shaping who we will become.

This simple truth, a unique characteristic of humans, both causes and solves many of the global issues we face today, and it will do so in the future. It also begs a pertinent question: who exactly have we become? How have the things we have created shaped not just our lifestyles, but our core properties as a human race? These qualities are entrenched across many generations through our institutions and traditions; dictating how we learn, how we work, how we govern, and how we treat each other on personal, group, and national levels. In other words, it shapes our education, economics, society, and politics.

We are rapidly evolving from having used only classical mechanics for centuries to using, more and more—as a global species—quantum mechanics as the basis of our new technologies, communications systems, and ways of interaction.

It explains more than you can imagine at first, delineating how we have achieved so much progress in the last two hundred years, but also why we feel like we have more problems now than ever before. It has shaped how and what we have learned for generations, how we have interacted from tribes to nations to states, as well as how our social priorities have been changing to define what is acceptable and what is not.

It also answers many other questions we are all asking ourselves and each other today: Why does it feel like we are jumping from one crisis to the next without a moment's breath? . . . Why do crises relentlessly overlap each other more than ever before? . . . Why does everything seem to be happening at an accelerated pace and at unexpected moments? . . . Why is it so hard to plan anything beyond one year in your business? . . . Why are politicians so unreliable and becoming more extreme or populist? . . . And why are we having more division in our societies than ever before, even if the basic needs of our lives have dramatically improved?

In quantum physics, the questions have always been more important than the answers, as each answer is the path to new questions. Can a better understanding of the world as being quantum help us improve our lives further or solve today's complex problems more effectively? How can we improve ourselves, our institutions, and our perspectives to understand the roots of these problems once and for all? How can we identify these hugely beneficial quantum phenomena taking place all around us and multiply them across other aspects of our lives to derive even more benefits?

We are at a turning point in our history, and if we do not act now, it may become too late to solve these problems or to more efficiently grasp the benefits we are seeing. Yet there is something fundamental holding us back, which could derail our beautiful story of human progress that has taken place over the last two centuries, and especially over the last thirty years.

Doubtless, throughout history this ominous bell has been rung many times, yet never before has the human race been able to connect so efficiently with each other and access a vast global pool of information. This makes today's situation unique in our history, and very critical.

As with all complicated questions, the answer may seem puzzling at first, but when it is broken down into clear parts, you will feel like you knew it all along. So, in the spirit of scientific discovery, let us start with our enigmatic hypothesis (that is, our answer) and then provide evidence to support its validity.

Our increasing progress and problems in social, political, and economic spheres, locally and globally, stem from the fact that we are living in a world exponentially influenced by the properties of quantum mechanics, while our perspectives, institutions, and belief systems are still organized and managed in accordance with classical (Newtonian) mechanics.

Reading this statement may cause the reader some confusion at first. What does Isaac Newton have to do with inequality, geopolitics, and financial crises in the twenty-first century? How can quantum mechanics explain why we have more social unrest and increasing populism in the 2020s? But most importantly, is this divergence something we really need to worry about? The answer is actually far simpler than it first seems and is explained by four simple observations.

1. All our institutions and belief systems are derived from human interaction and tradition.

Our social, political, and economic circumstances are a result of our interactions as a highly social species. These interactions have, over time, manifested into our belief systems, institutions, and networks. Today we call these things politics, money, religion, economics, business, education—virtually all other aspects of our lives that require a form of a social contract (at a minimum, *interaction*) to be present in order for a group of people to believe such a thing exists. This is the reason we call them *belief systems*.

The strongest and most important example of such a belief system is religion, which can hold extremely strong bonds among people from around the world, if they all hold such belief in the same values. A drastically different but also extremely strong belief system is money, which is essentially just printed paper; however, we all must believe that the currency, represented by the number that is printed on that paper (or on your screen), gives that paper value, in order for it to be an effective social tool. Laws are also belief systems because a large group of people depend on them and a smaller group enforce them, but in reality, they are just concepts. Similarly, a company is a legal entity, but it doesn't actually exist, it is an ethereal concept—owners, employees, consumers have to *believe* that the legal documents, which create such a company, give it existence. All these things need groups of people to hold common beliefs around an entity and apply common standards to it, giving it life through our interactions around these standards. For that entity to function and for us to base our relationships on such entities, we need two simple ingredients—a common *system* and *interaction*. Over time, these belief systems became institutions or social networks for interaction, as they are passed on through generations. We call this intergenerational transfer of belief systems simply tradition or culture.

In quantum physics, the questions have always been more important than the answers, as each answer is the path to new questions. Can a better understanding of the world as being quantum help us improve our lives further or solve today's complex problems more effectively?

Depending on where you are born and when in history, you are raised into a certain culture with specific beliefs and traditions. The traditions you follow were engrained into you by your parents, and later in life perhaps you follow other traditions through different people you encounter or experiences you accumulate. In short, tradition allows for consecutive generations to maintain their belief systems, preserving historic institutions and cultural values. Your education, familial structures, and language are all passed on to you in this way. It's important that we appreciate the extent to which our behavioral patterns have been engrained in us through traditions and belief systems from the moment we are born, rather than by our own personal choices.

Belief systems are largely controlled or centralized entities or concepts, which have a tacit or explicit buy-in from a population, in turn creating larger network effects. To create order (order being the number one priority of a classical state because without order there is chaos within which no stable governance can exist), these belief systems must be anchored by rule of God, rule of law, and social rules of conduct—rules that provide stability and comfort from their constancy. Social contracts are built around these belief systems in order to generate trust among individuals who engage around that certified trust. Without this stability, individuals cannot earn, pray, learn, or live peacefully.

2. Contemporary technologies influence how we interact, in turn directly impacting our belief systems.

Although these belief systems and institutions are embedded in tradition, they evolve around the technologies we harness, starting from the creation of language and fire, which separated us from our animal kin, stretching to smartphones and computers. Each stage of technological development generated within us a new form of interaction. The story of humanity can be told as a story of rapidly increasing and improving communication and interaction.

As humans evolved, we continuously developed better technologies, reaching a point where the technologies themselves are causing an increasing acceleration of our own slow evolutionary pace. Fire meant we consumed cooked food, which required the burning of fewer calories to digest the food. Thus, more energy was available to develop our brains, enabling us to create sophisticated languages, forging stronger bonds through improved communication. The invention of farming techniques and agricultural processes allowed us to form societies and civilizations, as we no longer had to travel great distances to hunt but could coalesce in one location and optimize tasks through division of labor. The steam engine sparked the Industrial Revolution and subsequent inventions in transportation spurred on globalization. Wheels, bridges, boats, and planes allowed us to physically interact with other cultures through trade, tourism, and war. The list continues to today when the internet and rapid improvements in computer processing power provide us with individualized and instant information sharing that has propelled us into the Digital Age.

This network effect between humans and our technologies may well result in a complete symbiosis between the two in due course. Inevitably, this symbiosis will create further inequality between those who can afford it and use it to enhance their own evolution, and those who cannot and remain at our slow human evolutionary pace. However, looking back we can see that each phase of technological progress dictated what form of interaction took place among humans as at that specific time. Therefore, the available contemporary technology is restricted and enabled by the scientific understanding at that time.

Today's prevailing scientific model is that of quantum theory.

For example, a stockbroker could not exist in the tenth century simply because the technology to trade shares did not exist, nor did the concept of a company as a legal entity. A king could not know in 1830 that his country was about to be attacked until the enemy had reached his shore, whereas today satellite imagery can provide live detailed mapping for anyone with a smartphone. A CEO in San Francisco in 2021 cannot 3D-print a steak in her office in three minutes, then have a holographic augmented-reality meeting with her team in Tokyo, before booking her space vacation with her children for the next day. She will soon. Our technologies dominate how we live, how we work, and most importantly, how we interact with each other.

They also represent our nature at that time because they are an extension of ourselves. As a species, we have prospered from the continuous (re)invention and improvement of tools to pull us from one phase of evolution to another, at a pace more accelerated than nature intended. The tools that empowered each phase of the human race, from weapons to agriculture to the steam engine, are the things that differentiate us from animals. In fact, each tool has been an augmentation of our human characteristics. We now have legs that can cross vast terrains in hours rather than months of walking or riding; we have arms that can construct structures larger than the pyramids or colosseums that required thousands of men; we have eyes to see across enigmatic galaxies yet also peer into the endless hall of mirrors of the substructures of our being.

Neither sea nor space is a barrier that hinders our connectivity, but rather they are mediums, which we can enhance through satellites and pipelines. Most recently, quantum theory has been used to develop technologies that have drastically changed our lives. The computer in your pocket (and the sheer number of them relative to the total population) has empowered individuality. Individuality, with the ability to receive and provide instant information from and to the world, is the core property of the quantum characteristics of the modern global society.

But why all this mention of physics impacting our daily lives? It's complicated enough to understand what quantum mechanics and quantum theory actually mean, so why this arbitrary association with politics or economics?

For the simple reason that it is thanks to scientific breakthroughs throughout human history, brought forth by the daring imagination of celebrated scientists, that technological progress was even possible in the first place. And today's prevailing scientific model is that of quantum theory.

3. The new technologies we develop are increasingly based on our current scientific understanding of reality—that of quantum theory and mechanics.

Originally, the science behind quantum physics was developed to account for the microscopic world of elementary particles. Thereafter, the concepts and rules behind quantum theory developed to underpin the chemical and technological advances of the twentieth century. Without quantum theory, we would not understand how electrons and other elementary particles behave, and we would not be able to create the vast array of chemical compounds that are used in nearly every manufacturing industry today.

So where is quantum mechanics used and what has it actually done for us? For a start, the two most widely used instruments by people all around the world—computers and smartphones—are created by quantum mechanics. These instruments use semiconductors, which in turn rely on the wave structure of electrons to enable us to shape the properties of silicon to behave in a certain way. We use quantum mechanics to pack layers of silicon with other elements via transistors to create processing microchips. These are in turn used in pretty much anything that has processing power today—smartphones, laptops, gadgets, toys, kitchen appliances, televisions, and even cars.

Whether you realize it or not, quantum mechanics dominates your life, especially if you live in a high-income country.

Other technologies that apply quantum mechanics are based around laser technology—a quantum phenomenon structured around photons, or units of light. Laser stands for Light Amplification by Stimulated Emission of Radiation, and this amplification of light (photons) at different wavelengths can be used in anything—from scanning barcodes, printing, DNA sequencing, surgery, and cosmetics, to countless other uses. The most accurate clocks in the world are atomic clocks, which use quantum theory to measure when electrons "jump" during radiation. Using this and even more complicated applications of quantum mechanics, we have opened the possibilities of the internet, GPS tracking, and MRIs, and are now at the precipice of quantum computing—a phenomenon that allows a computer to process information at indescribable speeds.

Whether you realize it or not, quantum mechanics dominates your life, especially if you live in a high-income country. These aforementioned technologies are all based on today's computing processing power. Governments and companies around the world are currently investing billions into developing quantum computing[1] abilities, which will amplify today's processors by unfathomable amounts and, alongside them, the technologies that quantum mechanics empowers.

But why does technology have such a big impact on *who* we are?

To answer this, we must look back to the early days of our understanding of reality. Initially, we described the forces of nature as the actions of angry or pleased gods, until the ancient atomist Greeks used rationality to kick off the philosophy of science in the sixth century BC. Copernicus then changed our thinking to consider that perhaps we are not the center of the universe with everything revolving around the earth, but instead we are a small part of something bigger revolving around a sun. Eventually, came Newton who elegantly described motion and causation through the theory of gravity, then Faraday and Maxwell who explained how everything is connected through electromagnetic fields and there is no empty space. Each one of these changes in scientific understandings of our reality had profound consequences on how we thought and then applied those theories to create new technologies. However, it was Albert Einstein (who was not a quantum physicist but paved the way for a new perspective of our reality) and the school of quantum theorists of the twentieth century who ushered in the era that we live in today, where we (mostly) no longer assume that a storm is a punishment for the village's misdeeds.

4. **Our social, political, educational, and professional lives increasingly use modern technologies that are based on quantum mechanics—making our interactions more quantum in nature—while our traditions and belief systems are still based on classical mechanics.**

If all this still seems somewhat philosophical to you, let us propose what science actually is. Scientific developments start off as philosophies because the initial spark of scientific progress is ignited by an inspired thought on how or why things are the way they are. It starts with a hypothesis or a theory on how things can be different or better. This theory is then discussed in the academic field and tested until proven right or wrong. Some theories warrant billions of dollars of research such as at CERN in Geneva; others simply require just a moment of clarity, such as a famous apple falling on someone's head. If proven right, it becomes our understanding of reality. Yet in our reality, no theory should be considered permanent as we strive to learn more and remain open to change our previous conceptions. This is the true spirit of science.

Otherwise, we restrict within us our greatest gift—imagination. Through its harnessing, we have managed to leap from flat earths and sun gods to flat screens and solar panels. All scientific processes—from Thales in the sixth century BC, who is credited with igniting the scientific process itself, to the great physicists of the twentieth century such as Max Planck, Niels Bohr, Paul Dirac, Albert Einstein, and Werner Heisenberg—started with imagining a different world. Being a good philosopher is part of being a good theoretical scientist. This is the path of human progress.

Subsequently, we use this scientific understanding to improve our existing technologies. The more people there are in the world having philosophical discussions and conducting tests of far-flung theories, the faster our technologies develop. For this reason, it is essential to utilize the human capacity for more creative work and critical thinking if we want to progress faster, rather than to train and provide mundane jobs that will eventually be automated. The easier such people openly connect and communicate with each other, the faster progress is achieved. It becomes exponential. This is why we have developed more technologies in the last one hundred years than in the previous one thousand years; and it is why the world in 2050 will look completely different than today's world.

We must reform many of the things we have taken for granted over the last few generations and be prepared for a new type of world—one which has already arrived.

But this chain reaction always starts with a courageous thought from someone who wants to think or act differently. A scientist or innovator must also be a philosopher in order to ask the right questions or think outside the box. Ultimately, science and philosophy are brother and sister. Anyone reading recent developments in quantum gravity, string theory, or many worlds theory will understand the transcendence into philosophy and science fiction—yet this is exactly what today's science is: yesterday's science fiction.

While we make rapid progress through innovation in our way of life, we do not apply the same philosophy or standards to our belief systems. Most of the belief systems and institutions we adhere to were developed at a time that did not include the quantum technologies we have adopted today and have changed how we interact. So, to summarize our four observations into one, we come to the following conclusion:

All our institutions and belief systems are based on human interaction and tradition, developed by technologies that were based on classical scientific understandings of reality. However, our current technologies are increasingly based on quantum mechanics, causing a deviation in how we actually interact compared to how our societies are designed for us to interact through our institutions and belief systems. Therefore, we must rethink or redesign parts of our societies and institutions to account for a more "quantum" world before the deviations become too extreme or we ignore unique opportunities for innovation, progress, and solutions to long-term global problems.

We have come to an unprecedented moment of tension. The roots of tradition are grating against the symbiotic evolution of humans and technology. There is a misalignment in the story of human progress and one that will have profound repercussions if left unattended. We must apply the same standards of the roots of our innovation to ourselves, our institutions, and our belief systems in order to achieve a more harmonious path of progress. We must reform many of the things we have taken for granted over the last few generations and be prepared for a new type of world—one that has already arrived.

But . . . Who Cares?

You may be thinking at this point, why does all of this matter to me? Why should I care about all these scientific, political, and philosophical theories, other than being nice dinner conversation? I still have to go to school and then work, make money, take care of my family, and try to enjoy life in between.

Simply put, it matters because, in the quantum world, you are an important quantum particle. You never had the chance to be this electron in the history of the universe, let alone the human race, until now. You have the opportunity to shape what work, money, family, and school look like to you and future generations, more than ever before. Humans have never been in a position to look in such detail across time into our origins and our history, while scanning across multiple fields of expertise to extrapolate patterns and insights that others may not have attempted to before—or have been too restricted by the prejudices they grew up with, both biological and cultural, to even try. This is the time to interact and think outside of the box and to challenge long-established norms, which were instilled in us by generational exchange of habit and limited access to information and education.

These restrictions have fallen away over the last one hundred years to a great degree and most specifically since the end of World War II. The 2020 pandemic and its consequences could be an opportunity to finally formalize the inevitable trend of the increasingly nurturing state, to disrupt traditional structures that are no longer relevant and that indirectly influence the trajectory of inequality within and between populations. The world wars and Great Depression of the twentieth century led to greater egalitarianism by changing the global mood toward collaboration. The exhaustion and division (by way of class, race, and even nationality) from the 2008 financial crisis to the 2020 pandemic will clear the path for a new way of life. What way this path of human progress takes is up to you more than ever before.

We are at a crossroads of multiple global events that converge to create a unique turning point in our history. We can influence what this history looks like if we apply these understandings, patterns, and insights onto a realistic assessment of what our reality is and how best to create positive externalities within it.

You are now a vibrant, engaging particle that is constantly a part of its environment; but you are also a quantum particle and can influence not only the immediate environment but one that is not physically next to you.

If you stand still, if you stop learning, if you stop interacting, there is only death.

You are constrained by your biology, but you are living in an environment of change and connectivity, freed by your irrational, creative mind and open to all possibilities in a highly connected world. Hopefully, through the power of insights during this journey and others explored tangentially, you will become unshackled from the chains of tradition and tribalism to see the quantum world for what it is: a place of uncertainty, asymmetry, and interaction, but one of great hope and possibilities. Yet the quantum world will also pose many challenges and global risks, and to mitigate them we must understand them in our quantum framework to develop more effective solutions that will help not just us, but future generations.

Can we make the Darwinian leap today much like our ancestors did millions of years ago, to begin our journey in this quantum world?

Armen Sarkissian is the President of Armenia. He is a physicist and computer scientist, and previously served as Prime Minister of Armenia from 1996 to 1997 and the Armenian Ambassador to the United Kingdom from 1998 to 2018.

Adapting Diplomatic Tools and Structures

Cathryn Clüver Ashbrook

Madeleine Albright says it often and well. In the digital age, citizens of democracies are speaking to their governments using twenty-first century technology, while governments—their diplomats very much included—have been listening via twentieth century technologies and responding with nineteenth century solutions.

For diplomacy and those who would effectively practice it, the time for that disjuncture must be over. The cost in public trust, diplomatic capacity, and respect for foreign policy expertise is just too high. To play a robust role in democratic national security structures, outwit authoritarian systems, regain public confidence, and bring twenty-first century solutions to problems of contemporary diplomacy, foreign ministries in democracies must adopt deeply data-driven analysis, embrace evidence-based policy making, and make themselves powerful centers of expertise by more radically embracing openness to the resources around them.

Classic diplomatic tradecraft remains utterly necessary. Measured assessment, interest-anticipation, and adroit negotiation remain foundational. But the context in which the "organized conduct of relations between states"[1] takes place has radically shifted.

On the one hand, there is the resurgence of familiar territorial, geopolitical, and geo-economic tensions in international relations, which often advantage the defense lever of any national security apparatus. On the other, there are the mounting transnational challenges—overlapping, simultaneous, sometimes causally linked—from climate change to pandemics to empowered extremism and migration management. These bring a new set of interlocutors to the national security and foreign policy arena, against the backdrop of technological transformation bringing social and economic changes we can yet only partially forecast.

This combination leaves the Westphalian-style, democratic nation-state increasingly challenged in its singular capacity to wield force, finance, and information. Authoritarian systems fight a loss of control by building out and tightening the reins of central administration. China, with its Great Firewall and interventionist economy, is the perfect example. Meanwhile, democratic systems fight a loss of public trust. The rapid advancement of technology—now, at the heart of the data revolution—accelerates these shifts at breakneck speed. Where accountability in a democracy is based around a bureaucratic system that slows down decision-making to spread consensus and accountability, while events overtake the process, the descent into dysfunction begins.

Taken together, these shifts affect many of the fundamental currencies of diplomacy, including discretion built on trust and limited, sequenced information necessary to marshaling the scope of any negotiation "at the table," the expertise and ability to design a deal and create value away from constant public scrutiny;[2] and an understanding of how these linked elements will play out "away from the table," particularly in multinational negotiations.[3]

The negotiations on the Transatlantic Trade and Investment Partnership (TTIP) may be the most vivid recent example. When US Secretary of State John Kerry and US Secretary of Defense Chuck Hagel endorsed the transatlantic trade pact at the Munich Security Conference in 2014—to the applause of hundreds of decision-makers in the room—they failed to foresee the degree to which digitally organized and financed activists could alter the negotiation environment "away from the table," shifting and constricting the policy options so dramatically, that passage ultimately became politically untenable. That cannot and should not happen to economic diplomats in the future—the stakes are too high. Faced with a systems competitor in tech-giant China, for instance, the EU-US Trade and Tech Council's work will have to be both feasible and effectively multi-stakeholder in execution and acceptance.

To play a robust role in democratic national security structures, outwit authoritarian systems, regain public confidence, and bring twenty-first century solutions to problems of contemporary diplomacy, foreign ministries in democracies must adopt deeply data-driven analysis, embrace evidence-based policy making, and make themselves powerful centers of expertise by more radically embracing openness to the resources around them.

In short, diplomacy as a practice and diplomatic institutions—ministries of foreign affairs (MFAs) and multilateral institutions—must embrace more radical

◂ Cathryn Clüver Ashbrook at the Munich Young Leaders Alumni Meeting in September 2019.

change and reform more fundamentally than the earlier attempts at crafting twenty-first century statecraft might suggest. MFAs across the world have used previous reform processes to better anchor themselves in their societies, increasing diversity efforts and democratic legitimacy through reauthorizations,[4] rethinking the usage of technology for digital listening, and the creation of rotational schemes between diplomacy, business, and other fields to maximize access to expertise. Those changes tackled the issues of yesterday. Now foreign ministries must become even more anticipatory organizations. They must reassert their own primacy and usefulness vis-à-vis powerful executive offices, defense ministries, and agencies with sectoral expertise. Further, to outwit the capacities of authoritarian societies, MFAs must become more—radically more—open than they are today.

MFAs are institutions with long histories—rightfully prestigious. But "messy problems" will require the ability to rely on other sorts of expertise, in which knowledge cannot be fully owned in one place. In short: the future of diplomacy will be marked by how an organization manages the risk of not knowing or owning everything. Marshaling more complex risk environments will become an increasingly important function of an MFA in a democracy.

MFAs should focus on evidence-based policy-making: Citizens were right to question the length and functionality of international engagement in Afghanistan. "How can we prevent the same mistakes in foreign policy over and over again?" must be answered by the effective transformation of foreign ministries into learning organizations, using systematic and thorough evaluation and the application of evidence, matching resources, and policy.[5] The combination of big data usage in diplomacy—that is, as practiced in Canada for visa applications and increasingly in trade negotiations—and accountability for usage will have be part of a newly emergent, diagnostic toolkit. Gaming and VR technology can help to more accurately forecast scenarios in classic foreign policy decision-making and in cybersecurity incidents, improving the "red team-blue team" exercises once piloted by the military. In the long term, getting it right—or getting it less wrong—will help to rebuild public trust. The multi-sector Centre of Competence on Humanitarian Negotiation (CCHN)[6] is a good example of how, through systemized analysis of crisis negotiation—often the most individual interactions in diplomacy—we can better train and prepare diplomats, based on a framework collaboratively developed with leading universities, to make the art of crisis negotiation more teachable and frontline diplomacy more functional. Other organizations, such as the WHO Hub for Pandemic Intelligence, are following that lead to pool expertise and build a basis for public credibility over the long term.

Ministries should embrace expertise: Climate change and pandemic prevention can only be effective with science, industry, and technology at the table—but diplomatic skill will be needed to negotiate access, secure resources, set legal and international standards. Providing the translation of expertise into negotiation capacity, also known as diplomacy, MFAs should reposition themselves as the nodes for this expertise. They cannot "own" this expertise in-house, but they must know how to convene and marshal it. Here, nuclear prevention diplomacy should be the model, not least the original JCPOA negotiations in which the expertise of US Energy Secretary Ernest Moniz and Iranian counterpart Ali Akbar Salehi were critical to the deal design. Different models will need to be developed to support more structural openness, but in a race with autocracies, this form of radical openness toward expertise is the only way forward.

And all diplomacy is local: Diplomacy is often likened to the art of persuasion: Getting the other side to have it your way. But what if—in the case of TTIP—the other side is your own public? When the lines between domestic and international relations blur, it becomes critical to seek foreign policy intelligence abroad and at home. Increasingly, mayors, NGOs, and activists are so internationally networked that they can impact negotiated outcomes at the table and away from the table. C40, the now powerful network of cities, has had an impact at every COP since Paris. MFAs should be exploiting the analysis these domestic actors acquire internationally to help persuade both domestic and foreign audiences of necessary foreign policy action.

By embracing new tools and engaging in a keen and strategic repositioning and reconceptualizing of their own institutional role, MFAs can become the architects—not the relics—of twenty-first century diplomacy, offering tangible, credible solutions to the world's most pressing problems.

Cathryn Clüver Ashbrook is the Director and CEO of the German Council on Foreign Relations. For eleven years, she served as the Executive Director of the Future of Diplomacy Project, which comparatively evaluated reform efforts in foreign policy institutions and trained the next generation of leaders in international relations at the Harvard Kennedy School. She was a Munich Young Leader in 2014.

MSC Health Security Roundtable at the Munich Security Conference in February 2020. ▸

3 Episodes of Diplomacy

msc
onferenz
BAYERISCHER
curity
ence
msc

Negotiating German Unity: The Art of Pragmatic Diplomacy

Robert B. Zoellick

Theory versus Diplomatic Practice

Professors usually teach foreign policy through the lens of international relations theories. These concepts are fun to debate; they can stimulate ideas. But diplomats are likely to find that the doctrines are of limited use when working on practical problems. US foreign policy has been most effective when Americans practiced pragmatic diplomacy. Perhaps it is not coincidental that pragmatism also represents the country's most significant contribution to philosophy.

William James and John Dewey described pragmatism as the study of the practical consequences that flow from experience. Their philosophical approach rejected dogmas, artificial intellectual conventions, and universal timeless truths. The pragmatic method begins by identifying problems and then looking to experience for ideas about how to fix situations.

Pragmatic philosophers recognize the roles of chance and contingency. They prize experimentation. The method anticipates dynamic situations and respects the pluralistic search for ideas. Impatient with abstractions, pragmatists value results over theories.

Pragmatic Diplomacy

In a similar way, pragmatic diplomacy seeks out what works. Pragmatic diplomats pay attention to realities "on the ground": of power, economics, military capacity, population, technologies, and votes. They study processes and institutions—and how they really work. Pragmatists need to know the interests and positions of others; they recognize the critical importance of timing.

Pragmatic political leaders may appreciate the appeal of visions and enjoy contests of ideas, but they pursue them flexibly. They must juggle multiple issues at once. Leaders may adhere to ideologies, but not rigidly. They aspire to achieve objectives that move situations closer to their vision. As such, pragmatists recognize the benefits of imperfect results in a far-from-perfect world. They study history to gain insights on how to do better, not with an acceptance of timeless obstacles.

The Pragmatists of 1989

The Americans who led the diplomacy of German unification were pragmatists. Consider how their actions in 1989–90 applied the art of pragmatic diplomacy.

In early 1989, the ice of the Cold War was cracking quickly. President Mikhail Gorbachev had created expectations of great change, but also uncertainties. Germans, in particular, welcomed the still-vague possibilities. In Washington the new president, George H.W. Bush, and the secretary of state, James Baker, recognized that the Federal Republic of Germany (FRG) would be the central European actor in the Western response to Gorbachev. Former secretary of state George Shultz and others in the Reagan administration had concluded that the Cold War was over. Bush and Baker viewed the situation differently. The Cold War had begun over the division of Berlin, Germany, and Europe; until the United States and its allies achieved "a Europe whole and free," including a democratic Germany, united in peace and freedom, the Cold War would not be finished.

US foreign policy has been most effective when Americans practiced pragmatic diplomacy. Perhaps it is not coincidental that pragmatism also represents the country's most significant contribution to philosophy.

The new US team recognized, however, that they faced a pressing problem with the FRG. The US-Soviet agreement in 1987 to eliminate intermediate-range missiles left only short-range nuclear forces (SNF) in Europe. NATO officials wanted to modernize those missiles, which were dwarfed in number by the Soviet arsenal. But as the German political leader Volker Rühe quipped, "The shorter the missiles, the deader the Germans." Most Germans wanted to negotiate SNF reductions and postpone the introduction of new missiles.

In May 1989, Bush offered a bold plan to cut drastically and equalize the NATO and Warsaw Pact armies. If the Soviets would agree to a parity of conventional arms at much lower levels, there would be less need for nuclear deterrence and SNF missiles. Furthermore, a major

◂ Robert B. Zoellick at the Munich Security Conference in February 2013.

withdrawal of the Red Army from Central and Eastern Europe would send an unmistakable signal to reformers pushing for democratization and independence. And a future Soviet leader would not be able to easily reverse the cuts and withdrawals. The move could help Gorbachev lower his crushing military budget as well. Bush also recognized that large US forces and maneuvers in the FRG created tensions; a smaller American footprint would be more politically sustainable.

After a debate at the NATO summit that went late into the night of May 29–30, the allies agreed to Bush's initiative. Prime Minister Margaret Thatcher had been particularly skeptical. In the end, Bush managed to lead the alliance through his creative proposal and Baker's adroit negotiations. NATO offered Gorbachev the prospect of a landmark treaty to cut conventional arms—the Conventional Armed Forces in Europe (CFE) Treaty—that would in fact be completed, in record time, by 1990. NATO also agreed to authorize a negotiation to partially reduce SNF forces but delayed the start until the two sides had begun to implement cuts in conventional forces.

After the NATO summit, Bush traveled to Chancellor Helmut Kohl's home state of Rheinland-Pfalz, where the President gave a major speech titled "Partners in Leadership." Within less than five months in office, Bush has positioned the United States and the FRG to work in close and trusted combination for the dramatic days to come.

Pragmatic political leaders may appreciate the appeal of visions and enjoy contests of ideas, but they pursue them flexibly.

First Moves toward Unification

During the summer and early fall of 1989, the flow of events in Central and Eastern Europe merged into a flood of transformation. The Solidarity movement in Poland won a smashing electoral victory and moved carefully to form the first noncommunist government in Eastern Europe. Hungary removed the barbed wire from its border, opening a release valve for East Germans who could flee to Austria. Bush visited both Poland and Hungary that summer. East Germans escaped to the FRG's embassy in Prague, leading to a carefully negotiated exit to the West. Brave East Germans demonstrated in increasing numbers at home. Then in November, Berliners opened the Wall. Within weeks Chancellor Kohl surprised everyone with a ten-point plan for German confederation, exciting Germans but sparking fears in Moscow and Western capitals alike.

As early as May, before the NATO summit, Bush, in an interview, had signaled his support for unification. In a briefing note for Secretary Baker, I had recommended that the United States lead on the topic so as to be better able to channel events. After Kohl's plan roiled the political waters, the United States offered four principles to frame a policy toward unification and to reassure the FRG's allies. The United States would support German self-determination without endorsing any specific outcome. Unification had to be consistent with Germany's membership in NATO and the EC, and with due regard for the legal role and responsibility of Allied powers. Moves toward unity should be gradual, peaceful, and step by step. And all border questions should respect the Helsinki Final Act principles of inviolability of frontiers while allowing for the possibility of peaceful change.

Our idea was to create a "safe haven" for the FRG with its allies while supporting unification within the strategic architecture of NATO and an increasingly integrated EC. Bush also sent the four principles to Gorbachev shortly after their Malta meeting on December 2–3. The alliance supported Bush's approach on December 4, and a few days later, the EC heads of government, after heated debate, agreed to a similar statement.

In a visit to Berlin on December 12, Secretary Baker took a further step: he embedded the US principles for unification within a larger architecture for a Europe whole and free. He recommended specific steps for NATO and European security. Baker also embraced the central role of the European Community in shaping a new Europe, and he proposed closer US-EC institutional ties as Europe moved toward union. And the United States envisaged expanded roles for the CSCE, the Helsinki process, in fostering East-West cooperation, security, and free elections.

That same day, Baker made a brief visit to Potsdam, where he encouraged the East German leaders to prepare free elections. He was the first US secretary of state to visit East Germany. Baker also met courageous Lutheran dissidents at the Nikolaikirche. That conversation left an important impression. The pastors and lay leaders were seeking a new "Third Way" policy for the GDR. But when I asked what their congregation wanted, the churchmen laughed and said "Oh, they want what they see on West German TV!" I recall thinking that German unification, if freely decided, would become a takeover by the FRG, not a merger of equals.

Consider the results and approach of America's pragmatic diplomacy at the end of 1989. The United States had aligned closely with its central alliance partner, the FRG. The United States had led and compromised within the alliance to support a bold negotiation on conventional arms in Europe; in doing so, NATO pushed the divisive SNF issue to the background. The United States had deployed policy principles to gain backing for the idea of German unification within NATO and a more integrated EC, and it had begun to outline an agenda for both reassurance and transformation. Bush and Baker had also started to forge a relationship of trust with Gorbachev and Foreign Minister Eduard Shevardnadze. But the first US priority in 1989 had been to shore up alliance cohesion.

The United States had connected these practical steps to a larger strategic design for dealing with "the German question." From the 1600s to 1871, the German question had referred to the manipulation of small German states by neighboring empires. After 1871 the German question became how to deal with a powerful state in the middle of Europe without natural borders. During the Cold War, the solution had been to have two German states, with the democratic FRG integrated within Western Europe and allied with America. In 1989 the United States advocated a strategy of a unified, democratic Germany within NATO and a European Union. We believed this outcome would benefit Germans, other Europeans, and the world while reassuring Germany's neighbors.

Bush and Baker combined this strategy with a pragmatic assessment of day-by-day conditions on the ground in Germany. The German people—both East and West—had become a diplomatic force; Berliners had already done so in 1949, 1953, and 1961. In 1989 a stalled process could have triggered a crisis. Frustrated Germans could have turned against Soviet soldiers or other foreigners. The Stasi or others might have fomented violence, which could have escalated quickly.

At the same time, the United States recognized that it could use German public pressure to urge other countries to make decisions that they were reluctant to face. In 1990 Bush and Baker had to work with Kohl and Foreign Minister Hans-Dietrich Genscher to persuade the Soviets and sometimes also the British, French, and other Europeans to reach the terms of a settlement for Germany and Europe.

1990: Negotiating German Unity and NATO Membership

To draw the diplomatic strands together, Secretary Baker decided early in 1990 that we needed to create a new process, the Two-Plus-Four, that included the two German states and the four victorious powers of World War II—the United States, the Soviet Union, Great Britain, and France. Some at the NSC opposed this initiative, fearing it would offer the Soviets and perhaps others a mechanism for delay. The State Department team recognized, however, that as a practical matter, the Soviets already had leverage, including 380,000 troops in East Germany and their four power rights from 1945, including over Berlin. If pressed into a corner, the Soviets might even argue for a form of unification while retaining residual rights. We needed terms of transition so that the Soviet army would go home, and Europeans would feel secure.

> German unification would not have been possible without trust among the key actors: Kohl and Genscher, Gorbachev and Shevardnadze, and Bush and Baker.

Therefore, the United States constructed the Two-Plus-Four process to connect the strategy with events on the ground. We placed the two Germanies in front to emphasize self-determination. They would negotiate the internal issues of unification on their own. The four powers would meet with the two Germanies to coordinate the external dimensions of unification, including a final settlement of four power rights.

Furthermore, we recognized that the East German elections in March 1990 would determine the nature and pace of unification. But after over a half century of the Third Reich and then communist control, East Germans might not believe they were truly free to choose. Some of us thought that the very announcement of the Two-Plus-Four process would signal to East Germans that the four powers were ready to accept unification. This was pragmatism at work: The creation of the Two-Plus-Four process would reinforce political momentum, which we could then use to keep the new diplomatic and negotiating process on track.

The United States and its partners had to coordinate and sequence complementary steps in other forums as well. We needed to complete the CFE negotiations to end the military confrontation; as part of CFE, the FRG would cap its forces at a lower level. NATO needed to adapt its doctrine, nuclear and force posture, and relations with newly free states in the East. CSCE became the OSCE with new missions and capabilities. The participants in the Two-Plus-Four process became an informal "steering group" to help synchronize the work on these tracks.

The biggest challenge in 1990 was to persuade Moscow to accept German unification within NATO. The Soviets recognized that, as a practical matter, unification was occurring. After elections in the East in March, the two German states began to negotiate the legal and economic terms. As some of us had foreseen the prior December, the legal process would be a takeover under Article 23 of the FRG's Basic Law (used for Saarland's accession in 1957), not under Article 146, which had provided for the negotiation of a new German constitution.

Baker urged Gorbachev and Shevardnadze to consider whether they wanted a united Germany to become an independent power overshadowing Central Europe—or a Germany remaining within NATO, linked to the United States. NATO, in turn, had to adapt to a post-Cold War world, which it began to do at the NATO summit on July 5–6, 1990.

In 1989 the United States advocated a strategy of a unified, democratic Germany within NATO and a European Union. We believed this outcome would benefit Germans, other Europeans, and the world while reassuring Germany's neighbors.

In mid-May, we made a guess about Soviet psychology. Events had been racing ahead; it was likely that the Soviets, who seemed off balance, had not fully comprehended the various proposals the United States and the FRG had been suggesting. So I packaged nine points, which we had already made, into one presentation—covering various arms control agreements, changes in NATO, transition arrangements in the former GDR, borders, CSCE, and economic support. Secretary Baker and I used these points in separate presentations to demonstrate that we were making a serious effort to address legitimate Soviet interests.

The United States, the FRG, and NATO followed through on each of the nine assurances. When Gorbachev finally agreed in June to the idea of a united Germany within NATO, he did so on the basis of the CSCE principle that countries should be free to choose their alliances. The economic assistance that the FRG promised to Gorbachev in July added a critical term.

The pragmatic diplomacy of 1989–90 was also mindful of another historical experience. We wanted to avoid what we termed a "Versailles Victory," meaning a settlement, like that after World War I, that planted the seeds of its own destruction. For Germany we wanted to avoid any discrimination—we used the term "singularization"—that in the future Germans might resent. In 1990 such objections seemed unlikely, but as time has passed, one can see that resentments and historical memories, including in Central and Eastern Europe, have fed hostile attitudes. For Poland, President Bush secretly mediated assurances about the existing Polish-German border with Prime Minister Tadeusz Mazowiecki and Chancellor Kohl. For Moscow, we sought to provide reassurance without offering a condominium that granted the Russians control over the Baltic states and others in Eastern Europe.

Building Trust

German unification would not have been possible without trust among the key actors: Kohl and Genscher, Gorbachev and Shevardnadze, and Bush and Baker. These men sought to listen to and understand the positions of their counterparts. They were in frequent contact, exploring ideas and trying to solve problems. Each pursued national and even personal interests but together they recognized mutual interests as well.

A Good Sense of Timing

Pragmatic diplomacy masters the imperatives of the clock. Only ten months passed between the opening of the Berlin Wall in November 1989 and the signing of the Two-Plus-Four Final Settlement in Moscow in September 1990. Germany united the next month.

We knew that an incident, coup, or dramatic turnaround in policy could halt, or at least divert, the rapid pace toward unification. In August 1990, Saddam Hussein overran Kuwait, forcing President Bush and Secretary Baker to turn their attention toward organizing a global coalition and domestic support for a reversal of Iraq's aggression. In December 1990, Shevardnadze resigned in the face of harsh domestic criticism. In August 1991, Gorbachev's opponents launched a coup; although it collapsed, so would the USSR by year end.

The window for the negotiation of unification was open only briefly.

The Pragmatic Diplomacy of German Unification

The story of German unification offers an example of the art of pragmatic diplomacy. The Americans and West Germans paid close attention to the surprising, transformative realities on the ground. They recognized the interests—and anxieties—of the key parties and sought to provide others with explanations for outcomes. The United States proposed the creation of a new diplomatic process, the Two-Plus-Four, to guide closure on critical issues. Washington also steered complementary actions in other forums—the CFE negotiations, NATO, and CSCE—so as to fit the pieces of the puzzle together. The FRG worked on the critical economic interests. By early 1990, France and Britain, two key allies, were also coordinating closely. The European Commission, led by President Jacques Delors, piloted unification within a more unified Europe.

Only ten months passed between the opening of the Berlin Wall in November 1989 and the signing of the Two-Plus-Four Final Settlement in Moscow in September 1990. Germany united the next month.

The United States and FRG were keenly attuned to timing throughout the diplomacy, capitalizing on the pace of events while seeking to avoid destabilizing the necessary cooperation.

The US strategy in 1989–90 included one other pragmatic calculation. We saw our actions as fulfilling a forty-year-long pledge to our German ally. At the same time, we expected that Germany—by reason of its size, economic power, and geography—would play a decisive role in Europe's future, as it had in Europe's past. Having forged a special partnership with a democratic Germany over decades of the Cold War, we hoped that our close cooperation in the closing chapter would leave a foundation for a future trans-Atlantic partnership. The Munich Security Conference—and Wolfgang Ischinger personally—have been examples of that bond.

Germans and Americans have benefited from mutual respect, strategic cooperation—and friendship. Both countries would be mistaken to ignore the consequences of drift, or worse, a lasting break in ties. I hope that a recollection of their cooperation at a vital historical moment will remind the officials of today and in the future of the ways and means of conducting pragmatic diplomacy together.

Robert B. Zoellick was the lead US negotiator in the Two-Plus-Four process; from 1989 to 1992, he was an Undersecretary of State and Deputy Chief of Staff of the White House. He later served as President of the World Bank, as US Deputy Secretary of State, and as US Trade Representative. His book, *America in the World: A History of U.S. Diplomacy and Foreign Policy*, was published in 2020.

Munich Security
Conference
Münchner Sicher
Münch
Konfe

Benefiting from Cross-Departmental Teamwork

Theo Waigel

There are challenges that diplomacy cannot solve single-handedly. The introduction of the euro and German reunification are examples of breakthroughs that were made possible only through skillful interplay between departments—and their ministers.

Back in the 1980s, the German minister of foreign affairs, Hans-Dietrich Genscher—not the finance minister, Gerhard Stoltenberg—proposed a memorandum advocating a monetary union in Europe. It was also due to the efforts of the minister of foreign affairs that, on the occasion of the 1988 European Summit in Hanover, the Delors Commission was established to develop an appropriate framework. The finance minister then made sure that this commission, which was led by the commission president, was staffed with the chairpersons of the central banks of the member states. At an early stage, in March, the commission presented its draft proposal to the European Council. In April the finance minister and the minister of foreign affairs discussed further action at several conferences. When the Intergovernmental Conference convened in Rome in December 1990, a division of competences took place. From now on, the minister of foreign affairs would be in charge of the concept of the political union while the finance minister took responsibility for economic and monetary union.

On February 7, 1992, Hans-Dietrich Genscher and I signed the draft for the treaty in Maastricht. Both of us were allowed to take home the historic fountain pen as a personal gift. Mine now resides in the Haus der Geschichte in Regensburg. Around ten years ago, Genscher called me and told me that his fountain pen had been stolen. He asked me to take pictures of my own pen so that the criminal investigation department could make inquiries. Several weeks later, the thieves returned the "Maastricht fountain pen"—whether this was because of its historic significance or because exploiting such a rarity had become too risky will likely never be clarified. Be that as it may, the interplay between the minister of foreign affairs and the finance minister was crowned with success.

A more serious example of an interaction of this kind ensued at the Maastricht European summit in May 1988. France was against the proposal to appoint Wim Duisenberg as the first president of the ECB. Discussions went on for hours. When a compromise—dividing the eight-year term between Duisenberg and Jean-Claude Trichet—was in the offing, incumbent minister of foreign affairs Klaus Kinkel and I asked Federal Chancellor Helmut Kohl to suspend the sitting and to confer with us. Having joined our forces, we tried to make it clear to him that a division of the term went against the treaties and must therefore not be seen as an option. At first, Kohl was annoyed, but he eventually accepted our legal interpretation. He prevailed against French President Chirac, and Duisenberg was appointed without limitation. Duisenberg declared that, in view of his age, he was not planning to stay in office for the full eight years, but that he would take his leave according to his discretion. This compromise finally cleared the way for the introduction of the euro.

The introduction of the euro and German reunification are examples of breakthroughs that were made possible only through skillful interplay between departments—and their ministers.

Without an ultimately productive and success-oriented interplay between the finance ministry and the ministry of foreign affairs, this fateful turn of European events could never have taken place. As early as 1946, the first chairman of the Christian Social Union, Josef Müller, had postulated a common European currency. Subsequent attempts had not been crowned with success. Only the skillful interplay between diplomacy and finance and currency politics, as well as the deep sense of trust among the players, have made this possible in the final decade of a crisis-ridden century.

Another example of the powerful impact of constructive cooperation between foreign, domestic, and finance politics is the reunification of Germany. The finance ministry conceptualized the economic, currency, and social union, the ministry of internal affairs prepared the Unification Treaty, and the ministry of foreign affairs negotiated the Two Plus Four Agreement. In the end, they all acted in concert, impressively underscoring what the departments and their leaders can achieve through skillful interplay.

Theo Waigel is a former member of the German Bundestag. He served as Federal Minister of Finance from 1989 to 1998 and as the Chairman of the Christian Social Union in Bavaria from 1988 to 1999.

◂ Theo Waigel at the Munich European Conference on the sidelines of the Munich Security Conference in February 2020.

Taking Sides as Mediators

Carl Bildt

There is no template for success in the art of diplomacy when it comes to conflict prevention and conflict resolution. Each situation has to be approached according to its own characteristics. Let me mention two cases I have been involved in.

The first case is the conflict that could have erupted in Estonia in the summer of 1993 soon after the country regained its independence. At worst, it could have resulted in the establishment of another Transnistria—a Russia-supported statelet—inside Estonia with vast ramifications for the political and security situation in the entire Nordic and Baltic area.

The immediate trigger for the crisis was Estonian legislation on citizenship, although tension between the Estonian majority and the Russian minority had been brewing ever since September 1991, when the country regained its independence in. In contrast to neighboring Latvia, Estonia never had had a significant Russian population, and the roughly one-third of its population who were Russian nationals in 1994 had arrived there during the Soviet period.

Many of them were concentrated in the northeast of the country with the border city of Narva at its center. Prior to World War II, this had been an almost exclusively Estonian-populated area, but after the intense destruction during those years, the Soviet authorities prevented the original population from coming back, and instead imported a new population that was predominantly Russian.

During the 1993 controversy over citizenship and related laws, the ex-Soviet local authorities in Narva and the surrounding area announced their intention to hold a referendum on the establishment of an autonomous area. As was the pattern in related conflicts in other parts of the former Soviet Union, this was accompanied by ominous statements coming out of militaristic and intensely nationalistic circles in Moscow promising to come to the help of their "threatened" Russian compatriots. There were signs of groups starting to gather.

This led, during the summer of 1993, to a period of intense diplomatic activity involving me in my position as prime minister of Sweden, Max van der Stoel in his position as the CSCE High Commissioner for National Minorities, the Estonian authorities with President Lennart Meri and Prime Minister Mart Laar, the Narva local leadership, and the Russian authorities with President Boris Yeltsin and Foreign Minister Andrzej Kozyrev.

Initially, the rhetoric coming out of the Kremlin on the issue had been fairly militant. President Yeltsin was under intense pressure from more nationalistic circles and could not be seen as being weak when it came to defending the rights of ethnic Russians in the former Soviet space. There was an obvious risk of the crisis sprawling out of control with a referendum endorsing a separate statelet, Russian "volunteers" of different sorts supporting the referendum, and nationalist Estonian elements trying to crush what they saw as a rebellion against their newly reestablished state. In retrospect, we now know that there were significant links with the forces that had been instrumental in setting up the Transnistria statelet in Moldova.

It's often said that the key to conflict resolution is for a mediator to have a neutral and equidistant position between the parties to the conflict. But the midsummer crisis of 1993 demonstrates that sometimes it is rather the reverse that is true.

From the Swedish side, we had very close personal and political links with the leadership in Estonia, and at the time also constructive relationships with the Russian leadership. We had been engaged in intense efforts to facilitate a peaceful solution to the difficult issue of the withdrawal of Russian military forces and assets, some of them of obvious strategic importance, from the Baltic states.

In this crisis, the formula that we worked on was trying to get the leadership in Estonia to make some revisions to their proposed laws and to use these in order to persuade the Kremlin to try to get the more nationalistic Russian forces in Estonia as well as across the border to quietly back down.

It wasn't easy. The laws in question were decided by a newly elected Estonian Parliament keen to establish rights that the Soviet regime had denied them for generations. Even apart from this crisis, the internal situation in the country wasn't entirely stable.

The shuttle diplomacy that followed had one of its high points when I flew into Tallinn and was able to persuade President Meri to refer the law already decided by the parliament to the Council of Europe for

◂ Carl Bildt at the Munich Security Conference in February 2019.

its assessment, securing an undertaking by President Yeltsin that this was going to be seen as a positive and constructive move. The final message from the Kremlin was delivered by phone to one of my assistants just as we entered the office of President Meri.

In parallel, we sought direct talks with the local leadership of Narva, trying to see if there were other ways to meet their concerns and grievances. They were—understandably—worried about not only their status in the new Estonian state, but even more by their employment and economic future as the entire ex-Soviet area was in a state of economic collapse. We told them that Swedish help and investment could be a possibility if the area was seen as stable, and later on, we delivered on that promise.

The referendum did take place and it had the expected result, but the turnout was less than expected, and by that time we had managed to secure both the promise of some changes in the controversial law and a distinct change of tone from Moscow. In all probability, the Kremlin had sent the messages that we had asked them to send to the local Russian leadership in Narva.

Thus, what could have been a severe crisis with profound long-term implications for the entire region was defused, and the midsummer crisis of 1993, as it is referred to, is today mostly forgotten. Narva is still an overwhelmingly Russian-populated area, many have sought and acquired Estonian citizenship, and apart from everything else there is an awareness of the fact that in spite many problems, the city and the region have done far better than the areas of Russia right across the Narva River.

It's often said that the key to conflict resolution is for a mediator to have a neutral and equidistant position between the parties to the conflict. But the midsummer crisis of 1993 demonstrates that sometimes it is rather the reverse that is true.

Key to the solution here wasn't that we were neutral mediators, but that we enjoyed the full confidence of the Estonian leadership while at the same time having the benefit of open channels to the Russian leadership. This made it possible for us to maneuver changes in Russia's position, particularly since the closeness of the relationship between Stockholm and Tallinn made us a relevant actor from Moscow's point of view.

The other case of interest is of course Bosnia, where three years of war and diplomacy eventually resulted in the agreement concluded in November 1995. I served as the special representative of the European Union and as co-chair of the negotiations, which occurred over three weeks in Dayton. Wolfgang Ischinger represented Germany, and the UK, France, and Russia each had senior representatives present.

The drawn-out saga of first trying to prevent war from breaking out in Bosnia as the entire edifice of Yugoslavia came crushing down, and then trying to stop the war and conclude some sort of peace, is as much a saga of conflicts among different international actors—and sometimes within them—as it is one of the conflict in Bosnia itself.

In the initial stages of the emerging Yugoslav crisis, it was the Europeans who were in the lead of the political efforts. The US was focused on the dangers inherent in the breakup of the nuclear-armed Soviet Union, and US Secretary of State James Baker frankly stated that "we have no dog in this fight." The Luxembourg Foreign Minister Jacques Poos rushed forward and said that "Europe's hour has arrived."

That turned out to be a misconception. There were severe divisions within the EU that had just emerged out of the Maastricht summit, with the Germans favoring swift recognition of the independence of Slovenia and Croatia, while the UK and France, strongly supported by the UN, urged caution and a wider diplomatic effort.

The initial efforts were focused on the conflict within Croatia between its Croat majority and Serb minority, and while it was possible to freeze that conflict with the deployment of a UN peacekeeping force, scant attention was devoted to the tensions building up in Bosnia. With its Muslim, Serb, and Croat nationalities, Bosnia was something of a mini-Yugoslavia with its stability dependent on the stability of the wider Yugoslav framework. A late attempt to forge a compromise inside Bosnia in early 1992, based on the setting of these three entities within a common framework, ultimately failed, and war broke out in the spring and escalated in fierce fighting and widespread ethnic cleansing, primarily but not only by the Serb side thereafter.

Frustrated with the failed efforts, the summer of 1992 saw the EU and the UN setting up a common framework for the conflict resolution efforts in the region, with the US still only playing a passive supporting role. By the time this had produced the so-called Vance/Owen peace plan in early 1993—based on ten different cantons—power had shifted in Washington and a new administration with a different agenda had taken over. The new administration quickly decided to abandon support for the Vance/Owen peace plan, thus settling its fate, and it all then entered a prolonged period of tension over the Atlantic on what could be done.

The US was determined not to get involved on the ground in Bosnia. It had just suffered a defeat in Somalia and wasn't keen on anything that might lead to a repetition of that experience. It focused instead on different military options of limited air strikes in combination with seeking to lift or circumvent the arms embargo on the region that the UN had imposed in the early stages of the conflict. But military measures alone could never achieve a political solution, and the Europeans insisted that a political solution was the only way to achieve peace.

With the common EU/UN framework sidelined, and with the US and the Europeans on a different page as to what to do, a so-called Contact Group was set up to try to forge a peace inside the international community on the issue. It consisted of the US, France, UK, Germany, and Russia.

By then it had become obvious that it was highly unlikely that the warring parties on the ground were going to accept a settlement as long as some of them believed that they could secure a better settlement somewhere down the road. The Bosniacs—as the Muslim side gradually preferred to be called—held out hope for a US military intervention, while the Serbs had solid support from Moscow. The Europeans sometimes had difficulty maneuvering in between.

A so-called peace plan produced by the Contact Group in the summer of 1994 after prolonged internal wrangling was nothing of the sort. It consisted of a rather complicated map, dividing the country into two different entities, but without any firm proposal on the critically important political structures of the country. It accordingly failed to gain traction.

What catalyzed the final peace efforts in the late summer of 1995 was less the catastrophe of Srebrenica, and more the realization in Washington that if the war was going to be prolonged even further, it would be pulled in also on the ground with unforeseeable consequences. On the political stage in Washington, there was firm support for the Bosniac position.

The conclusion was then to merge the key elements of a number of the previous peace efforts, none of which had been universally supported, into a consolidated effort under the firm leadership of US Assistant Secretary of State for European and Eurasian Affairs Richard Holbrooke. The Contact Group 49–51 plan of "territorial compromise" that partitioned Bosnia was combined with previous European ideas of a "thin" common state that should be acceptable to all parties to the conflict.

With the international community then for the first time speaking if not with one voice but at least with one common message, and with war fatigue setting in on all sides, a settlement was finally possible, although it took three weeks in Dayton to hammer out all the details. During these weeks, more attention was unfortunately given to the territorial division of the country and on how to separate the warring parties than to the political structures to hold the country together and secure also a long-term peace.

The Dayton settlement would not have been possible without the active participation of the United States. They had been absent when efforts to prevent the war had failed, had then been destructive to the efforts to close it down during its first year, and were essential to the settlement that was eventually reached. Having utilized air power, although with fairly limited effect, the US was in the position to persuade the Bosniac side into the crucial concession on accepting the term Republika Srpska for the 49 percent entity of the country dominated by the Serb side.

But to a degree, the same applies to the other international actors. The Russian side was consistently supportive of the combined efforts, thus leaving no real room for the Serb side to walk away even if they had wished to do so, and the Europeans were instrumental in pushing the US negotiators on the critically important constitutional issues.

In the case of the Bosnia war, there were no neutral mediators either. The different international actors had different degrees of sympathy for the different warring parties, with historical connections as well as domestic dynamics within them playing important parts.

As long as they had different ideas on what could be done, warring parties on the ground had little incentive to settle the conflict. It was only when all the international actors came together, resulting from a combination of the events in the conflict and of domestic pressures, that peace became possible.

Carl Bildt is Special Envoy for the ACT Accelerator of the World Health Organization. He previously served as both Prime Minister and Minister of Foreign Affairs of the Kingdom of Sweden. Bildt is Co-Chairman of the European Council on Foreign Relations and Member of the Munich Security Conference Advisory Council.

Pursuing Peace Against All Odds

Nasser bin Nasser

Observers of international diplomacy today must look at the recent state of the Arab-Israeli conflict and marvel that thirty years ago, the prospect of peace was even entertained as an option, let alone that the diplomatic feat of negotiating and concluding Palestinian-Israeli and Jordanian-Israeli peace treaties, respectively, was achieved against all odds.

Many officials who participated in the negotiations told me that the one critical factor that allowed for this achievement was leadership. One of the things that stands out in particular for me was the realism on display in the approach to peace and security. None of the three leaders were peace-loving idealists as their detractors tended to portray them. Quite the contrary—these were hardened military men who nonetheless recognized the limits of the military options in their toolkit. Whether it was the impact of the intifada for Israelis, the end of Cold War-era material and financial support for armed resistance movements for the Palestinians, or the end of strategic depth for Jordan following Iraq's defeat in the Gulf War, all three leaders appeared to arrive at the conclusion that the status quo was untenable. That peace, as a political solution, could bring security is not wholly unheard of for military men. Clausewitz's theory of war says that peace is the continuation of struggle through unarmed means. As King Hussein regularly remarked to some in his inner circle, "you don't make peace with friends, you make peace with your enemies," which strongly echoes this.

Another key leadership feature was the moral courage to not cede to populism, and instead to "sell" peace with the enemy to the respective publics, thereby working to shape rather than reflect public opinion. They also exhibited pragmatism and made difficult concessions out of necessity. An enduring example is Jordan's legal custodianship of the Haram El-Sharif in Jerusalem, which is enshrined in Jordan's peace treaty with Israel, and would not have been possible without both Palestinian and Israeli consent. The Palestinian leadership, for instance, recognized that Jordanian custodianship could better protect the holy sites despite the legitimizing impact it would offer them. This arrangement is likely to have been a major source of aggravation to Israel's recently outgoing prime minister and his bid to change the status of Jerusalem. It makes me consider whether it had been designed by all three sides to be a safeguard against populist leaders and their haphazard unilateral policies.

The leadership at the time was also characterized by candor, as the leaders seemed to call each other out and refrained from beating around the bush when needed. A Jordanian official told me that when Prime Minister Yitzhak Rabin protested some clauses to Prince Hassan bin Talal of Jordan, in a meeting with a small group of officials, claiming that he could never accept them because of the oft-repeated narrative that Israel was surrounded by enemies, Prince Hassan insisted, retorting that Jordan was surrounded by "frenemies" (friends/enemies).

Lastly, and perhaps most importantly, was the purposeful avoidance of zero-sum formulations in policy-making, which made negotiations and the short-lived peace era that followed possible. It was recounted to me that policymakers on all sides purportedly considered the impact of their policy options on their counterparts to ensure that they would not weaken, undermine, or even embarrass them. This was not because of affinity or rapport, but rather the realization that enduring stability in relations and the survival of the treaties would require for partners to be in a position of strength.

In more recent times, the formula that peace could bring security has been flipped such that the prevailing perception now is that security will bring peace. This is not only applicable to this conflict, but also seemingly to international diplomacy at large. The impact of populist thinking and the zero-sum approach to diplomacy exemplified in Donald Trump's *The Art of the Deal*, a transactional business approach to diplomacy flies in the face of any possible political accommodation that could otherwise be pursued through the aptly titled "art of diplomacy" context of this volume. The absence of justice and dignity for Palestinians has largely overshadowed any possible security benefits of peace treaties with Israel. Nonetheless, only diplomacy and leadership can salvage the situation, even in the face of today's insurmountable odds.

Nasser bin Nasser is the managing director of the Middle East Scientific Institute for Security based in Amman, Jordan. He was a Munich Young Leader in 2011.

◂ Nasser bin Nasser at the Munich Young Leaders Alumni Meeting in New York City in September 2019.

Conducting the Concert of Nations

Peter Ricketts

In all my years of working with Wolfgang Ischinger on the diplomatic circuit, I only once saw him seriously cross. It was in October 1998. As the crisis in Kosovo deepened, ministers from the six countries that made up the Contact Group (Britain, France, Germany, Italy, Russia, and the United States) assembled at Heathrow Airport to hear a report from Richard Holbrooke, the US envoy who was negotiating with President Milošević for a ceasefire and the withdrawal of Serbian security forces from Kosovo.

The venue suited busy ministers, but it was not ideal. The meeting room was alongside the main runway, and discussion was therefore interrupted every two minutes by the deafening roar of a jet taking off. It was also cramped, and only had space for ministers and their senior advisers, the political directors from foreign ministries. Holbrooke, with his customary tact, took one look round, declared that there were too many people in the room, and demanded that the meeting be ministers only. Since no one opposed him, political directors were ejected, and spent the next two hours on hard seats in the corridor drinking cold coffee.

Wolfgang was not amused. The Heathrow meeting was a form of diplomacy in which he excelled: trying to resolve international problems by calm, patient, but determined work among a selected group of countries that could exercise useful influence. He knew that, when ministers jetted off in their different directions, it would be the political directors who were left to follow up their decisions. Moreover, the German Foreign Ministry had been at the center of Kosovo diplomacy from early 1992. Germany had been the first to spot that the developing crisis in the former Yugoslavia could spill over into the Serbian province of Kosovo. In an effort to preempt tension between the Kosovo Albanian majority and the minority Serb community in Kosovo, the Germans proposed that the Conference on Security and Cooperation in Europe (CSCE, later the OSCE) should send observers to the province. This Europe-wide cooperative security body had recently expanded from 34 to 52 countries, as former Soviet allies flocked to join. However, Belgrade refused to grant visas to CSCE observers. Trying another tack, Germany pressed for Kosovo to be added to the agenda for the Dayton conference on Bosnia in 1995, but Holbrooke thought this would overload things.

The Contact Group had been set up to deal with the Bosnia crisis, but in 1997 Germany succeeded in persuading the other members to add Kosovo to the agenda. This sent a significant message, since it showed that Russia no longer accepted the Serbian argument that Kosovo was a purely domestic matter. Milošević totally failed to understand the signal, and in 1998 sent his security forces into Kosovo to embark on another round of violence and ethnic cleansing.

This was the backdrop to the Holbrooke mission and the Contact Group discussion at Heathrow. Ministers agreed that evening to send Holbrooke back to Belgrade. He finally succeeded in persuading Milošević to pull back Serbian forces and accept the deployment of an unarmed Kosovo Verification Mission under OSCE auspices (very much as Germany had advocated in 1992). But the lull in the violence was only temporary, and by January 1999, Serbian militias were once more terrorizing the Kosovo Albanian population. Events continued their inexorable deterioration to the point of NATO launching its air operations in March 1999 against the Serb forces in Kosovo.

In some ways the years of crisis management in the Balkans now feel like ancient history. But in my view, they offer some lessons in skillful use of the tools of diplomacy in tackling international crises that are still relevant for the new generation of politicians and diplomats as they grapple with a far more diverse range of threats and risks.

As I lived the Kosovo crisis as the UK Foreign Office's deputy political director, it seemed to me that it marked the Federal Republic's coming of age from a national security point of view. The NATO operation was famously the first time German forces were involved in a combat mission since the Second World War. The fact that this took place with a Red/Green coalition in power and Joschka Fischer as foreign minister seemed to me to make it all the more remarkable. It was only conceivable because German diplomacy had tried every possible way of achieving a peaceful resolution of the tensions between Belgrade and Pristina before the resort to military force. Moreover, the start of NATO combat operations did not mark the end of German efforts to find a solution to the crisis.

◂ Peter Ricketts during the "Open Book" Press Preview in Paris in June 2015.

Wolfgang Ischinger, as the new German government's state secretary at the Foreign Office, was once more at the heart of these efforts. He was helped in this by the fact that Germany held the rotating chairmanship of the G8 group of industrialized countries in 1999. This grouping had started life in 1973 as an informal gathering of six major industrialized economies (Britain, France, Germany, Italy, Japan, and the United States), and had become the G7 with the addition of Canada the following year. Russia had been added to the meetings of the G7 foreign ministers in 1997. While the NATO air operations were underway in the spring of 1999, the German Foreign Minister Joschka Fisher and his team devised a six-step peace plan and embarked on an intensive round of diplomacy to sell this to other partners, in particular the Russians. They presented their plan to a meeting of G8 foreign ministers at the top of the Petersberg outside Bonn in May 1999. The key demand was for Milošević to withdraw all Serbian troops and special police and to allow Kosovo Albanian refugees to return to their homes. The G8 meeting achieved a crucial breakthrough when Russian Foreign Minister Igor Ivanov accepted the principles of the peace plan and agreed that his envoy, former Russian Prime Minister Victor Chernomyrdin, should visit Belgrade with Finnish President Martti Ahtisaari to convince Milošević that the game was up.

The timing of this G8 initiative was just right, with the NATO bombing campaign in its second month and Serb forces evidently under real pressure. The messengers were well chosen: sending a senior Russian statesman and the President of a neutral European country made it more likely that Milošević would bow to the inevitable than if the ultimatum had been delivered by NATO member states. He did so, and the German diplomatic success was enhanced when, at the G8 summit in Cologne the following month, the Russians agreed to participate in the NATO-led KFOR stabilization force. At the same time, the G8 accepted a broader German-authored Stability Pact for Southeastern Europe. What can be distilled from this intensive period of international crisis management that can be applied to today's very different geopolitical situation? I suggest three lessons in particular.

First, although the tools of modern diplomacy have changed with the advent of digital communications and social media, the technique of listening to, and engaging with, those with very different views is as vital as ever. The contacts that German diplomats sustained in Belgrade, Pristina, and Moscow from 1992 onward made the Bonn government a trusted interlocutor for all sides. This was material when the moment came to leverage the pressures generated by military action to produce a political settlement. At the same time, there was never any ambiguity about Germany's total solidarity as a member of the NATO alliance, even while keeping channels open to the Milošević government.

Second, convening the right group of countries can be decisive in handling a crisis and finding a resolution. Throughout the Balkans wars, the Contact Group played an important part in keeping lines open between the two countries and Russia, even if it was slow to recognize German warnings about the gathering storm clouds in Kosovo. When the time came to force Milošević into accepting this terms, the G8 fortuitously had the right membership to bring the most powerful industrialized countries in the world together around the German peace plan and to have Russia convey it to Belgrade.

Talking only to one's own side will not solve today's global problems. Dialogue with authoritarian regimes is a signal of self-confidence, not a display of weakness.

Third, although the Contact Group and G8 were vital in building international pressure on Milošević, they needed the established international organizations to take the follow-up action. It was the OSCE that had the legitimacy (with its Europe-wide membership) and the capacity to mount a risky observer mission at short notice in an effort to resolve the tensions by peaceful means. When that failed, NATO was the only body capable of organizing first the air campaign and then the ground force stabilization mission, authorized by the UN Security Council.

Each of these points is still relevant as the democracies repair their structures of cooperation after the damage done by the pandemic and by Trump's cavalier approach to US commitments.

The first of my lessons, on keeping lines of communication open between all sides of an argument, is more topical than ever in a deeply polarized world in which China and Russia are challenging not only the existing rules-based order, but any concept of shared norms and values. It is a measure of how the strategic outlook has darkened since the 1990s that it would now be unthinkable that Russia would accept a Western-crafted peace plan and agree to present it to the leader of a Slav nation looking to Russia for assistance.

The need to keep channels of communication open with Moscow is even more challenging when Russian leaders seek to intimidate the West with a new arsenal of nuclear weapons, to destabilize our countries with reckless actions, and to undermine our societies by sowing discord and division. The strengthening force field of US/China confrontation is narrowing the space for European countries to maintain functioning relations with Beijing. And yet broad-based dialogue with both countries is necessary, not just to serve transactional interests, but to keep the pressure on these authoritarian regimes to recognize that they too have responsibilities for the stewardship of a fragile planet as the COVID-19 pandemic and the gathering climate crisis have so graphically shown.

My second lesson, on the importance of convening the right group of countries to handle a specific problem, is also linked to channels of communication. The current fashion is for like-minded countries to band together. The G8 shrunk once again to seven when Russia was excluded after the invasion of Crimea in 2014. There has been much talk of expanding its membership to include other democracies, for example to a D10 including Australia, South Korea, and India (this also reflects the current focus on the Indo-Pacific region). The UK took a step in that direction as host of the G7 Summit in June 2021 when it invited the three Asian nations plus South Africa as observers. President Biden held the first of two Summits for Democracy in late 2021. Meanwhile, Australia, India, Japan, and the US are stepping up their consultations on Asian security issues in a format known as the Quad. As US foreign policy is increasingly taken up with working out a new pattern of competitive coexistence with China, the emphasis on coordination among the democracies on China policy will continue. But the history of Balkans diplomacy in the 1990s shows that it is also vital to have international groupings that bridge ideological divides. Talking only to one's own side will not solve today's global problems. Dialogue with authoritarian regimes is a signal of self-confidence, not a display of weakness.

The third lesson from the Balkans years, on the importance of effective international institutions, has also lost none of its validity. The UN and NATO were the product of a very different postwar world, but have shown a remarkable capacity to survive and adapt. They both have serious weaknesses and are in urgent need of reform and reinvigoration. But they each offer something unique and irreplaceable that makes them worth the effort of preserving. The UN Security Council's crisis management role has been gravely undermined by the deep divisions among its permanent members. But the UN system still has the legitimacy of its global membership, and a precious asset in the network of Specialized Agencies. The World Health Organization, for example, has been much criticized over its handling of the COVID-19 pandemic. But it would be impossible to create another global public health body, so we need to do what is necessary to reform the WHO's governance and stabilize its funding so that it can act without fear or favor in preparing the world for another pandemic. Many of the other UN specialized agencies also play a key role in global resilience against disruptive threats. The other great postwar security organization, NATO, remains the only forum in which the US and its transatlantic allies can discuss their most important national security priorities as well as provide for collective defense. As a military alliance, it is in good shape, with levels of defense spending rising across Europe in response to the threat from Russia. But the trust among allies on which NATO's political strength relies was badly shaken by Trump and has been further eroded by a number of Allies (in particular Turkey) pursuing domestic policies that are hard to square with the founding principles of the Washington Treaty. The new emphasis in NATO on revitalizing political consultations is therefore welcome. Both the UN and NATO have the staff resources and the experience that informal groupings of countries like the G7 lack. Both are necessary if good ideas are to be turned into action that changes international behavior.

The most effective diplomats need the skill of an orchestral conductor, bringing together the different sections of the international system and achieving a harmony that no single instrument could achieve. That's what the Heathrow meeting was trying to achieve, despite the cacophony of the aircraft noise outside. And that's why the maestro conductor, Wolfgang Ischinger, was right to be exasperated at being excluded from the concert.

Peter Ricketts was a British diplomat for forty years and the UK's first National Security Advisor. He is now a Member of the House of Lords. His book *Hard Choices: What Britain Does Next* was published by Atlantic Books in 2021.

msc
Giesecke & Devrient

Dreaming of Dayton 30 Years On

Igor Ivanov

This is a brief report of a dream I had of the approaching anniversary of the Dayton agreements on Bosnia. In this dream, we were already close to thirty years after our quite protracted and complicated deliberations at the US military base in Dayton. I remember quite vividly these seemingly endless twenty-one days, when they deprived us of our cellphones and we had no chance to escape the location, even in the evening to enjoy the Dayton nightlife.

Still, as they say, "It's Great in Dayton!" From time to time, I recall our League of Extraordinary Gentlemen and Ladies—flamboyant and unpredictable Richard Holbrooke; meticulous and persistent Carl Bildt; decisive and straightforward Wesley Clark; charming, but strong-willed Pauline Neville-Jones; and the rest of our diverse, but very committed team. We did our best in Dayton, though at some points, our mission looked impossible and doomed to failure. In my view, Warren Christopher did a magnificent job to prevent a collapse of negotiations at the very last moment and to come to the final text of the agreement!

We did our best in Dayton, though at some points, our mission looked impossible and doomed to failure.

I have to say that only five years ago I was somewhat hesitant about whether we should go ahead with celebrating Dayton as a remarkable international accomplishment. After all, for a quarter of the century, Bosnia and Herzegovina existed essentially on an external life support system, remained highly fragile, and looked even somewhat artificial. The overall situation in the Western Balkans was not promising either—with plenty of local crises, clashes between neighboring states, and intense great power competition for the region. Many believed that in the beginning of the twenty-first century, the region remained the same dangerous powder keg of Europe that it had been a century ago.

In my dream, these dark times have passed. The transformation of the region over the last five years or so is truly remarkable. Not only have practically all the Balkan countries been shortlisted for EU accession, but the Western Balkans has also emerged as one of the most vibrant and dynamic economic development areas in Europe. Instead of being an eternal bone of contention and a source of tensions between Moscow and Brussels, it has become a natural economic and even cultural bridge between Russia and the West. It has also emerged as a critically important international lab for testing modern concepts of multiculturalism and confessional dialogue.

After all, miracles do happen even in our rational and material world. I do not want to imply that the miracle in the Balkans, which all of us can observe now happening, is a direct result of the Dayton agreements signed thirty years ago. Many factors contributed to the recent progress in the region, ranging from the gradual improvement of the geopolitical situation in Europe to the new cycle of globalization. Nations of the region were fast to grab many of the new opportunities in the post-COVID world. However, I believe that in Dayton we made our modest contribution to the current encouraging developments in the region. It took a long time for the seeds that we planted together to blossom, but we have always hoped that the harvest time would come someday. Now the region finally reaps the benefits of our decisions made thirty years ago.

I sincerely hope that all of us can get together in Dayton on November 21, 2025, at the same US military base that hospitably accommodated us thirty years ago. It is impossible to guarantee great weather in Dayton in November, but I am sure that it will be a great reunion for those of our group who are still around.

The forthcoming meeting in Dayton will be a great opportunity not only to reflect on the accomplishments of the past, but also to consider the challenges of the future. Specifically, I hope we can discuss whether we could apply the Dayton model to a number of unresolved conflicts in the MENA region and what we could do in strategic arms control in Europe beyond the the US-Russian INF-2 Treaty, concluded in my dream. This is hardly the right time for us to relax in retirement; too many international problems require our attention and, hopefully, our contribution. We must work hand in hand if we are to make dreams—like mine about Bosnia—a reality.

Igor Ivanov is President of the Russian International Affairs Council. He previously served the Russian Federation as First Deputy Minister of Foreign Affairs from 1993 to 1998, Minister of Foreign Affairs from 1998 to 2004, and Secretary of the Security Council from 2004 to 2007.

◂ Igor Ivanov (right) with Javier Solana at the Munich Security Conference in February 2016.

Atlantic Council
BROOKINGS

Ending a War

Strobe Talbott

In the last decade of the twentieth century, the Soviet Union and Yugoslavia erased themselves from the map of the world. But their leaders' intentions radically diverged. Boris Yeltsin tried to direct Russia and the other new Commonwealth of Independent States toward Western values, governance, and institutions, while Slobodan Milošević was a Serbian fascist, warring on his former compatriots.

The North Atlantic allies, the European Union, and the United Nations came to the Yeltsin administration's side to help its sweeping reforms. That assistance was exhilarating though daunting. At the same time, the West couldn't ignore the atrocities getting worse in the Balkans. The international community had to rein in the Serbs. That task was depressing and dangerous.

The Russians were willing to join peace conferences but determined to shield their Serbian cousins from NATO and an all-out war. As the 1990s were coming to an end, Milošević was losing ground to his enemies in Croatia and Bosnia, so he turned his wrath toward brutalizing his Muslim subjects in Kosovo. In January 1999, newspapers around the world carried photos of carnage after a massacre in the small village of Račak. Several Western diplomats tried a last-ditch peace effort with Milošević, but he was defiant.

In April Yeltsin appointed a special envoy to deal with the Kosovo conflict. His choice, Viktor Chernomyrdin—a former Russian prime minister and formidable personality—proposed that we have "an international personage" with whom he could work in tandem, "someone to accept the sword of surrender from Milošević." However, he couldn't play that role himself because he would never survive the political backlash at home. He was looking for a statesman from a nation outside of NATO who would agree with the conditions Milošević would have to accept if the bombing were to stop.

President Clinton and Secretary Albright quickly agreed that President Martti Ahtisaari of Finland was the best choice. He was the leader of a non-aligned country with a previous career in negotiating hot spots around the world for the UN, and in July he would take over, from Chancellor Gerhard Schröder, the rotating presidency of the European Union.

Chernomyrdin agreed instantly. Finland, as he put it, had "always conducted itself respectfully toward Russia," and Ahtisaari had excellent relations with Yeltsin. Clinton's national security adviser, Sandy Berger, came up with a nickname for the duo: Hammer and Anvil.

May was hectic and perilous. The sticking point was with the Russian Ministry of Defense. A group of officers were adamant that a contingent of the Serb army could remain in Kosovo when Western ground troops moved in. NATO would not budge on this point. Milošević's army was an enemy to be defeated, not to be invited on what was already a dangerous mission. The final meeting began on June 1 in the German government's guest house on the Petersberg, a mountain overlooking the Rhine. The invitation had come from Schröder, who wanted to make an appearance at what would be a breakthrough. Instead, as the day continued long into the night, it looked as though the Germans were hosting a fiasco. The Americans found themselves watching a brutal quarrel between Chernomyrdin and General Leonid Ivashov, a hardliner who had no truck with the Yeltsin government, or US diplomats and military officers.

In addition to refusing to endorse total withdrawal of Serb forces, the Russians refined their demand for a geographical division of labor and the command structure for a multination Kosovo force that would make it even less acceptable to NATO. The Russian military insisted that the whole operation must be under UN "political" control, and there must be a separate sector for a Russian contingent that would not be subordinate to NATO.

The US and NATO position was essentially the same as the one four years previously when Bill Perry got the Russians to accept a Bosnia peace agreement that made clear a unified NATO command for the whole operation, with the Russian peacekeepers reporting directly to an American officer and thus only indirectly to NATO. We called this arrangement "the Bosnia model."

General Ivashov, who did most of the talking for the Russian side on military questions, replied tartly that his ministry hadn't liked that model in Bosnia and wasn't going to accept it in Kosovo. In that case, we told Ivashov, Russia had the option of not participating. Regrettable as that would be, it was better than a separate Russian sector under a separate command. Since the Serbs would gravitate toward the Russian sector, that would be a recipe for the ethnic partition of Kosovo. In that case, said Ivashov, there was nothing

◂ Strobe Talbott at the MSC Core Group Meeting in Washington, DC, in November 2013.

more to talk about and they might as well go home. Chernomyrdin shut him down. He had instructions from his president to come up with a solution.

In the evening Schröder swooped in by helicopter, hoping to toast our success and participate in a press conference. We asked him politely to leave us alone, but he insisted on hosting an elaborate and stilted dinner. Chernomyrdin sat through it irritably, picking at his venison and muttering that we had real work to do.

The talks continued around a converted banquet table in a solarium. One of Chernomyrdin's aides set up a laptop computer and began typing a draft of the document spelling out the terms that Ahtisaari and Chernomyrdin would put to Milošević the next day in Belgrade. There were brackets around words in dispute, most notably the word "all" in the passage on withdrawing Serb troops from Kosovo. At 4 a.m., we decided to suggest an adjournment so that Chernomyrdin could phone home and we could all get some rest.

Over breakfast the Russians clustered by themselves, bleary-eyed and ill-tempered but clearly under instructions to keep negotiating. Chernomyrdin told me that he had been on the phone to Moscow almost non-stop and that the US terms were making his life very difficult. "This can't go on forever," he said. "We must smash all remaining problems this morning!" Meanwhile, the experts on three sides had gone back to haggling over the joint statement. Draft after draft kept emerging from the printer connected to the Russian laptop. Suddenly, out came a new version in which the brackets had disappeared around the word "all." Without warning or explanation, Chernomyrdin had accepted total withdrawals.

The closer we got to an agreed text, the more obstreperous General Ivashov became, and the more peremptory Chernomyrdin was in dismissing his objections. At one point, Chernomyrdin turned to Ivashov and said, "If you're going to keep interrupting me, you can go outside and smoke a cigarette."

Finally, Chernomyrdin leaned across the table and looked me hard in the eye. "If Milošević meets those conditions," he asked, "can you absolutely and immediately guarantee me that the bombing will stop?" "Yes, Victor Stepanovich," I replied, "once we've verified that he has indeed complied." "Okay," he said. "I'll hold you to that."

We were about to get up from the table and shake hands all around when General Ivashov made a formal statement dissociating himself from the document since the minister of defense had not cleared it. Chernomyrdin, a great bear of a man, pursed his lips and his face turned red at this final display of insubordination, but he said nothing.

For us on the American side of the table, the moment was as disturbing as it was dramatic: Chernomyrdin represented the president of Russia, who was also the commander in chief of the Russian military. Ivashov was committing an act of mutiny.

As the two delegations hurried to their cars, Jim Swigert, a veteran of Balkan diplomacy on our team, tried to cheer up the lone Russian foreign ministry representative, Boris Ivanovsky, who was looking very glum. "I'll tell you exactly what will happen, Jim," said Ivanovsky. "Milošević will accept this document, and I'll be fired. So, see you in Siberia."

Ahtisaari and Chernomyrdin each had a plane waiting at Cologne-Bonn Airport. Chernomyrdin had already flown four times to Belgrade to suss out Milošević. Now was the time for Hammer and Anvil. Ahtisaari had a smoother flight than his partner, at least inside the cabin. We later learned that Chernomyrdin and Ivashov got into a shouting match, this time while flying through the corridor that NATO bombers were using. The general returned to his seat muttering about Chernomyrdin, "I'd like to kill that son of a bitch."

The Americans didn't have to wait long for the first word from Belgrade. I was at dinner with my German counterpart and friend, Wolfgang Ischinger, at a restaurant near the Petersberg when a call came through from the Finns reporting that the first round with Milošević had gone "suspiciously well." Milošević seemed ready to give up, although he tried several times to suggest "improvements" in the document. Ahtisaari told him, "Not one comma can be changed." Milošević said he'd have to consult with his parliament, a pseudo-democratic body that was very much under his thumb.

The next day, Thursday, June 3, just as CNN began reporting that the parliament in Belgrade appeared to be close to approving the deal, I received a call from Chernomyrdin on a cellphone outside Milošević's office. I could make out voices jabbering in Serbian in the background. Chernomyrdin, said Milošević, "has taken the decision. I have just one suggestion for you." I feared what was coming next, but it turned out to be good news: Chernomyrdin said we needed to set up a meeting between NATO and the Serbian military as soon as possible to put a ceasefire into effect.

When Ahtisaari returned to Bonn, he gave me his full brief so I could tell Washington the latest. He reminded me of a veteran reporter of the hardboiled school on deadline dictating an eyewitness account of a dramatic, breaking story. He started with the facts and went straight to the bottom line: Milošević had accepted NATO's ultimatum in its entirety, without qualification.

The first evening in Belgrade, Ahtisaari had read the joint document aloud to Milošević and an assemblage of other Serbian leaders. He added four points: Chernomyrdin, who was sitting next to him, agreed to the terms; those terms were non-negotiable; they were the best Milošević could hope for; and if they were rejected, NATO's next offer would be worse from the Serbian standpoint. Milošević put up surprisingly little fight. He seemed interested in getting the deal done as quickly as possible. It was Ahtisaari's impression, from everything he'd heard and sensed in Belgrade, that Chernomyrdin's endorsement of the conditions was a crucial factor in Milošević's decision to throw in the towel.

"Our friend Victor was absolutely magnificent," said Ahtisaari. "He did everything he promised, without equivocation or complaint. The Serbs were clearly counting on him to offer them an out, and he didn't give them one."

Ahtisaari was whisked with a motorcycle escort to the EU meeting where the delegates waited in high suspense. I headed across the tarmac to our traveling team's plane to take us to Brussels. But before I boarded, I called the White House and was patched through to the Oval Office. The president was heartened by the news but also wary. We had to allow for the possibility that Milošević was yet again trying to fake us out, he said. We had to be sure that we pinned down the Serbs on everything they had to do before the bombing actually stopped.

When I arrived at NATO headquarters, I went first to Javier Solana's office. He was as exuberant as Ahtisaari was button-down, and he gave me a long, fierce hug. I suddenly had difficulty keeping my own emotions in check. We said barely a word to each other, but each knew what the other was thinking. For us both, Milošević's surrender was at least as much a relief as it was a victory. Dropping tons of high explosives on Serbia for nearly two and-a-half months—with all the attendant destruction, all the hardship for Serbia's people and neighbors, all the stress on the alliance, and all the strain in relations with Russia—had been necessary but wrenching for everyone who bore responsibility for the policy.

Javier would have gladly forgone the distinction of being NATO's first secretary general to help lead the alliance in a war, just as I would have much preferred to have vindicated the principle of diplomacy backed by force without having to make good on the threat. The seventy days of bombing and carnage were coming to the end.

Javier and I went to the main NATO conference room where the nineteen representatives of the allied states were waiting expectantly around a giant oval table. There was, I noticed, an empty chair next to Javier's. It was General Wes Clark's. He was upstairs talking on the phone to his Serbian counterpart, arranging for the border talks that would establish the procedures for the Serb withdrawal, the deployment of the international force, and the suspension of the bombing. Wes entered the room halfway through my report. All eyes turned to him. I stopped so that he could tell the group how he had stressed to the Serb general that "every hour we don't have the meeting is another hour I will be destroying your military machine."

After midnight, I flew from Brussels to Helsinki for what was supposed to be a valedictory session with the two envoys, but Chernomyrdin called me from Belgrade with his regrets. He had to get back to Moscow, he said, to "deal with certain matters there." He didn't say that back home his effigies were hanging from lampposts, and communists and nationalists in the Duma were accusing him of treason. Igor Ivanov told Secretary Albright that Chernomyrdin was "totally, absolutely finished."

Not quite. In 2001 Vladimir Putin appointed him Russia's ambassador to Ukraine. Chernomyrdin earned much more than that post. In tandem with Ahtisaari, he saved many Serbians' lives by forcing Milošević to give up on the war that he had started more than a decade earlier. Moreover, Milošević's days were numbered. He lost his presidency and spent the rest of his life conducting his own defense as a war criminal. He died in a prison cell in The Hague. While the country he had ruled was, finally, at peace.

Strobe Talbott is a distinguished fellow in the Foreign Policy program at the Brookings Institution. Previously, he served as president of the Brookings Institution from 2002 to 2017 and as US Deputy Secretary of State from 1994 to 2001. His most recent book, *Our Founders' Warning: The Age of Reason Meets the Age of Trump*, was published in 2020.

#NATOEngage

Reflecting on Journalistic Responsibility

Constanze Stelzenmüller

For journalists, diplomacy is strictly a spectator sport. There are distinguished exceptions, such as the former president of the Brookings Institution, Strobe Talbott, who was first a Russia correspondent and then undersecretary of state. But the rest of us are observers, not participants. And any kind of interference is obviously verboten.

As a journalist, I not only embraced this rule, but generally gave diplomats a wide berth. Frankly, I much preferred striking out on my own far from European capitals to trudging along at conferences behind an insomniac, irascible, or remote important official. So I was appalled when I found myself faced, in July 1998, with the possibility of single-handedly sabotaging a historic project of multilateral diplomacy.

My newspaper, the German weekly *DIE ZEIT*, had sent me to Rome to cover the negotiations on the creation of an International Criminal Court (ICC)—on the reasoning that, while I was quite junior, I happened to have a law degree, and this event was extremely unlikely to generate actual news. But by the time the conference headed toward the home stretch, things had become anything but boring: national security advisers and defense ministers around the world had woken up to the fact that some elements of the draft ICC statute might directly affect their ability to deploy military power.

On the Sunday before the final week and the vote on the statute, I went for a walk to clear my head. In a park, I ran into a younger member of the German delegation, who appeared extremely upset. When I asked whether he was all right, he wordlessly pulled out a sheet of paper and handed it to me.

One look told me that I was holding what the entire press corps covering the conference was hunting: proof of a wild rumor that the Americans had given some of their allies an ultimatum to join the US in voting against a key passage (universal jurisdiction for the court) in the statute.

After we parted, I sat on a bench for a long while. "US Secretary of Defense Threatens NATO Ally Germany with Troop Withdrawal" was front-page of *The New York Times* news. My editors would view my procuring this scoop as, finally, a proof of my reportorial manhood.

But other images kept intruding. Seventy-eight-year-old Benjamin Ferencz, a Holocaust survivor, one of the youngest prosecutors at the Nuremberg war crimes tribunal in 1946, and now an advisor to the US delegation, had told me how important it was to finally have a permanent court that could adjudicate genocide, war crimes, and crimes against humanity. (Having been to Rwanda and to Bosnia, I understood how he felt.)

Among the 160 countries represented at the ICC conference were a number of new democracies: Argentina, South Korea, Lesotho, Malawi. I had talked to their idealistic young delegates, who argued passionately that their countries needed a world criminal court as a last resort. I had watched the wily conference chairman, Canadian Philippe Kirsch, supported by the so-called Like-Minded Group of 65 states (to which Germany belonged), skillfully steer the negotiations toward the final vote. And I knew that American lawyers had made immense contributions to the preparatory work for the draft statute.

Back at the hotel, I took a deep breath and called my editor. I told him that I had proof of the scandalous rumor, and that to my knowledge I was the only one to have it; but that I was not going to admit that in public, much less write it. I listened to his objections, which were many and strenuous.

Then I said: US Secretary of Defense William Cohen's threat is outrageous, but the US has a point, and I think the dispute over universal jurisdiction will be resolved in negotiation. Whereas if we publish this, there will be such a global outcry that the conference could break down, probably ending forever a quest for international justice that began at the Nuremberg trials. Do we, a German weekly, want to be responsible for that? In a tiny-drama-queen voice, I added that I would rather resign.

That last threat was ridiculous, because I was expendable, and knew it. But the reference to Nazi war crimes worked.

In the final negotiating rounds, the US won the fight over universal jurisdiction. Yet the heavy-handed last-minute pressure from Washington paradoxically breathed new resolve into a lot of wavering delegations. The ICC statute was adopted in the early morning hours of July 17, 1998, with a vote of 120 to 7 (including the US), and 21 abstentions. It entered into force in 2002; today, 123 states are parties to the statute. As for me, I remain a devoted spectator of diplomacy.

Constanze Stelzenmüller is Fritz Stern Chair at the Brookings Institution. From 1994 to 2005, she was an editor for the political section of the German weekly *DIE ZEIT*, where she also served as Defense and International Security Editor and covered human rights issues and humanitarian crises.

◂ Constanze Stelzenmüller at NATO Engages in Washington, DC, in April 2019.

Wilson Center
Munich Security Conference msc
Münchner Sicherheitskonferenz

Trying to Rein in the Executive

Jane Harman

Members of Congress serve in a separate branch of government from our State Department and diplomatic corps. Yet what Congress does directly impacts the US posture with other nations and enhances or diminishes the work of our diplomatic corps. Sometimes what Congress does can offer an additional bargaining chip in negotiations or provide crucial backing at important junctures. Sometimes, however, Congress and the other branches are at odds over certain policies, thereby significantly hampering our diplomatic effectiveness. An interesting example is the effort to rein in what I came to view as rogue actions by Vice President Cheney and Secretary of Defense Rumsfeld during the early years of our war on terror.

On March 7, 2002, I was part of a congressional delegation that flew to the US naval base at Guantanamo Bay (GTMO) for a tour of the new detention facility there. After landing at the airstrip, we boarded a small boat for transport across the bay to the prison. A three-star army general was our guide. As we sped over the tropical water, I asked him, "How come the prison was set up here?" Without flinching, he replied, "To be beyond the reach of US law." I was stunned. But I didn't speak up then, nor did I do anything about it after returning to Washington DC. Looking back, it's clear that we—and I include myself—failed to recognize the unique legal and political challenges posed by international terror suspects and the enormous diplomatic fallout Guantanamo would bring with it over the years.

In the wake of 9/11, the Bush administration, with bipartisan congressional support, could have received ample authority and flexibility under a new legal framework that allowed for vigorous but humane interrogations, protection of classified information, prolonged detention if needed, and swift but fair trials of those who committed serious offenses. Such a framework would have to be revised over time in response to legitimate legal challenges or changed security circumstances. With both political parties so invested, America could have presented a united and principled front to friends and enemies alike and would not have opened itself up to (legitimate) criticism.

To be sure, the capture of dozens of suspected Al Qaeda militants and hundreds of Taliban fighters would have created a legal conundrum for any administration. These detainees did not fit the traditional legal categories of "criminal defendant" and "prisoner of war." The former gets a lawyer and Fifth Amendment protections against self-incrimination; the latter gets the protections of the Geneva Conventions designed for this purpose. Administration officials would later argue that prisoners captured in previous wars—like the thousands of German soldiers captured overseas and detained by the US for the duration of World War II—had never been supplied with lawyers or provided with access to courts. But those conflicts had a limited duration and there was no doubt that those prisoners, captured armed and in uniform, were in fact enemy combatants. The Bush administration's legal formulation was one-sided: all the advantages offered by the criminal justice and prisoner-of-war systems went to the government, with none of their protections provided to those detained.

In December 2001, I was a principal cosponsor of legislation requiring that military tribunals include habeas corpus rights and oversight by federal courts. I envisioned trials taking place either on American military bases overseas or on American aircraft carriers in open waters. We tied the use of tribunals closely to the acts passed by Congress three days after the 9/11 attacks. This would exclude any prisoners not associated with Al Qaeda, even if they were terrorists (for example, the Tamil Tigers in Sri Lanka or Basque separatists in Spain). Our bill went nowhere. But it was a statement early on that Congress would not be an idle bystander as a new wartime regime took root.

Almost two decades later, the problem still festers. There are now fewer than forty prisoners at GTMO, but the prison remains open. Congress has passed legislation barring their removal to the US for trial. Military tribunal proceedings at GTMO are endlessly delayed. The Biden administration has transferred one prisoner to a third country and is working on more transfers. Sadly, GTMO remains a recruiting tool for those who want to undermine the West and a problem for our diplomatic efforts and credibility on human rights issues around the world.

Jane Harman is Distinguished Fellow and President Emerita at the Wilson Center. She served as a nine-term member of Congress, as President Carter's Secretary of Cabinet and on many diplomatic missions to foreign countries. She is a member of the MSC Advisory Council. Her book, *Insanity Defense: Why Our Failure to Confront Hard National Security Problems Makes Us Less Safe*, was published in 2021.

◂ Jane Harman at the Munich Security Conference in February 2019.

Setting the Agenda of the United Nations General Assembly

Srgjan Kerim

To achieve their goals, diplomats must be prepared to tackle many hurdles, but they must also be prepared to try out many different routes. Where doors are closed, they must climb through windows, and even try out chimneys if no other route leads to the goal. Only those who are prepared to take byway after byway and for whom no path is too lengthy or complicated can be—or can become—successful diplomats.

For thirty years, I have tried to find the right byways in order to serve my country (or my countries) and the United Nations. Two of these byways in particular have stuck in my memory. Both originated during my presidency of the 62nd session of the United Nations General Assembly (2007–2008).

The most important task of the president of the UN General Assembly is to create a session agenda that is acceptable to all member states, which requires careful and prudent crafting. Most crucially, you have to leave the impression that all member states have had their say in it. This seemed to be mission impossible when it came to the important question of climate change. The US, China, Russia, India, and Brazil were strictly against including this topic in the agenda. Three of these countries are permanent members of the Security Council, which is regarded as the most important body of the United Nations. Notably, US President Bush didn't buy into my argument that discussing a subject didn't necessarily lead to obligations of any kind.

During their G8 presidency, the Germans tried to crack the same nut—without success. They likewise wanted to include half a sentence on climate change in the final communiqué of Heiligendamm, and, once again, the Americans were strictly opposed. I reached an agreement with Berlin to combine both problems in a way that would make it easier for Washington to accept the inclusion of the topic in the agenda of the General Assembly. In a conversation with US Secretary of State Condoleezza Rice, I stressed how strange it would look if the G8 didn't say a word about climate change, given that the United Nations would be discussing the subject shortly after. Since the US is especially fond of the G8's leading role, allowing the G8 to mention the subject first in order to pave the way for debate within the United Nations appeared to be the lesser evil, compared to being snubbed by the General Assembly. This small trick was enough to bring the US on board.

The next challenge was to convince Beijing that the time was ripe for a debate on climate change. In our face-to-face conversations, Chinese Prime Minister Wen Jiabao adamantly insisted that China could never make commitments on the international level. When I asked whether this was also true for national commitments, he answered with indignation that, as a matter of course, they planned to set themselves ambitious goals. When I explained to him that, considering the size of his country, these goals would have far-reaching consequences for our planet even without an international self-commitment, and would therefore be of interest to the General Assembly, he gave his consent to a corresponding item on the agenda as he didn't want to miss the opportunity to share his great plans.

As a diplomat, you have to be prepared to take any path or byway that presents itself to achieve the set goal. However, you must also have patience and content yourself with taking small steps toward the goal.

For entirely different reasons, all other countries gradually consented to including the climate-change item in the agenda. The challenge was to convince each country that it was genuinely in their interests to have this subject spoken about in the General Assembly. The moral is plain to see: As a diplomat, you have to be prepared to take any path or byway that presents itself to achieve the set goal. However, you must also have patience and content yourself with taking small steps toward the goal. This is illustrated by a second example.

In addition to negotiating the agenda of the upcoming session of the General Assembly, I had set a second major goal for my presidency: I wanted to achieve at least some progress toward reforming the Security Council—after a standstill of more than twenty years. To get to that point, two challenges had to be met. First, in the so-called Open-Ended Working Group (OWG)—which I chaired in my capacity as president of the General Assembly—we had to reach agreement on turning the endless exploratory talks into genuine negotiations about a possible expansion of the Security

◂ Srgjan Kerim at the United Nations General Assembly in September 2019.

Council. And second, we would then have to achieve a consensus on passing a corresponding resolution in the General Assembly.

Right at the beginning, I noticed that there were three groups of states, each with a totally different position. The first group, called G-4, consisted of the countries that saw themselves as candidates for permanent membership in an expanded Security Council: Brazil, Germany, India, and Japan. The second group, called G-3, included the US, Russia, and China, all of which, being permanent members of the Security Council, squarely rejected a General-Assembly vote on reforming the Security Council. The third group, which had named itself "United for Consensus," made the case for a decision on reforming the Security Council to be made by consensus and not by a simple majority.

Soon I realized that, given this setup, changing the status quo would be out of the question for some time to come for anyone unprepared to take a little byway. I was willing to do this, and, in my capacity as the president of the General Assembly and the chairman of the OWG, I was in a perfect position to do so. For a start, I decided to delay the talks in the OWG until the very last day of my mandate, thereby causing growing unrest and leading to unmistakable calls to replace me as chairman. The G-4 countries, in particular, accused me of actually not being interested in reforming the Security Council. I decided to escalate the provocation by threatening to step down. The G-4 reacted immediately and suggested that South Africa should take over the presidency. This, however, provoked bitter opposition from the "United for Consensus" group, which threatened to collectively leave the meeting. The chaos was complete, and there were increasing fears that the OWG was headed for an embarrassing failure.

The art of diplomacy often manifests itself in the small things, the long paths, and the cumbersome detours rather than in the quick shortcuts.

I announced a short break and asked the five permanent members of the Security Council to join me in my office. I then let them know that I was determined to suspend the OWG and to convene the General Assembly, which would be in a position to decide to turn the exploratory talks into genuine negotiations, considering that the OWG obviously could not be expected to produce results any time soon. I was perfectly entitled to proceed in this way—or to draft a resolution myself and to put it up for discussion, and, ultimately, to a vote. Resolution 62/557 demanded to move the deadlocked reform discussions from the OWG to intergovernmental negotiations, beginning with the 63rd session of the General Assembly. Confused by the escalation and the OWG's heated atmosphere, the five permanent members agreed to my proposal.

On September 15, 2008, my term as the president of the General Assembly ended with the adoption of this resolution by the General Assembly. Finally taking the matter from the clutches of the OWG and putting it into the hands of the member states paved the way for further steps. And even though little progress has been made since the adoption of resolution 62/557 thirteen years ago, I still believe that it represented the capstone of my diplomatic career. First, in my view, the matter was now where it belonged, and second, the blocking techniques of the various groups were now open to public scrutiny rather than hidden in a non-transparent OWG. To this day, I believe that, eventually, it will be possible to turn this into public pressure. While it may take some time, there is at least a realistic possibility of changing the composition of the Security Council from the current anachronism into a more representative composition. This alone was worth all the detours.

Both of these examples show how the art of diplomacy often manifests itself in the small things, the long paths, and the cumbersome detours rather than in the quick shortcuts, and why a diplomat needs, above all, patience and perseverance. If you possess both, and if you unswervingly hold your course, you are close to your goal.

Srgjan Kerim was the President of the 62nd Session of the United Nations General Assembly. He has also served as the Minister of Foreign Affairs of the Republic of Macedonia, as the Macedonian Ambassador to Germany, and as the Special Envoy of the UN Secretary General on Climate Change.

Wolfgang Ischinger (from left), Natalie Amiri, and António Guterres at the MSC Special Edition in February 2021. ▸

Surviving Difficult Diplomatic Visits

Louise Mushikiwabo

I am an African and a diplomat, which means that I am a professional storyteller. Storytelling and negotiating would be unthinkable without a good knowledge of language, and the ability to manipulate words and regulate your demeanor is a must for a good diplomat—the African touch to the exercise is an experience better lived than told. Still, I will attempt to share just a few diplomatic moments that have stuck with me over two decades in the trade.

My very first mission abroad as Rwanda's foreign minister was in the Democratic Republic of Congo, at a time of great tension between our countries. The travel was a bit tricky, and I was nervous. As my counterpart and I walked into the meeting room of a hotel in the capital Kinshasa, I was greeted by belligerent looks and whispering, and I immediately realized that I had to counter the hostility without compromising that crucial mission. I sat nervously waiting for the Congolese minister to conclude his minimal introduction of me and the meeting, before I walked to the podium prepared for the occasion and, improvising, said:

> Honorable minister, dear collaborators on both sides, my Congolese brothers, I bring you warm greetings from your relatives in Rwanda, and alongside this civility, the request from my government to resolve our issues as a family does so that I come back home with a breakthrough. I read and overheard some discontent and mistrust on the faces of some of you when I entered this room, but I am convinced that deep down you were happy to have me here, as a sister, especially that Kinshasa is my maiden trip in my current position. Surely you could not be unhappy with me, for as you and I know, in our culture we make the bride cry before the wedding day with nostalgic songs and memories of childhood with siblings, not because we want to hurt her, but because where we come from family sometimes regrets keeping apart from family. That is why I know the evil eyes and the whispering when I entered this room were all about reminding me that our countries have been apart in the last few years when we really should not be. I am here to tell you, from my side of the family, that we will have no choice but to get along.

At that point, the room filled with applause followed by a breeze of worrying silence. I had outdone myself and did not know what else to say to get the negotiations going, so I waited for the cheering to subside and said: "My dear brothers and sisters, let me conclude by sharing the conviction that no problem between us can be so complicated that we will not be able, together, to find a way out; we have no choice but to come back together as family. Of course, we are sovereign countries with sacred borders and our own rules but in the end, we remain family!"

Africa obviously is not one country, but by and large, it is not unusual that language and cultural similarities can turn an acrimonious bilateral meeting into a difficult family conversation.

Years after the Kinshasa family affair, very far away from Africa, I was confronted with an extremely delicate situation in an extremely powerful country with an extremely important ally of that country. My interlocutor came to our agreed meeting site with a dozen high-level diplomats and analysts. He carried an impressive pile of solidly bound and nicely covered thick documents, with logos and emblems that gave way to graphs and statistics, a multitude of colors, and sophisticated fonts.

Storytelling and negotiating would be unthinkable without a good knowledge of language, and the ability to manipulate words and regulate your demeanor is a must for a good diplomat.

There I was, a small woman from Africa, holding tightly to some neatly organized cards that bore talking points on numbered pages with underlined bolded words here and there as the only weapons to help me fight a war of words with a very tall Caucasian man carrying the previously mentioned arsenal. "Madam Minister," he said; "I wish first of all to thank you for accepting this lunch, and, as my time is very limited, let us get going."

Almost before I managed to utter a barely audible thank-you, my interlocutor began accusing my country of violations, of stubbornness, of having an attitude and a lack of understanding, and of not measuring consequences. Having studied and lived long in the West, I was not so much intimidated as I was surprised by the ease with which this man was being indelicate. His slow-talking manner suggested that he thought

◂ Louise Mushikiwabo at the MSC Core Group Meeting in Addis Ababa in April 2016.

this was the only way I would be able to understand him, and, further, that when big countries talk to small countries, the latter's job is to just listen and register (or not).

When my interlocutor paused for the next injunction, I dared to respond: "But Your Excellency and dear colleague . . .," which got him to stop and look at me finally with a distracted gaze. I was not sure whether it was to the "excellency" or to the "colleague" that I owed that second of attention, but I had already decided that I was going to tell this man what was on my mind—more about his attitude than my disagreement with him.

I told him that my delegation (of three) and I were grateful that he had found it fitting to have that meeting so that we could carry out that important exchange, but that since he did not have much time and I was in no disposition to accept the not-so-flattering reproaches made against my country, I wanted just to comment on one word he used that I thought was the only basis on which we might find common ground.

Africa obviously is not one country, but by and large, it is not unusual that language and cultural similarities can turn an acrimonious bilateral meeting into a difficult family conversation.

I ventured: "Your Excellency, I am surprised you would believe you know my country better than I, and I find it a bad premise to our discussion that you would use such aggressive adjectives about a friendly country, but since you called us 'partners,' we can begin by listening to each other's specific grievances, and the demands that follow. Again, I am only suggesting that we first take turns and express our countries' positions, and truly listen to each other, because that is what partnership is about."

The man switched from me to his warming salad and the said: "Indeed, I shall find a manner in which to clarify what you misunderstand, but in all partnership and friendship, you should understand that I have members of Parliament I am answerable to and who wonder what is wrong with your country."

At that point my fish was getting cold, and I told him that he should understand that I also have a Parliament to report to and the Foreign Relations Committee wanted to discuss with me why I allow my country to be mistreated by countries I always refer to as development "partners." The otherwise aloof man smiled and said, "let us eat."

Louise Mushikiwabo is the current Secretary General of La Francophonie. After living in the United States for twenty years, she moved to Tunisia in 2006 where she worked in the African Development Bank as the Director of Communications. In March 2008, she was called by the President of the Republic of Rwanda to join the government team where she successively served as Minister of Information from 2008 to 2009 and Minister of Foreign Affairs and International Cooperation from 2009 to 2018. She is a member of the MSC Advisory Council.

MSC Core Group Meeting in Addis Ababa in April 2016. ▸

msc
Giesecke+Devrient

Raising Interest for the Arctic

Ólafur Ragnar Grímsson

At their 2021 summit in Geneva, Presidents Biden and Putin devoted a considerable part of their relatively short meeting to the significance of the Arctic in the emerging geopolitical triangle of the United States, Russia, and China. In their subsequent press conferences, both leaders confirmed the high level of attention now given to the high North.

Many assume that Putin was expressing a long-standing interest and engagement in the Arctic, when, in fact, it has only been relatively recently that he gained this focus. At the beginning of his rule, it did not concern him at all. The evolution of his position and opinions on the Arctic is a fascinating case study in both the Russian art of diplomacy and the persistency of change in international relations.

More than twenty years ago, I went on a state visit to Russia—the first by a president of Iceland. Despite the Cold War, our countries had for decades enjoyed extensive trade and economic cooperation. Iceland sold Russia fish and in return got timber, iron, cars, oil, and petroleum. The fossil fuel from the Soviet Union helped to modernize Iceland. My fellow countrymen also had the ingenuity and audacity to resell part of the Soviet oil to the American military base, a core installation in the North Atlantic strategic balance. And with a considerable profit! Thus, for decades, the Pentagon depended on Soviet fuel for the Atlantic defense—courtesy of the Icelanders' ability to see a business opportunity where others only observed deadly conflict.

I eagerly looked forward to the encounter with Putin, whom the West was still trying to figure out. Convinced of the growing importance of the Arctic, I brought up the topic early in our discussion. Putin waved it off dismissively. He had absolutely no interest in the Arctic. It was not his concern: "You discuss that with the governors in the Arctic regions of Russia." I tried again. He changed the subject; turned the attention back to trade, fish, and timber.

Our next encounter was in 2010 during a conference on the Arctic organized by the distinguished explorer Artur Chilingarov under the auspices of the Russian Geographical Society—a traditional framework of science and exploration with no sign of geopolitical interest. Putin had then become prime minister but found the time to address this somewhat strange gathering of academics, scientists, and other Arctic nerds. I was the only president in attendance. Apart from Putin and me, no other politician turned up, neither Russian nor foreign. The media paid no attention.

Putin's speech clearly indicated that the Arctic had now gotten his attention and at the following conference—which took place the next year in Arkhangelsk—he invited Prince Albert to join the two of us on the plenary stage. His Serene Highness was following in the footsteps of his grandfather, who famously explored the Arctic. Iceland and Monaco! Not exactly a sign of new geopolitical relevance. But still, a smooth beginning of the diplomatic dance that accelerated in the coming years.

At the next conference, two years later in Salekhard, Putin used his regained presidential status to invite the president of Finland. Now there were three presidents—definitely an advance. By 2019 the conference was moved out of the shadows of small lecture halls in distant places to the large international conference center in St. Petersburg, the old capital of the czars. The presidents of Finland and Iceland and the prime ministers of Norway and Sweden were the honored guests, hosted by Putin for a long session on the grand stage in the main hall. All major ministers in the Russian government sat attentively among the audience and applauded when their president declared from the podium that the Arctic now had a bureaucratic home in the new Ministry for the Development of the Russian Far East and Arctic. Putin also emphasized how the Arctic had already become a strong pillar in the emerging economic axis between Russian and Asia.

Sitting now among the unofficial guests—having left office a few years before—I reflected on Putin's Arctic journey from our first meeting, when he had waved the Arctic off as a matter of little or no consequence, to this speech on how the future of Russia would be determined by the Arctic.

Why am I telling this story? Because it shows that, in international politics, positions often change, and opinions constantly evolve. It always pays to be mindful of this truth, whether in the Arctic or elsewhere.

Ólafur Ragnar Grímsson is Chairman of the Arctic Circle, which he founded in 2013 with various Arctic partners. He previously served as President of Iceland from 1996 to 2016.

◂ Ólafur Ragnar Grímsson with Madeleine Albright at the Munich Security Conference in February 2019.

WISN

Negotiating the Status of Kosovo

Frank G. Wisner

No part of Europe has vexed statesmen more than the Balkans—and for better than a century. Managing crises, building cooperation among the states of the region, and integrating the Balkans into the European and North Atlantic political and economic structures has been and continues to be a major challenge. Our collective inability to settle the problems of the Balkans means the dream of a Europe, fully whole, free, and secure will continue to be elusive.

It is to this challenge that many of Europe's and America's diplomats have over a generation been called—Wolfgang Ischinger is among them. When asked on behalf of the EU to deal with Kosovo's final status in 2007, Wolfgang Ischinger agreed. He brought to the table a successful career in diplomacy, a commitment to assertive European foreign policy, and a belief in Europe's shared agency with the United States.

No part of the multifaceted Balkan puzzle has proven more difficult to resolve than the question of Kosovo. For much of the past century, Kosovo was part of Serbia; its quest for independence began with the collapse of the erstwhile Yugoslav Federation. As a result of Serbia's attempt to suppress aspirations for independence of Kosovar Albanians, NATO intervened militarily in 1999, halted the carnage, forced Serbia out of Kosovo, and placed the country under UN tutelage. But Kosovo's drive for independence did not stop there. Fresh violence in the territory erupted five years later, forcing the international community to reopen the question of final status.

Managing crises, building cooperation among the states of the region, and integrating the Balkans into the European and North Atlantic political and economic structures has been and continues to be a major challenge.

In 2006 Condoleezza Rice asked me to represent the United States in negotiations to settle Kosovo's status, which the former President of Finland, Martti Ahtisaari, had been asked to lead. He produced a settlement plan twelve months later.

Although final status negotiations initially enjoyed the support of the Russian government, when it came time to agree to Ahtisaari's plan and set the stage for Kosovo's independence, Russia objected. Russia was unwilling to part company with Serbia, which bitterly opposed Kosovo's independence.

The question of Kosovo's future was then turned over to the US, the UK, Germany, France, and Russia for consideration at their 2007 summit. These governments agreed to undertake an additional round of negotiations in hopes of reaching a consensus. Wolfgang Ischinger was selected to represent the EU in the Troika. I represented the US and Alexander Botsan-Kharchenko joined as Russia's representative.

I had known Ambassador Ischinger during his tour of duty in Washington. We met again at his embassy in London in 2007 to discuss the way forward. The ambassador made it clear that he believed our diplomacy should be based in three principles. First, there would be strict alignment between the EU and the US. We needed to present a unified front to our Russian friends and to the Serbian and Kosovar sides. The second principle was a commitment to take a new look at all the issues affecting Kosovo's future. Although we would base our deliberations on the Ahtisaari plan, we would give the parties an opportunity to advance their conditions and arguments.

No part of the multifaceted Balkan puzzle has proven more difficult to resolve than the question of Kosovo.

The third element of our joint diplomacy was timing. The exploration we had in mind would be exhaustive and unbiased, but it had to be time limited. We set the end of 2007 as our target date. Failure to reach a reasonably early conclusion risked provoking violence in Kosovo.

Over the months that followed, with countless meetings held and thousands of kilometers traveled, the Troika adhered strictly to these principles.

Negotiations on any matter of importance are daunting. The final status talks over Kosovo were no exception. The difficulty of achieving consensus was made complex by two factors. The first was the intransigence of the parties. Both Serbia and the Kosovars held diametrically opposite views of what would constitute a settlement. The Serbs regarded Kosovo as a birthright. Denying its sovereignty was an existential matter and a

◂ Frank G. Wisner at the United Nations in New York in September 2007.

political impossibility. The Kosovars, on the other hand, regarded full independence as a matter of honor—indeed of ethnic survival.

The second complicating factor was the disposition of Moscow. Russia's leaders decided to stand by Serbia come what may. As Moscow saw matters, breaking with Belgrade would compromise Russian interests in the Balkans; furthermore, independence for Kosovo might be seen as a "victory" for NATO, something Russia could not bear.

The task before the Troika was therefore to find middle ground between polar opposites. Diplomacy is the art of the possible; sustainable diplomatic outcomes are often second-best solutions. Diplomacy requires compromise. The challenge the ambassador and I accepted was to identify a compromise position, and here Wolfgang Ischinger made a unique contribution.

Enjoying as he does the admirable qualities of empathy, patience, and persistence, the ambassador looked at the positions of Belgrade and Pristina and saw an example in Germany's experience to find a way forward. Drawing on record of his government's negotiations with East Germany, he proposed that the two parties set aside the issue of sovereignty and focus instead on arrangements that would let them live in peace, improve their lot, and advance them toward membership in the European Union. The arrangements Wolfgang Ischinger had in mind included a renunciation of the use of force, respect for existing borders, and agreements to trade, invest, deal with common concerns in public health and criminal justice, and provide for the free movement of citizens. The outcome he foresaw would result in de facto but not in de jure recognition. Serbia's face would be saved while Kosovo would achieve the substance of independence. Sovereignty would lose its salience if the two countries later joined the European Union.

Diplomacy is the art of the possible; sustainable diplomatic outcomes are often second-best solutions. Diplomacy requires compromise.

By avoiding the sensitive subject of sovereignty, Wolfgang Ischinger offered a way out of the Kosovo imbroglio. His proposal found favor with the Kosovars, and it is my impression that Moscow considered it. However, Prime Minister Vojislav Koštunica of Serbia and his colleagues rejected it, and Moscow closed ranks with them. The Ischinger-conceived compromise hit a brick wall and with its rejection, the Troika process came to an end. The United States and the Europeans refused a Russian and Serbian call for further negotiations. In February 2008, Kosovo declared its independence. Intransigence prevailed but at the cost of progress in settling one of the Balkans more intractable disputes—a dispute that debilitated both Serbia and Kosovo and undermined prospects for a better, more prosperous region.

The failure of the Ahtisaari plan and the Troika initiative to resolve final status is a dark reminder that not all international disputes have diplomatic solutions.

Serbia's opposition to Kosovar independence continues to this day. As a result, tensions persist and neither party has found a path to membership in the European Union. The failure of the Ahtisaari plan and the Troika initiative to resolve final status is a dark reminder that not all international disputes have diplomatic solutions. Wolfgang Ischinger's conception remains the best idea ever advanced to permit Serbia and Kosovo to live in peace and with mutual respect, and to achieve their European aspirations. It remains on the table today.

Frank G. Wisner served as US Ambassador to Zambia, Egypt, the Philippines, and India during his four-decade-long diplomatic career. He also served as Undersecretary of Defense for Policy and as Undersecretary of State for International Security Affairs of the United States of America.

MSC Balkan Security Roundtable at the Munich Security Conference in February 2020. ▸

Grlic Radman
Djukanovic
Dendias

Pursuing a European Future for Georgia

Eka Tkeshelashvili

While diplomats do occasionally stand in the limelight, particularly during international crises, most of the time their tireless work goes largely unnoticed and their voices mostly unheard. Back at home, they may be envied for their exotic lives and (perceived) privileges, but their views are rarely reflected in the public discourse and their entire skillset generally remains confined to the theoretical abroad. The early years of Georgian independence provide an example of diplomats contributing to the national interest at home and that the increasingly sophisticated disinformation campaigns of illiberal actors like Russia now make it even more important for public diplomacy to be focused not just on foreign populations and decision makers but on the home audience, too.

In 2021 Georgia celebrated thirty years of regaining its independence. The development of our young republic has been a remarkable, turbulent journey but marked with hope, pride, dedication, and appreciation of the unique historical momentum. For once, diplomacy was not only a valuable addendum to national policy but a vital component of our state-building process. Images of diplomats at the forefront of strategic policy deliberations, engaged in the establishment of bilateral and multilateral partnerships for our young nation, and negotiating the swift withdrawal of Russian soldiers from their Soviet-era bases is what shaped my perception of the power and the role of diplomacy and ignited my attraction to this noble profession.

As diplomats we had to work hard to consolidate the commitment of the Georgian public to democratic values, raise awareness on foreign policy priorities, and explain what it would take for us to integrate into the Euro-Atlantic community and why it mattered.

It is hard to overestimate how much enthusiasm, boldness, and dedication it took for so many of my colleagues to join the foreign service, to build it up from scratch, with scarce resources and limited experience or training in the art of diplomacy. But each of us had a clear understanding that foreign policy achievements were essential for building and securing a European future for Georgia. For most of us, there was no separation line between internal and foreign policy strategic objectives. Unlike most of my colleagues from Europe and the United States, we were at the very center of the domestic public discourse during these early days. As diplomats we had to work hard to consolidate the commitment of the Georgian public to democratic values, raise awareness on foreign policy priorities, and explain what it would take for us to integrate into the Euro-Atlantic community and why it mattered. Hardest of all was to build up public confidence when trust in the liberal global order was constantly tested and undermined by Russia.

But very few understood or appreciated this contribution of the diplomatic corps. While international partners helped to develop state institutions in many different sectors to promote and institutionalize Georgia's infant democracy, our diplomatic service fell outside the scope of most technical assistance programs—probably because diplomacy was once again seen in its traditional sense as somehow exogenous to the state-building context. Fortunately, a small number of partner countries realized the key importance of our diplomatic service, not just to defining our foreign relations, but also to building up a state (and its institutions) that our citizens could trust and identify with.

Thirty years later, this inward-looking work of the Georgian diplomatic service is more important than ever. Russian provocations and disinformation campaigns have not stopped. On the contrary, they are becoming more sophisticated by the day. Their objectives, however, remain unchanged—namely, to destabilize the Georgian state, fragment its society, and undermine its progress on the road towards a Euro-Atlantic future. By questioning the benefits of our democratic values and the sense in orienting ourselves toward the West, by instilling fear in vulnerable segments of our citizenry and by spreading rumors and fake news, Russia seeks to undo what Georgians have built up. Once again, the diplomatic service has an important role to play in persuading our population that the path we have chosen is the right one, that the hardships and frustrations are worth it, and that the easy solutions promulgated by those in Russia's hand and pay have no chance of success. We need diplomats to step into the public discourse and make the case for a path towards freedom, democracy, and prosperity that transcends electoral cycles and withstands the Russian onslaughts. Theirs will be the ultimate art of diplomacy.

Eka Tkeshelashvili is Head of the USAID-funded Anti-Corruption Program in Ukraine. Prior to this she was President of the Georgian Institute for Strategic Studies, Minister of Foreign Affairs, Vice Prime-Minister, and State Minister for Reintegration. She previously served as the National Security Adviser to the President of Georgia and as the Secretary of the National Security Council heading the National Strategic Review Process.

◂ Eka Tkeshelashvili (third from left) at the Munich Young Leaders Alumni Meeting in New York City in September 2019.

msc

Tearing Down Walls

Radosław Sikorski

1991: the end of history. Or so it seemed. It was also the year Poland signed the Association Agreement with the European Union. Unbeknownst to me at the time, it also marked the first step toward the Eastern Partnership (EaP). With the accession of the new Central and Eastern European Member States, the EU's focus started to shift eastward. Seventeen years later, a combined Polish-Swedish initiative—that I, with my foreign minister counterpart from Sweden, Carl Bildt, had conceived—was launched. How we got there is a tale of how to punch above one's weight.

The journey on the path of establishing the Eastern Partnership began over a decade before Carl and I tabled the first proposal to EU foreign ministers in May 2008. At that time, the EU had developed various neighborhood policies. Existing EU policies, however, left a void to be filled. Even though the countries covered by the EaP have diverse socioeconomic and cultural backgrounds, they were plagued by similar problems: they shared the challenge of a difficult rebirth as post-Soviet nations, including fragile government, economic underdevelopment, unresolved conflicts, and a lack of experience with democracy. The purpose of the EaP was to address these issues. The partnership was also important as developments in the EU's East were going to be of crucial relevance for the EU for years to come. In hindsight, we could not have been more correct in our assessment.

The Ukraine was obviously going to be a key part of the EaP. From a Polish perspective, it was clear that it had to be a part of any partnership with our post-Soviet neighborhood. It is our immediate neighbor, and not an insignificant country, albeit with its own economic, political, and administrative problems. This left us to consider which other countries could play a part. We started to brainstorm ideas in my ministry and came up with the following geographic reach based on potential and shared cultural bonds, among other criteria: Ukraine, Georgia, Moldova, Belarus, Armenia, and Azerbaijan.

Once we delineated the purpose and reach of the partnership, we needed to convince the EU's member states of its value. In my conversations with my then prime minister Donald Tusk, it became clear that Poland on its own—despite being a sizeable member state—did not have the political might to successfully push for this idea on its own. We needed an ally.

I decided to turn to a close political partner and friend: Carl. I knew that for the proposal to stand a chance in the Council of the EU, I needed the backing of a member state that had already been a member of the EU for some time. Sweden was also one of the wealthier member states—a net contributor to the EU budget. Having Sweden, a respected member state, on board would add more weight to the proposal, while at the same time removing the stigma of the idea being a solely Eastern European proposal. Otherwise, our idea could have been dismissed as a Polish fad rooted in history. When I outlined my idea, Carl immediately grasped the logic. He was on board.

More conversations followed with the then German and French foreign ministers Frank-Walter Steinmeier and Bernard Kouchner, but also other European leaders. I even invited Frank-Walter to my home in Poland to convince him. I would like to believe that the good Polish cuisine played its role in bringing him around to the idea. The most important part of those conversations was primarily to remove any potential obstacles to an EaP in the form of German or French opposition to the idea. Initially, there was some resistance from some member states—not only the aforementioned—based on a range of arguments: the initiative would duplicate existing EU policy efforts and the initiative would offer a fast-track path to EU membership for countries that were not ready for it, amongst others. Other events also played into our hands, such as the Russo-Georgian war in the summer of 2008. In the end, we managed to plead our case successfully. In order for an initiative to be successful, many stars have to align.

Finally, the moment came. The future EaP countries were on board, and EU member states approved the idea. In Prague in May 2009, the EU launched the Eastern Partnership under the umbrella of the European Neighborhood Policy. The Eastern Partnership was and still is the ambition of the EU and how it can exert its influence. It is also an example of how individual member states, with the right approach and the right ideas, can drive EU foreign policy.

Radosław Sikorski is former Minister of Foreign Affairs and former Minister of Defence of the Republic of Poland. He is currently a Member of the European Parliament, Member of the Committee on Foreign Affairs (AFET), the Special Committee on Artificial Intelligence in a Digital Age (AIDA), and the Subcommittee on Security and Defense (SEDE). He also chairs the Delegation for relations with the United States.

◂ Radoslaw Sikorski as a guest at MSC Events, among others at the Munich Strategy Forum in Elmau in 2016.

NATO Engages
The Alliance at 70
NATO
OTAN
Atlantic Council
msc

Negotiating the New START Treaty

Rose Gottemoeller

It is a well-known fact that the Munich Security Conference is a heavenly setting for diplomatic speed dating. If you are a senior official, within three short days you can see everyone you need, from heads of state to cabinet ministers to influential media figures. And let us not forget the representatives of big corporations and nongovernmental organizations.

The pace is hectic and efficient, the outcome, exhaustion. I well remember as a US Undersecretary of State or NATO Deputy Secretary General participating in meetings between my principal—Secretaries of State Clinton or Kerry, Secretary General Stoltenberg—and counterparts. Then I would race through the corridors, my own staff in tow, to get to the room where I had someone waiting to meet me. One always had to be on the lookout for the security details while dashing through the narrow places. They have very sharp elbows if they think that you are invading their space, getting too close to the big man (or woman).

Sometimes, however, the Hotel Bayerischer Hof is home not to new business, but to the wrap-up of old, a happy coda to celebrate when diplomacy has succeeded. Such was the case when the New START Treaty entered into force.

The process of treaty ratification had been wrapped up in both Moscow and Washington during December 2010. The US State Department and the Russian Ministry of Foreign Affairs could have exchanged dry diplomatic notes to bring the treaty into force, but we wanted to do better than that. We chose the Munich Security Conference because it was early in the year and we knew that Secretary of State Hillary Clinton and Minister of Foreign Affairs Sergei Lavrov already planned to be there. Thus, we could build a small ceremony into their schedules to celebrate the success of the New START Treaty.[1]

The New START Treaty came into force during a ceremony at the Munich Security Conference on February 5, 2011. Secretary of State Clinton and Minister of Foreign Affairs Lavrov signed the documents to record the entry into force, exchanging them afterwards with big smiles and applause all around. How long ago that seems. The Russian seizure of Crimea was three years away and some vestiges of the reset were still in operation, although Moscow was already complaining about US interference in Russia's affairs, especially on human rights issues. Indeed, Lavrov had just made some grumpy comments to that effect in the Munich plenary meeting hall.

It seemed possible, however, that something of the "spirit of Geneva"[2]—the practical, problem-solving relationship between the two delegations—could be preserved to advance US and Russian interests in further strategic arms control. President Obama was still intent on making progress on nuclear reductions with another treaty, and the Russians continued to be concerned about US missile defense developments, both in Europe and in the continental United States. They were not, as I had already discovered in Geneva, interested in pressing on with another treaty, but I thought that they could be convinced. Plenty of trends were emerging, especially new technologies, which could affect the nuclear balance. We both had an interest in maintaining that balance and the strategic stability that flowed from it.

> We negotiate with friends and allies, but just as often we are negotiating with those whose beliefs and goals differ from our own—sometimes intensely so. Nevertheless, if we are to solve problems without recourse to military force, then we have to talk.

So, after the ceremony was over that day, my counterpart Anatoly Antonov and I retired to the pub in the basement of the Hotel Bayerischer Hof, where the Munich Security Conference is held. We wanted to exchange a toast over the treaty's entry into force, but more importantly, we wanted to talk over next steps. Could we figure out a way to preserve the good working relationship that the two delegations had established at multiple levels, from the two of us, the chief negotiators, to the military experts who had a deep mutual understanding of the technical details? Neither of us knew whether our two capitals would support sustaining the relationship, but we agreed it was worth a try.

We talked about establishing a regular rhythm of meetings, perhaps twice a year, where the two delegations would come back together in Geneva for sustained discussion over one to two weeks. Such meetings could, we thought, be scheduled after the twice-yearly meetings of the Bilateral Consultative Commission, the New START implementing body, when the right people from both sides would be in Geneva anyway. The agenda

◂ Rose Gottemoeller as a guest at MSC Events, among others at NATO Engages in Washington, DC, in 2019.

would be agreed upon in advance, to address priority issues affecting strategic stability.

In my mind these meetings would be different from the talks already underway, chaired by Undersecretary of State Ellen Tauscher and Deputy Foreign Minister Sergei Ryabkov, to discuss cooperation on missile defenses. The talks I had in mind would cover a wider range of topics, including the emergence of new technologies, such as hypersonic glide vehicles, and new arms control challenges, such as limiting warheads. Republicans in the US Senate had already put us on notice that we must seek limits on Russian warheads in the next round of talks. Essentially, I thought a Geneva process could be used to build Russian interest in a new strategic arms reduction negotiation that would include new technologies and new problems that we had to tackle—warhead limits in particular.

While Antonov and I drank our Munich beer, a man sat down at the table next to us and opened a newspaper. He was so conspicuously close to us and so obviously intent on our conversation that Antonov said to me in a low voice, "Is he one of yours?" "No," I replied, "I don't think so. Is he one of yours?" He shrugged and we continued our conversation—there was nothing sensitive about it, except we knew we would have some convincing to do in Washington and Moscow.

To this day, I do not know whether that man was an intelligence operative or just some guy reading his newspaper. What I found out rather quickly, however, was that there was no interest in Washington in sustaining a Geneva process to scope out the next strategic reduction negotiation. Early on I approached Ellen Tauscher with the idea, and she told me gently that the attention now had to turn to the talks on missile defense, to try to develop some mutual understanding and cooperation with the Russians. Moreover, she said, that same set of talks would develop the strategic stability topics to prepare the way for the next negotiation. We will get the agenda for the next round ready to hand off to you, she said.

What ensued were good faith efforts by the United States to talk about missile defenses and to develop joint understanding and cooperation with the Russian Federation. Tauscher and her team were regularly accused on Capitol Hill of trying to limit US missile defenses, but in fact they were wholly focused on these two tasks—joint understanding and cooperation. They also began to open discussion about new technologies and their effect on the strategic balance.

Meanwhile, I headed off to try to convince our NATO allies that it was time to limit warheads at the negotiating table, which meant that the allies would have to countenance Russian inspectors at NATO nuclear facilities on their territories. This proved to be a tough and eventually insurmountable task, as the NATO countries at the time showed little interest in joining such an effort. It was politically difficult for many of them, given public opposition to the NATO nuclear mission, and raised too many uncomfortable questions. But that is a story for another day.

As I think back over that period, I believe one of the problems that I did not foresee was how foreign the notion of long-standing talks in Geneva had become to the Washington community. During the Cold War, delegations had sat for long years in Stockholm or Vienna or Geneva, working out conventional as well as nuclear arms limitations. They also worked on missile defense issues and shaping European security arrangements. The Mutual Balanced Force Reduction (MBFR) talks went on from 1973 to 1989, eventually resulting in the Conventional Forces in Europe Treaty (CFE).

By 2011 such ideas were out of favor with the Washington establishment. Indeed, MBFR and other long-running negotiations had probably contributed to poisoning the well by making such slow progress. I should have taken more seriously the senior White House official who stopped me outside the Situation Room to ask whether I really needed to sit in Geneva with so many people for so long. At the time I was perplexed that there wasn't a better understanding in the Obama administration of the advantages of an expert delegation with good, practical working links to its counterpart delegation. Now I know I shouldn't have downplayed his question.

What replaced delegation work were episodic visits to Moscow or other capitals in Europe, often Geneva, for a few days at a time, a few times a year. The results were not impressive, partially because the Russians became more and more recalcitrant, but also because it was difficult to develop progress from one short meeting to the next. A couple days of plenaries to exchange talking points and briefings, perhaps with some smaller meetings woven in involving the delegation heads, are important to put ideas on the table. However, they cannot be used to develop joint long-term solutions to complex technical problems, simply because it is too difficult to sustain momentum during the intervening period—especially if difficult political issues begin to get in the way.

This outcome during the Obama years was the beginning of my conviction that "drive-by negotiations" do not succeed. That conviction has only been strengthened by the experience of the Trump years. In 2020 the two presidents, Putin and Trump, interacted at the highest level through frequent phone calls to put in place the major anchor points of a new agreement, including a freeze on all nuclear warheads and an extension of New START. However, their two teams did not interact in the substantive and consistent way that could have produced the necessary implementing measures, particularly a verification regime. Instead, they got together for one or two days at a time in Geneva or Vienna, exchanged talking points, but never got down to the hard slog that produces substantive results. That hard slog cannot be avoided, and therefore I am sorry that the "spirit of Geneva" survives only in the decent working relationship between the two sides in the meetings of the Bilateral Consultative Commission. Perhaps it can be resurrected in future.

I believe that such resurrection will be necessary to tackle the tough issues that are raised by new technologies and by limits on warheads. It will also be necessary to try to control technologies that are not dependent on hardware such as missiles to perpetrate an attack—cyber weapons are a prime example. Joint development of the concepts of limitation, counting procedures when viable, and monitoring measures will all have to be done through detailed work among experts over a significant period of time.

For that reason, I will continue to press for bringing back sustained delegation work, not shying away from the necessity of sitting together for days, weeks, or even months, to get the right results for US national security.

These working relationships are not the same as friendships. We negotiate with friends and allies, but just as often we are negotiating with those whose beliefs and goals differ from our own—sometimes intensely so. Nevertheless, if we are to solve problems without recourse to military force, then we have to talk. That went for the Soviets during the Cold War, and it goes for the Russians now.

In coming times we will be negotiating about weapons with the Chinese, and we will no doubt return to the table with the North Koreans and Iranians. On some dark day in the future, we may have to negotiate with a terrorist chieftain who is threatening us with a nuclear attack. To talk him off that precipice will require us to build some trust, some relationship. Hostage negotiators know this, but nuclear negotiators have never had to wrestle with such a problem.

Whether at the big table of strategic arms reduction talks or a small table, facing a deadly terrorist, the principle is the same: Only through the development of relationships in a negotiation do we hit that sweet spot where all parties can say yes.

On February 3, 2021, President Biden and President Putin agreed to extend the New START Treaty. They did so according to terms already set in the treaty, which meant that it did not have to return to the US Senate for a ratification process. It will remain in force until February 4, 2026, which gives ample time for the next negotiations to produce results.

Thus, the stage is set to tackle the tough issues that new technologies have brought us, as well as old problems that we have wanted to tackle for a long time, especially limiting warheads. Despite deep differences between Washington and Moscow on issues ranging from human rights to the state sovereignty of Russia's neighbors, we must continue to make progress in controlling and limiting nuclear weapons. It is our responsibility to humanity.[3]

In this way and in addition to the entry into force of New START, my Russian counterpart Anatoly Antonov and I tried to use the February 2011 Munich Security Conference as an occasion to set the table for the next phase of strategic stability dialogues between the United States and Russia. With no reference to Antonov's efforts in Moscow, I have to say that I personally did not succeed in selling our ideas back in Washington.

No matter, ten years later, in the summer of 2021, we are again embarked on a US-Russia strategic stability dialogue. May the two teams have good fortune in working the issues both with colleagues in capitals and with their counterparts on the other side of the table. Who knows? Perhaps they will celebrate their efforts, with the global community, at a future Munich Security Conference.

Rose Gottemoeller was Deputy Secretary General of NATO from 2016 to 2019, after serving as the Under Secretary for Arms Control and International Security at the US Department of State for nearly five years. As Assistant Secretary of State for Arms Control, Verification and Compliance in 2009 and 2010, she was the chief US negotiator of the New Strategic Arms Reduction Treaty (New START) with the Russian Federation. She is now the Steven C. Házy Lecturer at Stanford University's Freeman Spogli Institute for International Studies. In 2021 her book *Negotiating the New START Treaty* was published by Cambria Press, parts of which are reproduced by permission.

Munich

ich Security
Conference
msc
chner Sicherheitskonferenz
www.securityconference.de

msc

Building NATO Consensus on Libya

Ivo H. Daalder

The French permanent representative to NATO, Ambassador Philippe Errera, gathered his papers, pushed back his chair, and stood up. To his right, Ambassador Martin Erdmann, his German counterpart, followed suit. Soon, the two ambassadors headed for the exit, leaving behind their twenty-six colleagues on the North Atlantic Council (NAC), myself among them, and the NATO Secretary General, Anders Fogh Rasmussen, whose outburst had caused their sudden departure.

The issue that had set off this disruption in diplomatic protocol was Libya—or, more precisely, whether NATO should have a role in the military intervention to end the country's civil upheaval. Rasmussen had called an informal NAC meeting on March 21, 2011, to discuss the matter. The meeting came four days after the UN Security Council, by a vote of 10-0 with five abstentions, had voted to authorize the use of "all necessary means" to protect Libyan civilians being attacked by the Libyan military. And it came two days after France, later followed by the United States and Britain, had launched airstrikes against Libyan forces, which threatened a forceful takeover of the eastern city of Benghazi where much of the opposition to Muammar Qadhafi, the country's long-ruling dictator, had taken shelter.

At the informal meeting, Rasmussen expressed his disappointment with Germany's decision to abstain on the UN vote and side instead with Russia and China against a resolution introduced by its allies, Britain, France, and the United States. And he also castigated France for having convened a meeting of several countries that favored intervening in Libya on March 19, but deliberately excluded key NATO allies and, not coincidentally, the secretary general himself. Rasmussen was known as someone who spoke his mind and while he had reason to be upset, he expressed himself in ways that could not but dismay the representatives of proud allied countries. Even so, walking out of an informal meeting solved nothing and a day later both ambassadors were back in their seats after an apology from the secretary general.

The drama underscored the seriousness of the issue confronting the NATO allies and the alliance itself. Libya's upheaval had followed the widespread demonstrations that toppled Arab dictators in neighboring Tunisia and Egypt. In Tripoli, however, large-scale demonstrations were met with brute force, as Qadhafi turned his military on his own people. France and Britain led the charge for intervention, calling for an arms embargo followed by a no-fly zone to prevent the Libyan air force from bombing its own people. Others, including the United States and Germany, were far more reluctant to intervene. At a NATO defense ministerial meeting earlier that March, skepticism of a more forceful NATO role was widespread. US Defense Secretary Robert Gates worried that a no-fly zone was costly to enforce and would be ineffective in addressing challenges on the ground. And he was adamant that the West not start a war against a third Muslim country without strong support from Arab countries.

Washington's assessment changed after the Arab League called for a no-fly zone, and France and Britain introduced a resolution at the UN Security Council to authorize its enforcement. President Obama agreed with Gates that a no-fly zone would do little to prevent Qadhafi from continuing to attack civilian areas with tanks, artillery, and ground forces. But rather than doing nothing, Obama wondered whether the UN might consider authorizing the use of military force to protect civilians in Libya. The United States, he suggested, would be willing to take the lead early on to destroy Libya's extensive, Soviet-supplied air defense network and would contribute its unique military capabilities for the duration. But he insisted that others more clamorous to intervene and with interests more closely affected by the turmoil in Libya carry the burden of the fight. And he made clear that the United States would need to hand off the lead of the operation to others in a matter of days.

France and Britain were keen to take the lead in launching bombing raids against Qadhafi's forces. Other NATO countries made clear that they were prepared to join in the fight, including Belgium, Canada, Denmark, and Norway. And key Arab nations—Jordan, Qatar, and the United Arab Emirates—let it be known that they could participate in strike missions. Yet other nations, NATO allies mainly but also Sweden and Morocco, made clear that they could contribute to enforcing the various UN mandates for an arms embargo and no-fly zone, but would not directly participate in bombing raids.

◂ Ivo H. Daalder at the MSC Core Group Meeting in Vienna in June 2015.

The big question, however, was who would lead this effort. Washington was adamant that it would need to hand off command and control of the operation to someone else. Unfortunately, in making that decision, the United States hadn't decided who could take over. France was eager to take control, and Britain was eager to stay tightly connected to France. But neither alone nor together did they have the capacity to command a complex, multinational military operation like this one. Aside from the United States, only NATO could do that. This much was clear to many of us working the issue at NATO headquarters in Brussels, and as soon as the UN had voted to authorize a military operation, we set out to convince our various capitals that NATO was the only viable answer for taking on an operation of this scale and scope.

Early discussions of NATO's possible role after the UN vote showed that there were important divisions among allies in Brussels. There was one group of nations, led by the United States and strongly supported by Belgium, Canada, Denmark, Luxembourg, Norway, and some others, that argued for the clarity and simplicity of NATO taking the lead. Belgium's Parliament had voted unanimously in favor of participating in the enforcement of all aspects of the UN resolution the day after its passage. Luxembourg spoke for many smaller allies when its representative said NATO offered the only viable way in which a country like his could participate directly in the enforcement of a resolution passed by the Security Council—it simply didn't have the capacity that some other nations had to set out on its own. Others emphasized that NATO had demonstrated in Afghanistan and elsewhere that it could incorporate non-NATO members easily in its operations, and thus offered the only opportunity to enlarge the coalition of those involved and enhance the operation's overall legitimacy. In Washington, the idea of NATO taking over from the United States received some resistance, reflecting concern that US dominance of the alliance might not accord with the president's desire to have others lead. But it was soon understood that there was no other country or organization that could do the job that needed to be done.

A second group of allies was more skeptical. Germany chose to abstain rather than support its long-standing allies at the Security Council. But Berlin was hardly alone in its skepticism. Many East European allies saw the alliance's involvement in a war to its South as further undermining the increasing need for NATO to focus on the growing menace to its East. Already, NATO seemed operationally extended and distracted, with its focus on the surge in Afghanistan, growing pressure to counter piracy in the Gulf of Aden, and other operations far from what they considered the main theater of potential conflict. Turkey, too, was skeptical. It had large interests in Libya that it wanted protected and worried that the aggressiveness of some allies, notably France, might infringe on those interests. Italy and Greece also had grave doubts, worried about an influx of refugees across the narrow passages in the Mediterranean and concerned that NATO might be biting off more than it could chew.

The final group was small, but critical. France, which had unilaterally launched a bombing operation against Libyan ground forces driving towards Benghazi, was adamantly opposed to a NATO role in the military operation. Part of it came from traditional Gaullist instincts not to be tied down by NATO, though Paris had two years earlier decided to return to the military command structure it had left in 1966. Part of it was traditional French pride. After all, it was France that had driven the effort toward a military intervention, and why should NATO now take over a French initiative. Part of it was fear that countries with different interests in Libya, notably Turkey but also Italy and Greece, might use their seat at the table to undermine the effort to forcibly intervene. And part of it was the conviction that Arab countries would shun involvement if the operation was led by NATO.

Though Britain shared few of these arguments and none of Paris's long-standing skepticism of NATO, Prime Minister David Cameron and his cabinet were adamant that there be no divisions on the issue between London and Paris. Instead of making clear that the only way to conduct this operation was under NATO command, London sought to stay on Paris's good side by trying to devise schemes to square the circle. One of these was the idea that NATO could lend its command system to a coalition of countries, which would set the political direction for the operation. That, of course, was a non-starter. No NATO member would agree to abandon the right of the North Atlantic Council to authorize and oversee military operations by the alliance. This was hardly news to British officials. But the point was that so long as France opposed a NATO lead, London wouldn't press for one.

As an organization that operates on consensus, NATO had little room to maneuver in view of these various divisions among the allies. The secretary general, in alienating two critical allies, had lost some of his ability to forge agreement. That left the advocates of a NATO role to try and get a consensus among the allies. Germany, helpfully, made clear that it would not interfere in the deliberations and would, in the end, join whatever consensus existed. East European allies, while weary and dragging their feet, were not likely to stand up against the United States in case Washington made clear it favored NATO to run the operation. Greece and Italy also indicated that if there was to be a military operation, it was better to have it run by an organization where they had a voice than to have it operate without their say.

That left Turkey and, critically, France as the two outliers. While Ankara had stridently attacked France for launching a bombing raid without the knowledge or input of its allies (and had been upset by Paris's decision not to invite it to the first major political meeting on Libya), it understood that it would have more input in the operation if it were a NATO effort and so was coming around to the idea of a NATO lead. With its strong relations with Arab countries, Turkey had also ascertained that the main Arab participants in a possible operation would welcome NATO taking over, because they were familiar with its operations as a result of their participation in NATO's mission in Afghanistan.

So, it all came down to France. There was little anyone could do about Paris's skepticism about NATO. But some of its other arguments soon lost their poignancy. Britain made clear that it did not see any alternative to a NATO command and control system. Neither Paris nor London had the ability, alone or together, to do what the United States or NATO could do. With Washington wanting out, only NATO could lead this operation. London was willing to see if the role of the NAC could be reduced in favor of a different coalition, but the NATO command structure would have to lead the operation. Arab countries, too, made clear that they far preferred operating within NATO than separately, thus undermining another French critique of NATO. And Turkey soon signaled that it didn't so much object to military intervention as to it lacking the coordination that only NATO could provide.

In the end, it took an intervention from Washington to get everyone on board. Three days after the French and German ambassadors had walked out of the NAC, Secretary of State Hillary Clinton convened a call with her British, French, and Turkish colleagues. She made clear we needed a package and she wanted everyone on board. NATO command and control was necessary for all military operations (arms embargo, no-fly zone, and civilian protection), and possible only if NATO military authorities responded to the political control of the North Atlantic Council. France would have to concede this point. The military needed broad latitude in conducting its operations and the NAC should therefore not interfere in setting the rules of engagement for the militaries involved. Turkey would need to agree on this point. A broad political grouping that included all parties concerned would need to provide political guidance without in any way interfering with or overseeing the NATO political-military machinery. Everyone would need to agree with this.

"Hillary, you are the consensus-builder," said Alain Juppé, the French foreign minister, in accepting Clinton's proposal. His Turkish counterpart, Ahmet Davutoğlu, agreed, as did William Hague, Britain's foreign secretary.

On Sunday evening, March 27, just ten days after the UN Security Council voted to authorize a military intervention in Libya to protect civilians from government forces, and little more than a week after French, British, and American forces had begun military operations, the North Atlantic Council voted to approve Operation Unified Protector and take over command and control of all military operations in Libya. The operation would last exactly seven months, lead to the ouster (and death) of Qadhafi, and the end of his brutal rule in Libya.

Ever since the end of NATO operations, there has been a debate about whether military intervention was the right thing to do and what responsibility those who intervened had for the chaotic aftermath that followed. Much did go wrong, and President Obama would later look back at the intervention and suggest that the failure to stabilize Libya after Qadhafi's fall was one of his greatest foreign policy regrets. But none of that should take away from the fact that the NATO operation itself proved effective in protecting civilians who had been deliberately targeted by the Libyan regime. And that through it all, an alliance deeply divided at the outset, remained unified in its response to the very end.

Ivo H. Daalder is President of the Chicago Council on Global Affairs. He served as the US Ambassador to NATO from 2009 to 2013.

msc
Conference
Munich Security
Conference
msc
msc

Reaching a Nuclear Deal with Iran

Helga Maria Schmid

The 2015 Joint Comprehensive Plan of Action (JCPOA) nuclear agreement with Iran is widely regarded as a major diplomatic success of the United States under Secretary of State John Kerry. While this is indisputable, the agreement is also—first and foremost, in fact—a success of multilateral and European diplomacy.

Over its one-hundred pages, the agreement lists detailed rules and defines a clear framework for limiting and monitoring the Iranian nuclear program, thereby providing the International Atomic Energy Agency (IAEA) with the most rigorous verification options. When I solved the final bracketed text with my Iranian negotiating partner, Deputy Foreign Minister Abbay Araghchi (in the Vienna Palais Coburg at two in the morning on July 14, 2012), it marked the close of a twelve-year arduous negotiating marathon for all those involved. On the morning of July 14, 2012, the ministers of the Group of Six (Germany, France, the United Kingdom, China, Russia, and the US, or E3+3), chaired by the high representative of the EU, formally accepted our negotiated text. Shortly before they jointly faced the media, John Kerry said to us, simply: "We avoided war."

Right from the start, the Europeans' diplomatic approach had been dual track—deploying both political and economic stimuli, as well as applying pressure.

The agreement has certainly made the world more secure, and it has eliminated one potentially dangerous source of uncontrolled nuclear proliferation.

In October 2003, the ministers of foreign affairs of Germany, France, and the United Kingdom made the first move—responding to reports of undeclared nuclear projects (Natanz, Arak) and fears that these facilities might enable Iran to run a non-civilian nuclear program. The primary initiative for this trip had come from Germany. I took part in it not as a textual negotiator, but in my capacity as Joschka Fischer's chief of staff. The result was that the chief Iranian negotiator, Hassan Rouhani, agreed to temporarily suspend the enrichment and reprocessing of uranium. The key sticking point, however, was our demand for a permanent halt to enrichment. After Mahmoud Ahmadinejad was elected president in 2005, nuclear capacities were extended, and uranium was now being enriched to up to 20 percent, which represented an essential step toward achieving nuclear weapons capability. It was not until 2013 that a negotiated solution again appeared possible. The ultimate breakthrough took place in Lausanne in April 2015, setting the scene for the final agreement, which was eventually concluded, after many nighttime sessions, at Palais Coburg on July 14, 2015.

Right from the start, the Europeans' diplomatic approach had been dual track—deploying both political and economic incentives, as well as applying pressure. During Ahmadinejad's presidency, it was the Europeans who imposed a comprehensive oil embargo to bring Iran back to the negotiation table. What sanctions alone could not achieve, US President Barack Obama—who was just as interested in a multilateral negotiated solution as the Europeans—did achieve with his reasonably differentiated Iran policy. His alignment with the Europeans was the key to success.

It has often, and justifiably, been speculated that it might have been possible to bring the negotiations to an earlier conclusion when the Iranian nuclear program was still in its early stages, under reformist President Mohammad Khatami. It is a question that, even today, is difficult to answer.

Europe was primarily interested in making sure that the Iranian nuclear program served purely civil purposes. For Iran security interests have always been in the foreground, primarily with its eye on Washington. Since reaching an agreement with Europe alone could never have been enough in the long run, the involvement of the US was crucial, as was the involvement of Russia and China from 2006 onward. The joint and united appearance of the E3+3 under the leadership of the EU was equally crucial. In 2004 it was mainly due to a German initiative that High Representative Javier Solana became involved in the negotiations. Since then, it has been the EU's role not only to chair the plenary sessions, but also to act as facilitator and to lead the negotiations.

The election of the former chief negotiator and security expert Rouhani as president in 2013 marked a foreign-policy power shift that paved the way for solution-oriented negotiations. During the last very intensive months of negotiation, we were often negoti-

◂ Helga Maria Schmid at the Munich Strategy Retreat in Elmau in December 2021.

ating well into the early hours—with the EU represented by a small team of experts. One of these experts—nuclear physicist Stephan Klement—also led the technical negotiations.

The EU had a significant role to play, because none of the involved countries would have been accepted as an "honest broker" in the negotiations. One reason was the lack of trust, which, at least initially, was predominant on both sides.

The negotiations took place on different levels—ministers of foreign affairs, political directors, and experts. On each level, the representatives of the EU oversaw internal consultation and coordination. This role became especially important when, on May 8, 2018, President Donald Trump announced the withdrawal of the US from the agreement. In November of the same year, sanctions were restored and tightened. Many commentators saw this as a purely politically motivated move—especially since the Vienna-based IAEA had repeatedly confirmed that Iran was complying with the terms of the JCPOA. Consequently, the other countries involved in the agreement unambiguously sided with the JCPOA.

Since reaching an agreement with Europe alone could never have been enough in the long run, the involvement of the US was crucial, as was the involvement of Russia and China from 2006 onward. The joint and united appearance of the E3+3 under the leadership of the EU was equally crucial.

On the day following the announcement of the US withdrawal, Federica Mogherini, then high representative of the EU, declared her regret and the EU's continued support of the agreement. While the US under President Trump returned to betting on "maximum pressure," the Europeans, Russia, and China remained committed to the nuclear deal.

As part of the JCPOA, a joint commission that included representatives from all parties was established to settle disputes and clarify contentious issues. In this context also, the EU (in the person of the high representative for foreign and security policy) once again took over the coordinating role.

The joint commission became particularly important after the withdrawal of the US. Since then, the E3+2 (without the US) met under my chairmanship in Vienna every three months at the political director level, and once or twice a year at the ministerial level.

One year after the US withdrawal from the JCPOA, Iran embarked on a policy of "gradual nuclear escalation," partly in response to obstacles caused by the sanctions in the financial sphere and in the oil trade—which has ground to an almost complete standstill—but also to put pressure on the remaining parties.

The agreement hung by a thread, but it has persisted.

Joe Biden's election as president brought with it a return to multilateralism, and thus made possible a renewed US commitment. There had never been an alternative to returning to the negotiation table—once again under the aegis of the European Union!

Helga Maria Schmid is now the Secretary General of the Organization for Security and Co-operation in Europe (OSCE). Prior to that appointment, she was the Secretary General of the European External Action Service (EEAS) and text negotiator of the JCPOA. She also serves as the Vice President of the Foundation Council of the Munich Security Conference Foundation.

Norbert Röttgen (left) and Ali Shamkhani at the MSC Core Group Meeting in Tehran in October 2015. ▸

Munich Security Conference
Münchner Sicherheitskonferenz
Röttgen
Shamkhani

msc
Giesecke+Devrient
Creating Confidence
Zerbo

Paving the Way for a Robust Diplomatic Process

Thomas Greminger

In 2014 war broke out in Europe. Russia's annexation of Crimea, tensions in eastern Ukraine, and the downing of Malaysia Airlines flight MH17 created a highly dangerous situation. On the one hand, it was feared that a further escalation could lead to a wider war with unforeseeable consequences. On the other hand, it was felt by many that the crisis in Ukraine was a reflection of deep distrust between Russia and the West. Both the causes and symptoms had to be addressed. Dialogue and de-escalation were urgently needed.

Attempts at Dialogue and De-Escalation

In 2014 Switzerland chaired the Organization for Security and Co-operation in Europe (OSCE). With its broad membership—including Russia, the United States, all countries of the European Union, as well as Ukraine—its permanent consultative bodies, and its well-stocked box of crisis management tools, the OSCE was well-positioned and well-equipped to deal with the crisis. For example, as Chairman of the Permanent Council, I managed to broker an agreement by consensus to deploy a multinational mission of observers from OSCE states. The first civilian monitors of the Special Monitoring Mission to Ukraine (SMM) were deployed within hours of the Permanent Council decision in March 2014. Another conflict-reducing measure was to appoint Ambassador Wolfgang Ischinger as the Representative of the Chairperson-in-Office for National Dialogue Roundtables. Together with former Ukrainian Presidents Leonid Kravchuk and Leonid Kuchma, in May 2014 he carried out a series of dialogues with local officials, church leaders, business leaders, and representatives of political parties and trade unions to facilitate consensus-building.

Unfortunately, national dialogue was not continued after the election of President Petro Poroshenko at the end of May 2015. Instead of reconciliation, fighting escalated in the summer. As a result attempts to promote dialogue within Ukraine were replaced by high-level diplomacy to stabilize the situation. On September 5, 2014, the Normandy Format comprising France, Germany, the Russian Federation, and Ukraine signed the Minsk Agreement.

While the Minsk Agreement led to a temporary reduction of hostilities, and while it was hoped that the SMM—which soon expanded to over seven hundred monitors augmented by unmanned aerial vehicles, cameras, and satellite imagery—could contain the conflict, there were bigger security issues that had to be addressed. How to restore dialogue and trust between Russia and the West? How to manage relations peacefully?

Some countries felt that discussing the future of European security or analyzing how things had gone so wrong was inappropriate while fighting still raged in Eastern Ukraine and Crimea remained occupied. But others felt that the war in Ukraine was symptomatic of a broader crisis of European security and therefore the two issues had to be addressed in parallel. There could be no peace in Europe until there was peace in Ukraine, and there could be no long-term stability in Ukraine without reconsolidating cooperative security in Europe.

While there was no consensus at the OSCE Ministerial Council meeting in Basel in December 2014 to create a Panel of Eminent Persons to address this politically sensitive security crisis, in early 2015 the OSCE Troika (comprising Switzerland, Serbia, and Germany) decided to go ahead and appoint a Panel of Eminent Persons on European Security as a Common Project.[1] Steering such a delicate process would require an experienced diplomat. We therefore called Ambassador Ischinger, who graciously agreed despite his busy schedule.

The panel's mandate was to "prepare the basis for an inclusive and constructive security dialogue across the Euro-Atlantic and Eurasian regions," reflect on how to rebuild trust to enhance peace and security in Europe on the grounds of the Helsinki Final Act (of 1975), explore perceived threats in the OSCE area and explore common responses, and "explore possibilities to reconfirm, refine, reinvigorate and complement elements of cooperative security."

Frank and Intense Discussions

Over a series of consultations between February and October 2015 (in Munich, Vienna, Kyiv, Geneva, Brussels, and Belgrade), the panel discussed the security situation in Europe and what to do about it. The confi-

◂ Thomas Greminger at the MSC Core Group Meeting in Minsk in October 2018.

dential discussions were often heated. Viewpoints were so divergent that it was not even possible to agree on a chronology on the sequence of events leading up to the annexation of Crimea and the military escalation in Eastern Ukraine. Perceptions on the wider crisis in European security were so antithetical that it was decided to include in the final report narratives on the main themes from three different standpoints: a view from the West, the view from Moscow, and the view from "states in-between." As Ischinger explained in the Foreword of the final report, the point was not so much the historical accuracy of the narratives, "but to illustrate how much our appreciation of the past diverges." As he observed, "these diametrically opposed narratives are a fact that, for the moment, we have to live with."[2]

While an effort was made to draft the report in a way that would reflect all viewpoints, some of the comments of the Russian participant were so divergent to those of the other members of the panel that it was agreed to add them as footnotes. This creative solution saved the project from collapse and gives the reader a glimpse into some of the differences of opinion. That said, it should be stressed that while the panel's views on the past diverged, they unanimously regarded the contemporary security situation as the most dangerous in several decades. As they recognized, "the vision of a 'common European home' may be more remote than it appeared two decades ago, but we still occupy a common space and need to find ways of living in it together."[3]

Back to Diplomacy

The final report, issued in November 2015, was entitled *Back to Diplomacy*. In his Foreword, Ambassador Ischinger proposed "a robust diplomatic process designed to replace mutual recrimination with rebuilding trust: not military activity, not propaganda, not rhetoric – but a process that explores our common problems carefully, confidentially and systematically."[4]

The report suggested that once the Minsk commitments are in place on the ground, a diplomatic process should be launched to rebuild the foundation of European security. Its ultimate aim should be to reestablish security on a cooperative basis, within the framework of OSCE principles. It was suggested that since the questions at issue are of a nature and urgency that requires the involvement of heads of state and government, the process should conclude with a summit.

Because the panel was created by the Troika rather than by a consensus-based decision of all fifty-seven OSCE participating states, the final report and recommendations of the Panel of Eminent Persons on European Security as a Common Project was never endorsed officially. But its legacy lives on. For example, in a decision at the OSCE Ministerial Council in Hamburg in December 2016, foreign ministers welcomed the launching of "a structured dialogue on the current and future challenges and risks to security in the OSCE area to foster a greater understanding on these issues that could serve as a common solid basis for a way forward." As a result, a process of Structured Dialogue was launched under Austria's chairmanship in 2017 and continues to this day.[5]

Thus far the results of the Structured Dialogue process have been limited. There have been discussions about how to reduce the risk of incidents and accidents, exchanges of views about threat perceptions, and talk about confidence-building measures. But the level of political engagement has been insufficient to produce significant results, there is little sense of urgency, and states accentuate their differences rather than seeking common ground. In short, the Structured Dialogue has been more fragile than the robust diplomatic process that Ambassador Ischinger and the panel called for.

Managing Differences and Identifying Converging Interests

A new tone was struck in May 2021 when US Secretary of State Antony Blinken met with Russian Foreign Minister Sergei Lavrov on the margins of an Arctic Council meeting in Reykjavik. Echoing sentiments from the historic meeting between Reagan and Gorbachev in the Icelandic capital in 1987, the two men noted that their countries have serious differences but for the sake of international peace and security, they need to find a way to get along. As Lavrov said, the United States and Russia have serious differences, but have to cooperate "in spheres where our interests collide." Put another way, they need to find ways to avoid collisions despite the existence of divergences while seeking areas where their interests converge. Blinken said Biden wanted "a predictable, stable relationship with Russia."

Such views were reiterated in the meeting between Presidents Biden and Putin in Geneva in June 2021. As the two leaders said in a joint statement, in the past, the US and Russia have demonstrated that "even in periods of tension, they are able to make progress on our shared goals of ensuring predictability in the strategic sphere, reducing the risk of armed conflicts and the threat of nuclear war." They therefore announced that the two countries would embark together on an integrated bilateral Strategic Stability Dialogue that will be "deliberate and robust." This has the potential to develop into what has been described as a "common unifying agenda," or converging interests.[6]

What could this look like? In the short term, urgent efforts should be made to agree on modalities to prevent and deal with incidents and accidents in the air and at sea, particularly in the Baltic and Black Sea areas. More effective use should be made of the Vienna Document on Confidence and Security-Building Measures (CSBMs). There should be more military to military contacts and dialogue. The United States and Russia should work together to resolve conflicts in existing negotiating frameworks that they are both part of, for example in relation to the crisis in Nagorno-Karabakh, or the situations in Moldova or Iran.

In the medium term, the two great powers should seek to rebuild the structure of treaties that were so crucial for building security in the 1990s, like the Open Skies Treaty, the CFE Treaty, and the New START Treaty. The adaption or modernization of such treaties as well as CSBMs could increase predictability and trust. The sides should also discuss ways of increasing transparency and trust on cyber issues, destabilizing weapons systems, and the use of new technologies.

As in the 1980s, an improvement of relations between Moscow and Washington is necessary but not sufficient to improve security in Europe. Discussions on arms control, conflict resolution (particularly in Ukraine), as well as dealing with transnational threats and challenges would require the involvement of a much wider group of countries with a stake in European security.

A Cooperative Security Agenda with "Fit-for-Purpose" Institutional Support

Therefore, as called for by Ambassador Ischinger and his panel, a diplomatic process should be launched to rebuild the foundations of European security based on principled cooperation. As in the buildup to the Helsinki Final Act in 1975, this exercise may take years. But the very process is crucial for building trust and working toward a common security agenda. It would also present an opportunity to discuss and agree on what these principles mean today. It could explore how certain principles like self-determination and territorial integrity can be reconciled. And it could try to overcome the security dilemma, and to square the circle between the indivisibility of security and the right of each state to choose its security arrangements freely. This will not be easy. But sweeping such issues under the carpet will not make them go away.

Therefore, at least a few countries need to demonstrate political courage and call for a forward-looking cooperative security agenda. As Ambassador Ischinger wrote in the *Back to Diplomacy* report, "above all we need confidence re-building in the political field – that is to say, diplomacy."[7] If successful, the efforts could be crowned by a summit, perhaps in 2025 if not before, marking the fiftieth anniversary of the Helsinki Final Act. The summit should result in the reaffirmation of common principles and a new foundational document for European security.

But to be credible, such a process and the follow-up to any high-level declarations or decisions will require a functional institutional basis. Therefore, the OSCE needs to be made fit for purpose—to ensure that it has the tools, structures, and procedures to help states put their political commitments into action. Institutional reforms are not a prerequisite for launching a robust diplomatic process, but the outcome of that process will have little chance of being implemented if negotiation bodies are gridlocked and executive structures cannot deliver. Therefore, reform of the pan-European security system and the OSCE will have to be complementary.[8]

Will it happen? Under Wolfgang Ischinger's leadership, the Munich Security Conference has witnessed some defining speeches in post-Cold War history, from President Putin's warning about world order in 2007 to then vice president Biden's "reset" speech in 2009. Let us hope that before Wolfgang turns 80, at least one world leader will stand on the stage of the Hotel Bayerischer Hof in Munich and have the courage to call for a cooperative security order in Europe based on the robust diplomatic process called for by Ambassador Ischinger and the Eminent Persons.

Thomas Greminger is Director of the Geneva Centre for Security Policy and former Secretary General of the Organization for Security and Co-operation in Europe (OSCE).

Making Use of Track Two Diplomacy

Alexander Dynkin

The concept of diplomacy—with its original *haute* elitist meaning—is changing drastically these days. There is an attempt to replace diplomacy with populist acts of pressure on politicians by slightly odd, pardon the expression, obsessed-with-their-ideas adolescents. Actors, sportsmen, and bloggers are all actively engaged in diplomacy. There is also megaphone diplomacy and Twitter diplomacy. All kinds of people are engaged in it, using exotic tools.

And, of course, advice to politicians comes from the internet. Against the backdrop of the pandemic, Infodemic—a gross conspiracy—is flourishing. The amount of deliberately false or simply ignorant information is enormous. One cannot just give it the air—professional diplomats serve their countries and governments, while the governments are elected by the citizens who read and often believe this nonsense. The diplomat used to be a member of the caste, but today he is forced to be a public figure, communicate with the mass media, and post on social media.

There is an attempt to replace diplomacy with populist acts of pressure on politicians by slightly odd, pardon the expression, obsessed-with-their-ideas adolescents. Actors, sportsmen, and bloggers are all actively engaged in diplomacy. There is also megaphone diplomacy and Twitter diplomacy.

I am far from being naive. And the old joke is still true: a diplomat who says yes means maybe, a diplomat who says maybe means no, and a diplomat who says no is no diplomat. At the same time, a highly professional diplomat and USSR Foreign Minister Andrei A. Gromyko was known as "Mr. No." Even so, A.A. Gromyko used to say, "better ten years of negotiations than one day of war." It is the art of negotiation that remains the essence of the art of diplomacy.

I am academician and economics expert, and I have not served in diplomacy. But I find extremely useful the global practice that exists in Russia and the United States, and which existed even in the Soviet Union. I refer specifically to the rotation between the expert academic community and the diplomatic service. The world's leading think tanks supply personnel to the diplomatic departments of their countries. When governments change, they go back to the think tanks. So do my close American colleagues—Tom Graham, Rose Gottemoeller, Richard Burt, and many others.

So did my mentor in science and in life, Yevgeny M. Primakov. This outstanding man was not tarnished during his lifetime or after his death, which is unique for a politician of such rank, although Primakov was always a public figure. He was not afraid; moreover, he loved and appreciated good journalists. He never lied, but as a true diplomat, of course, he kept many things quiet. In his life and work, he was guided by the principles of responsibility and adherence to the national interests, as well as by scientific outlook and profound knowledge. This helped him to conduct delicate negotiations with leaders of the Middle East region and beyond.

Diplomacy is the art of the possible. The utmost possible—within the limits of reality. Primakov's famous loop over the Atlantic[1] was, to my mind, an atypical act for him, because Primakov was always in favor of negotiations. But Washington's disruption of negotiations when they were already under way was beyond diplomacy.

After civil service, already as an aged man, Primakov did not just return—he rushed into science. He created and headed the Centre for Situation Analysis, which became part of IMEMO. It was Primakov who introduced the situation analysis method into Soviet and Russian science and practice. And reports on the results of situation analyses, often of critical content and with relevant recommendations, landed on the desks of decision makers at the highest levels.

But perhaps Primakov's most surprising and valuable quality was his ability to communicate and make friends with his colleagues, both Russian and American—his ability to listen and to hear, his ability to carry on a dialogue, and his focus on finding solutions.

And his willingness to joke and laugh. Primakov told that while meeting with US President Bill Clinton in 1996 in New York, he told him a joke. "A chicken is asked, 'what is your greatest achievement?' 'I laid an egg weighing 5 kilos.' 'And your greatest dream?' 'To lay an egg of 7 kilos.' Then the rooster is asked the same questions. To the question about the greatest dream, he answers, 'To punch the ostrich.'" Primakov said that Clinton laughed a lot, and then leaned over to Made-

◂ Alexander Dynkin at the Munich Strategy Forum in Elmau in December 2016.

leine Albright and asked her, “This joke is not about me, is it?”

Primakov was an optimist and believed that sooner or later solutions would be found. The same was stated by another patriarch of diplomacy and political science, his long-term counterpart, Henry Kissinger. In 2017, during a period of sharp deterioration in Russian-American relations, Kissinger came to Moscow for the Primakov Readings organized by IMEMO. “I have seen a lot of crises, but then relations came back to normal,” he said. And he continued almost in the words of Ecclesiastes: “All this has happened before. It will all pass.” “There are too many global problems that the US and Russia cannot solve without each other. We should have a common vision.” When I met him at the plane ladder in Domodedovo (at that time he was already ninety-four years old), I asked, “Dr. Kissinger, who are you now?” Without any hesitation, he answered: “I am an educator!” Instantly, I asked him to meet young IMEMO researchers. He agreed, spent two hours with thirty young people, answered their questions in detail, and signed books. This meeting remained an unforgettable event for them, and not just for their professional lives.

Track two diplomacy has confirmed its usefulness and will become an increasingly important tool, an aid to diplomacy. It combines scientific knowledge and great freedom, frankness, and rigor in the exchange of opinions, with a responsible approach of the parties and confidentiality—which is extremely important today. I am convinced that when diplomats fail to understand each other, experts should be given a chance.

In June 2014, traditions of Primakov diplomacy and academic school helped me and my colleagues from IMEMO hold the first track two negotiations on the settlement in Eastern Ukraine. It seems to me that track two diplomacy has confirmed its usefulness and will become an increasingly important tool, an aid to diplomacy. It combines scientific knowledge and great freedom, frankness, and rigor in the exchange of opinions, with a responsible approach of the parties and confidentiality—which is extremely important today. I am convinced that when diplomats fail to understand each other, experts should be given a chance before calling in the military. Track two is not for the public. It is for probing all possible options, identifying “red lines,” but at the same time outlining even the most unlikely possibilities for solving the problem. All this in an informal atmosphere, often over dinner. A.A. Gromyko, by the way, is also famous for another aphorism: “A diplomat digs his own grave with a spoon, a fork, and especially with a glass.”

Well, every profession has its own costs.

Such was the confidential US-Russian meeting on Boisto Island, Finland, in the summer of 2014, when the war in Donbass was at its most active phase. The first talks on Ukraine, which on the American side included, among others, Tom Graham (former special assistant to the US president and senior director for Russia on the National Security Council staff) and Andrew Weiss (vice president for studies at the Carnegie Endowment; former director for Russian, Ukrainian, and Eurasian Affairs on the National Security Council staff). The Russian party was represented, from the IMEMO team—besides me—by Vyacheslav Trubnikov (ambassador extraordinary and plenipotentiary, former head of the Russian Foreign Intelligence Service), academician Alexei Arbatov (former deputy chairman of the Russian State Duma Defense Committee, member of the delegation to the START negotiations), and our young colleague, current IMEMO director, corresponding member of RAS Fyodor Voitolovsky.

This is a classic example of track two negotiations. We managed to develop (without demagogy and polemical positioning) a plan of stopping the war and the first steps for restoring peace. Many of the twenty-four steps of the Boisto Plan proved practical and were used by the parties in developing the Minsk Protocol of September 5 and the Memorandum of September 19, 2014.

The world faces a growing number of problems that require professional negotiations in the format of track two diplomacy. Agreements to launch such projects are often reached on the sidelines of major international conferences such as the Munich Security Conference or Primakov Readings. It is a real way to resolve conflicts, a way to avoid the trap of Infodemic.

Alexander Dynkin is the President of the Primakov National Research Institute of World Economy and International Relations (IMEMO) at the Russian Academy of Sciences. He is a member of the Presidium of the Russian Academy of Sciences, the Russian Foreign Minister’s Scientific Council and the Advisory Board of the Russian Security Council. He served as Economic Assistant to the Russian Prime-Minister Primakov from 1998 to 1999.

Dmitry A. Medvedev at the Munich Security Conference in February 2016. ▸

POLIZEI
BY
1321
POLIZEI
BY
1321
msc

Conducting Small Power Diplomacy in an Age of Great Power Rivalry

Ine Eriksen Søreide

I have had the pleasure of attending the Munich Security Conference every year since 2014. The conference is a unique forum for frank discussions and informal meetings, and provides a vantage point for assessing the ever-changing security landscape. Some of the changes we have seen in these past years have been dramatic.

A few weeks into my tenure as Norwegian minister of defense, I attended the 2013 NATO-Russia Council (NRC) meeting in Brussels. NRC ministerial meetings had just resumed after a hiatus of two years, and the mood was unusually upbeat. Interventions focused on future cooperation, lighthearted jokes were traded across the table, and Russian Defense Minister Sergey Shoygu even spiced up his address by handing the secretary general a rose-painted military helmet. The optimistic atmosphere on that October day in 2013 proved short-lived, and soon gave way to a dramatic shift. A few months later, as we gathered around the table in Brussels for the NATO Defense Ministers' meeting, reports broke that Russian special forces had taken control of key sites in Crimea.

In eras of great power rivalry, neutrality has often been deemed a safe bet for small and medium-sized countries. However, alliances have served such countries well and remain a credible option for the future.

Russia's annexation of Crimea, a serious violation of international law, has led to significant changes in Europe since 2014. Russia has continued its military modernization, while NATO has revamped its collective defense and ramped up defense spending. Other components of the European security architecture have been eroded. The CFE Treaty was already under severe strain in 2014, and efforts to get it back on track have stalled. In 2019 the US pulled out of the INF Treaty due to Russian noncompliance and went on to withdraw from the Open Skies Treaty as well. Russia followed suit a year later. Confidence-building talks have continued but have failed to produce results that are adequately adapted to a radically different security climate.

These changes in Europe reflect broader trends that will put foreign policy and diplomacy to the test in the years to come. Rapid technological development is placing new capabilities into the hands of not only Russia, but also a growing list of opponents to Western power. International relations are increasingly being shaped by an ever-deeper rivalry between the US and China, and multilateral cooperation is likely to remain under pressure for a long time to come.

The return of great power rivalry is rarely good news for small and medium-sized countries. For such countries, these periods tend to be associated with less freedom and less influence in the world. However, it is possible to operate effectively in a more divisive environment. It just requires more sophisticated answers. Finding them, though, is no easy task.

When we gained our independence in 1905, neutrality was considered the best way forward. As a young state, Norway had mixed experience of alliances with other countries and was determined never to fall prey to great power politics again. Indeed, the power of contemporary thought was such that some even debated whether Norway needed diplomats or a foreign policy at all. Would not trade alone and a simple consular corps be sufficient for a small and globalized economy?

Confidence in neutrality grew stronger as Norway avoided the hostilities of World War I and went on to join the League of Nations. The early debate on the raison d'être of Norwegian diplomacy subsided but was soon replaced by a similar debate on the military, followed by massive defense cuts in the 1920s and early 1930s.

It would take another world war to deliver a deadly blow to this policy of neutrality, and in the spring of 1949, Norway joined NATO as a founding member, with the US as our most important ally. We went on to build robust relations with our Nordic neighbors, develop constructive practical cooperation with Russia, and forge an ever-closer relationship with Europe.

It is possible to a draw a line from the early days of Norwegian diplomacy to contemporary discussions on the place of small and medium-sized countries in a world of growing great power rivalry. When we formally launched Norway's campaign for a non-permanent seat on the UN Security Council in 2019, a surprising debate, reminiscent of the early days of our foreign ser-

◂ Ine Eriksen Søreide as a guest at MSC events, among others at the Munich Security Conference in February 2016.

vice, ensued: should a small country aspire to a seat on the UN Security Council and risk being subjected to increased pressure from others?

While this is a legitimate concern, the question disregarded two fundamental realities: pressure from other actors has always been a part of international relations, and the best way to deal with this is not to disengage, but to be an active member of the international community.

Indeed, multilateral engagement has not limited Norway's room for maneuver in foreign policy. It has opened opportunities. Our room for maneuver has always been determined by our ability and willingness to form alliances. We can never avoid pressure altogether, but we can greatly reduce and more easily withstand it when we are a part of a larger community.

NATO is one such community. It is the bedrock of our security, but it is far more than that. The alliance has a legacy of expanding Europe's political room for maneuver, notably in the aftermath of World War II, when it paved the way for reconstruction and European integration.

For Norway, NATO has played an even more important and direct role, by helping to balance an otherwise inherently asymmetrical relationship with a great power, our neighbor Russia. This has made it possible for Norway to engage in practical cooperation with Russia in areas in which our two countries have common interests in the north, such as fisheries, nuclear safety, and search and rescue.

The security provided by our membership in NATO has also allowed us to engage in confidence building vis-à-vis Russia and we have reached agreement on a number of bilateral transparency measures that enhance stability and predictability in our part of the world. The Arctic, a region of great strategic importance, is by no means an institutional or legal vacuum. It is a well-regulated region governed by international law, with the Arctic Council as the key international body for handling Arctic issues.

Now, as a new era of great power rivalry dawns, we need to adapt, both in terms of foreign policy and diplomatic tradecraft, in order to maintain our room for maneuver. As foreign minister, this has been one of my main priorities.

International law and multilateral institutions remain vital, both for ensuring a level playing field and for tackling the major challenges of our time. Some of these challenges, such as climate change, can only be addressed if all the major powers are on board. For this reason, we should not be averse to cooperating with countries like China in areas in which we share an interest in finding constructive solutions. I have also argued that we should be pragmatic when it comes to allowing emerging powers to join existing multilateral institutions. The engagement of all great powers in international governance is a strength that sets the multilateral system of the last seventy years apart from the failures of the past.

However, pragmatism should not be mistaken for neutrality. A new era of great power rivalry also calls for stronger transatlantic bonds. NATO has a long track record as a bulwark against pressure and coercion, and we should make policy choices that reinforce its capacity to provide such protection in the future.

Collective defense and deterrence remain fundamental to our political strength. Much has been achieved since 2014, but in the face of growing military competition powered by new technology, we cannot afford to backtrack. Allied defense spending will have to be maintained at about 2 percent of GDP for a long time, and substantial resources will need to be invested in research and development. Promoting stronger competition across the Euro-Atlantic defense market could further increase the effect of our defense spending and bring down the cost of new capabilities.

Furthermore, we need to strengthen NATO's political deterrence. We can do so by expanding political dialogue as security policy extends into new areas. Dialogue on all types of security issues has traditionally been considered a matter of promoting cohesion within the alliance. However, this dialogue is also an effective antidote to external pressure, and we should make the most of its deterrent potential. I have been encouraged to see growing allied coordination with regard to attributing cyberattacks, rebutting disinformation, and countering espionage. This is an effective way to reduce the risk of external pressure, and we should develop this further.

How we handle differences within the alliance is also essential to our political deterrence. NATO's success relies almost as much on its tolerance of diversity as on its unity. During the Cold War, we overcame significant internal challenges, such as the Suez Crisis and political turmoil in member states. This would not have been possible without a culture of patience and tolerance within the alliance. I am concerned that, in recent years, we have too often allowed bilateral issues unrelated to security and defense to interfere with our work in NATO. Member states should never hold allied defense planning or cooperation with partners hostage to domestic or bilateral issues because this can make us vulnerable to external forces that are seeking to heighten discord and hamper allied decision making.

The US has led by example and should continue to do so. The unique nature of US leadership extends beyond its agenda-setting power and ability to rally allies around a common cause. Its commitment to the freedom of its allies and relative restraint when it comes to exerting pressure also set it apart from past powers. For Norway, tolerance of differences remains vital both for ensuring popular support for NATO and for managing our relations with Russia.

Since 1949, when Norway was one of the founders of NATO, our security policy has been based on the need to strike a balance between deterrence and reassurance towards Russia. In the face of Russia's military modernization and more assertive foreign policy, NATO's security guarantee remains vital. However, our membership in NATO also provides room for reassurance measures, which are important for avoiding escalation in our region. Norway, for instance, does not allow foreign combat forces to establish permanent bases on its soil in peacetime; nor do we allow the stockpiling or deployment of nuclear weapons in peacetime. We also maintain certain limitations on military activities.

A new era of great power rivalry also calls for stronger transatlantic bonds. NATO has a long track record as a bulwark against pressure and coercion, and we should make policy choices that reinforce its capacity to provide such protection in the future.

Collective security and an allied culture of tolerance and understanding of differences have also opened opportunities in other parts of our foreign policy, not least in terms of creating space for peace diplomacy and mediation, which have been important elements of Norwegian foreign policy for the past decades.

While the diversity of our experiences as allies has been a strength to NATO, there is a need to address differences in threat perceptions. The extent of these differences has often been exaggerated. In my experience, threat perceptions tend to converge, rather than diverge, over time. However, differing perceptions remain a risk in a more diverse alliance and security environment.

Common situational awareness is key to the way NATO works. Allied consensus is not primarily reached through persuasion or pressure, but rather through painstaking efforts to build common awareness. We therefore need to invest in measures to achieve this.

This is one of the reasons why Norway has increased its intelligence capabilities, why we promote intelligence sharing among allies, and why we want to see an even closer dialogue between NATO and the EU. NATO-EU relations have expanded considerably since 2014, but gaps remain, especially when it comes to issues that lie at the interface between security, trade, and technology. This is somewhat surprising; these are highly strategic issues for which allies sometimes reach different conclusions, and where differences may be used against us. To my mind, it is worth considering whether allowing allies that are not EU members to participate in the EU-US Trade and Technology Council could bridge part of the gap and improve our collective resilience.

Political deterrence is essential to ensuring that our alliance is fit to tackle a more complex future. We should make every effort to counter pressure and minimize the risk of internal division. However, our efforts will have little effect if our adversaries can achieve their objectives by playing on domestic sentiments. In most cases, political pressure at home still has greater impact than external pressure, and it is far more likely to affect fundamental foreign policy choices.

During my tenure as a minister, I have seen a worrying resurgence of populism and isolationism across the Western hemisphere, growing polarization, loss of trust in public authorities, and even democratic backsliding in some member states. All of this not only runs counter to the ideals of our alliance, but it also affects our security. Poor governance fuels grievances and divisions that adversaries can exploit to their benefit. In a time when hybrid threats loom large, we cannot leave such risks unaddressed.

As we tailor our foreign policy and diplomacy to a new and more challenging security environment, we should be equally invested in building a strong foundation at home. The principles enshrined in the preamble to the North Atlantic Treaty—our joint commitment to democracy, individual liberty, and the rule of law—are not empty words. Defending these core values is essential to our collective security and future resilience.

Ine Eriksen Søreide is Chair of the Foreign Affairs and Defense Committee in the Norwegian Parliament (The Storting). She served as Norway's Minister for Defense from 2013 to 2017 and Minister for Foreign Affairs from 2017 to 2021.

msc
msc
msc
msc
Juma
Neumann

Fighting Terrorism

Peter Neumann

Whenever there is no political way forward between states, it is frequently suggested that cooperation should be practiced in fighting terrorism: this is commonly seen as a diplomatic "easy win," given that groups like al-Qaeda and ISIS represent a threat to everybody, and given that there are no fundamental objections to be made by any side against an improved cooperation in fighting terrorism.

However, the difficulties of putting anti-terrorism cooperation into practice became clear to me when the Austrian Council Presidency of the Organization for Security and Co-operation in Europe (OSCE) appointed me Special Representative on Countering Violent Radicalization. As a scientist, I had been researching terrorism for nearly twenty years, and the idea of being able to help implement politics intrigued me. At that time, the ISIS terror campaign was at its apex, and there appeared to be not only a consensus, but also an urgency when it came to fighting terrorism.

My first visits to Vienna seemed to confirm that impression. Everybody was excited, and many people told me that the OSCE—the only security organization in which Russia and the West were sitting at the same table—was uniquely predestined for this task.

Quite soon, however, it became obvious that enormous obstacles existed. Opinions on what terrorism is differed greatly. If Azerbaijanis talked about terrorism, they meant Armenia. Central Asians were concerned about Islamic opposition groups. And for Turkey, the focus was on President Erdoğan's adversaries. During a visit to Ankara, I had to listen to a three-hour presentation, half of which was about the so-called Gülen organization.

Additionally, there was less unanimity than expected when it came to fighting terrorism. Prior to my visit to Russia, the Austrian foreign ministry had explicitly asked me to get together with the civil society. However, the only appointment dates the Russians had arranged were with government officials, who proudly told me that Russia had "solved" its terrorism problem by applying the method of the "carrot and stick." One general complained about the Europeans' failure to feed their terrorism data into the computer system that Russia had created. After my visit, I could well understand why.

Moreover, the topic was constantly overlaid with other conflicts and disputes. In several capitals, I had to apologize for right-wing extremist attacks on mosques in France and the Netherlands. In Ankara, I was confronted about an exposition on the suppression of the Kurds organized by the European Parliament two years earlier. Conversations that started with the fight against terrorism eventually led to debates about Islam, the role of the US, and European colonial history. This was not my idea of an "easy win."

My final report therefore contained fewer specific ideas and solution proposals than I had initially expected. I avoided controversial topics and focused instead on "good practices"—good examples, which I hoped would encourage other countries to embark on a similar path. However, even this—in my view—innocuous approach has provoked controversy and led to the rejection of my report by several countries.

Despite this diplomatic defeat, I learned a lot along the way. First, cooperating in the fight against terrorism is not the easiest, but one of the most difficult diplomatic challenges, because there is hardy any conflict line drawn in domestic, foreign, and security politics that is unrelated to the topic of terrorism. Second, diplomats who have made progress in this area deserve the highest recognition.

A dozen conventions regarding the fight against terrorism now exist on the international level. The prevention approach is firmly established internationally. UN Security Council resolutions on terrorist foreign fighters, for instance, have prompted dozens of countries to pass corresponding laws. And the US-led global coalition against ISIS has resulted in the group losing its territory in Syria and Iraq.

The international fight against terrorism is certainly no easy win. However, the progress that diplomats have fought hard to achieve over the recent years—and decades—has made us all more secure.

Peter Neumann is Professor of Security Studies at the Department of War Studies, King's College London. He founded the International Centre for the Study of Radicalisation (ICSR), serving as its Director from 2008 to 2018. In 2017 he also served as the Special Representative on Countering Violent Extremism for the Organization for Security and Co-operation in Europe (OSCE).

◂ Peter Neumann at the MSC Core Group Meeting in Addis Ababa in April 2016.

Accepting Failure in Cyprus

Espen Barth Eide

It's July 6, 2017. A crisp sun has risen over the Swiss alpine resort of Crans-Montana, where the final phase of the Conference on Cyprus has been underway since late June. United Nations Secretary-General António Guterres returns to the conference to encourage the parties to seal a deal that would ensure the reunification of the long-divided island in the Eastern Mediterranean. As the secretary-general descends in a Swiss Air Force helicopter on his last leg from New York via Geneva that beautiful morning, it seems that this will be the day. The essential pieces of the grand puzzle of the "CyProb" are largely in place. We who had helped facilitate the Cyprus talks had known from the very start that at some point, a final, decisive moment would be required. In complex, multi-level negotiating processes, the most contentious questions being settled are always mutually dependent on each other. Talks can be incremental, but only up to a point: Neither party can risk showing their most precious cards without simultaneously seeing those of the other side. Hence, we knew that we had to prepare for a moment of truth, with all the key players around the same table.

In complex, multi-level negotiating processes, the most contentious questions being settled are always mutually dependent on each other.

Finally, that day had arrived! A marathon of bilateral meetings with the leaders of the two communities in Cyprus, as well as with the three guarantor states, Greece, Turkey, and the United Kingdom, was now to pave the way for the conclusion of that strategic deal.

Or so we thought. What a difference a day makes. Well into the next morning, at a dramatic final working dinner, the secretary-general concluded that the Conference on Cyprus had failed. Despite the solutions that now seemed available to every element of the agreed "Guterres framework," a strategic settlement did not emerge. The secretary-general concluded that, given what he had observed at that meeting, reconvening the conference later would not lead to a different outcome. Everyone present concurred. Yet another round of talks had proven unsuccessful.

I was the SASG—the Special Advisor to the Secretary General on Cyprus—from August 2014 to August 2017, working with Secretary-Generals Ban Ki-moon and Antonio Guterres on one of the UN's most protracted peace processes ever. The following is a personal reflection on the trajectory that led us to Crans-Montana as well as on what we can learn from it.

The 2015–2017 round of negotiations is the last effort to date in the long struggle to reunify Cyprus. A decade earlier, the "Annan Plan" had tried to capitalize on the 2004 eastern expansion of the European Union as a rallying ground for reunifying the island and joining the EU in one go. The Annan Plan was to hold two simultaneous referenda, one in the Turkish-controlled Turkish-Cypriot North and one in the Greek-Cypriot South. While the Turkish-Cypriot (TC) referendum returned a resounding yes to unification and EU entry, the majority of the Greek-Cypriot (GC) side voted no to unification. Immediately afterward, and paradoxically to some, only the GC-dominated Republic of Cyprus entered the European Union. The Turkish Cypriots side remained on the outside, despite their yes in the referendum. Discussions continue to this day about how this major opportunity was lost. A new attempt took place in 2008, between the then-leaders Mehmet Ali Talat and Dimitris Christofias. While these did not lead to a breakthrough at the time, they provided a well-structured framework for future negotiations that we then used also to structure the 2015–2017 talks.

Some ten years after the failure of the Annan Plan, there was new movement. A "joint declaration" was negotiated between Nicos Anastasiades, the President of Cyprus and in this context the leader of the GC community, and Derviş Eroğlu, the TC leader at the time. The February 11, 2014, joint declaration fundamentally set out all the key parameters for further negotiations, building on the 2008 framework. UN Secretary-General Ban Ki-moon then asked me to facilitate a new round of talks, which we originally thought could start that same autumn.

A crisis over hydrocarbons exploration during the winter of 2014–15 postponed the initial attempt to start fresh negotiations. The Republic of Cyprus (RoC) argued its sovereign right to explore potential petroleum reserves in its economic zone, whereas the TC and Turkish side argued that these resources belonged to the entirety of Cyprus and that a settlement should be concluded before any exploration began. Working

◂ Espen Barth Eide at the MSC Energy Security Summit in Stavanger in August 2018.

with Turkey, therefore, the Turkish-Cypriot side started seismic activities on their own in order to drive home the point, which in turn created harsh reactions on the GC side. The hydrocarbons crisis mobilized every element of the intractable competition for historical narratives, legality, and legitimacy that so much characterizes the Cyprus problem. In the ensuing climate, it proved impossible to launch a new round of talks. It also reminded the broader international community of the regional risks involved in leaving Cyprus unresolved.

A series of discrete, behind-the-scenes efforts the following winter eventually defused the crisis, and the exploration activities subsided temporarily. The hard drop in petroleum prices during the winter of 2015 came in handy, as it took some steam out of the rush for natural gas reserves. By April 2015, the mood in Cyprus had changed for the better and the two sides declared themselves ready for a new round of talks. Before they could start, however, elections were to be held on the TC side. Possibly helped by this newfound optimism, the clear winner was Mr. Mustafa Akıncı, a declaredly pro-solution social democrat who had settlement as his main agenda. Mr. Akıncı had years earlier served as the Mayor of Northern Nicosia, and he had used this platform to strengthen cooperation across the divided capital city in a way that had earned him a positive reputation in both the South and the North. Mr. Akıncı was also perceived, in the North and the South alike, as a true Turkish Cypriot, rather than an "Ankara-obedient Turk." This perception was confirmed by Mr. Akıncı's preparedness also to occasionally speak out against Ankara and Turkey's president Recep Tayyip Erdoğan.

Cyprus has often been referred to as a "diplomat's graveyard" after so many failed attempts . . . At the same time, however, the Cyprus question is almost unique in the world in how "organized" it is. This is particularly apparent if we compare it to many of the far messier conflicts of today.

Shortly after Mr. Akıncı's victory, on May 11, 2015, I organized a dinner between the two leaders, Mustafa Akıncı and Nicos Anastasiades, in which they agreed to go straight to work. The first leaders' meeting was held on May 15 at the UN headquarters in the buffer zone. Mr. Anastasiades, who had been President of Cyprus since 2013, was also known for his vocal support of the Annan Plan back in 2004.

Led by two declaredly pro-solution leaders, both of whom had voted yes to and argued in favor of the Annan Plan ten years earlier, the talks were off to a truly good start that summer and subsequent autumn.

Cyprus has often been referred to as a "diplomat's graveyard" after so many failed attempts. The argument has its merit, as long as the problem remains unsolved. At the same time, however, the Cyprus question is almost unique in the world in how "organized" it is. This is particularly apparent if we compare it to many of the far messier conflicts of today. In Cyprus, there are two sides, not several: the Greek Cypriot community in the South, and the Turkish Cypriot community in the North. While personalities and policies change, the sides remain constant over time. It is clear who is in charge on either side. No alternative actors come into the scene competing for their roles. There is, of course, deep disagreement over the existence of a "state" in the North. The "Turkish Republic of Northern Cyprus" is not internationally recognized, and the GCs see it as illegal, while the TCs and Turkey on the other hand do not recognize the Republic of Cyprus. Despite all of this, within the framework of UN-led talks, it is agreed that there are two "communities" on the island and that they are both led by a "leader," the legitimacy of whom is also mutually recognized, if only in that capacity. Hence, the leaders, their negotiators, and their teams are equals at the table. Beyond the two sides, there are the guarantor states, Greece, Turkey, and the UK, as there have been since Cyprus' independence in 1960. Furthermore, inasmuch as a future united Cyprus is supposed to be a full-fledged EU member state, the European Union has become increasingly involved in the process as well—an involvement that proved to be extremely helpful as seen from the UN side, as many historically difficult questions were now to be settled by jointly adhering to the EU's *acquis communautaire*.

The sides were even in agreement on what they were after, namely unification in the form of a "bi-communal, bi-zonal federation with political equality." This future united Cyprus was to be a full member of the UN and the EU and to have a single international legal personality and a single sovereignty. Even the organization of themes to be discussed was fully agreed: the chapters are governance and power-sharing, economy, European Union matters, property, territory, and finally, security and guarantees. Again, such a high level of agreement on the outcome even before talks start is rather unique in comparison to most other contemporary conflicts.

However, it is important to understand that it still precisely that: a conflict. It is a deep, unresolved dispute in which significant violence has been used in the past and where future violence cannot be ruled out. Even if, thankfully, there hasn't been fresh blood spilled for well over two decades, there is no shortage of historical grievances. The capital, Nicosia, as well as the entire island, is divided like Berlin in the Cold War with soldiers from the two sides on watchful guard, separated by UNFICYP, the oldest ongoing armed UN peacekeeping mission in the world.

Cyprus' location in the deeply troubled Eastern Mediterranean, characterized by a set of complex power dynamics, is essential. To see the problem resolved actually matters to the international community, way beyond the importance of the island as such. Suffice it here to mention that the constant challenges of Greco-Turkish (and by implication, EU-NATO) relations, at least in part, have their origin in competing views on Cyprus.

The role of the UN in Cyprus is broadly respected. As the chief UN envoy to the peace process, I did not have to compete with a number of alternative processes, facilitators, or mediators, as often is the case in conflict situations. The Security Council was firmly united behind the effort, not something to be taken for granted in today's geopolitical environment. The rest of the international community, like the European Union, leading states, and the international financial institutions, all played a strong and constructive role in the process. And at the end of the day, the Cypriots as well as the international community agree that the process is and should remain leader-led; the UN is there in a supporting role, as a service to this Cypriot-owned and leader-led process.

In the summer of 2015, spirits were high. Mr. Akıncı and Mr. Anastasiades both demonstrated their will to move forward in the talks. They started by confirming or updating past convergences and agreeing on some of the less-contentious questions. They met socially and they even crossed over to the other side attending well-covered public events together, which helped create an early ambiance of progress. The act of crossing the line is a big deal for Cypriot leaders, even if the crossings have been open since 2003. Two highly professional and experienced chief negotiators, Andreas Mavroyannis and Özdil Nami, with their expert teams, conducted the day-to-day negotiations, leading up to and preparing leaders' meetings every two weeks or so. Bonds were created between their negotiation teams, both of whom impressed me by their dedication and professionalism.

This apparently ideal circumstance for successful talks should not mask, however, the underlying, inherent problem: namely that the dispute represents different things to different people. The two communities' historical narratives and recollections diverge strongly, which again influences their visions of the future. In order to identify the essence of the question to each side, one needs to understand what form of security they are seeking from the settlement.

Many Greek Cypriots see the era prior to the division into North and South as relatively happy days: in their view, the republic established after independence from the United Kingdom in 1960 worked, by and large, in the early days. GCs and TCs lived all over the island in their ancestral homes and in mixed villages and life was good until the TC leaders left the political institutions in 1963 and tensions grew. In this view, the troubles that led the UN to dispatch a peacekeeping force in 1964 were unfortunate, but fundamentally, they were passing skirmishes. Their founding catastrophe on the GC side is therefore the events of 1974, when a failed military coup, supported by the Greek Junta, triggered the Turkish invasion, which in turn led to Turkish occupation. It also provoked mass movement of people and massive loss of property.

The two communities' historical narratives and recollections diverge strongly, which again influences their visions of the future. In order to identify the essence of the question to each side, one needs to understand what form of security they are seeking from the settlement.

Many Turkish Cypriots, on the other hand, remember the early days as an era of increasing marginalization, oppression, and violence, principally directed against the Turkish Cypriots at the hands of the GC majority. Their tragedy started in the 1960s, and for them, the advent of the Turkish Army after the failed 1974 coup was in some respects a relief; finally, they could now live a life without fear in their own community. On both sides, you will find people who are strong supporters of reunification, but you will also find many who long ago decided that it is probably better to leave things more or less as they are now—you know what you have, and not what you will get.

Hence, to understand what the two sides are after, one must acknowledge the continued contemporary relevance of these founding narratives. For the GC side, a stable, independent, and well-functioning state is goal number one, free from any form of Turkish interference, democratic in the sense that the majority have the upper hand, albeit with some rights ensured for the smaller TC community. They would also prefer a settlement that facilitates reinstatement of lost property over economic compensation, even if that property is on what will remain the TC side. Many of the GC goals, therefore, are oriented precisely toward ensuring that a new 1974 does not happen again.

On the Turkish-Cypriot side, the main effort has been to secure a sense of "security of community"; that is, the continued security not only of life but also of the cultural and political identity of the Turkish-Cypriots, being, after all, the numerically smaller community. This requires solid provisions securing that 1963 will not happen again. This means that the governance and power-sharing system must ensure that the larger GC community cannot undermine the political equality of the TCs, now or in the future. A democratic state, from a TC perspective, must therefore be federal, with clear and unalterable rights and prerogatives for each constituent state enshrined in basic law. The TCs would also prefer that the settlement provide for economic compensation over reinstatement of lost property, even if they are open to a mix of both. This is to ensure that the TC community in effect will remain the larger group on their side, even if there will be free movement of people across the island. On territory, the sides agree that some of the territory of the TC side should be transferred back to the future GC constituent state in the event of a settlement, even if the exact demarcation of this is a topic for negotiations.

So while the two sides agree on the broad framework of an outcome (bi-zonal, bi-communal federation, or "BBF" in CyProb jargon), what matters most to each side is not the same. That is not necessarily a problem. Through a well-structured negotiating process, this can even be an advantage, as what matters most for one can be realized through securing that what matters most for the other side is also achieved—precisely since it is not the same thing.

Unfortunately, it was not possible to bring in the essential questions of security per se before the very end. This was by design: as these questions have much to do with the future role of the guarantors and on foreign troops. Turkey in particular made clear that it would only be ready to discuss these questions once they were sufficiently convinced that all key intra-island questions had been resolved. The only way we could prepare these issues was through shuttle diplomacy, speaking to one at a time, be it the sides on the island, Athens, Ankara, or London, while the talks therefore focused on the internal aspects of the settlement.

Swift progress continued during 2015 and moving into 2016. In January 2016, the two leaders addressed the World Economic Forum's annual meeting in Davos together, declaring their shared determination to settle the issue and to do so in the course of that very year. Both leaders concurred that the benign opportunities that had facilitated a return to talks would not last forever. Internal political dynamics—like election schedules—and key international circumstances would eventually change, and time now was of the essence.

Despite this strong public commitment, we saw a somewhat paradoxical pattern evolve. As the actual talks at the negotiation table continued to progress, the mood surrounding the talks deteriorated. Over time, there were fewer joint appearances between the leaders, media critique grew, and relatively minor disagreements on day-to-day questions outside the scope of the talks as such were increasingly accentuated. Relations between the communities were souring again. The political impulse started to fade. Two rounds of meetings were then held in late 2016 at Mont-Pèlerin, Swizerland. These were to enter into the highly sensitive question of territorial adjustment, but despite a major opening on this front, these talks did not lead to the expected sense of strategic progress. Doubts started to grow on whether time was indeed running out.

Through a series of UN-led efforts to salvage the process, many observers were therefore positively surprised when the leaders on December 1 declared that they were close enough now on the "intra-Cyprus" or domestic issues that time was ripe for the final, international Conference on Cyprus—with the guarantors present—to be opened in January 2017. Prior to that, the two sides were to exchange their proposed maps for a territorial settlement, which they also did. This was an act many observers saw as a potentially defining moment in the history of Cyprus talks. This event then paved the way for finally bringing the three guarantor states, as well as the European Union in the role of an observer, into the process.

The Conference on Cyprus started on January 12, 2017, in Geneva, chaired by the new Secretary-General Antonio Guterres, in what was only his second week in office. The guarantors were present at the level of foreign ministers, the EU with the President of the Commission, and the High Representative of Foreign Affairs as observers. The main outcome of the first meeting of the conference was to establish the overarching principle that "the security of one community could not come at the expense of the security of the other." It also established that the solutions envisaged needed to "address both communities' traditional security fears, while developing a shared security vision for the future." A very productive follow-up meeting of deputies the next week dove more deeply into these questions, and some of the contours of a security settlement gradually emerged, even if in a guarded manner. It became clearer, for instance, that the traditional system of "guarantees," which de facto implies a unilateral right of intervention from the guarantors if things go wrong, is not compatible with EU membership status. Similarly, it emerged that foreign troops had to be significantly reduced and eventually repurposed, until the day that they would no longer be required. New ideas were developed on how the international community could successfully back up and ensure implementation of the process until such a point where the settlement would work on its own, hence taking away the old argument for having "guarantor states." While difficult, we finally felt that we were now dealing with the most essential elements of a future settlement.

Again, however, we saw the same pattern outside of the talks themselves. The fact that most domestic issues were so advanced that maps in line with agreed spatial provisions had been exchanged, and that security was finally and seriously on the table, should have given anyone actually hoping for a solution solid reasons for optimism. But, quite the contrary, the surrounding mood deteriorated further. A move in the GC Parliament to commemorate the day of "Enosis"—the old vision of unification of the Island with Greece, supported by President Anastasiasiades' own party—led to a new crisis that nearly derailed the process. It became increasingly clear that there was a growing wariness in many quarters that the talks would actually lead to unification. After all, a continued status quo also has its strong proponents.

After so many attempts, setbacks, and failures, key players got more and more used to the idea that the problem was probably unsolvable, and that while it was worth trying, mostly to show goodwill, it would probably never work. The necessary concessions from the other side would never materialize anyway, many thought.

The entire process was now at the brink of collapse. Only with the direct intervention of the secretary-general, was it possible to get the sides to agree to move to the crucial, final chapter of the Conference on Cyprus, this time to be held in Crans-Montana.

Once convened, a few weeks later, the conference was off to a good start. All participants accepted the proposed "Guterres framework" that suggested the manner in which the few but essential outstanding questions, including those of security and guarantees, were to be addressed. Two parallel "tables" were established, one for the Cypriots and one where they also met with the guarantor states, so that the guarantors did not become involved in domestic matters. Still, progress proved more difficult than we had hoped. Even at this stage, the sides continued to hold back, expecting someone else to move first. Real movement only happened the last week. Critical elements of a possible solution on security and guarantees started to emerge, to the degree that the UN had reason to believe that if the participants actually wanted to conclude a strategic agreement, they could do it now.

And yet, it failed. Since Crans-Montana, many have tried to identify that one single item, that missing link that could explain the collapse. Was it in property? Territory? Security and guarantees? As I see it, it was none of these.

Rather, I believe that a significant part of the answer lies in the absence of real preparedness for success. After so many attempts, setbacks, and failures, key players got more and more used to the idea that the problem was probably unsolvable, and that while it was worth trying, mostly to show goodwill, it would probably never work. The necessary concessions from the other side would never materialize anyway, many thought. This pessimistic view was sustained by large parts of the media and by key politicians back in Cyprus. Hence, at times, not only at the leader level but also in the broader surrounding environment, there was a sense that realism had to prevail over excessive optimism. This is, of course, often a sound instinct. In Cyprus, however, it was at times practiced to the degree that it actually ended up undermining any glimmer of hope. So when the opportunity suddenly was there, on the table, it was as if it was too much to handle. Below the level of strategic agreement, there are always outstanding details to be settled. Those outstanding questions can either be solved through a shared can-do approach or aggravated to become a major problem. Their importance is in the eyes of the beholder. If you do not want to solve a problem, there is always an argument for not doing it.

While I genuinely think that there is relatively solid support for unification, given that a few key sine-quanon requirements for each side are met, this does not always translate into a sense of strategic urgency. After all, on the beautiful and mostly peaceful Mediterranean island, life goes on. This might lead key actors to think that there will always be a better time and a better deal out there in the distant future, only to discover, yet again, that there is no time like the present.

If you do not want to solve a problem, there is always an argument for not doing it.

I also learned to emphasize the size of the challenge that face leaders in such rare, history-defining moments. Seen from the outside world, the leader who shakes hands with his counterpart sealing a major breakthrough will typically be the hero of the story—

the one who changes history for the better. Internally, at home, the opposite perception could equally well prevail. In that very act of agreeing to a practicable, real-world settlement, he is necessarily giving up on at least some of the multiple "red lines" that his predecessors have spelled out so many times, and which, in earnest, never could have been met simultaneously. To take that big leap, he will also think about whether it will be possible to convince the broader public back home about the virtues of a settlement over the status quo, given the experiences of the past. Such decisions—at the highest levels of leadership—are always very lonely decisions.

I have come to conclude that success cannot solely be sought at the negotiating table. It also has to be embedded in broader society, and that dimension needs careful cultivation. And that has to be done locally, by Cypriots on both sides themselves. The international community must be very careful not to come across as wanting a settlement more than those affected by it do.

Five years after Crans-Montana, the process remains at a standstill. A few meetings of the leaders have not led to a new round of actual talks. Political circumstances have deteriorated. Mustafa Akıncı has been replaced by a more hardline and Ankara-oriented Turkish Cypriot, Mr. Ersin Tatar. He, as well as Turkey, now seem far less inclined to find a federal solution in line with the established parameters of the past. In its place, they now argue for an agreed, two-state solution. And, needless to say, the surrounding geopolitical landscape has not improved much either.

Seen from the outside world, the leader who shakes hands with his counterpart sealing a major breakthrough will typically be the hero of the story—the one who changes history for the better. Internally, at home, the opposite perception could equally well prevail.

I hope there will be a new attempt one day. There is a vast body of work that is already completed and that can be capitalized on again, if the will is there. The problem is clearly solvable. However, you cannot just do the same thing over and over again and expect a different outcome. It will take more than two equally committed leaders to lead; leaders also need support. Society must be far more engaged than last time, so that success can be embedded among the people who ultimately must vote yes. Furthermore, strong and sustained international support will be required not only for reaching a deal but even more so for supporting the implementation.

Absent these factors, I am afraid that we are stuck with an ever-more permanent non-solution, as the current status quo, year by year, turns into the new normal.

Espen Barth Eide is the Norwegian Minister of Climate and Environment. He previously served as Deputy Minister of Foreign Affairs in Prime Minister Jens Stoltenberg's first government and then as Deputy Minister of Defense in Stoltenberg's second government. He held the position of Minister of Defense between 2011 and 2012 and that of Minister of Foreign Affairs between 2012 and 2013. He has been a Labour Party (Arbeiderpartiet) parliamentarian since 2017. From 2014 to 2017, he served as the United Nations Special Adviser on Cyprus.

MSC Core Group Meeting in Doha in October 2019. ▸

Munich Security
Conference
msc
Münchner Sicherheitskonferenz
Bilat

Saying No to Turkey

Alexander Graf Lambsdorff

Political scientists describe Turkey, that important country between Asia and Europe, as a bridgehead of the West, as a buffer state, as a bulwark, or in other abstract terms. There is nothing wrong with these descriptions. However, in day-to-day political life, dialogue partners in Ankara and Istanbul would prefer to appear as representatives of a proud nation, the history of which spans millennia, which highly values its sovereignty, and where national pride is readily regarded as a good thing. Although Turkey's highly professional diplomats are, of course, aware of the role they play, they do not wish to be reduced to it. However, this is exactly what the EU has done, when the bloc, encouraged by the US and Great Britain, initiated accession talks with Turkey.

The concept of Turkey's accession can only be explained by geopolitical logic. It does not make any sense, either from the perspective of Turkish domestic politics (even prior to Erdoğan) or from the perspective of European integration. It is based solely on the idea that a close integration of Turkey may expand Europe's geopolitical scope. Additionally, some people expected that negotiations would also result in strengthening liberal tendencies within Turkey. After sixteen years of fruitless negotiations, diplomatic relationships are extremely strained, Turkish domestic liberalism is shattered, and public opinion in the EU is clearly against Turkey's accession. The accession process is a rubbish heap that the member states lack the courage to dispose of. The problem is that the termination of negotiations can only be decided unanimously. One member state would suffice to force upon all others the continuation of this process that has long since become zombie-like.

In the European Parliament (EP), the situation is different. While the EP itself cannot terminate the negotiation process, the elected representatives must approve the inclusion of a country in the EU. Just as it did in the UN Security Council, the fiercest debates took place between French and British representatives, whose positions resembled those of their governments. German opinions were as widely varied as opinions throughout Europe. As a result, in my capacity as a German representative, I was able to talk to all sides, eventually taking on the role of rapporteur on Turkey for my ALDE Group. This allowed me to become the driving force behind a complicated but exciting compromise-seeking process.

I was personally against the idea of an accession. The main argument was and still is that Turkey's accession would lead to an overexpansion of the EU and to less acceptance of the EU by its people, and that Turkey didn't need the accession in the first place as its key security and economic needs were already fulfilled by way of its membership in NATO and in the EU Customs Union. As a rapporteur, I was able over the years to make these arguments more audible in the EP. Moreover, in the light of dramatic curtailments of rights and freedoms by the Turkish government, skepticism became more plausible, with "progress reports" increasingly becoming "regression reports."

The turning point of the debate in the EP was the coup in Turkey in 2016. Erdoğan's announcement of a constitutional reform, by which he practically abolished the separation of powers, led to a parliamentary majority urging the European Commission and the UN Security Council to immediately suspend accession negotiations if the package was implemented without changes. It was a necessary signal if European values are still in any way to be taken seriously. I helped to bring about this "if-then" vote within the negotiations concerning the report. The following year, I left the EP to join the Bundestag. I was all the happier when, years later, the "then" materialized in the EP entirely without my doing: the Report on Turkey of March 13, 2019, demanded—backed by the votes of Liberals, Social Democrats, and Conservatives, with the Greens abstaining—the immediate termination of negotiations with Turkey. Today—not only in Paris, but in the EP—the saying is, "La Turquie, c'est . . . non." However, one of the most important tasks of the coming years will be to complement this "no" to membership with a "yes" to an improved cooperation with our proud neighbor.

Alexander Graf Lambsdorff is a Member of the Bundestag and the Deputy Chairperson of the Free Democratic Party parliamentary group in charge of foreign, security, Europe, and development policies. He was previously a Member of the European Parliament from 2004 to 2017 and, in 2014, was made one of its Vice Presidents.

◂ Alexander Graf Lambsdorff at the Munich Strategy Retreat in Heiligendamm in October 2021.

Paving the Way for the Agreement between Greece and North Macedonia

Johannes Hahn

Even pizza can become a means of diplomacy. Take, for instance, the negotiations for the intra-Macedonean Pržino agreement, which created the realpolitik conditions for the historic Treaty of Prespa between Greece and North Macedonia. During long negotiation nights, pizza relaxed the atmosphere, thereby creating trust—the magic formula for successful diplomacy.

If the right chemistry between negotiators can be created, then that chemistry works like a catalyst for compromise. As a commissioner for accession negotiations, I have always attached great importance to creating this kind of trust. That was the reason I encouraged internal negotiations in North Macedonia, leading to an agreement of the four biggest parties: the Pržino agreement. I facilitated these negotiations in Strasbourg, Brussels, and Skopje—and we even rededicated my cabinet members' workspaces to provide each party with a room to retreat. When necessary, we shuttled back and forth until the parties had sufficiently moved in each other's direction to again sit around a common table. The negotiating parties finally achieved the Pržino agreement—stipulating the preparations of elections. That led to a change of government, which paved the way for negotiations between North Macedonia and Greece and finally enabled the success of the treaty of Prespa.

Many a flight had to be postponed as the negotiations began to see movement. This kind of "shuttle diplomacy"—with perseverance and flexibility as its core virtues—helped us to ferret out what each party was able to do and where their red lines were. Those in charge would eventually have to muster the backbone required to stand by what had been decided in the face of criticism from the opposition and the public. In this respect, the Treaty of Prespa eventually proved remarkably successful. Despite domestic obstacles, both countries were able to implement it. This historic and internationally acclaimed agreement marked the end of a long-standing dispute over the country name and facilitated closer cooperation between both countries. This success had a signal effect for the whole region.

When the European Union took over the honest broker's role in the negotiations leading to the Pržino agreement, its neutral position proved particularly important whenever emotions ran high. During the UN-led dialogue between Greece and North Macedonian leading to the Treaty of Prespa, we were successfully acting behind the scenes.

Each time the parties became obsessed with the categories of "winner" and "loser"—which, unfortunately, still happens in the rhetoric of the region—we were able to shift the focus to the fact that, in good negotiations, both parties win. This requires not only a keen sense of the past, but also a still greater sense of the future, since it is the political actors' responsibility to make decisions not only in the here and now, but with a view to tomorrow. In this specific case, it was the prospect of a better future as neighbors and partners within the European Union that helped to overcome limited national perspectives. It was not least due to the Treaty of Prespa that North Macedonia gained international recognition and attention for its ambition of joining the EU.

The European Union has proven its worth as diplomatic mediator in many instances—especially because we tend to leverage our "soft power" instead of threatening to apply "hard power." Our union is in diplomatic nonstop mode, with the capacity to compromise as its centerpiece. Henry Kissinger reportedly said that a successful international negotiation is "one which leaves all negotiating parties equally unhappy with the outcome." According to this definition, we are continually producing well-balanced and long-lasting compromises, to judge by the amount of criticism voiced against EU summit decisions.

The success of the European Union proves us right. Not only are we the world's biggest internal market and a sought-after trading partner, but we also ensure peace and prosperity for the European people. We are able to do so because of the trust that we have built for decades, and which radiates well beyond our union. Our ability to forge compromise, used as a foreign policy asset, gives us additional weight on the global stage. Seen in this way, we Europeans can and should be more self-confident as a geopolitical shaping force.

Johannes Hahn is the European Commissioner for Budget and Administration. He previously served as the European Commissioner for European Neighborhood Policy and Enlargement Negotiations, as the European Commissioner for Regional Policy, and as the Austrian Minister for Science and Research.

◂ Johannes Hahn at the Munich Strategy Forum in Elmau in November 2015.

Ottilia Maunga

Moving from Enmity to Accountability

Ottilia Anna Maunganidze

On August 3, Sudan's transitional cabinet voted unanimously to join the International Criminal Court (ICC).[1] This was followed a week later by an announcement by Sudan's minister of foreign affairs, Mariam al-Sadiq al-Mahdi, that the country would hand over all suspects charged by the ICC for crimes committed in Darfur. These complementary moves were heralded by many as a step in the right direction for accountability, not only in Sudan, but in Africa and globally. For international criminal justice observers and international relations buffs, these were no ordinary moves. Until April 2019, the idea that Sudan would ever support the ICC, let alone consider becoming a state party to the Rome Statute of the ICC, was implausible.[2] Sudan's former president, Omar Hassan al-Bashir, was the first sitting head of state to face possible prosecution at the court.[3] Between 2008, when it became apparent that the ICC prosecutor at the time intended to charge al-Bashir, and 2019, when al-Bashir was ousted from office following a popular revolt, the government of Sudan was the ICC's greatest critic. Some would even argue, its greatest nemesis.

Fast forward to August 2021 and the transitional government of Sudan not only confirmed its support for the ICC and committed to cooperation (including in arresting and surrendering ICC suspects to the court), it also took initial steps to sign up as the court's newest member. Beyond pressure from Sudanese civil society, local and international non-governmental organizations, and international partners, artful diplomacy paved the path to this about-turn.

The agents of this diplomacy were varied—and included some who were not the usual political suspects of international diplomacy. These included the ICC's prosecutor (both Fatou Bensouda since 2012, and her successor, Karim Ahmad Khan, who took over in June 2021), who traveled to Sudan in 2020 and 2021 for closed discussions with the Sudanese authorities. These discussions were aimed at securing the cooperation of the Sudanese authorities in investigations, arrests, and the subsequent prosecutions of ICC suspects.[4] They also included representatives of Sudanese civil society and non-governmental organizations from within and outside Sudan, who previously had no direct access to the Sudanese government under al-Bashir, but could now meet with the Sudanese authorities whose ascent to office was incidentally paved by concerted pressure from civil society.

In February 2020 (just a month before the world shutdown due to the global COVID-19 pandemic), Sudan's transitional authority attended the 56th Munich Security Conference (MSC).[5] It was the first time that the government of Sudan had attended the MSC and contributed substantively to discussions. Led by Prime Minister Abdalla Hamdok (who I had previously met when he worked at the UN Economic Commission for Africa in Addis Ababa), Sudan's high-powered delegation engaged in discussions on peaceful transition, transnational security, sustainable peace, and justice in the Horn of Africa, North Africa, and globally. One such engagement was a high-level discussion I moderated on "Peacing It Together: Regional Security in Northeast Africa," organized by the *Deutsche Gesellschaft für Internationale Zusammenarbeit GmbH (GIZ)*—the German Corporation for International Cooperation—in which representatives from the African Union (AU), the Sudan, Egypt, the World Bank, and the European Institute of Peace (EIP) spoke candidly. The then state minister for foreign affairs of the Sudan, Omer Gamar-Eldin Ismail, who was part of the Sudan's diplomatic tour de force at the MSC, asserted Sudan's "return" and its commitment to regional peace, security, and justice. The message from the regional leaders, the AU, and key international partners was clear: to establish sustainable peace and security in Northeast Africa would now require having Sudan on board.

Until April 2019, the idea that Sudan would ever support the ICC, let alone consider becoming a state party to the Rome Statute of the ICC, was implausible.

The Sudan, a pariah state until recently, was making a solid foray back into global politics and retaking its long vacant seat at the table. The charm offensive immediately paid off with Chancellor Angela Merkel expressing Germany's commitment to partnering with the Sudan. This was immediately followed in late February by the state visit of the federal president of Germany, Frank-Walter Steinmeier, to the Sudan.[6] This visit was the first of its kind since 1985.[7] Then in June 2020, following an earlier resolution by Germany's Parliament to lift the ban on development aid to Sudan,

◂ Ottilia Anna Maunganidze at the Munich Young Leaders Alumni Meeting in New York City in September 2019.

Germany pledged €150 million in aid.[8] Germany was not alone in this change of policy and practice. While the EU had, prior to 2019, collaborated and funded Sudanese civil society and human rights organizations, as well as providing some limited funding to Sudan for a climate change and food security program, and a trust fund contributing to peace, stability, and economic development,[9] it wasn't until after the change of government that relations started to thaw and normalize. This occurred through enhanced humanitarian support, and in the development of a short-term strategy connected to the country's transition.[10]

Of course, part of what led to Sudan being largely cast out from global engagements and diplomacy, and gravely affected its ability to access foreign direct investment and support, was that, since 1993, it was on the United States' list of state sponsors of terrorism.[11] This listing meant that engagements with, among others, the US, Germany, and the EU, were gravely constrained. In December 2020, following diplomatic engagements with the transitional government, the US government removed Sudan from this list. Now the US and Sudan look to reestablish full diplomatic relations, which Washington suspended when it closed its embassy in Khartoum in 1996 before reopening a downgraded mission in 2002.[12]

The message from the regional leaders, the AU, and key international partners was clear: to establish sustainable peace and security in Northeast Africa would now require having Sudan on board.

These good-faith gestures are the cornerstone of international diplomacy. They equally require a quid pro quo from the Sudanese authorities. After more than three decades as a global diplomacy outcast, the Sudanese authorities must now do more to assert and cement their legitimacy in a challenging political context. To do this, they need to demonstrate how different they are from the past government. What easier way to demonstrate this than to advance accountability and to change tactics on the ICC? For Sudan the move is both politically expedient and strategic at home and within the international community.[13]

At home the Sudanese authorities are still building trust with the society by ticking off tasks set for it by protestors in 2018 and 2019, and codified in its 2019 Constitution. One of those tasks is pursuing justice and accountability for past crimes. This extends beyond the crimes the ICC has charged al-Bashir and others for, and includes crimes dating back to June 30, 1989.[14] Al-Bashir was already convicted for corruption and sentenced to two years in prison in 2019.[15] He and sixteen others still face the prospect of prosecution for the crimes committed in 1989 when he took power through a coup d'état. For the international community, calls for accountability for crimes committed in Darfur and the Kordofan regions continue, including by the UN Secretary General's Special Representative for Sudan, Dr. Volker Perthes. Surrendering al-Bashir to the ICC would be seen as a step toward accountability, at least for the crimes in Darfur. An easy win.

What does the Sudan example show? First, that nothing is set in stone in international politics (or international law). Second, that efforts towards accountability are best initiated at home. Third, and perhaps most poignant for diplomacy, that there are no eternal enemies in international governance.

When the UN Security Council referred the situation in Darfur, Sudan, to the ICC in March 2005,[16] the hope was that action would be swift and that, though implicated, Sudanese authorities would comply. As the fourteen years since the referral showed, reality couldn't have been further from this hope. The Sudanese authorities resisted, insistent that the Darfur conflict was blown out of proportion and that their "internal" matters should not be dealt with externally. Sudan's status as a pariah state solidified. By 2009 it had very few friends globally. By 2019 far fewer, if any, were left. Having dealt with any dissent and protests viciously in the past, the success of the 2018/19 protests in toppling al-Bashir caught many by surprise. However, for those who had worked tirelessly behind the scenes to negotiate a peaceful (or at least largely peaceful) transition, it was the first sign that things can and will change. It just takes time. The fast shift by the Sudanese authorities to try to assert legitimacy, curry favor with past foes, and get Sudan back on track, was to be expected. Likewise, the embrace of the new Sudanese authorities by the international community. Of course, the truest test will be in how long these changes will hold and what new relationships will be forged with Sudan at the table. What's certain, though, is that through diplomacy, Sudan is no longer perceived as "al-Bashir's Sudan."

The eventual decision to prosecute or hand over ICC suspects was driven by a need to respond to calls for accountability at home. While the ICC had done its part to try to ensure justice for crimes in Darfur, it was effectively local organizations that forced the new administration's hand. Ironically, the complementarity system envisaged in the ICC statute clearly articulates that the ICC is a court of last resort, intervening only where a state is unable or unwilling to proceed.[17] So far, both in rhetoric and in practice, the transitional authority in Sudan has shown a willingness to prosecute past crimes, including those that occurred during the transition before handover to civilian authorities, such as the June 3, 2019, massacre in Khartoum. However, for international crimes, it likely does not have the resources, experience, and expertise to proceed on its own. This would gravely impact the ability to deliver effectively. The ICC, one hopes, has had over a decade to build solid cases and with more resources at its disposal would be the pragmatic choice for the prosecutions.

For years, as far as the crimes in Darfur were concerned, with Sudan's government not regarded as legitimate enough to be trusted to ensure accountability (and with the president then enjoying absolute immunity from prosecution), the ICC was positioned as if it were the court of first instance. Now, things have changed. The Sudanese authorities have full right to make a call on whether to proceed with domestic trials, initiate hybrid processes, or surrender suspects to the better-equipped ICC. This means that even when they opt for ICC prosecutions over domestic ones, they are still reasserting the primacy of national jurisdictions in the way originally envisaged under the Rome Statute system. Of course, to succeed, the Sudanese authorities must show more than just willingness to ensure accountability—they must actually do it. It's practice over policy that demonstrates real change.

These good-faith gestures are the cornerstone of international diplomacy. After more than three decades as a global diplomacy outcast, the Sudanese authorities must now do more to assert and cement their legitimacy in a challenging political context.

A change in government has seen Sudan start to change course. This shift has seen changes in engagement from other countries near and far, including removal of sanctions, the delisting from the United States' list of state sponsors of terrorism, and resumption of aid through the state. Former enemies have fast become friends. Pointedly though, the Sudan—once the ICC's harshest critic under al-Bashir, but now, potentially its newest member and under new leadership—could be the country that breathes new life into a court still struggling to assert its own legitimacy. That would be a win for diplomacy.

Anecdotally, my personal decision to work in the field of international justice was inspired, in large part, by my support for calls for al-Bashir's arrest. Working in a non-governmental organization dedicated to promoting peace, security, stability, and justice in Africa, I had signed many petitions for accountability for crimes in Darfur. I had never been to Sudan nor met al-Bashir. I had, however, written and commented extensively on both.

In April 2018, I found myself in the same room with al-Bashir. I was attending the Tana High-Level Forum on Security in Africa (an initiative supported by the MSC, and one I attended as both the ISS Head of Special Projects and as an alumnus of the Munich Young Leaders program). At the time, among many peace and security issues on the continent, the worsening crisis in the Horn of Africa was on the agenda. While views differed, tempers didn't really flare at the Tana Forum. Neither al-Bashir nor I (nor anyone, really) knew then that that would be his last Tana Forum. Neither he nor I could have known that a year later, almost to the very date, he would be out of office, soon to be arrested, and later prosecuted for corruption. I think about that day often. While it took me aback to see someone I regard as a war criminal right across the room from me, that moment was perhaps one of the starkest examples of how diplomacy often requires you to have constructive conversations with your adversaries. At the time, Sudan and Ethiopia were, together with Egypt, engaged in last-ditch efforts to agree on the future of the Grand Ethiopian Renaissance Dam (GERD) project along the Nile River. While those negotiations failed, and Ethiopia proceeded without the agreement of both Sudan and Egypt, the presence of the Sudanese president at the Tana Forum on the banks of one of the Nile's lakes was at the very least symbolic.

What does the Sudan example show? First, that nothing is set in stone in international politics (or international law). Second, that efforts towards accountability are best initiated at home. Third, and perhaps most poignant for diplomacy, that there are no eternal enemies in international governance.

Ottilia Anna Maunganidze is Head of Special Projects at the Institute for Security Studies in Pretoria, South Africa. She was a Munich Young Leader in 2017.

Körber Stiftung
msc

Futureproofing NATO

Benedetta Berti

One of the keys to NATO's success has been its ability to continuously adapt to ensure Euro-Atlantic security in a constantly evolving strategic landscape. Today, the world is again changing rapidly. It is becoming more competitive, with assertive and authoritarian powers contesting international norms and institutions; and more complex, as we face novel challenges, including climate change, more sophisticated hybrid and cyber-attacks, and the exponential impact of emerging and disruptive technologies on security and defense.

Continuing to adapt the alliance to prepare for the challenges of the next decade and beyond is therefore essential. And this is exactly what NATO has been doing with the NATO 2030 agenda endorsed at the Brussels Summit in 2021. Concretely, with NATO 2030, the thirty NATO allies took steps to increase, broaden, and deepen the political role of NATO as the unique transatlantic platform for consultation, coordination, and joint action between North America and Europe on all matters that affect our defense and security. They focused on accelerating the alliance's military adaptation, enhancing cyber defenses and boosting resilience. They also agreed that climate change and security should be a priority for the alliance and put in motion an ambitious plan to ensure that NATO becomes the leading international organization when it comes to understanding, adapting, and mitigating the impact of climate change on security. The 2021 summit also placed a strong emphasis on technological innovation, with the decision to launch the civil-military Defence Innovation Accelerator and the Innovation Fund to promote transatlantic cooperation on critical technologies. To better tackle global challenges, allies also agreed to strengthen their focus on upholding the rules-based international order and to reach out more to like-minded partners and international organizations across the globe. And finally, to capture the adaptation made over the past decade and set a clear guidance for the future, allies also asked Secretary General Jens Stoltenberg to lead a process to update the NATO Strategic Concept, NATO's key political and strategic document.

But how did allies agree on these priorities, and how were these ideas generated in the first place? Futureproofing an alliance like NATO requires a unique and multi-stage diplomatic process, involving a multitude of stakeholders, inside and outside the alliance. In the case of NATO 2030, the secretary general developed a set of proposals, which were then negotiated and agreed by allies.

To ensure that these proposals captured the right priorities to adapt the alliance, the secretary general engaged deeply with all NATO allies. But he also reached out widely to gather ideas and input from stakeholders across the Euro-Atlantic area and beyond. He convened an independent group of senior experts from the public and private sectors, academia, and think tanks; established a group of young leaders aged twenty five to thirty five from a diverse range of sectors; organized series of outreach events with representatives from civil society, the private sector, youth, and partner institutions including the UN, the OSCE, and the EU; and received recommendations from parliamentarians, through the NATO Parliamentary Assembly. He also utilized innovative tools to gather input; for example, by organizing NATO's first-ever policy hackathon. This allowed eighty students from ten universities across the alliance to pitch new policy ideas, contributing to the formation of the alliance's thinking.

Engaging in an open and inclusive process allowed us to both gather new ideas and get a better sense of what different stakeholders within our societies expected from the alliance. This had concrete results, which included raising our level of ambition when it comes to issues like climate change and security or technological innovation. It also allowed us to present allies with a forward-looking and comprehensive set of ideas to discuss, refine, and negotiate together, and led to extensive and open consultations on NATO's priorities now and into the future.

As such, the NATO 2030 decisions are a prime example of successful modern diplomacy. They represent an ambitious compromise reached through a broad consultative process, drawing on input from both traditional and less-traditional actors in the diplomatic arena. This inclusive approach is key to prepare the alliance for a more competitive and unpredictable world, characterized by global challenges requiring comprehensive responses.

Benedetta Berti serves as Head of Policy Planning in the Office of the Secretary General at NATO. She was a Munich Young Leader in 2013.

◂ Benedetta Berti (right) at the Munich Young Leaders Alumni Meeting in New York City in September 2019.

Building Institutions in the Realm of Economic and Monetary Policy

Christine Lagarde

"Nothing is possible without (wo)men; nothing is lasting without institutions." [1]

Jean Monnet

Introduction

This essay explores briefly—from the perspective of a central banker and former economic policymaker—how, during Wolfgang Ischinger's lifetime, diplomacy in the realm of economic policy and central banking have helped build up international and European institutions that have served to promote European integration and the global financial system, thereby enhancing security, stability, and prosperity in Europe and around the globe.

Without the element of diplomacy in this realm too—including tireless preparations, discussions, and negotiations, both formal and informal, regular and irregular, at the lowest and especially at the highest level of policymakers—neither the post-World War II global financial governance nor European integration would have been possible, nor would they have accomplished as much as they have to this day. Successful economic diplomacy outcomes were either the result of, or went hand in hand with, effective institution building, which in turn provided the basis for longer-lasting policy solutions.[2]

Diplomacy will continue to play a key role in the realm of economic policy and must continue to be founded not only on interpersonal skills, teamwork, and a detailed understanding of complex issues, but also on solid institutions that can steer the relevant debates and negotiations toward productive outcomes for all stakeholders involved.

We are nearing the end of the first quarter of the twenty-first century, during which time the European Union (EU) has grappled with and continues to face momentous challenges: from the coming of the digital revolution to climate change, migration waves, and major new partners and competitors at the global level. Diplomacy will continue to play a key role in the realm of economic policy and must continue to be founded not only on interpersonal skills, teamwork, and a detailed understanding of complex issues, but also on solid institutions that can steer the relevant debates and negotiations toward productive outcomes for all stakeholders involved.

Diplomacy and the Global Financial Architecture

Diplomacy has been essential in building up the institutions of the post-World War II international monetary and financial order. Not only political leaders but also economic policy makers and central bankers engaged at Bretton Woods before the end of the war, where they arrived at the economic solutions and institutions that provide the bedrock of international cooperation to this day. And although the preferences of some negotiating parties lost out to those of others back then, the fundamental innovation at this juncture of international economic cooperation was the very creation of well-functioning, credible institutions with the necessary mandate and tools to support economies in trouble and to implement economic reforms.[3]

Ever since, agreement at the international level to deal with adverse economic conditions such as balance of payments crises or financial instability, be it locally, regionally, or globally, has been a somewhat less tortuous process given the multitude of counterparties and interests involved. Still, international financial architecture reform now "is immensely more complicated than in 1944 by virtue of the sheer numbers involved. Where in 1944 there were basically one-and-a-half countries at the table, the world today is a more multi-polar place. This undeniable fact of modern political and financial life greatly complicates the process of reaching agreement."[4] Agreement on how to improve the global financial system nowadays requires not only more acute diplomacy but also well-established institutions that are able to align preferences, strike compromises, and keep up with a fast-changing financial environment.

The IMF, G7, and G20

Bretton Woods was a balancing act between recovery in the post-World War II era and a recalibration of the reach of the then great powers. Importantly, it resulted in the establishment of previously absent institutions, namely the International Monetary Fund (IMF) and (what later became known as) the World Bank. While the IMF in particular has been a subject of—at times heated—debate in relation to both its governance and its policies, in time it has proved to be a key institution for reaching decisions about the global financial architecture.

◂ Christine Lagarde at the Munich Security Conference in February 2019.

The so-called Bretton Woods institutions have thus outlasted most institutions of international cooperation in recent history. One reason why they have been so resilient is that, as time went by and new challenges emerged and crises erupted, they exhibited the necessary qualities that characterize successful international institutions: strong governance; the ability to align the preferences of a diverse membership greatly differing in economic size and power, catering for both economically weaker and stronger countries and for both creditors and debtors in a world of competing interests and multiple constituencies; the ability to adapt; and the resilience to change. In this task, policymakers were served by a solid body of independent staff that provided cutting-edge policy analysis and recommendations, led by people who exhibited both courage and humility. Showing the extent to which such qualities may be required in diplomacy, the IMF itself came into being "as a result of a supreme act of faith," according to one observer.[5]

Agreement on how to improve the global financial system nowadays requires not only more acute diplomacy but also well-established institutions that are able to align preferences, strike compromises, and keep up with a fast-changing financial environment.

Policymakers have also adapted their policy prescriptions to the realities of their time and occasionally evolved, through initiative and leadership, but also in the face of major crises. Indeed, in terms of institutional evolution, the oil shocks and financial crisis of the 1970s were a second key moment, after Bretton Woods, in shaping the post-World War II financial architecture. The stagflationary and geopolitically challenging environment of the time led President Valéry Giscard d'Estaing and Chancellor Helmut Schmidt to instigate the G7, facilitating the alignment of diverse preferences in the face of a global asymmetric shock. Moreover, the nature of discussions and the approach to institutions also had to evolve over time to meet increasing demands for legitimacy and accountability. One such moment was when the G7 started to issue communiques after the 1985 Plaza Accord.

A third key moment for the evolution of international economic governance, following Bretton Woods and the 1970s crisis,[6] came with the peak of the great financial crisis of 2008–09, when the G20 emerged as the key forum for very intense cooperation among leaders.[7]

As a direct witness to the formation of the first G20 leaders meeting, eventually settled between President Nicolas Sarkozy and President George W. Bush, I can attest that the combination of leadership and diplomatic channels expedited a process that necessity called for, and from which remarkable progress resulted.[8] This momentum lasted for a number of years, but a certain reform fatigue then set in again. The COVID-19 pandemic brought back the need and desire for cooperation.

The path of global institutional cooperation has not always been as smooth as one would hope. First, setbacks in policy acceptance and implementation occurred when, for example, the "Washington Consensus" came up against severe headwinds in the 1990s and some of its basic premises had to be rethought. The degree of inclusiveness of international forums was also a challenge. Although the end of the Cold War ushered in a new beginning for many countries,[9] it was not always smooth sailing, as the example of the Russian Federation and the creation of the G8 showed.[10] The reemergence of global players such as China, and their reentry after a very long absence from the international community, brought about a new global status quo and dramatically changed the Western-centered world of the post-Industrial Revolution period.

Second, the emergence of forums like the G7 and G20 showed that patience was called for, and informal settings had to be pursued when compromises and solutions were needed at critical moments. Formal institutional change did not always follow, decisions remained less binding, and decision making was not followed by effective implementation.

Third, less formal settings of cooperation may have the drawback of not being visible enough and their outcomes may be difficult to communicate, because they are perceived to lack an "own face." The rotating presidencies of such forums also created variable leadership and sense of purpose. By contrast, treaty-based executive institutions tend to be much more relatable to the wider public. They potentially enjoy more acceptance, especially when the choices faced leave them caught "between a rock and a hard place."

Fourth, international institutions tend to be governed more intergovernmentally, meaning that reaching agreement may be more difficult due to the veto powers of individual members. They may also enjoy only indirect legitimacy and accountability, which means that they require leadership and skillful diplomacy both at home and abroad.

International agreements often face obstacles when implemented nationally and might not be consistently implemented by all parties, especially in situations in which domestic institutional capacity is lacking and where political and economic debates may be misconceived or misrepresented. In other words, international agreements, especially those of a more informal nature, need to pass the tests of democratic legitimacy and accountability, given that these dimensions of political and economic life may be perceived as lacking at the international level, as they are usually satisfied only indirectly. It therefore requires a great deal of diplomatic skill, well-coordinated actions, and appropriate institutional processes to receive the mandate and reach international agreements (for example, on trade or financial standards) that will also pass the test of national approval through the necessary democratic processes.

The Role of Central Bankers and Central Banks

As key and highly technocratic institutions with long traditions, central banks have long played their own role in helping to build up the global monetary and financial system, irrespective of their degree of independence from government. They have remained largely in the background of the high-level politics of the day, despite the view that currencies and politics are relatively connected.[11] Acting within their remits, they have analyzed and advised on key topics, for example, in the development of bilateral or multilateral monetary arrangements, within and through institutions such as the IMF, and in the context of forums such as the G20 meetings of finance ministers and central bank governors. Institutionally, alongside the IMF, the Bank for International Settlements (BIS) has played a key role since 1930 in bringing together the central banking community to assist in the smooth functioning of the global monetary and financial system.[12] Another notable body, the Financial Stability Board (FSB), and its subcommittees, bring together not only finance ministers and central bank governors but also financial supervisory and regulatory authorities. With all the main players setting financial stability policies across different sectors of the financial system at one table, the FSB is uniquely placed to also inform and advise the G20 leaders on matters of international financial stability.

At the heart of monetary and financial cooperation have been currency exchange rate arrangements, especially since the collapse of the fixed regime of Bretton Woods. These arrangements have required the ability to speak in confidence and on the basis of far-reaching trust. Following a long process that has led towards increasingly free-floating arrangements, relative stability has been largely observed in recent years, at least among the major reserve currencies. Two factors are worth highlighting in this regard. First, the introduction of the euro at the turn of the century played a central role in achieving this stability by very quickly eliminating nominal exchange rate fluctuations within Europe and becoming a trusted and credible reserve currency around the world.[13] And second, forums such as the G7 and G20, meeting also in central bank composition, steered the international community through the turbulence insofar as the agreed commitments were mostly observed by its members.

As key and highly technocratic institutions with long traditions, central banks have long played their own role in helping to build up the global monetary and financial system, irrespective of their degree of independence from government.

Central bank cooperation on a number of other key—albeit less visible—topics has also been permanently ongoing. Central banks have cooperated, intensely in the face of crises, in liquidity provision and have developed extensive networks of swap lines,[14] while addressing key components of the financial architecture such as international reserve management and payment systems, to support financial development and stability.

Finally, any mention of the BIS's role in fostering cooperation would be incomplete without noting the very difficult, detailed, and technical negotiations that have taken place within its bodies to advance common financial standards, aiming toward a level and safe global financial playing field, through the Basel Accords. The work of the BIS continues to keep up with the times and is now also focusing on central bank digital currencies (CBDCs), financial innovation in general, and cybersecurity specifically.

From Trade and the WTO to the UN and Climate Change

Ever since Bretton Woods, the global monetary and financial agenda has developed in parallel with negotiations on international trade. Despite the fact that no institution as such emerged at the time to promote trade relations (contrary to the preference of some for establishing an "International Trade Organization"), the General Agreement on Tariffs and Trade (GATT) signed by 23 nations in 1947 proved to be a good start in promoting international trade over the next few decades,[15] eventually leading to the creation of the World Trade Organization (WTO), which now has a membership of more than 160 countries.

Here too, as the strong impact of the reduction in tariffs in the decades after World War II subsided and the drive for trade liberalization waned—and again when the Cold War ended, while new challenges began to emerge in the areas of, for example, intellectual property rights—policymakers grasped the opportunity to turn the GATT into an institution with governing bodies and staff as well as arbitration and dispute resolution mechanisms (albeit with no direct powers of sanctioning).[16]

These experiences serve as useful lessons for the most pressing long-term global issue faced by current policymakers and future generations—climate change. For those who still have doubts about the magnitude of the challenge, it is useful to consider for a moment the economic fallout of the COVID-19 pandemic. An organism that effectively has a single source and measures some 100 nanometres[17] was responsible for a global fall in output of -3.1 percent in 2020, the sharpest one-year decline in decades and a much larger one than experienced, for example, during the great financial crisis of 2007–10.[18] Defending against it has required enormous responses not only by health authorities but also by fiscal and monetary authorities. The response has required increasingly coordinated efforts, including at the international level, as the cooperation between the IMF and the World Health Organization (WHO) shows.[19] Nevertheless, the response across the globe, for example as regards vaccination, remains uneven and therefore threatens our ability to overcome the pandemic.[20] On the economic front, the response has seen the IMF deploy or adjust various lending instruments, especially in countries that have been unable to respond appropriately with, for example, fiscal policies.[21]

Against this background, isn't it worth considering how we can expect to meet the challenge of climate change—which, like the pandemic, affects the entire global population, but also involves the earth's enormously complex but singular climatological system[22]—with the current fragmented global governance setup in matters of emissions reduction? We cannot afford to miss our emissions reduction goals, as this would result in devastating consequences for our economies and a vast amount of human suffering. Since there is no greater negative externality currently being faced, the response needs to be built around effective international institutions that can internalize negative externalities in order to gradually eliminate them.

European Integration

The rebuilding of Europe that took place after World War II, in parallel to institutional construction at the international level, was also an act of diplomacy and negotiation, both in the economic and the political realm, as the nation states of Europe sought solutions on how to share their sovereignty for a greater, collective, and mutually beneficial purpose. European integration was an economic project that also aimed at internal and external security.[23] It was first institutionalized through the European Coal and Steel Community of 1951. By sharing sovereignty over coal and steel, European nations ensured that war would not only become unthinkable, but also materially impossible. Robert Schuman, French foreign minister at the time and former prime minister, issued the declaration on May 9, 1950, with Jean Monnet, the French economy minister, at his side. This and the integration steps that followed, including the introduction of the euro itself, were essentially aimed at continuing along that path of securing peace in the first instance, and not only prosperity, in Europe and beyond.

The key difference between this very close integration in post-war Europe and other cross-national cooperation and regional integration models was the foundation and development of solid political, legal, and economic institutions. These increasingly required a far-reaching degree of sovereignty sharing as the issues became more significant and political. Pillars of institutionalized statehood were established and developed over the years to nurture peace and prosperity in a fair way, thus promoting the European socioeconomic model:[24] the European Commission, the European Parliament, the Council of the European Union, the Court of Justice of the European Union, the European Court of Auditors, the European Council, and the European Central Bank. Despite all the limitations of this institutional framework, it is not an exaggeration to say that without it, the EU would not have survived its most extreme crises, nor would it have been able to adequately align interests and preferences in a multi-country, multi-level governance framework and to act together in the face of a number of internal and external challenges.

Maastricht and Beyond

It took several rounds of EU treaty negotiations—including among economic policymakers and central bankers—to arrive at the creation of the Economic and Monetary Union (EMU) and the introduction of the single currency in Europe. After previous attempts with fixed exchange rate mechanisms such as "the snake" and the European Monetary System, the Maastricht Treaty eventually brought about monetary unification and stability once and for all. Once again, it was leadership at the highest level and the gradual but precise and clearly defined development toward solid institutional solutions, rather than loose arrangements of cooperation, that brought about the introduction of the euro as a new and stable currency.

Nevertheless, while the monetary framework of EMU proved to be resilient in times of crisis, some of the key aspects of EMU, especially as regards economic and fiscal policy, exhibited shortcomings and indeed a lack of institutions, especially during crisis periods.[25] In the areas of shared fiscal, financial, and economic policies, this gap gradually began to be covered by further integrative steps, including the help of the existing institutional setup.[26]

High-level diplomacy and political negotiations, as well as detailed technical discussions and continuous late-night and sometimes shuttle diplomacy, went into defending against the great financial crisis of 2007–09 and the ensuing European debt crisis of 2010–12. Examples include the emergency swap lines and coordinated liquidity provision by central banks; the creation of the European Financial Stability Facility (EFSF), European Financial Stabilisation Mechanism (EFSM), and the European Stability Mechanism (ESM); and the financial assistance programs of the EU and the IMF. Eventually, single European banking supervision and resolution mechanisms were also established.

The continuing efforts have been worth it. Banking supervision in the euro area has taken a notable step toward facing the new challenges of the twenty-first century, with progress made on issues ranging from healthier and gradually greener balance sheets to the prevention of cyberattacks. The challenge of fully completing the banking union and capital markets union, however, remains an ongoing affair. I am regularly in Brussels discussing with counterparts the setting up of the third leg of the banking union, beyond supervision and resolution—that of pan-European deposit insurance. Here too, robust institutional solutions need to be the outcome of the negotiations. This is because one key lesson from the institution building we have seen at the European and international level is that it is only worth building institutions that have clear and focused mandates as well as the tools to deliver on those mandates. Otherwise, institution building may have the exact opposite of the intended effect.

Currently, the incremental steps being debated and negotiated regularly in the Eurogroup and the Economic and Financial Affairs Council (ECOFIN), and occasionally in the European Council of the EU leaders, are relatively moderate. But it was not so long ago that the COVID-19 pandemic prompted some difficult decisions both in Frankfurt and in Brussels. At the European Central Bank (ECB), I underlined that there are no limits to our commitment to the euro, and, in March 2020, we deployed within days one of the most powerful monetary policy tools suitable for the circumstances—the pandemic emergency purchase program (PEPP). In the face of yet another crisis, and unlike ten years or so ago, the EU fiscal authorities also took relatively little time to come up with a far-reaching and solid response, first at the national level and then at the European level with the NextGenerationEU package. It marked a new level of fiscal cooperation in Europe, and one of substantial fiscal support in the shape of both grants and loans, funded by EU borrowing backed by the EU budget, and overseen by the directly elected representatives of EU citizens in the European Parliament. Thus, comparing the crisis responses in 2010 and 2020, we see that institutions can also have this effect: they help us to better remember the past and to not repeat errors. To borrow from Jean Monnet twice: with the help of solid institutions, people may after all appreciate the necessity for change, and not only when crisis is already upon them.[27]

High-level diplomacy and political negotiations, as well as detailed technical discussions and continuous late-night and sometimes shuttle diplomacy, went into defending against the great financial crisis of 2007–09 and the ensuing European debt crisis of 2010–12.

More generally, the response to the COVID-19 pandemic in the EU showed (again) that where there is a will in Europe, there is a way, and the institutional framework facilitates the realization of that will. Whether longer or shorter, and whether there are more heated or cooler heads around the table, the Brussels processes can be arduous. But this also means that, eventually, everyone can be on board. This inclusiveness also helps increase the degree of successful policy implementation.

As with the meetings held at the international level, the institutional processes in Brussels require continuous monitoring, good preparation, and effective communication. They require convincing economic arguments that take into account the political economy of a union of countries with different economic sizes and structures, political cultures (and geopolitical reach), and national institutional arrangements. In the end, however, at least one key element and one realization usually help to produce results. The key element is the solid institutional framework of the EU based on the treaties (and the primacy of EU law); the realization is that in today's globalized world and in the face of major global challenges and uncertainty, none of the member states is large enough to go it alone.[28]

Diplomacy in the realm of economic and monetary policy will continue to play a vital role in the global monetary, financial, and trade system, with new powerful players being integrated and new challenges facing each of us, from climate change and digitalized financial systems—including digital currencies—to intellectual property rights and industrial policy.

In turn, the European institutional setup—and for that matter any institutional setup—needs to provide both for stability and for change. It is a fine balance that has always been called for between institutional stasis and evolution, and hence between allocative and adaptive efficiency in the institutional framework that serves the public. For this balance to work, skillful diplomacy has been and will continue to be required.

Challenges Ahead

Diplomacy in the realm of economic and monetary policy will continue to play a vital role in the global monetary, financial, and trade system, with new powerful players being integrated and new challenges facing each of us, from climate change and digitalized financial systems—including digital currencies—to intellectual property rights and industrial policy. We already have the well-developed institutional infrastructure required to address some of these challenges; however, we need to find the right and continuing balance between stability and evolution. For other challenges, the willingness to negotiate and compromise must come from the world's leaders, in order to move to the stage of institution building.

In the area of climate change, for example, one could go beyond international agreements and establish an institution, possibly under the auspices of the UN and similar to the WTO, to defend against (hopefully) temporary policy and political setbacks arising in individual countries, monitor progress more closely, ensure conformity and implementation, and drive the agenda forward more rigorously. To be more effective, such an institution could also require the authority to enforce agreements.

In Europe diplomacy in the broader sense will continue to play a role in pooling sovereignty toward completing the EMU, both in terms of policy areas (such as the banking, capital markets, and fiscal unions) and in terms of new members. While not directly in the realm of high-level politics, dialogue and good policy solutions and implementation in the economic sphere will remain—even if in the background—an essential part of these negotiations.

The necessary deepening of EMU will require, at some point, the creation of a proper fiscal capacity. In this sense, it meets one of the conditions presumably necessary also for the goal of European strategic autonomy.[29] In the first instance, EMU and EU strategic autonomy may seem unrelated, but there are instances in which they can possibly reinforce each other.[30] Indeed, the COVID-19 crisis also shows that both at the international and the European level, policy response is most effective when institutions work well and when they work—if not together—at least in the same direction. This is impossible without women and men willing to enter the diplomatic fray and lead such institutions.[31]

Christine Lagarde is the President of the European Central Bank (ECB). Prior to that, she was Finance Minister of the French Republic from 2007 to 2011 and Managing Director of the International Monetary Fund from 2011 to 2019.

Olaf Scholz, Kristalina Georgieva, and Christine Lagarde at the Munich Security Conference in February 2019. ▸

Munich Security Conference msc
Münchner Sicherheitskonferenz

NATO Engages
SCHLOSS ELMAU
msc
Heusgen
UNICEF

Bringing a Breath of Fresh Air to the United Nations Security Council

Christoph Heusgen

In April 2019, Germany took over the presidency of the UN Security Council for one month. The presidency is rotated monthly. During their two-year membership on what is arguably the most important of all UN panels, non-permanent members have the opportunity (normally twice) to use their month of presidency to set the agenda and to define priorities. This, of course, relates first of all to the substance—the issues—to be discussed. In addition to addressing current crises, we chose the fight against sexual violence in conflict zones as our focal topic.

In a rather symbolic step, we also wanted to make Security Council meetings more transparent and lively. In the face of opposition from a tradition-minded UN Secretariat and from some of the permanent Security Council members, we managed to open the heavy curtains of the time-honored hall. Light was suddenly flowing through the "chamber," changing the atmosphere completely. To make debates more dynamic, we made use of an oversized hourglass produced by a small Thuringian business, the five-minute running time of which served to urge speakers to keep it short. Moreover, as the chairman of the Security Council, I asked colleagues to put their manuscripts aside and to speak freely, to respond to previous speakers' points, and to encourage true debate.

Open curtains, hourglasses, and enlivened discussions alone cannot solve the more deep-rooted, fundamental problems facing the Security Council. There is no questioning the fact that the Security Council is currently undergoing a phase of weakness.

I must admit that these measures didn't have much of a lasting effect. Going against entrenched habits is never easy. The pandemic, which meant that meetings could only take place virtually, made most of the debates even duller and less of a genuine exchange. However, we succeeded in attracting media attention and initiating a discussion on the workings of the Security Council. As the aspects mentioned are now regularly criticized, I am confident that future presidencies will follow up on them, and that this could eventually lead to a change.

Of course, open curtains, hourglasses, and enlivened discussions alone cannot solve the more deep-rooted, fundamental problems facing the Security Council. There is no questioning the fact that the Security Council is currently undergoing a phase of weakness. If we recollect, the UN Security Council was created in the wake of World War II to make sure that future conflicts would no longer be fought on the battleground, but at the negotiating table. It was envisaged as adopting legally binding resolutions that would form the basis for settling conflicts, to which the community of states was expected to adhere. What had been spectacularly achieved in Europe by establishing the European Union—namely the settling of disputes not through the use of force, but through political action by the European Commission and the various Council bodies, and, if needed, by the European Court of Justice—was to be implemented on a global level. Even during the Cold War, it became obvious that a lack of political will on the part of one or several of the permanent members possessing the right of veto meant no hope of a solution. The Security Council nevertheless turned out to be a success, especially as long as no immediate interests of the five permanent members were affected. Over the decades, it has proven possible to regulate conflicts, conclude agreements, and make arrangements—on specific as well as general topics—through negotiations conducted inside and outside the Security Council, thereby establishing a rule-based international order.

When I say that the Security Council is currently experiencing a phase of weakness, this has much to do with an alarming tendency that has become obvious in recent years on the part of Russia, China, and the United States to brush away agreements, arrangements, and resolutions previously achieved in the Security Council as soon as they no longer fit their agenda. And if "big" nations no longer play by the rules, why should "smaller" ones do so?

By invading and occupying parts of Ukraine and annexing Crimea, Russia has arguably committed the most severe violation of international law in Europe since the end of World War II. Statements from Moscow leave little hope for settling this conflict in the foreseeable future. Further questions regarding Russia's attitude toward international law are raised by its military support for the Assad regime, which has committed atrocious war crimes, and its related attacks in

◂ Christoph Heusgen as a guest at MSC events, among others at the Munich Young Leaders Alumni Meeting in 2019.

the UN Security Council (and elsewhere) on the OPCW, the international organization whose mission is to ensure adherence to the Chemical Weapons Convention. By sending troops (the "Wagner Group") to Libya, Russia has infringed on binding Security Council resolutions. Russian global cyberattacks, the murders of opposition members and intelligence service defectors, and the abrogation of basic political rights in Russia itself are also highly alarming.

As China's political and economic power increases, it also turns away from international law whenever the country's national interests are at stake (contrary to its assurances). This is particularly obvious in the South China Sea, where China continually tries to enforce the "right of the strongest" against applicable marine law. Moreover, China has unscrupulously overridden its agreement with Hong Kong ("one country, two systems"). By locking up hundreds of thousands of Uyghur people in reeducation and work camps, China is committing crimes against humanity. Those suppressed by Beijing not only include Uyghurs, but also Tibetans, Mongols, and other minorities.

Under the Trump administration, the United States has turned away from multilateral cooperation in many fields and has ignored international law: it left the Paris Agreement, the World Health Organization, and the Geneva Human Rights Council. The US administration unilaterally repealed the nuclear agreement with Iran that had become legally binding through a Security Council resolution. Against valid Security Council resolutions (that is, decisions the US had backed itself), the US embassy was transferred from Tel Aviv to Jerusalem, and Israel's territorial sovereignty over the Golan Heights was acknowledged. The same situation occurred regarding Western Sahara. Here too, the United States infringed on a legally binding Security Council resolution by acknowledging Moroccan sovereignty over the region. Unfortunately, this list of international law infringements is not complete. On the other hand, it is of course to be welcomed that the US administration under President Biden has revoked some of the most severe infringements of the previous government—though, unfortunately, not all of them. Given the heated and polarized political atmosphere in the US, nobody can say with certainty that Trumpian foreign policy will remain a one-time accident.

The Security Council needs to be reformed. In its current composition, it no longer reflects the realities of today's world.

Against the background of this gloomy analysis, a question arises: how should the international community of states react to the described trends? One possibility is to no longer commit to a rule-based international order and to leave the United Nations to its fate, with the prospect of it coming to an end like its predecessor, the League of Nations. In this case, we would return to an "order" in which the "right of the strongest" prevails. Alone or with like-minded partners, each state would seek to defend its interests to make sure it doesn't fall victim to those prepared to exert their influence by any means. One has no wish to imagine such an order, let alone to see it unfold once again.

For this reason, and, above all, because of our experiences and our responsibility from German history, we must not give up on our commitment to multilateralism, a rule-based international order, and the United Nations. It is only in a joint effort that the great challenges facing humanity—such as climate change, underdevelopment, and pandemics—can be met with some prospect of success. By agreeing on long-term development goals—the so-called Sustainable Development Goals (SDGs)—the United Nations have already defined a common agenda. That alone marks an outstanding success of the community of states. For the future, it will be essential to persuade the international community, and, in particular, those states that tend to unilateralism (or, at best, common action according to their discretion) that adherence to international rules and standards and a joint effort to cope with the great tasks of the world community will be in their true interest. Good words and appeals alone will not suffice; there is also need for political pressure.

Preserving peace and security is among the most important future tasks. The UN Security Council will remain the forum legitimized by international law for peacefully settling conflicts. The deficits described must not prevent us from consistently standing up for a rule-based international order, adherence to Security Council resolutions, and defending human rights. As evidenced by the US government's renewed closeness with the United Nations, continued effort is worthwhile. Why shouldn't China and Russia eventually come to the conclusion that respecting international law is in their own interests?

Regardless of the attitude shown by the permanent members of the Security Council toward international law, the Security Council needs to be reformed. In its current composition, it no longer reflects the realities of today's world. It was last reformed in the 1960s. If the forces of inertia—in particular, China, which sees its privileged position as threatened by the potential granting of a permanent membership to India and Japan, and Russia, which backs China—continue to prevail, the Security Council will eventually lose its legitimacy, since the African nations in particular do not feel adequately represented. Already, Africans often refuse to put conflicts on their continent onto the Security Council's agenda, as can most recently be seen with the disputes that have erupted in Ethiopia. This trend of Africans turning to the African Union or regional African organizations for solutions to their conflicts will intensify. Understandably, there is increasing opposition from African countries to the Chinese policy of dissuading Africans from strongly demanding a reform of the Security Council in the General Assembly. It is also regrettable, however, that countries such as Italy, Spain, Mexico, Canada, Argentina, and South Korea oppose reforms, which they fear will not serve their interests. States supporting an international rule-based order must be reminded of their responsibility towards the community of states. They should declare their willingness to take part in substantial negotiations, rather than opposing them.

Time and again, the question of a "European seat" in the UN Security Council is discussed—an idea flowing from the evolution of the European Union's common foreign and security policy in recent years. The call for such a seat, however, ignores the fact that the United Nations Charter only allows for membership of single states. Any attempt to change the charter in this respect would surely fail, as China and Russia would never agree. Nor would other states that are not democratically led and do not respect human rights stand up for a European seat. Finally, permanent member France is not interested in relativizing its position. However, there is potential for a stronger European voice in the Security Council. Although the Security Council's three non-permanent African members regularly speak with one voice in the form of common declarations, European members seem incapable of doing the same. France, in particular, which attaches much importance to its permanent seat, has long opposed an increased "Europeanization." What can be built upon, however, is the increasing frequency with which EU members within the Security Council have issued joint press statements in recent years. Another positive development can be seen in the continually growing influence and importance of the European External Action Service in New York.

As described, Germany has tried to make meetings more dynamic and transparent during its term in the Security Council. This endeavor was also helped by preferentially inviting female representatives of the civil society to act as "briefers," according to our regular habit. Moreover—and most importantly—it was by making substantial contributions that we helped to advance the Security Council and the peaceful settlement of conflicts. In so many ways—through our engagement for solving the Ukrainian conflict; for Libya, Sudan, and Afghanistan; by deploying German army soldiers to UN missions in Mali and Lebanon; by dispatching a frigate into the South China Sea; by putting important topics such as the use of sexual violence in conflicts and the link between climate and security on the Security Council's agenda; and by consistently standing up for human rights—we have assumed responsibility and contributed to strengthening the international rule-based order and the Security Council.

Germany's contributions are widely acknowledged. The German nation is recognized for being the second-largest financial contributor to the United Nations. It's because of our highly valued neutral stance and our strong commitment to international law that we are regularly asked to help resolve conflicts. More than ever in an era in which the permanent members of the Security Council do not focus their efforts on rule-based order, Germany must continue to play this part consistently. Yet we will never achieve results alone, but only through working together with partners—which, of course, include our traditional allies in the EU, in NATO, and in the G7. However, we should increasingly build on partnerships beyond the classical "West": namely, partnerships with nations in Africa, Asia, Australia, and South America that are committed to good governance and to rule-based international order. The United Nations Charter and the Universal Declaration of Human Rights ultimately form a universal body of applicable rules, to which all states have committed themselves. They are not rules of "the West." Working together, it should be possible to reinforce the relevance of the UN Security Council.

The United Nations Charter and the Universal Declaration of Human Rights ultimately form a universal body of applicable rules, to which all states have committed themselves. They are not rules of "the West."

Christoph Heusgen, a German career diplomat, served for more than a decade as foreign and security policy advisor to Chancellor Angela Merkel and, more recently, as Permanent Representative of the Federal Republic of Germany to the United Nations in New York. He is Chairman of the Board of Trustees of the Munich Security Conference Foundation and will be Wolfgang Ischinger's successor as Chairman of the MSC after the Munich Security Conference 2022.

4 Lessons for Diplomacy

50th Munich Security
Conference
50. Münchner Siche
January 31
31. Januar
Munich Security
Conference msc
Münchner Sicherheitskonferenz
BAYERISCHER HOF

The EU and Three Lessons in Foreign Policy

Catherine Ashton

The future of Europe is dependent not just on the internal dynamics between nations, but on the relationships and pressures that stretch beyond its borders. Each country is affected by a unique combination of history, geography, and politics. The scale of ambition, strength of connections, and depth of animosities are all factors to be taken into account in any analysis of why Europe makes the choices it does. As a consequence, it is not always easy to predict a united position, even where the members of the EU have arguably clear common interests.

Beyond the EU, countries like the UK, Norway, and Switzerland stay close to the values and ideals that underpin the principles on which the EU is built. Other European countries have aspirations to be part of the EU, or to orbit closely to it, looking for strong economic or political links. Some of these aspirations strain the relationships within the EU, either because of their weariness of enlargement or fears of adding new problems when the member states are already dealing with enough internal challenges.

Outside observers and internal critics might argue that there is a question mark over the capacity of Europe to play a stronger role in a world increasingly looking for new leadership. Without common positions and clear ideas, it is difficult to decide whether Europe is ready to step forward. Whether it can succeed depends on its management of a series of relationships—with nations, with crises and challenges, with issues and ideals.

Without common positions and clear ideas, it is difficult to decide whether Europe is ready to step forward. Whether it can succeed depends on its management of a series of relationships—with nations, with crises and challenges, with issues and ideals.

Three major outside relationships will continue to dominate the agenda—with the US, Russia, and China. All three have the capacity, in different ways, to inflict damage on the idea of strong European countries, a strong European identity, and the EU as a foreign policy actor. Each has sought to split the alliance of the EU, forming individual relationships or alternative groupings. China created the China-Central and Eastern European Countries (China-CEEC) initiative as a way of bringing together some European nations both within and outside the EU to promote the Belt and Road initiative and promote collaboration on areas like infrastructure. It has been embraced by many European countries as a way to meet directly with China, rather than the indirect route through the structures of the EU. Some see it as a direct threat to the integrity of the EU with an agenda that benefits China. In the meantime, the EU has struggled to develop a long-term strategy towards China, in part reflecting its ongoing dilemmas about whether to sail close to the US or to chart its own course in what could be tempestuous seas.

Russia creates the most immediate and challenging problems for Europe. By its actions in Ukraine, poisoning and imprisonment of opposition leader Alexei Navalny, and cyberattacks in Europe, it has caused a substantial rethinking of defense and security strategies. Individual European countries have long established links, particularly on energy, and some have seen significant investment in recent years, which play into decisions on the immediate (sanctions) and the future (trade and energy). Finding a common position is tricky for the EU in this context.

The most dramatic development has been in the relationship across the Atlantic with the US. The transatlantic partnership has been a crucial force pushing Europe to stand together in resolving its problems and to be a partner in promoting economic growth and democracy. The interest of successive US presidents in the future of Europe, combined with a complacency within Europe that the US would always protect its allies across the Atlantic, has created a strong reliance on American support. While US presidents have consistently warned that Europe needed to carry more of the burden of its own security, the Trump administration hammered this home in blunt and direct ways. Things have not returned to where they were, on either side. It remains to be seen whether this is an opportunity for Europe to take more responsibility for areas of foreign and defense policy that it has traditionally left to American leadership—especially after the scenes in Afghanistan.

Close to home are the challenges that Europe faces from its neighborhood. From war and chaos in Syria and Libya, to frozen conflicts in Georgia, Moldova, and

◂ Catherine Ashton with Hashim Thaçi at the Munich Security Conference in February 2014.

increasingly Ukraine, Europe is directly impacted by the tragedies playing out in its backyard. Memories of the war and the horror of the collapse of Yugoslavia are still strong, and the need to ensure that all the nations of the Western Balkans find their way into the EU is still an ambition—even if, for some, it is low on their agenda.

These issues play into the domestic politics in every country. At any given moment, one or other will be facing elections, either national or local, presidential or parliamentary. At any point a government could fall, vulnerable to a change in coalition politics or the precarious nature of its majority.

Even the most secure among them is aware of what concerns their population, and, in every country, migration is a live and difficult issue. Populism stalks the lands of Europe, whipping up anger and blame and using the chaos in the neighborhood as a means to inspire fear that large, uncontrolled numbers of refugees can alter the very nature of their countries. With movement of people creating opportunities for the young and entrepreneurial to work in other EU countries, anxiety about what the future will look like in countries they have left has added to the clamor for others to take greater responsibility or for the issue to be dealt with "elsewhere."

Finding strong foreign policy and security responses to the neighborhood is the most visible way that Europe demonstrates its capacity to answer the question of whether it wishes to be taken seriously as a key foreign policy player. The capacity to tackle neighborhood issues has always been about finding the compromises between issues that are at the top of some countries' agendas and low on others; differences of perspective on the cause of the problem and who is best placed to fix it; taking action that might damage domestic economies as a price for a collective response. Yet the neighborhood is where Europe has the chance to show its strength, its values, and its determination to be a strong force for democracy and human rights. I learned a great deal about the capacity for the EU to act, and the potential for it to do more. Even from the shores of a country no longer a part of the EU, I watch with anticipation for the potential to be realized. Working with the reality of the EU as well as the possibility of what it could do in the future, I learned a great deal. These three lessons from foreign policy are especially important.

A System of Collaboration

There are no serious issues individual nations face that can be resolved alone. From the global challenges of climate change and COVID-19, to threats from serious crime and terrorism, and the benefits of trade and economic partnerships, every country must collaborate to achieve its goals.

Collaboration has been at the heart of the European project since its beginning. As more complex questions have come onto the agenda, and as more states have joined with their own priorities, so this collaboration has become more challenging. It has also become more necessary. Solutions to migration created by chaos and war, drought, flood, or economic need, require a broad consensus. Getting to concrete proposals to deal with our changed climate and prevent further, potentially catastrophic change, needs sustained effort. None of this is easy. Politicians representing their home country do not leave their home priorities and politics at the door of the Council meeting room on Rue de la Loi in Brussels. Rather, they arrive mindful of their government's strength or precariousness, and the domestic realities they face. This is not to excuse those who fail to see collaboration as vital to their own success as well as that of the EU, but rather to be clear-eyed about the pressures each face. Collaboration often requires political courage and the farsightedness of those sitting around the table. It also requires the recognition that a convergence of interests and values creates a framework for action.

Collaboration has been at the heart of the European project since its beginning. As more complex questions have come onto the agenda, and as more states have joined with their own priorities, so this collaboration has become more challenging. It has also become more necessary.

The Green Deal is a prime example of the kind of cooperative, long-term, large-scale thinking required, with its clear goals and targets. A comprehensive plan—applicable across twenty seven nations, with ambitious targets for phasing out fossil fuels, ramped-up investment in clean energy, and a clear role for the private sector—it is a good example of the kind of multi-nation, multi-industry thinking that must be in evidence across the globe. It will not be easy to implement and already finds itself challenged from within some member states for going too far, and from some in the European Parliament for not going far enough. But the fact that it exists and will be a major part of the discussions at the beginning of November when the UN Climate Change Conference, also known as COP26, opens in Glasgow, Scotland, demonstrates its importance. As each day passes and the conference creeps closer, the need to find sustainable, long-term, practical solutions becomes more urgent. NASA tells us that, despite our efforts so far, the last seven years were the warmest on record. The demand, therefore, to throw all available resources at the climate crisis is unavoidable.

While individual nations must approach COP26 with well thought-out, ambitious goals and commitments, it is in collaboration and partnership that many of the real solutions lie. Harnessing and joining expertise across sectors, countries, and regions needs to gain momentum. The EU Green Deal shows how that collaboration can work.

In the wider international system, there has been some level of acceptance for the last seventy plus years that the values and norms attributable to the notion of Western democracies lies at the core of the framework that holds it together. This acceptance has been subject to increasing challenge, particularly over recent years. Sergei Lavrov, foreign minister of Russia, wrote recently that the West should recognize other forms of governance. He argued that Russia and China, among others, had their own values and traditions that dated back a thousand years. Any attempt to decide whose values were better was a pointless exercise, in his view. China has been clear that they want a say in the setting of international rules. In the European Union, Poland and Hungary have questioned who decides "which" European values and "whose" rule of law should apply. They have put their own perspectives above the common interest when considering how to act as one in international affairs. Long-running disputes about judicial independence in Poland or press freedom in Hungary have grown into fundamental differences at the heart of the Union. The Dutch Prime Minister, Mark Rutte, publicly declared that Hungary had no place in the EU anymore due its legislation attacking LGTBQ rights. In reality, removing any nation from the EU would require a unanimous decision after a tortuous process, with all concerned trying to avoid such an outcome. But frustrations now run deep and the chances of concerted, joint action to address external challenges are reduced.

Collaboration often requires political courage and the farsightedness of those sitting around the table. It also requires the recognition that a convergence of interests and values creates a framework for action.

For the international community to act, whether through the UN and especially the UN Security Council, or through the unanimous view of the European Union, it must start by having a common acceptance of both the problem and the solution. That appears to be harder to achieve. It has always been the case that changes of government in any country can lead to a difference in policy, both domestic and foreign. But there has been an assumption at the heart of the system that the US and Europe would fundamentally remain committed to the values and ideals of the recent past.

The US cannot guarantee that a new administration in four years will stick to its commitments on climate, on foreign policy, or on strategic alliances. This will be a consideration in the determination or lack of it from other countries to take their own significant action. As international organizations come under question resolving complex problems, from the future of Afghanistan to ending the conflict in Ukraine or in Syria, is even more difficult when the route through formal international bodies looks impossible.

This may be the time to reexamine the tried and tested models of collaboration of which there are three versions. The first is formal collaboration when states are prepared to work together within a framework of established rules. United Nations operations or EU Missions are the most obvious examples, providing civilian and military support to people in need, agreeing to sanctions, and putting in place aid programs. Working together in the EU on defense through the European Defence Agency is an area in which the economies of scale and opportunities to share knowledge with allies have proved invaluable. Research into IEDs, training of helicopter pilots, and ensuring that all member states have the capacity for midair refueling have benefited missions for NATO as well as the EU and individual nations' capacity.

The second is the informal process or the coalition of the willing. These groupings have also covered the spectrum of activity from military and civilian to humanitarian aid. The recent G7 meeting is an example of the informal grouping, with membership confined to those who already share the same ideas. Without formal rules, the G8 was able to remove Russia simply by disinvitation and become again the G7. The advantages are obvious; working together only on issues on which they agree, determining membership to suit their interests, and choosing their issues rather than being expected to deal with all of them. The disadvantages are clear too. Without the formal structures, they do not carry the legal or moral authority nor necessarily have the depth and staying power to continue to tackle a problem over many years. They are like yachts, able to maneuver quickly and provide support at speed, unlike the formal models, which are more reminiscent of tankers—hard to get moving and slow to change direction, but willing to stay at sea for a long time. In the EU, the European Commission is the tanker, while the EEAS has the qualities of a yacht, able to move more quickly. But it is the combination that provides the best response, bringing speed of initial action together with longer-term support. Each model has limitations. The crisis in Libya began with a formal UN Security Council process to support the people of Benghazi under attack from Gadaffi's forces. It became a response by a coalition of the willing, moving from the formal to the informal, or from the tanker to the yacht. The problem came when initial enthusiasm for a military mission was not followed by long-term support as the coalition fell away, and there was no government on the ground willing to allow international bodies to put practical support in place. Libya spiraled into chaos. Thinking through any response requires an understanding of each model's strengths and weaknesses, and arguably a willingness to use both to tackle the same issue.

There is a third model, which is a hybrid of the two and best exemplified in the Iran negotiations that led to the Joint Comprehensive Plan of Action (JCPOA). Authority was given to the coalition of six countries, led under the EU's chairmanship, to negotiate an agreement. It was not a formal model, because there was no serious obligation on the six countries to stick with the agreement—as witnessed by the lack of action when the US withdrew. It relied on the informal model of a coalition willing to work together to get the job done, and the formal acceptance that it had authority to act on behalf of the UN. The advantage it took from the informal model was the ability to compartmentalize issues, so when Russia took Crimea and invaded parts of Eastern Ukraine, the talks continued largely unaffected. I flew between Kyiv where I condemned Russia's actions, and Vienna, where I sat beside Russia on the Iran deal. It was necessary to find ways to achieve this clarity between issues if we were to have a chance of resolving at least one of them. Whether this will be possible in any future disputes is perhaps more questionable.

It should not be surprising that countries with no history of democracy struggle to escape their past quickly. But in offering advice and support, we need to offer our understanding that the road to a strong democracy requires vigilance and sustained effort.

The Conference on Climate Change will itself use this model as it tries to move the world to more radical, sustained solutions. On one hand, the signatories to the United Nations Framework Convention on Climate Change—a treaty in force from 1994—and the EU as a major participant with an agreed plan, are formal structures. On the other hand, this is a coalition of the willing, prepared to do what is necessary to save the planet from the biggest crisis we face. To achieve a positive outcome, disputes and conflicts between nations will be put aside or put into a different compartment, at least for the duration of getting the agreement. Commitments will be made that the world will hope to be honored by those political leaders who will follow in their footsteps. But, as always in the informal, sanctions on those who don't will be hard to agree to and even harder to implement.

Over the coming years, as the list of crises, frozen conflicts, and issues of concern grows, it may be time for the models to be examined, tested, and refined. Without collaboration we have little chance of finding any serious, long-lasting solutions. Using the right models at the right time could help. In our interconnected world, no nation can stand alone.

Deep Democracy

Across rallies and demonstrations from Tunisia to Ukraine, I heard "election and democracy" in the same sentence as if one automatically led to the other or that the two were cause and effect. While elections are a fundamental part of democratic life, they are insufficient on their own. It doesn't mean that we have to wait centuries for countries to establish democracy, but it does mean we need to keep nurturing and supporting it to ensure that it grows deep roots.

It is not surprising that the calls for elections were loud, and that those who wanted to lead the country were keen to get their legitimacy established as fast as possible. Elections are the most visible manifestation of what should be an interwoven group of ideas, institutions, laws, and organizations that enable people to exercise their vote with confidence. It is a system I call "deep democracy." What that means was described to me by a young man who had recently emerged from eight years in a prison in Libya. We were standing in a Benghazi hotel looking out at buildings shattered by the bombings in a country shortly to disintegrate into chaos. "We want what you have—democracy as part of our everyday life."

In his perfect English, he made the point that is crucial to the debate on democracy—that it is part of everyday life. Deeply rooted in our institutions, media, civil society, and political structures, it doesn't happen by accident. It requires time and effort and vigilance. It gives confidence, even in times of great challenge, in the institutions and political framework of society.

The journey can be long. In the UK it is over 800 years since Magna Carta, the Great Charter, proclaimed the importance of the rule of law, documented liberties that pertained to free men, and gave freedom to the individual against the arbitrary decisions of those in power. It was a key moment in the development of democracy. But modern British democracy took centuries to evolve: more than 400 years for Parliament to wrest power from the monarch, almost 500 years to achieve a free press, and 713 years before women secured equal voting rights as men, as recently as 1928. It should not be surprising that countries with no history of democracy struggle to escape their past quickly. But in offering advice and support, we need to offer our understanding that the road to a strong democracy requires vigilance and sustained effort. And we need to identify what we regard as fundamental to establishing a strong democracy that will last.

Many crises erupt after years or underlying problems, others are impossible to predict, while more come as a surprise in the moment, but have deep roots that in hindsight are obvious. In most circumstances, it is clear from the beginning that dealing with the immediate impact is a necessary but insufficient approach. "Sticking plaster" on the problem is unlikely to have much effect.

Underpinning it all needs to be a strong legal framework, where the rule of law is backed up by an independent judiciary and where the rules for elections and government are set out and observed. Attacks on the role of judges and the validity of the courts are common among those who seek to take control. The same is true for a free media. However difficult it might be for those in positions of authority, a strong media with the resources to investigate wrongdoing is part of the infrastructure that makes democracy effective.

A funded, supported civil society, focused on communities and issues, representing the vulnerable to those in authority and highlighting concerns, is a sign of a thriving democracy. Representative organizations for individuals, charities, and businesses help to lobby governments for change, and bring under public gaze injustice and inequality. Across mature democracies, the mark that civil society has made is clear, from votes for women, to support for the disabled, better housing, developments in education, and rights for the LGTBQI community.

And of course, rules for free and fair elections need to be in place to give confidence in the process and get results that reflect the will of the people. Elections must give voters the practical opportunity, and not just the theoretical right, to throw politicians out of office and replace them. An elderly politician in Egypt, at the time of the overthrow of President Mubarak, said to me, "what we need is a retired president—someone who voluntarily leaves office when their time is up. We have never had that."

As Europe's own history shows only too clearly, democracy is fragile. It needs to be supported by an interwoven infrastructure that includes these elements—and more. These things must command support at home: they cannot, and should not, be imposed from outside. Europe's role should be to act as a beacon by insisting on, and so demonstrating, best practice within its own borders—and so inspire those, such as the young man in Benghazi, who seek to grow democracy in their own countries.

A Comprehensive Approach—Economics Meets Politics

In a crisis, the focus is on the immediate. Many crises erupt after years or underlying problems, others are impossible to predict, while more come as a surprise in the moment, but have deep roots that in hindsight are obvious. In most circumstances, it is clear from the beginning that dealing with the immediate impact is a necessary but insufficient approach. "Sticking plaster" on the problem is unlikely to have much effect.

The Lisbon Treaty brought closer working between member states and institutions, which made it simpler for officials and commissioners leading crisis management, long-term development, and diplomacy together. Over time it became easier to pool resources, share requests for help, and put in place better planning. This helped to make the EU response in a crisis more effective.

An example in which a comprehensive strategy made a difference was in Somalia where pirates operated off the coast threatening the World Food Programme, whose lifesaving supplies were under threat. Shipping and trade lost huge sums as ships were hijacked and crew, cargo, and ships were held for ransom. International efforts, including the EU Atalanta Mission, were able to deter and capture pirates at sea and, over time, the situation improved. But the real challenge was to try and support a fledgling government in a country that had known twenty years of civil war and where little functioned because the causes of piracy lay on the land, not at sea.

The EU had been a constant support to the UN efforts to drive back Al Shabaab, a terrorist organization trying to take control of the country. Development teams supported local communities, including young men who were lured into piracy by the promise of money they had no hope of earning on the land. At sea, military missions deterred, disrupted, and captured pirates attempting to hijack ships and take the vessels, crew, and cargo hostage, at a cost of billions of euros to trade and shipping.

Developing a comprehensive approach enabled the EU to bring all these efforts together and weave them into a more effective response. Young men were offered greater opportunities, ships were better protected, and the government was helped as it promoted education and jobs. New campaigns to get children back into school, under the slogan "give up your guns and go to school," helped a new generation find alternatives to piracy or joining Al Shabaab. Prisons for pirates were built with rehabilitation and training programs as a standard part of their approach. All these ideas and many more helped improve the chances of a people who had known nothing but chaos. At its heart was the idea that by pooling ideas and weaving together programs, a better response would lead to more lasting outcomes.

The Arab Spring traces its beginnings to the middle of December 2010 in Tunisia when a young man called Mohamed Bouazizi was harassed yet again by police who confiscated his stock of fruit and vegetables, claiming he needed a permit. Bouazizi, frustrated and in despair of ever being able to support his family, set fire to himself in protest. He died weeks later from his terrible injuries. His plight became a rallying call across the country, and soon across the region others protested against corruption and lack of opportunity, demanding rights in a truly democratic future.

While the political imperative for changes in leadership and greater democracy became louder, the reason that Bouazizi took such drastic action was his inability to look after his family. His were economic problems born of the political choices made by those in power. Economics and politics are two sides of the coin. In responding to the waves of protests and dramatic events of the Arab Spring, the EU found a new mechanism to try and recognize these twin challenges. They were termed task forces and were put together for Egypt, Tunisia, Jordan, and later Myanmar.

The propositions behind them were simple. European business was interested in investing in these countries, but would only do so if there was stability and rule of law governing their engagement. Leaders needed to attract foreign direct investment, and welcomed the support of the World Bank, the IMF, the EBRD, and other financial bodies. They had to show that they had plans for the economy and would back up those plans with commitments to develop infrastructure and business opportunities. Alongside the business and economic drive, it was necessary to show that democracy was working, that rights were respected, and that civil society was beginning to flourish.

The task forces were a collaboration between the commission services for industry and business, development, and the European External Action Service, with member states participating throughout. Business leaders from across Europe came to a formal meeting, together with members of the European Parliament, civil society representatives, and member states' ministers and ambassadors. Over the course of several days, there were opportunities to discuss, reach agreement, form teams—in Myanmar the EU/Myanmar chamber of commerce was launched—and make plans. The EBRD, agreeing to an extension of its geographic mandate, was able to explore investments in infrastructure and energy. Some years later, as a result of this early work, Egypt became the country of highest investment.

There were a number of messages in this approach. First, the recognition that economics and politics meet together in the aspirations and demands of the population. People want a future for themselves and their children with education, jobs, security, and stability. Second, that thinking through a comprehensive approach allows resources to be focused on tackling underlying and connected issues. Third, by demonstrating support and showing those in position of authority what should and can be done, it is possible to influence future decisions.

Aftermath

In a post-Brexit, post-President Trump world, the three lessons seem as pertinent as they were when in 2014 I left the position of EU High Representative/Vice President (HRVP). Whatever course the UK charts, collaboration will be vital to its capacity to act and to thrive. Economics and politics will remain closely linked. There is a lot to do to find the best relationship with the EU, but it may be that over time, together with the US, the EU and the UK become an effective grouping to promote democracy, stability, and security in the world. As the lessons in collaboration taught me, there are many different groupings that work for a specific purpose. They need not be incompatible. Recent decisions by Australia, the US, and the UK to work together in the Indo Pacific are not really surprising considering the focus each has had over the last months. Using the models of collaboration may help distinguish between informal agreements that serve one purpose and the deeper collaborations that are likely to sustain.

Democracy remains our best method of giving power and control to the people. They should never be afraid of their government. It is always under attack for that very reason. Attempts to stop judges from being impartial, journalists from exposing the truth, and people from having a say will always be in the toolkit of those who seek to take control for themselves. Every nation is an unfinished project, nowhere more so than in its democratic journey.

Catherine Ashton served as the European Union's first High Representative for Foreign Affairs and Security Policy from 2009 to 2014. As a negotiator, she led the P5+1 talks on Iran's nuclear program and galvanized agreement between Serbia and Kosovo. Previously, Ashton served as the first woman Commissioner for Trade in the European Commission and the first woman British European Commissioner.

Munich Security
Conference
msc

Has Diplomacy Had Its Day?

Jens Stoltenberg

In this age of renewed authoritarianism, identity politics, and wolf warrior tactics, you may be forgiven for thinking that the golden age of quiet diplomacy and dedicated multilateralism is a relic of the past. However, in today's multipolar world, the need to work with allies and partners to defend is more important than ever.

I was baptized into the world of diplomacy at an early age. My father was a diplomat and later defense and foreign minister of Norway. He developed his own unique brand of "kitchen table" diplomacy. Growing up as a boy in the 1960s and 1970s, I regularly encountered political leaders and freedom fighters from all over the world who my father brought home for breakfast. This is where I first met Nelson Mandela, over Norwegian mackerel, brown cheese, and coffee. Admittedly, the breakfast may not sound the most appealing, but the experience of welcoming people into our home and breaking bread together as a way to break down barriers and solve collective challenges is something that has stuck with me ever since. It was then that I learned to listen, to be patient, and to embrace others' points of view. Above all, I learned the importance of compromise. These are all valuable lessons in the art of diplomacy.

Even when we disagree with our neighbors, it is important to understand their position and seek common ground.

Throughout my career, I have had the privilege to work with some of the world's finest diplomats, and diplomacy has always been central to my roles. Before joining NATO, I was the UN Special Envoy for Climate Change. Determined diplomacy has led global leaders to agree to ambitious reductions in greenhouse gas emissions, our best chance to combat climate change. As an environment minister and later prime minister of Norway, I was able to negotiate agreements with Russia on maritime, fisheries, and environmental issues. Even when we disagree with our neighbors, it is important to understand their position and seek common ground. It is always good to talk, and I remain convinced that diplomacy and dialogue are particularly important in difficult times. We have to keep trying.

It was creative and determined diplomacy that led to the creation of NATO from the spoils of war. It made allies of former adversaries and brought them together to solve their differences around a table rather than in the trenches.

In my current role at NATO, I see diplomacy in action every day. From high-level summits of allied leaders to the daily interactions of national representatives, NATO is the only platform where North America and Europe come together every day to consult, coordinate, and, when needed, act on matters that affect their defense and security. Building consensus among so many different democracies can be noisy, difficult, and slow. However, when we reach agreement through dialogue, our voice is thirty nations' strong, our decisions are better, and our actions more effective.

It is the unseen work of diplomacy that makes breakthroughs and keeps us from the path to war. But in the words of Theodore Roosevelt: "To go far, we must speak softly and carry a big stick." Indeed, sometimes, diplomacy alone is not enough. At NATO our military strength provides the conditions for our diplomatic achievements. With Russia we combine credible deterrence and defense with dialogue. To fight terrorism, we use political tools alongside military ones. When dealing with China, we seek to respond to Beijing's coercive policies and pushback on the rules-based order, while at the same time, maximizing opportunities for dialogue on issues such as arms control and climate change. A mix of credible defense and relentless diplomacy is how we keep our nations safe.

As we look to a more uncertain and competitive world, we will need even more creativity, even greater unity, and even stronger determination in the years ahead. Working even closer together, as a transatlantic community and with likeminded partners across the world, is the best—if not the only—way forward.

If war is the failure of diplomacy, then the absence of war is diplomacy's success. Nothing symbolizes this more than NATO, which has guaranteed the defense and security of the Alliance for over seventy years.

Jens Stoltenberg is Secretary General of NATO. He previously served as Prime Minister of Norway from 2000 to 2001 and from 2005 until 2013.

◂ Jens Stoltenberg at the Munich Security Conference in February 2018.

Why Do We Succeed or Fail in Negotiation and Mediation?

Jan Eliasson

Several years ago, I was visiting professor at the Department of Peace and Conflict Research at Uppsala University, Sweden. The head of the department, Professor Peter Wallensteen, asked me for the reasons why I had succeeded or failed in different negotiation and mediation missions. He wanted me to give a lecture on the subject. I had mediated for the UN in the Iran/Iraq War in the 1980s and in the Darfur conflict in 2007/2008. I had also conducted humanitarian diplomacy for the UN in Somalia, Sudan, and Myanmar in the 1990s.

I spent a week going through my notes and experiences in these missions. I wrote a draft lecture and felt reasonably comfortable with my conclusions. Experiences in multilateral diplomacy as president of the UN General Assembly (2005–2006) and as deputy secretary-general (2012–2016) confirmed my findings in Uppsala.

My starting point for a successful negotiation is that the parties to a conflict must have sufficient political will and substantial interest to come to a negotiated solution. "You can lead a horse to water, but you can't make him drink," is an old and wise saying.

A further basic reason for success is that the mediator has a thorough and deep knowledge of the problems and issues at hand in the conflict.

A third important factor is that outside parties or states are not undermining or sabotaging the mediation efforts. The phenomenon of "proxy wars" has been a serious obstacle to mediation, not least in the Middle East. The regional tensions between Saudi Arabia and Iran as well as the rivalry between the US and the Russian Federation in the UN Security Council have made negotiating a solution to the Syrian war almost impossible.

With these three caveats, I venture to suggest four main reasons for success or failure in mediation or negotiation. They are the words we use, the timing we choose, the cultural sensitivity we display, and the personal relations we develop.

The Power of the Word

It is obvious that the spoken and written word is the most important tool in diplomacy. As a child, I started to "collect" words, later in life realizing that I had a useful toolbox in negotiation and mediation. This is important of course for our native languages, but also for key international languages. In the UN, fluent English is necessary. French is a key working language in the UN, particularly in Geneva, and is indispensable in Brussels within the EU.

Choosing the right word in negotiations can open the door to progress in the same way that the wrong word can close it. To be able to quickly present synonyms or alternative wording can prevent breakups or long delays.

Listening carefully to nuances in language coming from the parties to a conflict can provide the basis for new openings.

I would go so far as to claim that words can save lives. In 1993, as UN secretary-general for humanitarian affairs, I traveled with a team to Khartoum and Juba in Sudan in order to alleviate a serious starvation crisis in the South caused by the violent civil war. A specific area with around 75,000 people was in particular danger. The area was plagued by intense fighting but also isolated by the proliferation of landmines in the area. What we strived to achieve was a local cease-fire, in order to reach the affected population with urgent food, water, and medicine by air transport from neighboring Kenya.

Choosing the right word in negotiations can open the door to progress in the same way that the wrong word can close it.

Very soon it was evident that the leadership in Khartoum would not accept a local cease-fire. "The terrorists" would be given unacceptable legitimacy by an agreement of this kind, they said. Furthermore, how would a cease-fire be monitored? Could the UN organize observers within a couple of weeks?

I realized that we had to switch focus in the talks. After long talks within the UN delegation, we agreed on a different approach, a different concept. We suggested a humanitarian corridor in which all villages, whether government or rebel controlled, would be assisted. And no agreement between the parties was necessary. A commitment to the UN would be sufficient.

This proposal was accepted, first by the government, then by the SPLA, the liberation movement in the South. A week later, planes and helicopters were flying from Kenya into the affected area in Sudan with much-needed humanitarian assistance.

◂ Jan Eliasson at the Munich Security Conference in February 2015.

What in the end had saved lives was in fact the right words, the "humanitarian corridor." These two words were the key to the solution to the crisis on the ground.

Timing

Timing of a proposal is crucial in negotiations. Mistakes are made by waiting too long and not acting preventively or in time. But it is equally common to make proposals too early when the situation is not ready for progress.

I recall how, during the spring of 2012, Kofi Annan—the first UN Envoy for Syria and the former UN secretary-general—worked hard with the parties on a formula for a political process. In Geneva at the end of June, he achieved support for a text which, in the best of worlds, would have been adopted by the UN Security Council and led to a binding council resolution. This did not happen, mainly due to the belief of both the government and the opposition—and their supporters—that the war would be decided by military means.

Mistakes are made by waiting too long and not acting preventively or in time. But it is equally common to make proposals too early when the situation is not ready for progress.

There was not any room for compromises on ending the Syrian conflict at this early stage.

Cultural Sensitivity

Trust building is a key in reaching solutions in negotiation and mediation. One wise and effective way of building trust is to display sensitivity for history, culture, and traditions of the parties on the other side of the table. Cultural sensitivity introduces an element of deeper purpose to the talks as well as a human element of pride of origin, customs, and history.

I remember negotiations in the Iran/Iraq mediation where a visit to a museum or a quote from the Koran made progress possible in the talks. Once in Iran, I asked to make a break in the talks to visit the famous carpet museum in Teheran. In the end, I had three guides from the Iranian delegation accompanying me to the museum. There was a drastic change of atmosphere after this museum visit. The talks went exceptionally smoothly after this display of cultural sensitivity in the eyes of the Iranians.

On the issue of withdrawal to the international boundaries, our UN delegation, then led by Prime Minister Olof Palme, quoted a chapter "sura" of the Koran. It claimed that you must not attack an enemy who turns his back to you and returns home. This quote had a much greater effect than references to international law.

Personal Relations

In the end, personal relations often are decisive in reaching an agreement. To make concessions or agree to compromises can be painful, difficult, and sometimes dangerous for the parties. They must have complete trust in the mediator or chief negotiator as well as in their judgment and commitment to a balanced solution. Honesty and discretion as well as an unfailing attachment to truth are indispensable.

It is sometimes difficult to mobilize sympathy for political leaders who are known for cruelty to their own population. Saddam Hussein of Iraq is one example. Even if sympathy could not evolve with him, I am reasonably certain that he respected the impartiality and fairness of the UN mediators.

A personal touch sometimes can change the atmosphere to the positive. Swedish author Eyvind Johnson, writing about a successful personality in his Krilon trilogy, said that "It was only when he dared be personal that he started to conquer the world."

By this I do not mean using lighthearted jokes, which often can be misunderstood—rather I advise caution regarding cultural differences of humor. But expressions of interest or concern if fellow negotiators fall sick or lose a relative can be deeply appreciated.

I was once met at the airport by an Algerian colleague six years after our cooperation at the UN in New York. In the car to my hotel, he confided that he never forgot the letter I wrote him after his wife's near fatal car crash outside New York. That is why he personally had gone to the airport to receive me—not because we had navigated a number of resolutions through the UN General Assembly.

Jan Eliasson was Deputy Secretary-General of the United Nations from 2012 to 2016. He also served as mediator in several international conflicts, including as the UN Special Envoy for Darfur. He is now the Chair of the Governing Board of the Stockholm International Peace Research Institute (SIPRI).

Ban Ki-moon and Frank-Walter Steinmeier at the Munich Security Conference in February 2020. ▸

msc
msc
Police

The Diplomatic Toolbox

Wolfgang Ischinger

As an art, diplomacy does not lend itself easily to scientific exploration. Not unlike an actor on stage, the diplomat needs to be able to evoke or provoke the entire spectrum of human emotions—from the threat of conflict and the fear of war, through the safety of trusted partnership, to the exuberance of success and the glory of victory. But quite unlike the actor, the diplomat employs emotions not as an entertainment program, but as tools in the service of decisions about peace and war, about life and death. As such, diplomacy is possibly the deadliest of all forms of art. Nobody has circumscribed this better than W.H. Auden in his "Sonnets from China" (Sonnet XV), highlighting the potential consequences of the "conversations of the highly trained." As he concludes: "And on the issue of their charm depended, A land laid waste with all its young men slain, Its women weeping and its towns in terror."

Much has been made in recent years about the predominance that ought to be granted diplomacy vis-à-vis the use of military force. Those governments that clamor most loudly about the necessary predominance of diplomacy are often militarily weak, even incapable of defending their own territory. The other extreme can be found with countries with huge military capabilities. The United States provides the best example of a system in which the defense department plays a predominant role, sometimes relegating diplomatic considerations to the backseat. Yes indeed: If you are holding a pen, you will try to look for a piece of paper to write on. But if you are holding a hammer, your first instinct will be to look for nails to drive into the wood.

And while we are busy pondering how to teach the world to use the pen rather than the hammer as instruments of statecraft, the world around us appears to become rougher every day. We are confronted with an international system without unchallenged and responsible global leadership, a world without a rules-based international order, and with growing risks of great power and other conflicts. In this sense, the question of the optimal use of the range of instruments of statecraft to foster peace has emerged as an ever more important issue.

Against this background, I would like to offer a few humble suggestions regarding the practical use of the diplomatic toolbox. First, if you have the tool of diplomacy, use it! In recent years, the practice of German chancellors has increasingly been to ignore their own ambassadors when visiting foreign countries. Chancellor Merkel, for example, has often been accompanied abroad only by her own small circle of advisors. Keeping your own ambassador from offering advice and from participating in your meetings is not a good idea. Not only because the ambassador will in most cases be better equipped than visiting delegations to understand what is said or written between the lines; even more importantly, for the ambassador himself and his local role, being kept away from meetings will tend to undermine his professional effectiveness and his opportunity to enjoy the respect of the local leadership. In short, an unnecessarily humiliating and counterproductive practice.

If we insist, as we do, that we wish to strengthen the European Union and its credibility as a foreign policy actor, it should be a no-brainer for EU heads of government or foreign ministers to invite the local EU ambassador to participate in visits and meetings, and thus to highlight our determination to build not a national, but an EU foreign policy. In short: Smart use of the diplomatic toolbox would suggest having not only your own ambassador at your side, but also the most senior representative of the European Union.

An additional option provided by the diplomatic toolbox is the use of senior special envoys. The European Union, with twenty-seven current members, has the luxury of being able to call on a significant number of former presidents, prime ministers, chancellors, foreign ministers, and senior diplomats. But is this huge reservoir of experienced elder statesmen or women being used appropriately? Sadly, not really. In ten years of the Syrian tragedy, the European Union has found itself unable to appoint a senior figure to represent the European Union in discussions and negotiations, and to support the EU's high representative. A more systematic use of senior envoys might enhance the ability of the European Union to avoid standing on the sidelines, and instead to help shape the influence of negotiated outcomes.

One more example of the intelligent use of the diplomatic toolbox pertains to the conduct of diplomatic

◂ Wolfgang Ischinger with Joseph R. Biden Jr. at the Munich Security Conference in February 2018.

Munich Security Conference msc
Münchner Sicherheitskonferenz
BAYERISCHER HOF

negotiations. Heads of state and government, as well as their foreign ministers, should always resist the temptation to lead negotiations or to draft documents themselves—even if they believe that they are smarter or more experienced than their diplomatic staff. Two examples from the last ten or fifteen years may help to illustrate this point.

In early 2008, NATO ambassadors were unable to reach agreement in Brussels on a draft communiqué for the NATO summit to be held in Bucharest in April 2008. Instead of revising their instructions to the ambassadors, the heads of state and government personally negotiated the disputed text, finally reaching agreement in Bucharest during the summit itself, under enormous time pressure. Unfortunately, the text in question—about possible future membership of Ukraine and Georgia in NATO—ended up leaving more questions unanswered and creating more problems than any of the earlier draft versions considered at the ambassadorial level. Heads of state and government felt that their text was going to be somewhat acceptable to Russia because there was no date for future membership included in the text. From a Russian point of view, the opposite was true: this text looked like a clear provocation of Russia. The communiqué established that Ukraine and Georgia would end up being NATO members—totally unacceptable for Moscow. Some have argued that the lack of clarity of the NATO communiqué language even contributed to the military confrontation between Russia and Georgia in August of 2008.

A more recent example is the so-called "Minsk Agreement" of 2014/2015, personally negotiated by the leaders of France, Germany, Russia, and Ukraine. The Minsk Agreement has turned out not to be implementable. Neither Ukraine nor Russia have taken the required steps to reach agreement and end the Donbass conflict. The problem here is the following: If a text negotiated at the ambassadorial level is seen as unsatisfactory, there is always the option of taking the issue to the level of the foreign ministers or even to the heads of state and government. But if a text has been drafted by the heads of state and government themselves, there is no escalation or revision option left: bad use of the toolbox.

The successful use of the diplomatic toolbox depends on one key element: trust. With trust much can be achieved. Take the example of the peaceful unification of the two German states, which would have never worked without international leaders putting trust in West Germany and its leadership. On the other hand, without trust nothing works in international crisis negotiations. Even the most experienced leaders will not be able to reach sustainable agreements or negotiate successful peace arrangements without being able to trust each other. In other words, trust is the currency of diplomacy and thus the single most important ingredient in the diplomatic toolbox.

Moreover, it is important to note that, contrary to war fighting, smart diplomacy must never be defined as a zero-sum game in which victory through deterrence or defeat of the adversary is what matters. Instead, diplomacy seeks to obtain long-term benefits without humiliating the adversary on the other side of the table: a classic win-win definition. Young diplomats are often taught that you always meet twice in your diplomatic career—therefore, make sure no one seeks revenge against you when you meet next time.

Such advice may appear quite banal. Putting smart diplomacy into practice in a world of light-speed communication and social media disinformation is actually quite demanding. Above all, diplomacy requires the underrated ability to listen—and to understand not only what is said or written, but also what is either not said at all or only between the lines. Intercultural competence and comprehension, including language proficiency, is a key precondition for the successful conduct of the diplomatic mission.

Finally, personality matters. Diplomatic success is often the result not only of good planning and preparation, but also of the ability to pull your interlocutor into your magnetic orbit and offer him the opportunity to trust you. In military terms, diplomacy is the art of winning without producing casualties. In the twenty-first century, diplomacy therefore deserves to be in the driver's seat as the international community struggles to prevent war and to preserve a global order of peace, prosperity, and stability.

Wolfgang Ischinger has been Chairman of the Munich Security Conference since 2008. Passing the baton to Christoph Heusgen after the Munich Security Conference 2022, he will continue to serve as President of the Foundation Council of the Munich Security Conference Foundation. As a German diplomat, he served in various roles, including as State Secretary from 1998 to 2001, German Ambassador to the United States from 2001 to 2006 and to the United Kingdom from 2006 to 2008. His most recent book, *World in Danger. Germany and Europe in an Uncertain Time,* was published in 2020.

◂ Angela Merkel and Wolfgang Ischinger at the Munich Security Conference in February 2019.

5 Addendum

Acknowledgments

It is often said that it takes a village to raise a child. To compile and realize this book almost took a city. We are enormously grateful and indebted to all its citizens and will happily pick out a few who have been particularly helpful over the last few months.

Naturally, our greatest thanks must go to all contributors (and their staff) who took time out of their busy schedules to reflect on the art of diplomacy and share so many insightful anecdotes with us. Some of them followed our detailed instructions to the point of perfection, others proved their creativity by totally ignoring them. We love the result and hope you will too.

We would also like to thank our partners at Econ Verlag and Bonnier Media. Jürgen Diessl enthusiastically supported the idea from the beginning and Marco Krönfeld actually made it happen. The contributions to the book immensely benefited from the comments and editorial skills of Rick Madsen, our copy editor, and Nikolas Bertheau, who translated some of the contributions into English. We are also grateful to Alan Fortuna for smoothly managing the copyediting process and to Theodor Bayer-Eynck for typesetting and layout.

Diplomacy is an art—and so is photography. We are thrilled that this book has become a piece of art itself through the inclusion of so many photographs taken by the MSC's own "court photographer" and art director Michael Kuhlmann. His photos have shaped the public perception of the MSC for the last decade and we very much hope that they will continue to do so for many decades to come.

We would like to thank the Munich Security Conference Foundation for supporting this project.

Last but not least, we owe an immense debt of gratitude to the entire team of the Munich Security Conference. Our colleagues regularly make possible the impossible and this is particularly true for our special forces team led by Ulrike Strauss and Nardine Luca. Uli and Nardine kept this project on track, sent countless friendly reminders to our authors (and even more to us), and made sure that this book (almost) appeared on time. How they kept a straight face through it all is beyond us.

Finally, thanks to Wolfgang Ischinger for the inspiration—for a lot of what we do and for this book in particular. It is, quite obviously, dedicated to him and the type of diplomacy he stands for.

Berlin and Munich, November 2021
T.B. and B.F.

Image Sources

8-9	MSC/Michael Kuhlmann
10	MSC/Michael Kuhlmann
13	MSC/Michael Kuhlmann
16	MSC/Michael Kuhlmann
18-19	MSC/Michael Kuhlmann
20	MSC/Michael Kuhlmann
22	MSC/Michael Kuhlmann
24	MSC/Michael Kuhlmann
26	MSC/Michael Kuhlmann
32	MSC/Michael Kuhlmann
35	MSC/Michael Kuhlmann
36	MSC/Michael Kuhlmann, Henning Schacht
38	MSC/Michael Kuhlmann
42-43	MSC/Michael Kuhlmann
44	MSC/Michael Kuhlmann
46	MSC/Michael Kuhlmann
48	MSC/Michael Kuhlmann
50-51	MSC/Michael Kuhlmann
52	MSC/Michael Kuhlmann
55	MSC/Michael Kuhlmann
56-57	MSC/Michael Kuhlmann
58	MSC/Michael Kuhlmann
62	MSC/Michael Kuhlmann
65	MSC/Michael Kuhlmann
66	MSC/Michael Kuhlmann
68	MSC/Michael Kuhlmann
71	MSC/Michael Kuhlmann
72-73	MSC/Michael Kuhlmann
74	MSC/Michael Kuhlmann
76	MSC/Michael Kuhlmann
78	MSC/Michael Kuhlmann
82	MSC/Michael Kuhlmann
84	MSC/Michael Kuhlmann
86	MSC/Marc Müller
88	MSC/Michael Kuhlmann
91	MSC/Michael Kuhlmann
92	MSC/Michael Kuhlmann
96	MSC/Michael Kuhlmann
102	MSC/Michael Kuhlmann
104-105	MSC/Michael Kuhlmann
106	MSC/Michael Kuhlmann
111	MSC/Joerg Koch
112	MSC/Michael Kuhlmann
115	MSC/Michael Kuhlmann
116	MSC/Michael Kuhlmann
122-123	MSC/Michael Kuhlmann
124	MSC/Michael Kuhlmann
126-127	MSC/Michael Kuhlmann
128	MSC/Karl-Josef Hildenbrand
132	MSC/Michael Kuhlmann
134	Henny Ray Abrams/Getty Images
136	MSC/Michael Kuhlmann
140-141	MSC/Michael Kuhlmann
142	MSC/Michael Kuhlmann
145	MSC/Michael Kuhlmann
146	MSC/Michael Kuhlmann
148	MSC/Daniel Karmann
150	MSC/Michael Kuhlmann
157	MSC/Michael Kuhlmann
158-159	MSC/Michael Kuhlmann
160	MSC/Michael Kuhlmann
162	Bayerische Staatskanzlei
164	MSC/Michael Kuhlmann
166	MSC/Michael Kuhlmann
168	MSC/Michael Kuhlmann
170	MSC/Michael Kuhlmann
172	MSC/Matthias Balk
174	MSC/Michael Kuhlmann
179	MSC/Michael Kuhlmann
180	MSC/Michael Kuhlmann
188	MSC/Michael Kuhlmann
194	MSC/Michael Kuhlmann
197	MSC/Michael Kuhlmann
198	MSC/Michael Kuhlmann
204	MSC/Michael Kuhlmann
210	MSC/Michael Kuhlmann
213	MSC/Michael Kuhlmann
214-215	MSC/Michael Kuhlmann
216	MSC/Michael Kuhlmann
218	MSC/Michael Kuhlmann
220	MSC/Michael Kuhlmann
222	MSC/Daniel Karmann
224	MSC/Michael Kuhlmann
226	MSC/Alexander Koerner
234	MSC/Michael Kuhlmann
237	MSC/Michael Kuhlmann
240	MSC/Harald Dettenborn
246	MSC/Thomas Niedermueller
248	MSC/Michael Kuhlmann
252	MSC/Michael Kuhlmann
254	Aurelien Meunier/Getty Images
258	MSC/Michael Kuhlmann
260	MSC/Michael Kuhlmann
264	MSC/Michael Kuhlmann
266	MSC/Lennart Preiss
268	Srgjan Kerim/Private
271	MSC/Michael Kuhlmann
272	MSC/Michael Kuhlmann
275	MSC/Michael Kuhlmann
276	MSC/Michael Kuhlmann
278	Stan Honda/Getty Images
281	MSC/Michael Kuhlmann
282	MSC/Michael Kuhlmann
284	MSC/Michael Kuhlmann

286	MSC/Michael Kuhlmann
290-291	MSC/Sebastian Zwez
292	MSC/Michael Kuhlmann
296	MSC/Michael Kuhlmann
299	MSC/Tobias Kleinschmidt
300	MSC/Michael Kuhlmann
304	MSC/Michael Kuhlmann
307	MSC/Michael Kuhlmann
308	MSC/Michael Kuhlmann
312	MSC/Michael Kuhlmann
314-315	MSC/Michael Kuhlmann
316	MSC/Michael Kuhlmann
323	MSC/Michael Kuhlmann
324	MSC/Michael Kuhlmann
326	MSC/Michael Kuhlmann
328	MSC/Michael Kuhlmann
332-333	MSC/Michael Kuhlmann
334	MSC/Michael Kuhlmann
336-337	MSC/Michael Kuhlmann
338	MSC/Lukas Barth
345	MSC/Lennart Preiss
346	MSC/Michael Kuhlmann
352	MSC/Marc Müller
360	MSC/Michael Kuhlmann
362	MSC/Michael Kuhlmann
365	MSC/Michael Kuhlmann
366	MSC/Lennart Preiss
368	MSC/Michael Kuhlmann
376-377	MSC/Lukas Schulze
390-391	MSC/Michael Kuhlmann

Photo Captions

8-9	Angela Merkel at the Munich Security Conference in February 2019.
18-19	Munich Strategy Retreat in Heiligendamm in October 2021.
42-43	Wolfgang Ischinger at the Munich Security Conference in February 2019.
50-51	MSC Concert and Panel Discussion at the Munich Security Conference in February 2020.
56-57	MSC Core Group Meeting in Cairo in October 2019.
72-73	MSC Core Group Meeting in Washington, DC, in May 2017.
104-105	MSC Core Group Meeting in Vienna in June 2015.
122-123	Fu Ying and Henry Kissinger at the MSC Core Group Meeting in Washington, DC, in May 2017.
126-127	MSC Core Group Meeting in Beijing in November 2016.
140-141	John McCain at the MSC Core Group Meeting in Washington, DC, in May 2017.
158-159	Joseph R. Biden Jr., Angela Merkel, and Emmanuel Macron with Wolfgang Ischinger during the MSC Special Edition in February 2021.
214-215	Emmanuel Macron and Wolfgang Ischinger at the Munich Security Conference in February 2020.
290-291	New START Treaty: Sergey Lavrov and Hillary Clinton at the Munich Security Conference in February 2011.
314-315	MSC Core Group Meeting in Addis Ababa in April 2016.
332-333	MSC at Tana Forum in Bahir Dar in May 2019.
336-337	MSC at NATO Engages: The Alliance at 70 in Washington, DC, in April 2019.
376-377	Wang Yi with Wolfgang Ischinger at the Munich Security Conference in February 2020.
390-391	MSC Conversation on the Future of German Foreign and Security Policy in Berlin in June 2021.

Munich Security Conference msc
Münchner Sicherheitskonferenz
Munich Security Conference msc
Münchner Sicherheitskonferenz

BAYERISCHER HOF
Munich Security Conference msc
Münchner Sicherheitskonferenz

Endnotes

Page 8
Speak Softly and Carry a Big Book
Tobias Bunde and Benedikt Franke

1 Roosevelt, then William McKinley's vice president, first used this proverb in 1901, addressing an audience at the Minnesota State Fair. As president, he would repeatedly take it up again. See Eliot A. Cohen, *The Big Stick. The Limits of Soft Power & the Necessity of Military Force*, New York: Basic Books, 2016, ix.

Page 26
The Utility of Ambassadors
Robert Cooper

1 The interested reader should google: "You meaner beauties of the night."
2 That is, the five permanent members of the UN Security Council, plus Germany.
3 Joint Comprehensive Programme of Action.
4 Sorry that there are no women! This is ten or fifteen years ago: now the British ambassadors in Washington, New York, Beijing, and Moscow are all women.
5 Later Peter turned respectable, serving as EU ambassador in Skopje, Sarajevo, and Geneva.

Page 38
The Language of Power
Josep Borrell Fontelles

1 See Robert Kagan, *The Jungle Grows Back: America and Our Imperiled World*, New York: Knopf, 2018.
2 See Anu Bradford, *The Brussels Effect. How the European Union Rules the World*, Oxford: Oxford University Press, 2020.

Page 44
The Power of Language
Jasmine El-Gamal

1 Barack Obama, "Remarks by the President to the White House Press Corps," August 20, 2012, https://obamawhitehouse.archives.gov/the-press-office/2012/08/20/remarks-president-white-house-press-corps.
2 Quoted in Patrick Wintour, "John Kerry Gives Syria Week to Hand Over Chemical Weapons or Face Attack," *The Guardian*, September 9, 2013, https://www.theguardian.com/world/2013/sep/09/us-syria-chemical-weapons-attack-john-kerry.

Page 66
Back-Channel Diplomacy
Karl Kaiser

1 Quoted in Hans Monath, "Zankapfel Kissinger. Der Ex-Außenminister der USA wird Namenspatron an der Universität Bonn. Daran scheiden sich die Geister," *Der Tagesspiegel*, June 2, 2014; author's translation, emphasis added.
2 See Henry A. Kissinger, "Memorial Remarks for Egon Bahr," September 17, 2015, https://www.henryakissinger.com/remembrances/memorial-remarks-for-egon-bahr/.

Page 74
Track Two Diplomacy
Sam Nunn

1 See Des Browne, Igor Ivanov, Wolfgang Ischinger, and Sam Nunn, "Building Mutual Security in the Euro-Atlantic Region: Report Prepared for Presidents, Prime Ministers, Parliamentarians, and Publics," Washington, DC: Nuclear Threat Initiative, April 3, 2013, https://www.nti.org/analysis/articles/building-mutual-security-euro-atlantic-region-report-prepared-presidents-prime-ministers-parliamentarians-and-publics/.
2 For more information on the EASLG, see http://www.nti.org/EASLG.

Page 76
The Younger Generation
Desmond Browne

1 See "Younger Generation Leaders Network on Euro-Atlantic Security." Available at: https://www.europeanleadershipnetwork.org/networks/ygln/.

Page 78
People's Diplomacy
Izumi Nakamitsu

1 Dag Hammarskjöld, "At UN Correspondents Association Luncheon in His Honor at the Beginning of His Second Term, New York, April 9, 1958," in *Public Papers of the Secretaries General of the United Nations. Vol. 4: 1958-1960*, Dag Hammarskjöld, ed. Andrew Cordier and Wilder Foote (New York: Columbia University Press, 2010), 63–64.

Page 80
Choosing the Right Historical Analogies
Ivan Krastev

1 One can easily imagine that if a mass political protest had erupted in Moscow in the year 2017 (the centenary of the Bolshevik revolution), we would have been tempted to believe that history had yet again changed its course and our view of what was happening on the streets would have been dramatically shaped by the

books about Lenin, Stalin, and Trotsky that topped the bestsellers lists.
2 Richard E. Neustadt and Ernest R. May, *Thinking in Time: The Uses of History for Decision-Makers*, New York: The Free Press, 1986.
3 See Barbara Tuchman, *The Guns of August*, New York: Macmillan, 1962.
4 Robert F. Kennedy, *Thirteen Days: A Memoir of the Cuban Missile Crisis*, New York: W. W. Norton, 1969, 127.

Page 88
Securing Fragile Peace
Charles Kupchan

1 See Richard N. Haass and Charles A. Kupchan, "The New Concert of Powers. How to Prevent Catastrophe and Promote Stability in a Multipolar World," Foreign Affairs, March 23, 2021, https://www.foreignaffairs.com/articles/world/2021-03-23/new-concert-powers; and Richard N. Haass and Charles A. Kupchan, "A Concert of Powers for a Global Era," Project Syndicate, March 25, 2021, https://www.project-syndicate.org/commentary/concert-of-powers-for-global-era-by-richard-haass-and-charles-a-kupchan-2021-03.

Page 92
Pursuing Diplomacy in a G-Zero World
Ian Bremmer

1 Charles P. Kindleberger, *The World in Depression, 1929-1939. 40th Anniversary Edition*, Berkeley: University of California Press, 2013, 292.
2 Ian Bremmer and David Gordon, "G-Zero," *Foreign Policy*, January 7, 2011.
3 Jackie Calmes and Steven Lee Myers, "Divisions Aside, U.S. and China Moving Closer; Agreement Is Elusive on Cyberspying," *The New York Times*, June 9, 2013.
4 "Coronavirus (COVID-19) Vaccinations," Our World in Data, December 11, 2021, https://ourworldindata.org/covid-vaccinations.
5 "Text of Havel's Speech to Congress," *The Washington Post*, February 22, 1990.
6 *"Where Is the G7 Headed?"* Council on Foreign Relations, June 14, 2021, https://www.cfr.org/backgrounder/where-g7-headed.
7 George H. W. Bush, "Address Before a Joint Session of the Congress on the Persian Gulf Crisis and the Federal Budget Deficit," Washington, DC, September 11, 1990, https://bush41library.tamu.edu/archives/public-papers/2217; Wolfgang Ischinger, "Foreword," in: Tobias Bunde et al., "Munich Security Report 2020: Westlessness," Munich: Munich Security Conference, 2020, https://doi.org/10.47342/IAQX5691, 5.
8 Wolfgang Ischinger, *World in Danger: Germany and Europe in an Uncertain Time*, Washington, DC: Brookings Institution Press, 2020, 233.

Page 106
Putting Ourselves in Others' Shoes
Sigmar Gabriel

1 "Munich Security Conference Named 'Best Think Tank Conference'," January 29, 2021, https://securityconference.org/en/news/full/best-think-tank-conference/. See James G. McGann, "2020 Global Go To Think Tank Index Report," Think Tanks and Civil Society Program, University of Pennsylvannia, January 28, 2021, https://repository.upenn.edu/think_tanks/18/.
2 Julian Reichelt, "Weltpolitik mit dem Charme eines Skilehrers," *Bild*, February 14, 2019, https://www.bild.de/politik/inland/politik-inland/wolfgang-ischinger-weltpolitik-mit-dem-charme-des-skilehrers-60151418.bild.html.
3 On the origins of the term, see "Q. Who Originated the Term VUCA (Volatility, Uncertainty, Complexity and Ambiguity)?," U.S. Army Heritage & Education Center, May 7, 2019, https://usawc.libanswers.com/faq/84869.
4 Wolfgang Ischinger, *World in Danger. Germany and Europe in an Uncertain Time*, Washington, DC: Brookings Institution Press, 2020.
5 Vladimir Putin, "Speech in the Bundestag of the Federal Republic of Germany," September 25, 2001, http://en.kremlin.ru/events/president/transcripts/21340.
6 Vladimir Putin, "Speech and the Following Discussion at the Munich Security Conference on Security Policy," February 10, 2007, http://en.kremlin.ru/events/president/transcripts/24034.

Page 112
Keeping Communication Channels Open
Nora Müller

1 W.H. Lawrence, "Churchill Urges Patience in Coping with Red Dangers," *The New York Times*, June 27, 1954.
2 "USA/China: Ein harter und direkter Schlagabtausch," https://www.dw.com/de/usa-china-harter-schlagabtausch-alaska/a-56935964.
3 Michael Thumann, "Wie eine neue Ostpolitik aussehen könnte," https://www.zeit.de/politik/2021-07/ostpolitik-eu-russland-deutschland-wladimir-putin-nato-cyberwar.
4 "Remarks by President Biden in Press Conference," The White House Briefing Room, June 16, 2021, https://

www.whitehouse.gov/briefing-room/speeches-remarks/2021/06/16/remarks-by-president-biden-in-press-conference-4/.

5 Thomas Wright, "Order from Chaos: The US and China Finally Get Real with Each Other," https://www.brookings.edu/blog/order-from-chaos/2021/03/22/the-us-and-china-finally-get-real-with-each-other/.

6 Andrew H. Kydd, "Trust and Mistrust in International Relations," https://press.princeton.edu/books/paperback/9780691133881/trust-and-mistrust-in-international-relations.

7 Samm Sacks and Anne-Marie Slaughter, "The Broader Dialogue the US-China Relationship Needs," https://www.channelnewsasia.com/commentary/us-china-relationship-cooperation-conflict-alaska-anchorage-196436.

8 Matthias Gebauer and Christoph Schult, "Konflikte in Zeiten von Corona: Kontaktlose Diplomatie," https://www.spiegel.de/politik/deutschland/konflikte-in-zeiten-von-corona-kontaktlose-diplomatie-a-b7c65940-a540-49db-a38e-0ba4f477b7cc.

9 Samm Sacks and Anne-Marie Slaughter, "The Broader Dialogue the US-China Relationship Needs," https://www.channelnewsasia.com/commentary/us-china-relationship-cooperation-conflict-alaska-anchorage-196436.

10 See https://www.koerber-stiftung.de/en/munich-young-leaders.

Page 116
Promoting Mutual Understanding between China and the West
Fu Ying

1 See "Panel Discussion: 'America, Europe, and Asia,'" February 1, 2014, https://securityconference.org/en/medialibrary/asset/panel-discussion-america-europe-and-asia-1215-01-02-2014/.

2 See "Statement and Discussion with Wang Yi," February 15, 2020, https://securityconference.org/en/medialibrary/asset/statement-and-discussion-20200215-1245/.

3 See "Speaker Pelosi Remarks at Munich Security Conference," February 14, 2020, https://www.speaker.gov/newsroom/21420-1.

4 Ibid.

5 Ibid.

6 Ibid.

7 Ibid.

8 Ibid.

9 Ibid.

10 Ibid.

11 See Tobias Bunde et al., "Munich Security Report 2020: Westlessness," Munich: Munich Security Conference, February 2020, https://doi.org/10.47342/IAQX5691.

Page 136
Not Giving Up on Democracy and Equality in the Middle East
Tawakkol Karman

1 Condoleezza Rice, "Remarks at the American University in Cairo," June 20, 2005, https://2001-2009.state.gov/secretary/rm/2005/48328.htm.

Page 146
Diplomacy at the MSC in 2038
Anne-Marie Slaughter

1 See "History of the Munich Security Conference," https://securityconference.org/en/about-us/history/.

2 Ibid.

3 See Jean-Dominique Morency, Éric Caron Malenfant and Samuel MacIsaac, "Immigration and Diversity: Population Projections for Canada and its Regions, 2011 to 2036," Statistics Canada, January 25, 2017, https://www150.statcan.gc.ca/n1/pub/91-551-x/91-551-x2017001-eng.htm.

4 See Gianmarco Ottaviano, "How Does Immigration Affect Trade in Services?," World Economic Forum, June 18, 2015, https://www.weforum.org/agenda/2015/06/how-does-immigration-affect-trade-in-services/.

Page 148
Recalibrating Western Ambition
Thomas Kleine-Brockhoff

1 Fritz Stern, *Kulturpessimismus als politische Waffe*, Bern/Stuttgart: Scherz, 1963, 1–15.

Page 150
Overcoming Westlessness
Tobias Bunde

1 This contribution builds on my introductory essays to the Munich Security Reports 2019, 2020, and 2021, as well as the readout from the MSC Special Edition in 2021. See Tobias Bunde et al., "Munich Security Report 2019: The Great Puzzle – Who Will Pick Up the Pieces?," Munich: Munich Security Conference, February 2019, https://doi.org/10.47342/RYTY8045; Tobias Bunde et al., "Munich Security Report 2020: Westlessness," Munich: Munich Security Conference, February 2020, https://doi.org/10.47342/IAQX5691; Tobias Bunde et al., "Munich Security Report 2021: Between States of Matter –

Competition and Cooperation," München: Münchner Sicherheitskonferenz (MSC), June 2021, https://doi.org/10.47342/CYPE1056; Tobias Bunde, "Beyond Westlessness: A Readout From the MSC Special Edition 2021," Munich: Munich Security Conference, February 2021, https://doi.org/10.47342/NLUJ4791.

2 Roger Cohen, "Munich or a Requiem for the West," *The New York Times*, February 15, 2019, https://perma.cc/KW8L-QPNA.

3 See Toluse Olorunnipa et al., "G-7 Summit Ends with Little Consensus amid Trump's Mixed Messaging on the Trade War," *The Washington Post*, August 26, 2019, https://perma.cc/9K75-LBFG.

4 "Emmanuel Macron in His Own Words (English)," *The Economist*, November 7, 2019, https://perma.cc/9PXT-BQTA.

5 Bunde et al., "Munich Security Report 2020: Westlessness," 6.

6 Frank-Walter Steinmeier, "Opening of the Munich Security Conference," Munich, February 14, 2020, https://perma.cc/6PRW-SH8B.

7 David E. Sanger and Steven Erlanger, "'The West Is Winning,' Pompeo Said. The West Wasn't Buying It," *The New York Times*, February 15, 2020, https://perma.cc/D2MG-98SR.

8 Kang Kyung-wha, "Panel Discussion 'Westlessness in the World: Multilateralism in a Changing International Order,'" Munich: Munich Security Conference, February 14, 2020, https://perma.cc/C5YB-43E8.

9 See the comments by Indian Minister of External Affairs Subrahmanyam Jaishankar at the same panel. A transcript is available at the website of the Indian Ministry of External Affairs: https://mea.gov.in/Speeches-Statements.htm?dtl/32483. Jaishankar defined "Westfulness" as an era in which "the West was so sure that it would sort of extend into infinity. That it actually didn't cultivate broader constituencies of support in the rest of the world." According to him, the West would do well to "look beyond the alliances and work with partners beyond alliances, who will come from a different place with a different history."

10 Cooperation among liberal democracies in the face of authoritarian threats has been the core theme of the Munich Security Conference since its beginnings as "Wehrkundetagung" in the early 1960s. See the contributions in Wolfgang Ischinger, with Tobias Bunde, Antje Lein-Struck, and Adrian Oroz (eds.), *Toward Mutual Security: Fifty Years of Munich Security Conference*, Göttingen: Vandenhoeck & Ruprecht, 2014.

11 Jeremy Cliffe, "The Return of the West: Can the G7 Nations Rebuild a Global Alliance?," *The New Statesman*, June 2, 2021, https://perma.cc/NZ55-E2DE.

12 Andreas Kluth, "If Aukus, China and Russia Don't Take Europe Seriously, Guess Who's to Blame," *Bloomberg Opinion*, September 21, 2021, https://perma.cc/9WM8-3C5S. See also Jeremy Cliffe, "The Return of the West": "With the subsequent 12 months culminating in the storming of the Capitol in Washington, DC in January 2021 – a sort of grotesque parody of the liberal democratic revolutions of 1989 – any doubts about the reality of Westlessness were laid to rest."

13 See, for example, Benjamin Herborth and Gunther Hellmann, "Introduction: Uses of the West," in Gunter Hellmann and Benjamin Herborth (eds.), *Uses of the West: Security and the Politics of Order*, Cambridge: Cambridge University Press, 2017, 1–9, 1: "In everyday political language 'the West' is usually understood to refer to a grouping of states and societies in Europe and North America, which share a few characteristics, are tightly connected among each other, and have amassed the overwhelming bulk of military capabilities, economic power, and cultural attraction. Defying geographical common sense, however, Australia, New Zealand, and possibly even Japan are widely considered to be 'Western' outliers in the Pacific. While the idea of 'the West' as well as the array of images, practices, and institutions associated with it did originate in Western Europe, today the imaginary dimension of 'the West' has taken on a life of its own."

14 See in detail Bunde et al., "Munich Security Report 2020: Westlessness," 6–10.

15 Robert Kagan, "Our Constitutional Crisis Is Already Here," *The Washington Post*, September 23, 2021, https://perma.cc/52CX-4ECB. See also Steven Levitsky and Daniel Ziblatt, "The Biggest Threat to Democracy Is the GOP Stealing the Next Election," *The Atlantic*, July 9, 2021, https://perma.cc/U8S4-7AKC.

16 Bunde et al., "Munich Security Report 2021: Between States of Matter – Competition and Cooperation," 17.

17 Joseph R. Biden, "Remarks by President Biden at the 2021 Virtual Munich Security Conference," Washington, DC, February 19, 2021, https://perma.cc/WRV5-9ZEM.

18 See https://freedomhouse.org/country/hungary/freedom-world/2020.

19 See, for example, Kishore Mahbubani, "The West's Incompetent Response to the Pandemic Will Hasten the Power-Shift to the East," *The Economist*, April 20, 2020, https://perma.cc/WD6W-X2YV.

20 Anne Applebaum, "The West Has Lost Confidence in Its Values. Syria Is Paying the Price," *The Washington Post*, September 6, 2019.

21 See Evan Hill and Christiaan Triebert, "12 Hours. 4

Syrian Hospitals Bombed. One Culprit: Russia," *The New York Times*, October 13, 2019, https://nyti.ms/2IM8M21. At the end of last year, NYT journalists published additional in-depth evidence. See Malachy Browne et al., "Hospitals and Schools Are Being Bombed in Syria. A U.N. Inquiry Is Limited. We Took a Deeper Look," *The New York Times*, December 31, 2019, https://perma.cc/JK4R-VF8E. See Bunde et al., "Munich Security Report 2020: Westlessness," 12–17, for more examples.

22 David Miliband, "The New Arrogance of Power: Global Politics in the Age of Impunity," International Rescue Committee, 19, 20, and 21 June 2019, https://perma.cc/J4CM-FN3V.

23 See Wolfgang Ischinger's comments at the Aurora Dialogues in Berlin. Global Perspectives Initiative, "Aurora Dialogues Berlin 2018. Humanity in a Fragile World. Partnering for Change. A Summary of the Results," February 2019, https://bit.ly/GPI-FollowUP, 11; Tom Ginsburg, "Authoritarian International Law?," *American Journal of International Law* 114, no. 2 (April 2020), 221–260.

24 Quoted in "A Transatlantic Conversation on the Geopolitical and Business Effects of COVID-19," Munich Security Conference, April 28, 2020, https://perma.cc/RD59-5Z8D.

25 Claus Kleber, "ZDF heute journal," *ZDF*, February 19, 2021, https://perma.cc/7F7A-96RQ.

26 For a more detailed readout from the MSC Special Edition, see Bunde, "Beyond Westlessness."

27 See Andrew Small, "Europe's China Deal: How Not to Work with the Biden Administration," *ECFR Commentary*, January 21, 2021, https://perma.cc/G7DZ-QRCR; Nicholas Vinocur, "Why Europe's China Deal Will Poison Transatlantic Relations," *Politico*, January 14, 2021, https://perma.cc/K4W4-4XXE. For a few proposals on how to develop a common transatlantic strategy on China, see Wolfgang Ischinger and Joseph S. Nye, Jr. (eds.), "Mind the Gap: Priorities for Transatlantic China Policy – Report of the Distinguished Reflection Group on Transatlantic China Policy," Munich, Berlin, and Washington, DC: Munich Security Conference, Mercator Institute for China Studies, and Aspen Strategy Group, July 2021, https://doi.org/10.47342/GXWK1490.

28 Matthew Karnitschnig, "Disbelief and Betrayal: Europe Reacts to Biden's Afghanistan 'Miscalculation,'" *Politico*, August 17, 2021, https://perma.cc/L5VV-397R.

29 Charles Michel, "The Chaotic Withdrawal in Afghanistan Forces Us to Accelerate Honest Thinking about European Defence," September 2, 2021, https://perma.cc/3FPL-8HFB.

30 See, for example, "China Is Betting that the West Is in Irreversible Decline," *The Economist*, March 31, 2021; Sabine Fischer and Angela Stanzel, "Afghanistan: The West Fails – a Win for China and Russia?," *SWP Comment 2021/C50*, September 22, 2021, doi:10.18449/2021C50.

31 National Intelligence Council, "Global Trends 2040: A More Contested World," Washington, DC: Office of the Director of National Intelligence, March 2021, https://www.dni.gov/files/images/globalTrends/GT2040/GlobalTrends_2040_for_web1.pdf, 110–111.

32 Joseph R. Biden, "Why America Must Lead Again: Rescuing U.S. Foreign Policy After Trump," *Foreign Affairs* 99, no. 2 (March/April 2020), 64–76, https://perma.cc/D9MX-NMPT.

33 Biden, "Remarks by President Biden at the 2021 Virtual Munich Security Conference," Boris Johnson, "Prime Minister's Speech at the Munich Security Conference: 19 February 2021," https://www.gov.uk/government/speeches/prime-ministers-speech-at-the-munich-security-conference-19-february-2021; Jens Stoltenberg, "NATO 2030: Future-Proofing the Alliance: Remarks by NATO Secretary General Jens Stoltenberg at the Munich Security Conference 2021 (Online Event)," February 19, 2021, https://perma.cc/SHY9-QL5L.

34 Carl Bildt, "China Is a Rising Digital Superpower. Europe and the U.S. Must Catch Up – Together," *The Washington Post*, February 1, 2021, https://perma.cc/BJG5JQTJ; Anders Fogh Rasmussen, "Building a Democratic High-Tech Alliance," *Project Syndicate*, March 29, 2021, https://perma.cc/R7QR-VEKE; Toomas H. Ilves, "Opinion: We Need a Global League to Protect against Cyberthreats to Democracy," *The Washington Post*, October 5, 2017, https://perma.cc/FKG6-82LU.

35 Patrick Wintour, "Boris Johnson to Visit India in January in Bid to Transform G7," *The Guardian*, December 15, 2020, https://perma.cc/Q96A-ZG93. On the origins of the D10, see Ash Jain, "Like-Minded and Capable Democracies. A New Framework for Advancing a Liberal World Order," New York: Council on Foreign Relations, January 2013, https://perma.cc/F4A3-42LG.

36 "Ergebnis der Sondierungen zwischen SPD, Bündnis 90/Die Grünen und FDP," Berlin, October 15, 2021, available at https://www.tagesschau.de/sondierungen-153.pdf, 12, author's translation.

37 Edward Fishman and Siddharth Mohandas, "A Council of Democracies Can Save Multilateralism: Boris Johnson's 'D-10' Is the Club the World Desperately Needs," *Foreign Affairs*, August 3, 2020, https://perma.cc/S3LV-XDB4.

38 Nahal Toosi, "Are You on the List? Biden's Democracy Summit Spurs Anxieties – and Skepticism," *Politico*, November 28, 2020, https://perma.cc/LYT3-F7ML.
39 James Goldgeier and Bruce W. Jentleson, "A Democracy Summit Is Not What the Doctor Ordered: America, Heal Thyself," *Foreign Affairs*, December 14, 2020, https://perma.cc/UN6Y-WWAE. But see Frances Z. Brown, Thomas Carothers, and Alex Pascal, "America Needs a Democracy Summit More Than Ever," *Foreign Affairs*, January 15, 2021, https://perma.cc/APU9-ACR6.
40 G. John Ikenberry, *A World Safe for Democracy: Liberal Internationalism and the Crises of Global Order*, New Haven: Yale University Press, 2020, xi.
41 Brands and Edel, "A Grand Strategy of Democratic Solidarity," *The Washington Quarterly* 44, no. 1 (Spring 2021), 29–47, 34.
42 Emmanuel Macron, "President Sets Out French Foreign Policy Goals," Paris: Ambassadors' Conference, August 27, 2019, https://perma.cc/XUS3-GKDK.
43 Rym Momtaz, "Macron: EU Shouldn't Gang Up on China With US," *Politico*, February 4, 2021, https://perma.cc/TJ3Z-UDLV.
44 Stuart Lau and Laurenz Gehrke, "Merkel Sides with Xi on Avoiding Cold War Blocs," *Politico*, January 26, 2021, https://perma.cc/5K4U-2QHK.
45 Goldgeier and Jentleson, "A Democracy Summit Is Not What the Doctor Ordered." See also Richard N. Haass and Charles A. Kupchan, "The New Concert of Powers. How to Prevent Catastrophe and Promote Stability in a Multipolar World," *Foreign Affairs*, March 23, 2021, https://perma.cc/3CBY-26VV; as well as Charles Kupchan's contribution to this volume.
46 Jeff Colgan and Robert Keohane, "The Liberal Order Is Rigged: Fix It Now or Watch It Wither," *Foreign Affairs* 96, no. 3 (May/June 2017), 36–44.
47 Hal Brands and Charles Edel, "A Grand Strategy of Democratic Solidarity," 40.

Page: 160
Developing a Weltpolitikfähigkeitsverlustvermeidungsstrategie
Timothy Garton Ash

1 A recording of the event is available at the MSC website: https://securityconference.org/en/medialibrary/asset/msc-kick-off-2019-in-berlin-1130-11-02-2019/.
2 See Tobias Bunde et al. "Munich Security Report 2020: Westlessness," Munich: Munich Security Conference, February 2020, https://doi.org/10.47342/IAQX5691.

Page: 164
Forging a Common European Strategic Culture
Franziska Brantner

1 Tobias Bunde et al., "Munich Security Report 2020: Westlessness," Munich: Munich Security Conference, 2020, https://doi.org/10.47342/IAQX5691, 6.
2 Angela Merkel, "Wir Europäer müssen unser Schicksal in unsere eigene Hand nehmen," *Handelsblatt*, May 28, 2017, https://www.handelsblatt.com/politik/deutschland/angela-merkel-wir-europaeer-muessen-unser-schicksal-in-unsere-eigene-hand-nehmen/19861340.html?ticket=ST-495496-dSMAc-9Q6EryCiiKGRdRr-ap6.
3 Emmanuel Macron, "Speech on New Initiative for Europe," September 26, 2017, https://www.elysee.fr/en/emmanuel-macron/2017/09/26/president-macron-gives-speech-on-new-initiative-for-europe.
4 Franco-German Parliamentary Assembly, "Beschluss vom 22. September 2020 zur Einsetzung einer Arbeitsgruppe 'Außen- und Verteidigungspolitik'," Document No 2020/12, https://www.bundestag.de/resource/blob/794758/f61889f82dd97a8d9b6bdb2afee82407/nr_2020_12-data.pdf.
5 Ursula von der Leyen, "Rede der Bundesministerin der Verteidigung Dr. Ursula von der Leyen auf der 54. Münchner Sicherheitskonferenz am 16. Februar 2018," https://www.bmvg.de/resource/blob/22178/909a56e9af7501819eba0563f9724109/20180216-download-eroeffnungsrede-deutsch-data.pdf.

Page 170
Reforming Germany's National Security Architecture
Boris Ruge

1 The context is worth noting: The SPD-Green coalition agreement of October 1998 called for "the Federal Security Council to be restored to its original coordinating role." Social Democratic Party of Germany and Alliance 90/The Greens, "Aufbruch und Erneuerung – Deutschlands Weg ins 21. Jahrhundert: Koalitionsvereinbarung zwischen der Sozialdemokratischen Partei Deutschlands und Bündnis90/Die GRÜNEN," http://library.fes.de/pdf-files/bibliothek/downl/koalitionsvertrag1998.pdf, 46.
2 Bundesregierung, "2016 White Paper on Security Policy and the Future of the Bundeswehr," Berlin: Federal Ministry of Defense, 2016, https:// perma.cc/82Z7-8437, 57.
3 Julianne C. Smith, "German Foreign Policy is Stuck in Neutral," *War on the Rocks*, February 18, 2019, https://warontherocks.com/2019/02/german-foreign-policy-

is-stuck-in-neutral/.

4 Tobias Bunde et al., "Zeitenwende | Wendezeiten: Special Edition of the Munich Security Report," Munich: Munich Security Conference, 2020, https://doi.org/10.47342/SBID8214, 159.

Page: 172
Navigating Propaganda and Social Media
Steven Erlanger

1 Steven Erlanger, "German Leader's Warning: War Plan Is a Huge Mistake," *The New York Times*, September 2, 2002, https://www.nytimes.com/2002/09/05/international/europe/german-leaders-warning-war-plan-is-a-huge-mistake.html.

Page 174
Mitigating Hybrid Threats
Teija Tiilikainen

1 See G. John Ikenberry, "The End of the Liberal World Order," *International Affairs* 94, no. 1 (2018): 7–23, 10; Katja Creutz et al., "The Changing Global Order and Its Implications for the EU," FIIA Report 59, Helsinki: Finnish Institute for International Affairs, March 2019, 29; Joseph R. Nye, *The Future of Power*, New York: Public Affairs, 2011, 114.

2 See for example Mark Galeotti, *Russian Political War. Moving Beyond the Hybrid*, London: Routledge, 2019. The origins of the concept are in "hybrid warfare," which was characterized by Frank Hoffman as "a range of different modes of warfare, including conventional capabilities, irregular tactics and formations, terrorist acts including indiscriminate violence and coercion, and criminal disorder." Frank Hoffman, "Conflict in the 21st Century: The Rise of Hybrid Wars," Arlington, VA: Potomac Institute for Policy Studies, 2007, 14.

3 Hanna Smith, "In the Era of Hybrid Threats: Power of the Powerful or Power of the 'Weak'?," Hybrid CoE Strategic Analysis 1, Helsinki: The European Centre of Excellence for Countering Hybrid Threats, October 2017, 5.

4 Brian Barry discusses the concept of the state in political philosophy. See Brian Barry and Marcel Wissenburg, "The Concept of the State in Political Philosophy," *European Political Science* 10 (2011), 92–102.

5 See Mark Galeotti, "Controlling Chaos: How Russia Manages Its Political War in Europe?," Policy Brief, London: European Council on Foreign Relations, 2017; Dmitri Trenin, "Russia's National Security Strategy: A Manifesto for a New Era," Moscow: Carnegie Moscow Center, 2021, 1; Niklas Nilsson et al., "Security Challenges in the Grey Zone: Hybrid Threats and Hybrid Warfare," in *Hybrid Warfare: Security and Asymmetric Conflict in International Relations*, ed. Mikael Weissmann et al. (London: I.B. Tauris, 2021), 1–18, 4.

6 Jukka Aukia, "China as a Hybrid Influencer: Non-state Actors as State Proxies," Hybrid CoE Research Report 1, Helsinki: The European Centre of Excellence for Countering Hybrid Threats, 2021, 14.

7 Aukia, "China as a Hybrid Influencer, 12; Anthony H. Cordesman, with the assistance of Grace Hwang, "Chronology of Possible Chinese Gray Area and Hybrid Warfare Operations, Working Draft, Washington, DC: Center for Strategic International Studies, September 28, 2020, 5.

8 See Rouzbeh Parsi and John Rydqvist, "Introduction: The Converging and Diverging Interests of Iran and the West," in *Iran and the West. Regional Interests and Global Controversies*, ed. Rouzbeh Parsi and John Rydqvist (Stockholm: FOI, 2011), 12–14.

9 See the "Mueller Report 2019" (Special Counsel Robert S. Mueller, III, "Report on the Investigation into Russian Interference in the 2016 Presidential Election," Washington, DC, 2019); "Covert Foreign Money: Financial Loopholes Exploited by Authoritarians to Fund Political Interference in Democracies," Washington, DC: German Marshall Fund, Alliance for Security Democracy, 2020, 6.

10 Kim Wijnja, "Countering Hybrid Threats: Does Strategic Culture Matter?," Defence Studies, online first, 2021, https://doi.org/10.1080/14702436.2021.1945452.

11 Aurel Sari, "Legal Resilience in an Era of Grey Zone Conflicts and Hybrid Threats," *Cambridge Review of International Affairs* 33, no. 6 (2020), 846–867; Aurel Sari, "Hybrid Threats and the Law: Building Legal Resilience," Hybrid CoE Research Report 3, Helsinki: The European Centre of Excellence for Countering Hybrid Threats, 2021.

12 Paul Stronsky and Richard Sokolsky, *Multipolarity in Practice: Understanding Russia's Engagement With Regional Institutions*, Washington, DC: Carnegie Endowment for International Peace, 2020.

13 Philip Remler, "Russia at the United Nations: Law, Sovereignty, and Legitimacy," Washington, DC: Carnegie Endowment for International Peace, 2020.

14 Gary D. Brown, "International Law and Cyber Conflict," in *Routledge Handbook of Cyber Security*, ed. Eneken Tikk and Mika Kerttunen (London: Routledge, 2020), 171.

15 John Raine, "War or Peace? Understanding the Grey Zone," International Institute for Strategic Studies, April 3, 2019; Mikael Weissman, "Hybrid Warfare and

Hybrid Threats Today and Tomorrow: Towards an Analytical Framework," *Journal on Baltic Security* 5 (2019), no. 1, 17–26.
16 "Joint Declaration by the President of the European Council, the President of the European Commission, and the Secretary General of the North Atlantic Treaty Organization," Warsaw, July 8, 2016.

Page 180
Understanding the Digitization of War
Toomas Hendrik Ilves
1 Richard Dawkins, *The Selfish Gene: 40th Anniversary Edition*, Oxford: Oxford University Press, 2016.
2 Wolfgang Ischinger, "It's Time to Security Proof the EU's Future," *Politico*, October 26, 2021, https://www.politico.eu/article/security-proof-eu-future/.
3 Ulrike Franke and José Ignacio Torreblanca, "Geo-Tech Politics: Why Technology Shapes European Power," ECFR Policy Brief, July 15, 2021, https://ecfr.eu/publication/geo-tech-politics-why-technology-shapes-european-power/.

Page 188
The Art of Deniability
Thomas Rid
1 This short piece is adapted from a longer, more tightly argued chapter, which will appear in Hal Brands, ed., *Makers of Modern Strategy*, 3rd ed. (Princeton: Princeton University Press, 2023).
2 Richard Helms, "Communist Forgeries," Committee on the Judiciary, U.S. Senate (Washington, DC: Government Printing Office, June 2, 1961).
3 https://web.archive.org/web/20150712001908/http://www.wikisaleaks.com/.
4 For a detailed account, see Thomas Rid, *Active Measures*, New York: FSG, 2020, chapter 13.
5 "Facebook takedowns reveal sophistication of Russian trolls," *AP*, March 12, 2020.
6 See, as an example, several presentations at the 2021 "CYBERWARCON" conference, held in Arlington, Virginia, on November 16, https://web.archive.org/web/20211020161336/https://www.cyberwarcon.com/2021-agenda.

Page 194
Treating Cyber Problems as Geopolitical Problems
Dmitri Alperovitch
1 "Remarks by President Obama and President Xi of the People's Republic of China in Joint Press Conference," September 25, 2015, https://obamawhitehouse.archives.gov/the-press-office/2015/09/25/remarks-president-obama-and-president-xi-peoples-republic-china-joint.

Page 198
Maintaining the Negotiating Edge in the Age of Tech-Geopolitics
Sorin Ducaru
1 Harold Nicolson, *Diplomacy*, Oxford: Oxford University Press, 1939.
2 See "Rudolf Kjellén and the Origin of Geopolitics," Center for Research on Geopolitics, April 21, 2015, https://geopoliticsresearch.wordpress.com/2015/04/21/rudolf-kjellen-and-the-origin-of-geopolitics/.
3 See "Paris Call for Trust and Security in Cyberspace," https://pariscall.international/en/.

Page 210
Paving the Way for Trusted Connectivity
Kersti Kaljulaid
1 See "The Tallinn Consensus on Trusted Connectivity," September 7, 2021, https://www.digitalsummit.ee/the-tallinn-consensus-on-trusted-connectivity/.
2 Editorial Board, "Opinion: Russia's Massive Hack Demands a Reckoning for U.S. Cyber Defenses," *The Washington Post*, December 16, 2020, https://www.washingtonpost.com/opinions/russia-solar-winds-hack-us-cyber-defenses/2020/12/16/e3bfabe8-3fd2-11eb-8bc0-ae155bee4aff_story.html.
3 David E. Sanger and Nicole Perlroth, "Pipeline Attack Yields Urgent Lessons About U.S. Cybersecurity," *The New York Times*, May 14, 2021, https://www.nytimes.com/2021/05/14/us/politics/pipeline-hack.html.
4 See Gallup, "Congress and the Public," https://news.gallup.com/poll/1600/congress-public.aspx; Rick Edmonds, "US Ranks Last among 46 Countries in Trust in Media, Reuters Institute Report Finds," *Poynter*, June 24, 2021, https://www.poynter.org/ethics-trust/2021/us-ranks-last-among-46-countries-in-trust-in-media-reuters-institute-report-finds/.
5 See "Carbis Bay G7 Summit Communiqué," June 13, 2021, https://www.whitehouse.gov/briefing-room/statements-releases/2021/06/13/carbis-bay-g7-summit-communique/.
6 See "Fact Sheet: President Biden and G7 Leaders Launch Build Back Better World (B3W) Partnership," June 12, 2021; and the website of the Australian Infrastructure Financing Facility for the Pacific, https://www.aiffp.gov.au/.
7 See "OECD and the Blue Dot Network," https://www.oecd.org/corporate/oecd-and-the-blue-dot-network.htm.
8 See "G20 Principles for Quality Infrastructure Invest-

ments," https://www.mof.go.jp/english/international_policy/convention/g20/annex6_1.pdf; "The Policy Framework for Investment (PFI)," https://www.oecd.org/investment/pfi.htm; "The Equator Principles," July 2020, https://equator-principles.com/wp-content/uploads/2021/02/The-Equator-Principles-July-2020.pdf.

9 See "Smart Connectivity," https://3seas.eu/about/smart-connectivity.

10 See "Priority Projects," https://3seas.eu/about/progressreport.

Page 216

Balancing the Geopolitical Power of Tech Companies

Marietje Schaake

1 See "Senator Asks How Facebook Remains Free, Mark Zuckerberg Smirks: 'We Run Ads,'" *NBC News*, April 10, 2018, https://youtu.be/n2H8wx1aBiQ; Andrew Griffin, "'Will You Commit to Ending Finsta': US Senator Sparks Panic and Confusion With Strange Question to Facebook Executive," *The Independent*, October 1, 2021, https://www.independent.co.uk/life-style/gadgets-and-tech/finsta-meaning-instagram-richard-blumenthal-b1930619.html.

2 See Christopher A. Thomas and Xander Wu, "How Global Tech Executives View U.S.-China Tech Competition," *Tech Stream*, February 25, 2021, https://www.brookings.edu/techstream/how-global-tech-executives-view-u-s-china-tech-competition/.

3 See Alex Hern and Dan Sabbagh, "Zuckerberg's Refusal to Testify Before UK MPs 'absolutely astonishing,'" *The Guardian*, March 27, 2018, https://www.theguardian.com/technology/2018/mar/27/facebook-mark-zuckerberg-declines-to-appear-before-uk-fake-news-inquiry-mps.

Page 220

Promoting a Comprehensive Understanding of Security

Achim Steiner

1 See Wolfgang Ischinger, "Mehr Eigenverantwortung für und in Europa," in Wolfgang Ischinger and Dirk Messner, eds., *Deutschlands neue Verantwortung: Die Zukunft der deutschen und europäischen Außen-, Entwicklungs- und Sicherheitspolitik*, Berlin: Econ, 2017. For more details see Tobias Bunde et al., "Zeitenwende | Wendezeiten: Special Edition of the Munich Security Report," Munich: Munich Security Conference, 2020, https://doi.org/10.47342/SBID8214, chapter 4.

Page 226

Making Sense of the Quantum World

Armen Sarkissian

1 Quantum computing uses the quantum properties of entanglement and superposition to process computations in parallel rather than one after another.

Page 234

Adapting Diplomatic Tools and Structures

Cathryn Clüver Ashbrook

1 See Harold Nicolson, *Diplomacy*, Oxford: Oxford University Press, 1939.

2 See Robert D. Putnam, "Diplomacy and Domestic Politics: The Logic of Two-Level Games," *International Organization* 42, 3 (Summer 1988), 427–460.

3 See David A. Lax and James K. Sebenius, *3-D Negotiation: Powerful Tools to Change the Game in Your Most Important Deals*, Cambridge, MA: Harvard Business Press, 2006.

4 Nicholas Burns, Marc Grossman, and Marcie Ries, "A U.S. Diplomatic Service for the 21st Century," Report, Cambridge, MA: Belfer Center for Science and International Affairs, November 2020, https://www.belfercenter.org/publication/us-diplomatic-service-21st-century.

5 See "Memorandum on Restoring Trust in Government Through Scientific Integrity and Evidence-Based Policymaking," Washington, DC: The White House, January 27, 2021, https://www.whitehouse.gov/briefing-room/presidential-actions/2021/01/27/memorandum-on-restoring-trust-in-government-through-scientific-integrity-and-evidence-based-policymaking/.

6 For more information, see https://frontline-negotiations.org/.

Page 286

Negotiating the New START Treaty

Rose Gottemoeller

1 The following paragraphs are reproduced by permission from Rose Gottemoeller, *Negotiating the New START Treaty*, Amherst, NY: Cambria Press, 2021, 189–194.

2 For an in-depth recollection of the negotiations, including the sessions in Geneva leading up to the New START Treaty, see Gottemoeller, *Negotiating the New START Treaty*.

3 Here ends the excerpt from *Negotiating the New START Treaty*.

Page 300

Paving the Way for a Robust Diplomatic Process

Thomas Greminger

1 More information on the Panel of Eminent Persons is available at https://www.osce.org/networks/pep.

2 Wolfgang Ischinger, "Foreword," in Panel of Eminent Persons, "Back to Diplomacy. Final Report and Recommendations of the Panel of Eminent Persons on European Security as a Common Project," OSCE: Vienna, 2015, https://www.osce.org/networks/205846, 2.

3 Panel of Eminent Persons, "Back to Diplomacy," 12.

4 Ischinger, "Foreword," 3.

5 More information on the Structured Dialogue is available at https://www.osce.org/structured-dialogue.

6 "U.S.-Russia Presidential Joint Statement on Strategic Stability," June 16, 2021, https://www.whitehouse.gov/briefing-room/statements-releases/2021/06/16/ u-s-russia-presidential-joint-statement-on-strategic-stability/.

7 Ischinger, "Foreword," 3.

8 See Thomas Greminger, "Strengthening Cooperative Security in Difficult Times: Three Years as Secretary General of the OSCE (2017-2020) a Critical Appraisal," in *Multilateralism in Transition: Challenges and Opportunities for the OSCE*, ed. Simon J. A. Mason and Lisa Watanabe (Zurich: Center for Security Studies at ETH Zürich, 2021), https://doi.org/10.3929/ethz-b-000489477, 22–84.

Page 328

Moving from Enmity to Accountability

Ottilia Anna Maunganidze

1 "Sudan Cabinet Unanimous on Bill to Join Rome Statute of ICC," *Dabanga*, August 3, 2021, https://www.dabangasudan.org/en/all-news/article/sudan-cabinet-unanimous-on-bill-to-join-rome-statute-of-icc.

2 See Ottilia Anna Maunganidze, "Will Justice Rise With Al-Bashir's Fall?," *ISS Today*, April 16, 2019, https://issafrica.org/iss-today/will-justice-rise-with-al-bashirs-fall.

3 Ottilia Anna Maunganidze & Max du Plessis, "Independent Judges at the ICC Confirm that Al-Bashir Should be Arrested for Genocide," *ISS Today*, July 15, 2010, https://issafrica.org/iss-today/independent-judges-at-the-icc-confirm-that-al-bashir-should-be-arrested-for-genocide.

4 Theresa Squatrito, "Judicial Diplomacy: International Courts and Legitimation," *Review of International Studies* 47, no. 1 (2021): 64–84.

5 Sudan Council of Ministers, "Merkel: Germany Will Be a Partner With Sudan," February 2020, http://www.sudan.gov.sd/index.php/en/home/news_details/1933.

6 Mohammed Amin, "Germany President in Sudan After 30 Years - German Leader Urges International Community to Help Sudan," *Anadolu Agency*, February 29, 2020, https://www.aa.com.tr/en/africa/germany-president-in-sudan-after-30-years-/1749319.

7 "Visit to the Republic of the Sudan," February 27, 2020, https://www.bundespraesident.de/SharedDocs/Berichte/EN/Frank-Walter-Steinmeier/2020/200226-28-Visit-Sudan.html.

8 "Germany Pledges €150 Million in Aid for Sudan," *Deutsche Welle*, June 25, 2020, https://www.dw.com/en/germany-pledges-150-million-in-aid-for-sudan/a-53940760.

9 See for example, "Action Fiche for the Implementation of the Horn of Africa Window EUTF05 – HoA – SD –38," https://ec.europa.eu/international-partnerships/system/files/eutf-hoa-sd-38-sudan-tcf_en.pdf.

10 European Commission, "Sudan," https://ec.europa.eu/international-partnerships/where-we-work/sudan_en.

11 "Diplomacy Could Unlock Aid for Sudan," *Borgen Magazine*, November 23, 2020, https://www.borgenmagazine.com/aid-for-sudan/.

12 Robbie Gramer, "Top Counterterrorism Envoy Could Be First U.S. Ambassador to Sudan in Decades," *Foreign Policy*, July 30, 2021, https://foreignpolicy.com/2021/07/30/biden-sudan-ambassador-east-africa-diplomacy/.

13 Maram Mahdi & Ottilia Anna Maunganidze, "Why Has Sudan Decided to Hand Over Al-Bashir to the ICC?," Institute for Security Studies, https://issafrica.org/iss-today/why-has-sudan-decided-to-hand-over-al-bashir-to-the-icc, *ISS Today*, September 21, 2021; See also DW interview with PM Hamdok, https://www.youtube.com/watch?v=vG09mloNdAk, February 2020.

14 "Sudan's Bashir Faces Death Sentence Over His 1989 Coup," *Africanews*, July 21, 2020, https://www.africanews.com/2020/07/21/sudan-s-bashir-faces-death-sentence-over-his-1989-coup/.

15 See Khalid Abdelaziz, "Former Sudan President Bashir Sentenced to Two Years in Detention for Corruption," *Reuters*, December 14, 2019, https://www.reuters.com/article/us-sudan-politics-bashir-idUSKBN1YI087.

16 UNSC Resolution 1593 (2005), March 31, 2005, https://www.icc-cpi.int/nr/rdonlyres/85febd1a-29f8-4ec4-9566-48edf55cc587/283244/n0529273.pdf.

17 See Dire Tladi, "Complementarity and Cooperation in International Criminal Justice. Assessing Initiatives to Fill the Impunity Gap," *ISS Paper 277*, November 2014, https://issafrica.org/research/papers/complementarity-and-cooperation-in-international-criminal-justice.

Page 338
Building Institutions in the Realm of Economic and Monetary Policy
Christine Lagarde

1 Jean Monnet, *Memoirs*, Garden City: Doubleday, 1978.
2 There are different definitions of the term "economic diplomacy" (see, for example, Tony Wayne, "What Is Economic Diplomacy and How Does It Work?," *The Foreign Service Journal*, January/February 2019, https://afsa.org/what-economic-diplomacy-and-how-does-it-work). In this essay, I define economic diplomacy as the interaction that has taken place since World War II, mainly among economic policymakers, in order to come to agreements and build international and European institutions dealing with monetary, financial, broader economic, and trade affairs.
3 For a vivid (and some would say controversial) account of the negotiations at Bretton Woods, see Benn Steil, *The Battle of Bretton Woods: John Maynard Keynes, Harry Dexter White and the Making of a New World Order*, Princeton, NJ: Princeton University Press, 2013. Steil claims both that Keynes enjoyed celebrity status at the time and understood best the economic situation of the UK economy, but also that he may have been "the world's worst diplomat." See his book presentation at Politics & Prose bookstore on April 21, 2013, https://youtu.be/FLse54Eobk4. In terms of the outcome, the views of Keynes, an academic economist who had also served as a Director of the Bank of England and was in favor of an international clearing mechanism for surpluses, lost out to the plan of his US counterpart, Harry Dexter White, leading to the creation of the IMF as a powerful institution (and the IBRD, which became the lending arm of the World Bank). See also J.K. Horsefield, *The International Monetary Fund: 1945-1965. Twenty Years of International Monetary Cooperation. Volume I: Chronicle,* Washington, DC: International Monetary Fund, 1969. For the perspective of France in the negotiations, see Michael D. Bordo et al., "France and the Breakdown of the Bretton Woods International Monetary System," International Monetary Fund, 1994, https://doi.org/10.5089/9781451935363.001.
4 Barry Eichengreen, "Strengthening the International Financial Architecture: Where Do We Stand?," *ASEAN Economic Bulletin*, Vol. 17, No 2, 2000, pp. 175–192.
5 Horsefield explains as follows: The IMF "came into being as a result of a supreme act of faith – the decision to surrender to an untried and imperfectly visualized international body the supervision of one of the most cherished attributes of national sovereignty, the right to change the rate of exchange. That this surrender was hedged round with safeguards is not surprising; that it was made at all and was accompanied by vesting in the same body an appreciable fraction of the members' international reserves, can be explained only by the coincidence of the hour and the men." Horsefield, *The International Monetary Fund: 1945-1965*, 3.
6 Harold James, "Bretton Woods to Brexit," *IMF Finance and Development*, Vol. 54, No 3, 2017, https://www.imf.org/external/pubs/ft/fandd/2017/09/pdf/james.pdf.
7 See "Canada G7 Meeting May Be Group's Swansong," *Financial Times*, February 5, 2010, https://www.ft.com/content/0f3020f2-1279-11df-a611-00144feab49a, article quoting Jean Claude Trichet: "The prime grouping for international co-operation is the G20. It is no more the G7, at least in this format of ministers and governments."
8 See "London Summit – Leaders' Statement," April 2, 2009, https://www.imf.org/external/np/sec/pr/2009/pdf/g20_040209.pdf.
9 James M. Boughton, *Tearing Down Walls: The International Monetary Fund 1990-1999*, Washington, DC: International Monetary Fund, 2012, https://www.imf.org/external/pubs/ft/history/2012/.
10 The Russian Federation joined the G7 in 1998 and left in 2014.
11 For a perspective on the links between currencies and politics, see, for example, Benjamin J. Cohen, *Currency Power: Understanding Monetary Rivalry*, Princeton: Princeton University Press, 2015.
12 The BIS also played a role in setting up the euro in that it facilitated the meetings of the Committee of (EU) Governors in Basel held in the 1980s with the goal of setting up the European Monetary Institute (EMI) in Stage II of EMU, which preceded the ECB/Eurosystem (Stage III).
13 See "The International Role of the Euro," European Central Bank, June 2021, https://www.ecb.europa.eu/pub/ire/html/ecb.ire202106~a058f84c61.en.html. On far-reaching ideas about how to eliminate further international nominal exchange rate volatility, see Robert Mundell, "The Case for a World Currency," *Journal of Policy Modeling*, Vol. 34, No 4, 2012, pp. 568–578.
14 On the euro area's swap line and repurchase agreement network, see "Central Bank Liquidity Lines," https://www.ecb.europa.eu/mopo/implement/liquidity_lines/html/index.en.html.
15 Robert O. Keohane, *After Hegemony: Cooperation and Discord in the World Political Economy*, Princeton: Princeton University Press, 1984, and Judith L. Goldstein, Douglas Rivers, and Michael Tomz, *Institutions in International Relations: Understanding the Effects of the GATT and the WTO on World Trade*, Cambridge:

Cambridge University Press, 2007.

16 See Deborah E. Siegel, "Legal Aspects of the IMF/WTO Relationship: The Fund's Articles of Agreement and the WTO Agreements," *American Journal of International Law*, Vol. 96, No 3, 2002, pp. 561–599, https://www.imf.org/external/np/leg/sem/2002/cdmfl/eng/siegel.pdf.

17 Yinon M. Bar-On et al., "SARS-CoV-2 (COVID-19) by the Numbers," *eLife*, April 2, 2020, https://www.ncbi.nlm.nih.gov/pmc/articles/PMC7224694/.

18 The decline in global GDP at the peak of the global financial crisis in 2009 was 0.1 percent. See "World Economic Outlook: Recovery During a Pandemic," October 2021, International Monetary Fund, https://www.imf.org/en/Publications/WEO/Issues/2021/10/12/world-economic-outlook-october-2021.

19 See, for example, their cooperation as regards vaccination, "The IMF and COVID-19 (Coronavirus)," https://www.imf.org/en/Topics/imf-and-covid19.

20 See "IMF-WHO COVID-19 Vaccine Supply Tracker," https://www.imf.org/en/Topics/imf-and-covid19/IMF-WHO-COVID-19-Vaccine-Supply-Tracker.

21 See "COVID-19 Financial Assistance and Debt Service Relief," https://www.imf.org/en/Topics/imf-and-covid19/COVID-Lending-Tracker.

22 For the latest assessment of the UN's Intergovernmental Panel on Climate Change (IPCC), responsible for assessing the science related to climate change, see https://www.ipcc.ch/report/ar6/wg1/#SPM.

23 See Monnet, *Memoirs*; Dennis Swann, *The Single European Market and Beyond. A Study of the Wider Implications of the Singe European Act*, London: Routledge, 1992; Desmond Dinan, *Ever Closer Union: An Introduction to European Integration,* Boulder: Lynne Rienner, 1999; Maurice Schiff and Alan L. Winters, "Regional Integration as Diplomacy," *World Bank Economic Review*, Vol. 12, No. 2, May 1998, 271–295.

24 The EU accounts for about 7 percent of the world's population, 30 percent of its economy, and some 50 percent of global social welfare spending (recalling a quote by Angela Merkel in the early 2010s). The exact figure on social spending has since become the subject of debate. See, for example, Indemit S. Gill and Martin Raiser, "Golden Growth: Restoring the Lustre of the European Economic Model," Washington, DC: World Bank Group, http://documents.worldbank.org/curated/en/539371468036253854/Main-report.

25 For a transatlantic perspective on the negotiations during the crisis, see C. Randall Henning, *Tangled Governance: International Regime Complexity, the Troika, and the Euro Crisis*, Oxford: Oxford University Press, 2017.

26 It may be noted that the establishment of strong institutions often allows these institutions themselves to become drivers of integration. On the role of institutions in furthering global and European integration, see Ernst B. Haas, *The Uniting of Europe*, Indiana: University of Notre Dame Press, 1958; Ernst B. Haas, "International Integration: The European and the Universal Process," *International Organization*, Volume 15, Issue 3, Summer 1961, 366–392; and more recently, Arne Niemann and D. Ioannou, "European economic integration in times of crisis: a case of neofunctionalism?," *Journal of European Public Policy*, Volume 22, Issue 2, 2015, 196–218.

27 "People only accept change when they are faced with necessity, and only recognise necessity when a crisis is upon them." And "Nothing is possible without (wo) men; nothing is lasting without institutions." See Jean Monnet, *Memoirs*.

28 This has also increased the degree to which Europeans begin to feel and act with a common identity and as a single polity. On the impact of external factors driving European integration, see also C. Randall Henning, "US Policy in the Euro Crisis and the Institutional Deepening of the Monetary Union," *Journal of Economic Policy Reform*, Vol. 23, No, 3, 2020, 325–341.

29 Such autonomy would require far-reaching constitutional changes both at the European and the national level, giving exclusive competence to the EU in foreign and security policy. It would also require a fiscal capacity with notable powers. Such deep cooperation and integration in Europe, which could also serve other purposes, has been shown to work and deliver synergies and economic benefits; it would help to strengthen the foundations of EMU on the one hand, and also, presumably, to avoid disjointed responses by EU member states toward external partners.

30 For an overview by the European Commission of "strengthening the EU's open strategic autonomy," see https://ec.europa.eu/info/strategy/priorities-2019-2024/europe-fit-digital-age/european-industrial-strategy_en#strengthening-eus-open-strategic-autonomy.

31 One example in which strategic autonomy meets economic policy is the extraterritorial reach of law (for example, US law and Iran; see Sascha Lohmann, "Extraterritorial U.S. Sanctions. Only Domestic Courts Could Effectively Curb the Enforcement of U.S. Law Abroad," *SWP Comment*, No 5, February 2019, doi:10.18449/2019C05.

msc

Imprint

Econ is part of the
Ullstein Buchverlage GmbH Group.
ISBN 978-3-430-21077-5

Editors
Tobias Bunde & Benedikt Franke
Munich Security Conference

Editorial team
Ulrike Strauss & Nardine Luca
Munich Security Conference

Copyediting
Rick Madsen @ Fortuna Communication, Tübingen

Translation
Nikolas Bertheau

Photography and art consulting
Michael Kuhlmann

Art direction
Morian & Bayer-Eynck, Coesfeld

Book jacket and type-setting
Morian & Bayer-Eynck, Coesfeld
Set in msc realist and Tiempos Text

Print and binding
Eberl & Kösel, Krugzell
Printed in Germany

Editorial closing December 15, 2021. This book went to print in December 2021. The contributions of the authors reflect their personal opinions.

Our promise for more sustainability
• Climate neutral product
• FSC® certified paper
• Made in Germany

FSC www.fsc.org MIX Paper from responsible sources FSC® C013736